An Introducti
AutoCAD LT 97

An Introduction to AutoCAD LT 97

A. Yarwood

Registered Developer

Addison Wesley Longman Limited
Edinburgh Gate, Harlow
Essex CM20 2JE, England
and Associated Companies throughout the world

First published 1998

British Library Cataloguing in Publication Data
A catalogue entry for this title is available from the British Library

ISBN 0-582-35731-4

Set by 24 in 10/13pt Melior
Produced by Longman Singapore Publishers (Pte) Ltd
Printed in Singapore

Contents

List of plates

Colour plates are between pages 112 and 113.

Preface

What is AutoCAD LT 97?

AutoCAD LT 97 is a two-dimensional (2D) computer-aided design (CAD) software package which works within either Windows 95 or Windows NT (version 4). LT 97 is fully compatible with AutoCAD Release 14. LT 97 replaces LT Release 3 (Windows 95 version) and contains a number of enhancements over LT 3 bringing it up to date with modern CAD technology.

The reader

This book is designed specifically for the beginner wishing to learn how to construct technical drawings with the aid of the 2D CAD software package known as AutoCAD LT 97. Its contents are suitable for use by pupils in the sixth forms of schools, students in colleges of Further Education and colleges of Higher Education and for the general reader.

System requirements

Software

AutoCAD LT 97 will run in Windows 95 or Windows NT (version 4.0). If wishing to use the Internet or Intranet facilities available with AutoCAD LT 97, a browser such as Internet Explorer or Netscape Navigator must also be loaded on the computer being used.

Hardware

CPU: Intel 486 with coprocessor or better. Pentium preferred, or better.
RAM: 16 Mbytes.
Hard disk space:
Up to 56 Mbytes for LT files.

64 Mbytes for swap files.
8 Mbytes for each LT session being run concurrently with others.
5 Mbytes for loading during installation – removed when installation completed.

New features

There have been a considerable number of enhancements over previous releases of LT incorporated with LT 97. Among these enhancements are the following:

Fully compatible with AutoCAD Release 14.
File compatibility with earlier releases of both AutoCAD and AutoCAD LT.
Increased, faster performance over previous releases of LT, with less of a memory footprint.
AutoSnap™ can be set, together with its Marker, Snap tip, Magnet and Cycling through snap points properties.
PolarSnap™ can be set, together with its Angle snap, Distance snap and Polar distance properties.
Layer and Linetype management have been considerably improved over earlier releases.
A Layer Tab has been included with LT 97.
Enhanced Object Properties Toolbar to include listing and editing of properties of selected drawing entities.
Microsoft IntelliMouse can be used as a digitiser.
The ability to Solid Fill areas of drawings in any available colour has been included.
Proportional Scaling of embedded objects through dragging of the object handles ensures that embedded objects retain their proportionality.
Display Order Control allows embedded objects in a drawing to be plotted in conjunction with drawing entities in the order desired by the operator.
Content Explorer displays the contents of a drawing in either icon or name form and allows blocks within the Explorer to be dragged into the drawing.
An updated Plot Preview which is faster and allows Pan and Zoom within the Preview.
Enhanced text usability.
Internet tools – Drawing Web File format (DWF) supported for output from and input to LT 97, allowing exchange of drawings via the Internet. The command Browser allows the Internet browser to be launched within LT 97.

Stand alone installation – no personalisation disk required.

Full compliance with Microsoft Office.

Right-click menus for all commands are available with the setvar PICKFIRST set to 1.

A CD-ROM 'AutoCAD Learning Assistance' is available for helping the operator to learn how to use LT 97.

A. Yarwood
Salisbury 1998

Acknowledgements

The author wishes to acknowledge with grateful thanks the help given to him by members of the staff at Autodesk Ltd.

The author would also like to thank Janet Levitton for her assistance with the preparation of the manuscript of this book.

Trademarks

A. Yarwood is a Master Developer with Autodesk Ltd.

CHAPTER 1

Introduction

Starting AutoCAD LT 97

If the computer being used is configured to start up with Windows 95, when it is switched on, the Windows 95 programme loads and a desktop window appears similar to that shown in Fig. 1.1. The number and type of icons depends upon the applications loaded into the computer and also whether they can be started from the Windows desktop Start-up window. The icons representing applications in the desktop window have been placed as **Shortcuts**, which allow applications to be started, either with a *double-click* on the application shortcut icon, or by a *right-click* on the shortcut icon, which brings up a menu from which a *left-click* on the application name loads the application. Figure 1.1 shows the menu resulting from a *right-click* on the **AutoCAD LT 97** shortcut icon.

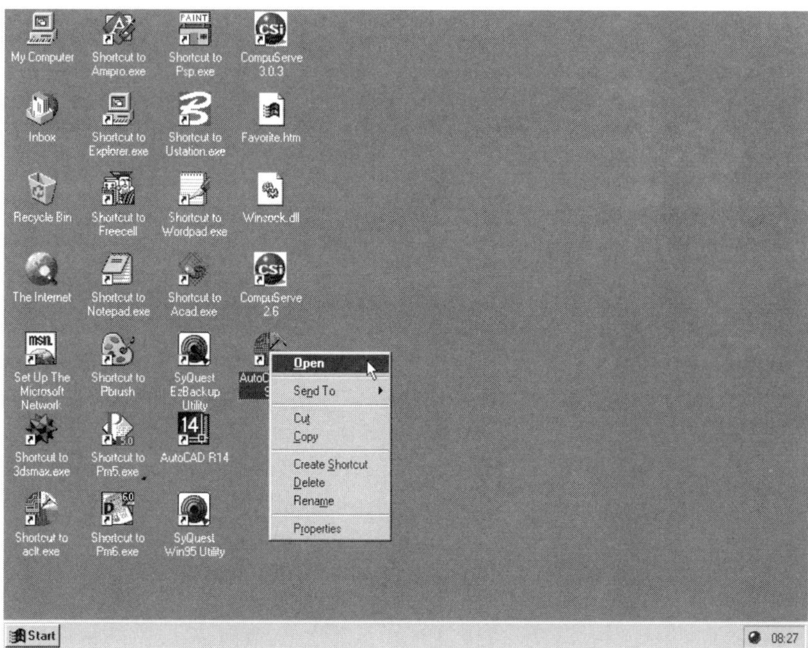

Fig. 1.1 The Windows 95 desktop Start-up window

A second method of starting **AutoCAD LT 97** is to *left-click* on the **Start** button at the bottom left of the Windows 95 desktop window, followed by another *left-click* on **Programs** in the menu which appears. This results in another menu appearing showing all applications loaded on the computer. *Left-click* on the name **AutoCAD LT 97,** and from this third menu, *left-click* on the name **AutoCAD LT 97** (Fig. 1.2). LT commences loading. This will take some seconds depending upon the speed of the computer. The resulting LT 97 window is shown in Fig. 1.3.

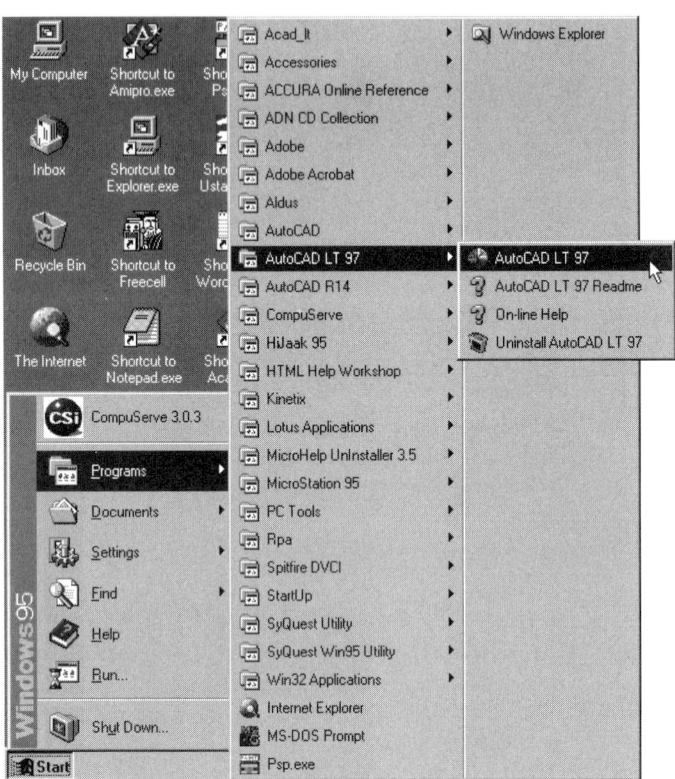

Fig. 1.2 The **Programs** menus resulting from a *left-click* on the Windows 95 **Start** button

Configuring LT 97

The **Start Up** dialogue box which appears in the centre of the **LT 97** window on start up contains five buttons arrayed on the left-hand side of the dialogue box. Upon start up, the **Use a Template** button is usually active, allowing a drawing template to be loaded from the selection available with LT 97. More about LT drawing templates later.

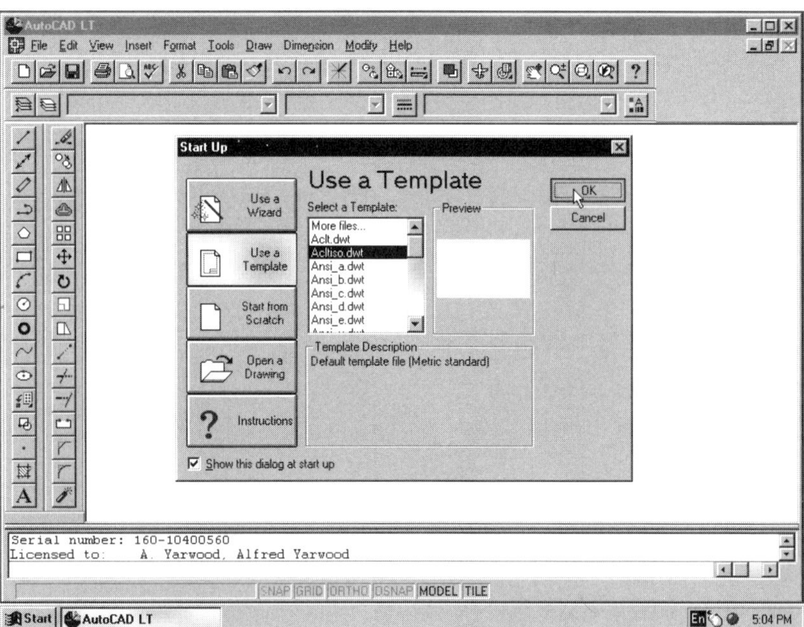

Fig. 1.3 The AutoCAD LT 97 start up window

The five buttons in the Start Up dialogue box

Use a Wizard button

A *left-click* on this button and the dialogue box changes to **Use a Wizard**. If the **Advanced Setup** name is selected (Fig. 1.4) *double-click* on the name, or *left-click* on the name, followed by another *left-click* on the **OK** button and the **Advanced Setup** dialogue box appears (Fig. 1.5). This dialogue contains a number of further dialogues, which can be chosen with *left-clicks* on the tabs at the top of the dialogue box, allowing configuration of the parameters of the LT 97 window the operator wishes to work in. Make settings for the time being as follows:

Step 1: Units – set to **Decimal** with **Precision** set to **0** (Fig. 1.5).
Step 2: Angle – set **Decimal Degrees** to **0** (not illustrated).
Step 3: Angle Measure – accept the default **East** (not illustrated).
Step 4: Angle Direction – accept the default **Counter-clockwise** (not illustrated).
Step 5: Area – *enter* **Width 420**; **Length 300** (Fig. 1.6). These sizes are the millimetre dimensions of an A4 sheet in portrait format.
Step 6: Title Block – set to **No title block** and **No title block name** (Fig. 1.7).

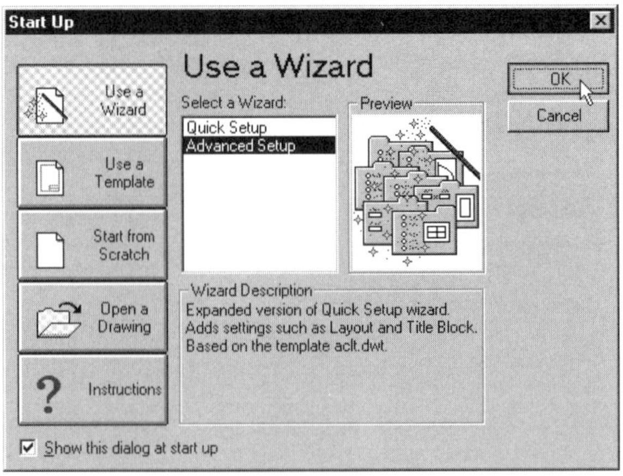

Fig. 1.4 Selecting the **Advanced Setup** option from the **Use a Wizard** dialogue box

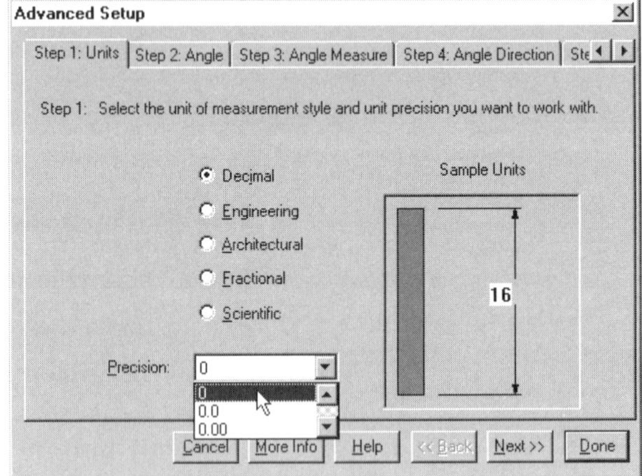

Fig. 1.5 The **Advanced Setup** dialogue box. **Step 1: Units**

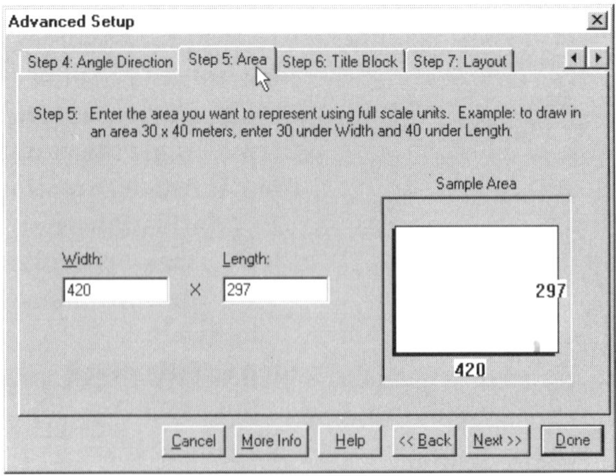

Fig. 1.6 The **Advanced Setup** dialogue box. **Step 5: Area**

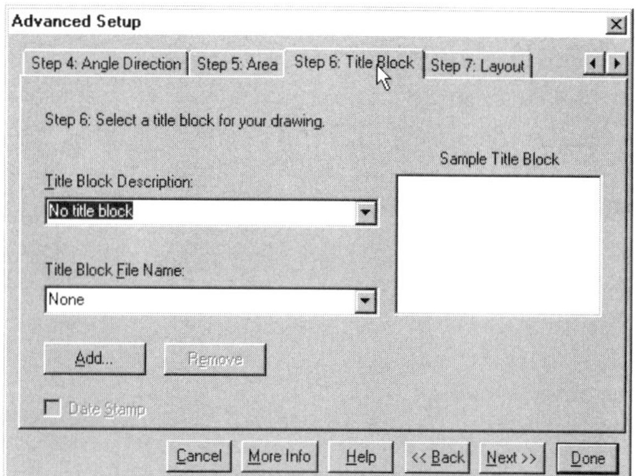

Fig. 1.7 The **Advanced Setup** dialogue box. **Step 6: Title Block**

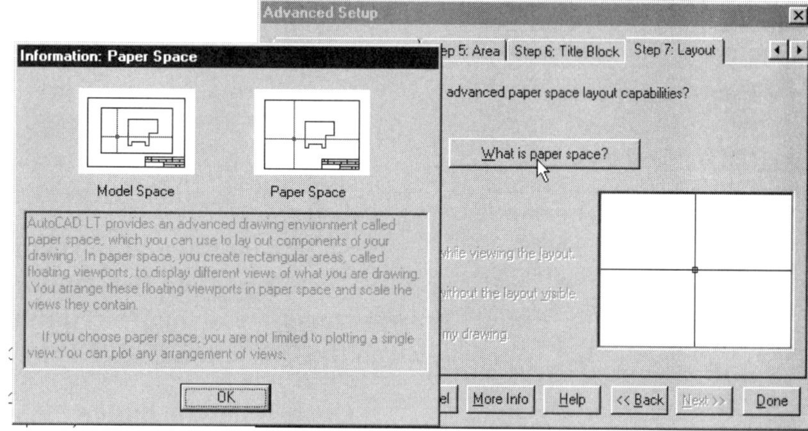

Fig. 1.8 The **Advanced Setup** dialogue box. **Step 7: Layout**

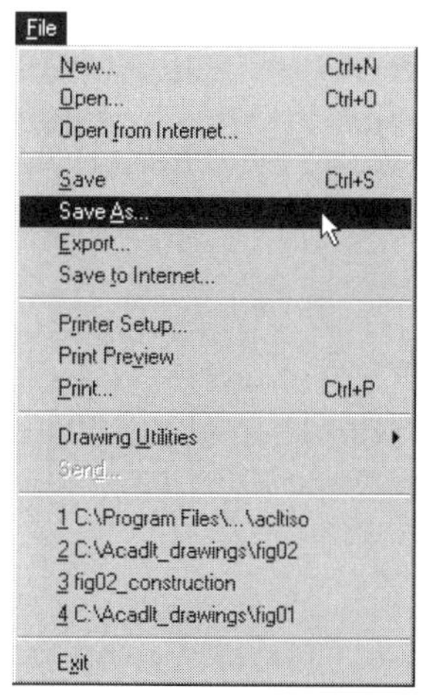

Fig. 1.9 Selecting **Save As...** from the **File** pull-down menu

Step 7: Layout – set to **No** in answer to **Do you want to use advanced paper space layout capabilities?**. Note that if the **What is paper space?** button is selected a box containing a description appears (Fig. 1.8).

Now *left-click* on the **Done** button. The settings from the **Use a Wizard** dialogue boxes will be reflected in the LT 97 window which appears. Before going any further, *left-click* on **File** in the menu bar (left-hand top of LT 97 window). The **File** pull-down menu appears (Fig. 1.9). *Left-click* on **Save As...** from the menu, which brings the **Save File As** dialogue box on screen (Fig. 1.10).

Left-click in the **Save as type:** box. A popup list appears, *left-click* on **Drawing Template File[*.dwt]** and *enter* your initials in the **File name:** box. My initials are **ay**, so I have saved the template to the file name **ay.dwt**.

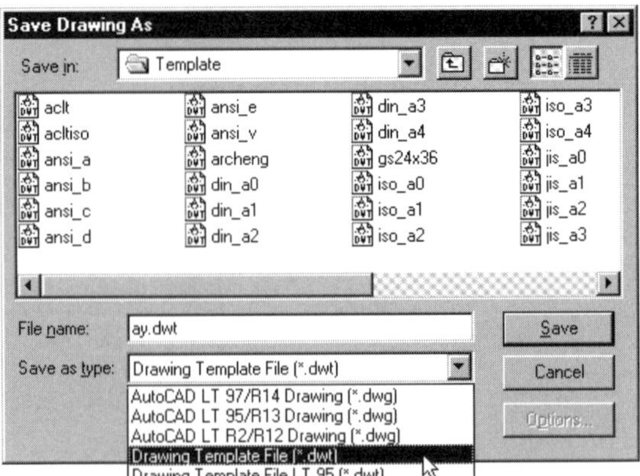

Fig. 1.10 The **Save Drawing As** dialogue box

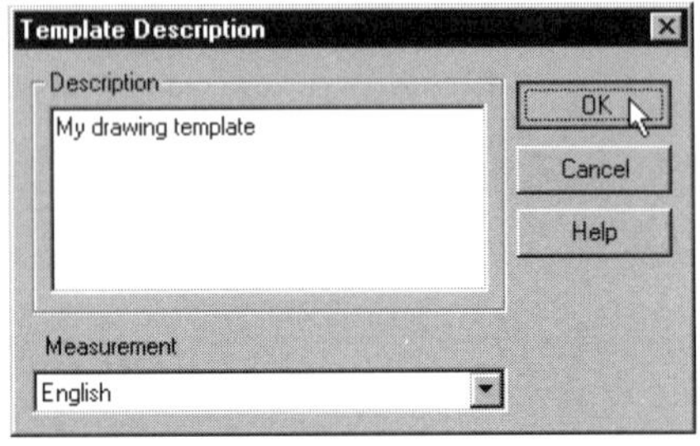

Fig. 1.11 The **Template Description** box

Left-click on the **Save** button of the dialogue box and another box appears – the **Template Description** box. *Enter* a note such as **My drawing template** in the **Description** box, followed by another *left-click* on the **OK** button (Fig. 1.11).

Use a Template button

A *left-click* on the **Use a Template** button and the dialogue box changes to **Use a Template**. A list of templates available appears in the **Select a Template:** list box from which a template can be selected for working in. If your own template had been saved prior to starting LT 97, it could be selected from the list.

Start from Scratch button

Left-click on this button, select **Metric** (Fig. 1.12) and *left-click* on the **OK** button. The LT 97 window opens with the area set to 420 by 300. Other settings for this window can be made later from the **Preferences** dialogue box (see later in this chapter).

The Open a Drawing button

A *left-click* on this button and the dialogue box is renamed **Open a Drawing**. If this is the very first session of setting up LT 97, only

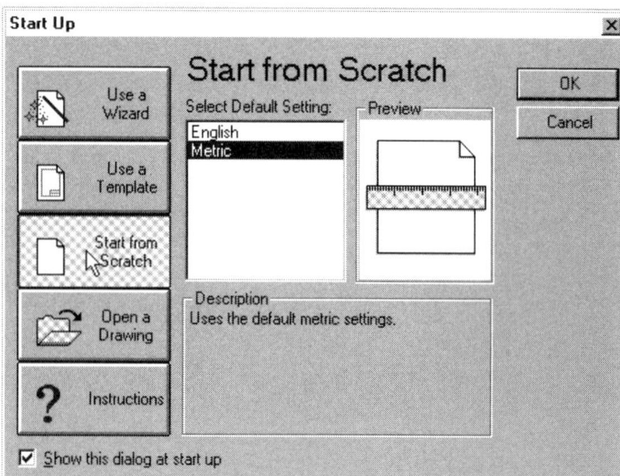

Fig. 1.12 The **Start from Scratch** dialogue box

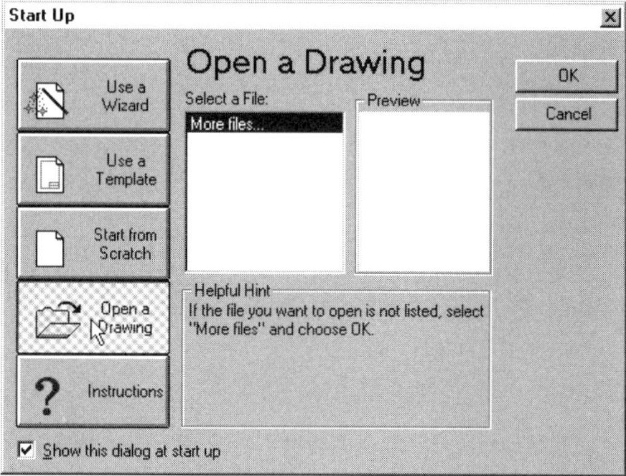

Fig. 1.13 The **Open a Drawing** dialogue box

More files... will appear in the **Select a file:** list, but if LT 97 has been previously used a number of recently opened drawing files will also appear. A *left-click* on the name **More files...** brings up the **Select File** dialogue box, from which a previously saved file can be opened.

The Instructions button

A *left-click* on this button and the dialogue box changes to **Instructions** and several notes on how to use the **Set Up** buttons shows in the box (Fig. 1.14).

Preferences

Left-click on **Tools** in the menu bar, and from the pull-down menu which appears, select **Preferences...** (Fig. 1.15). The **Preferences** dialogue box appears (Fig. 1.16). This, like the **Advanced Setup**

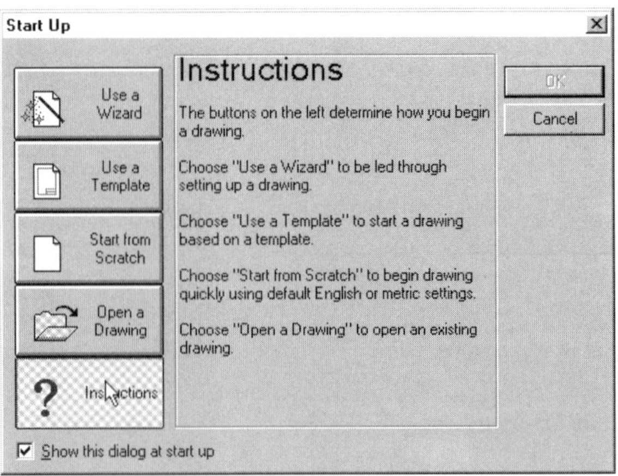

Fig. 1.14 The **Instructions** dialogue box

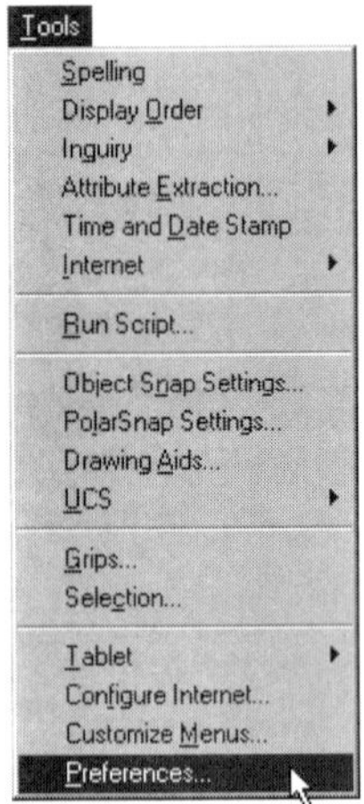

Fig. 1.15 Selecting **Preferences...** from the **Tools** pull-down menu

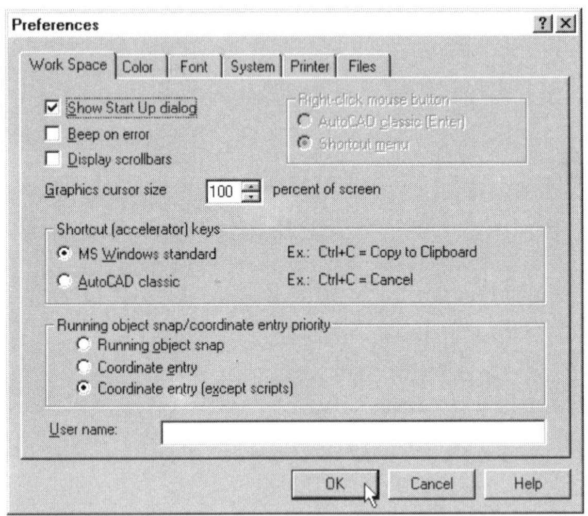

Fig. 1.16 The **Preferences** dialogue box

dialogue box (Fig. 1.5, page 4) has a number of tabs along the upper part of the box, a *left-click* on any of which brings up another dialogue. A variety of settings can be made from these dialogue boxes. For setting up preferences for our template (my **ay.dwt**) the following settings were made.

Work Space box: make sure a tick is in the check box to the left of **Show Start Up dialogue**, but clear the ticks in the other two check boxes – **Beep on error** and **Display scrollbars**. These three settings are at the operator's discretion. I am showing here my own preferences. Another setting in the **Work Space** box, which I prefer to make is to set the **Graphics cursor size** to **100** – that is stretching right across the screen from side to side and from top to bottom (Fig. 1.16).

Colors box: I prefer the LT 97 window to be mostly white, but there is an advantage in working in a black **Graphics window background**

in that some colours show more clearly against a black background. To change a colour of any part of the window, first *left-click* in that part of the window to be changed. The name of the part appears in the **Windows Element:** list box. Then *left-click* in the colour box of your choice under **Basic Colors:** and that part of the window changes colour (Fig. 1.17).

I find it best to leave the other settings in the **Preferences** dialogue box to the default settings, i.e. those set when the software is delivered to the user. However, the choice is the operator's.

Now save the window again to the template name **initials.dwt** (in my case **ay.dwt**) in the **Save Drawing As** dialogue box.

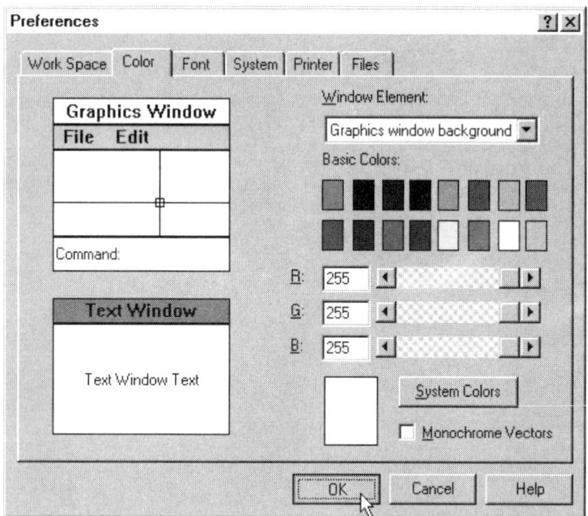

Fig. 1.17 The **Colors** box of **Preferences**

Set Grid and Snap

Still getting together my drawing template, *left-click* against the word **Command:** in the Command window (at bottom of LT 97 window – Fig. 1.18) and *enter* the grid and *right-click*. The following line appears:

Grid spacing (X) or ON/Off?Snap/Aspect <10>:

Fig. 1.18 The Command window at the bottom of the LT 97 window

Right-click and a grid at 10 unit intervals appears on screen.

Then *enter* the word snap against **Command:**. The following line appears:

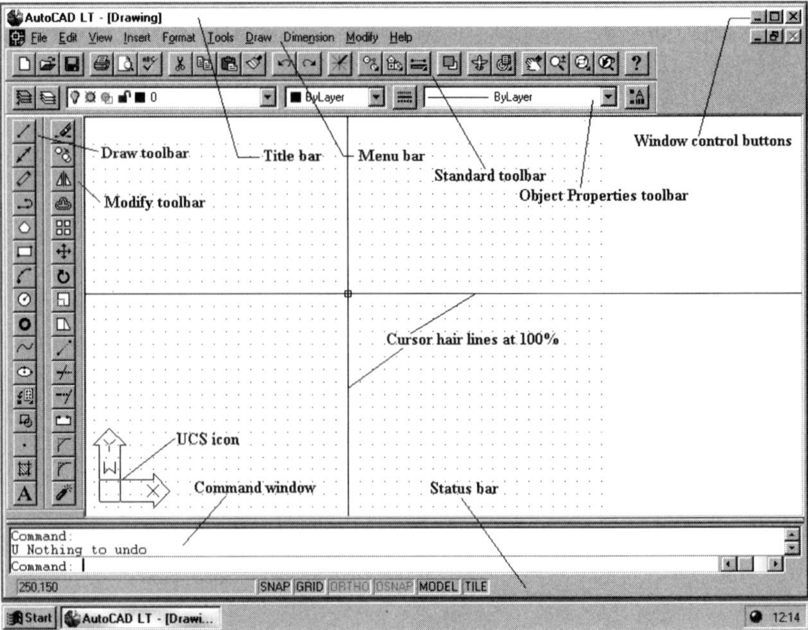

Fig. 1.19 The LT 97 window as set up for the **ay.dwt** template

Fig. 1.20 All the pull-down menus

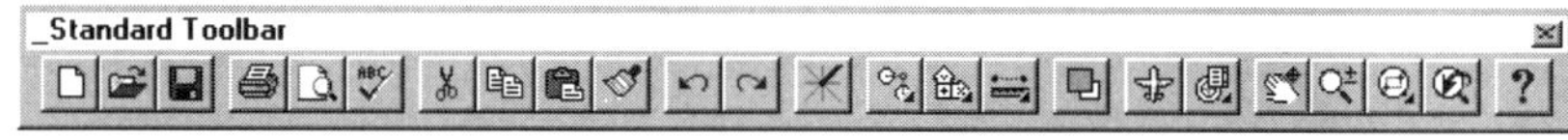

Fig. 1.21 The **Standard toolbar**

Snap spacing or ON/OFF/Aspect/Rotate/Style <10>:

Enter 5, followed by a *right-click*.

Now, again save the window to your template name to store the grid and snap entries in the template file.

The ay.dwt LT 97 window

Figure 1.19 shows the resulting LT 97 window after the above settings have been made, with names of the parts included in the illustration. Note the following parts of the window:

Title bar: Shows the name of the current drawing. When any drawing template is opened the name will be **Drawing**.

Menu bar: Showing the names of all the pull-down menus. All the pull-down menus from the menu bar are shown in Fig. 1.20.

Window control buttons: These are the **Minimise**, the **Maximise** and the **Close** buttons, common to all Windows 95 applications.

Standard toolbar: Figure 1.21. This contains some of the most frequently used tools in LT 97. The names of the tools in the toolbar are shown in Fig. 1.22.

Object Properties toolbar: Figure 1.23. Details of the popup menus and tools from this toolbar will be described in Chapter 5.

Draw and **Modify toolbars**: These are usually (but not necessarily always) docked against the left-hand side of the LT 97 window. The tools from the two toolbars are shown in Fig. 1.24.

Cursor hair lines: The cross hairs move in response to movement of the mouse. Points on a drawing can be determined by moving the mouse so that the intersection point of the cross hairs is at the required position.

UCS icon: More about this in Chapter 15.

Command window: Commands can be *entered* in this window. It is a window which can be extended upwards to show previously *entered* commands.

Status bar: Below the Command window. Contains the position of the intersection of the cursor cross hairs as coordinate numbers, together with five buttons for setting **SNAP**, **GRID**, **ORTHO**, **MODEL Space** or **PAPER Space**. When the cursor, under mouse control is placed over a tool icon, the coordinate numbers are replaced by a prompt informing the operator of the function of the tool.

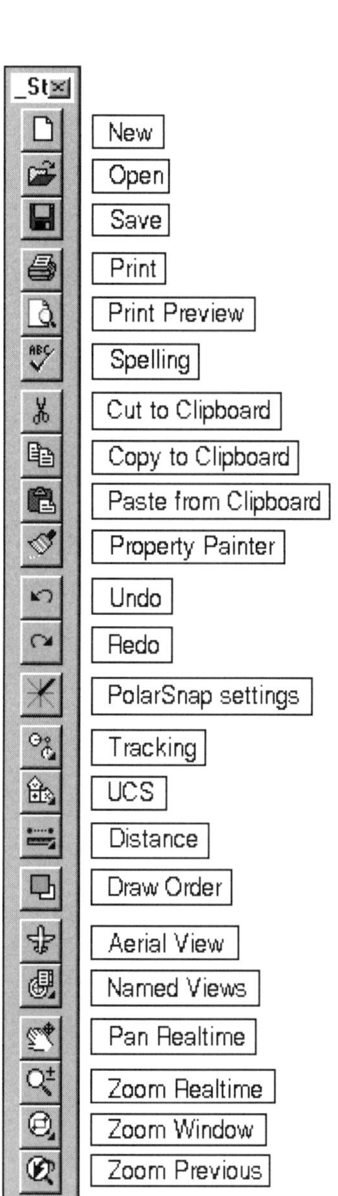

Fig. 1.22 Names of the tools in the **Standard** toolbar

Fig. 1.23 The **Object Properties** toolbar

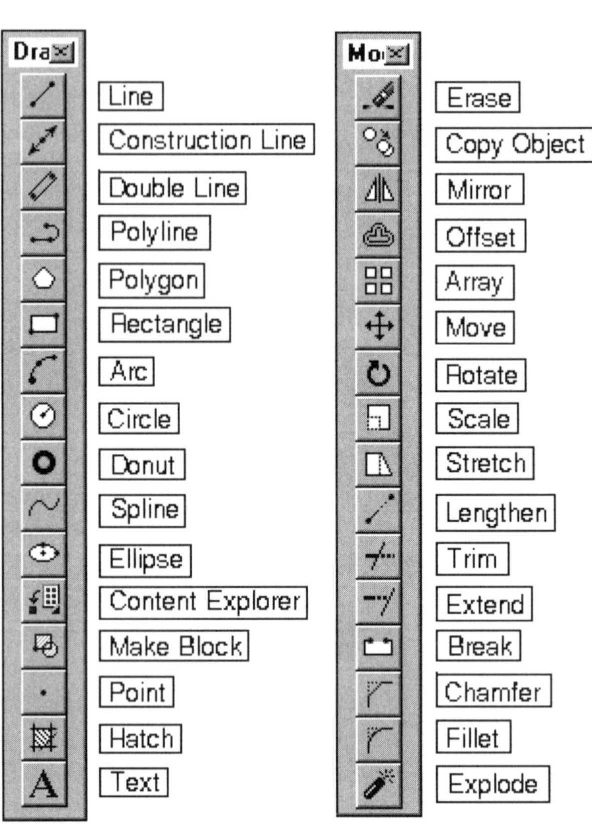

Fig. 1.24 The tools in the **Draw** and **Modify** toolbars

Task bar: In the Windows task bar, shown at the bottom of the window in Fig. 1.19, when LT 97 is on screen, the LT 97 icon, the name **AutoCAD LT** and the drawing name show in a box. If the LT 97 window is minimised by a *left-click* on the **Minimise** button, the highlighted name in the task bar changes and the LT 97 window goes off screen. A *left-click* on the name of the application in the task bar brings the LT 97 window back to screen.

The mouse as a digitiser

Although other types of digitiser can be used when working with AutoCAD LT 97, in this book only methods of working with a two-button mouse as the digitiser are given. In general when working with a two-button mouse, the left-hand button is the **Pick** button and the right-hand button the **Return** button (Fig. 1.25).

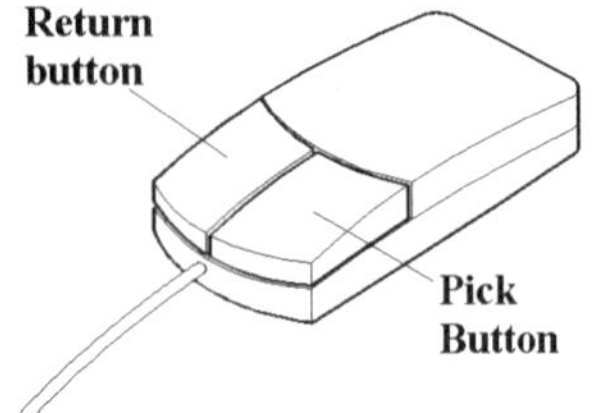

Fig. 1.25 A two-button mouse and the names of its buttons

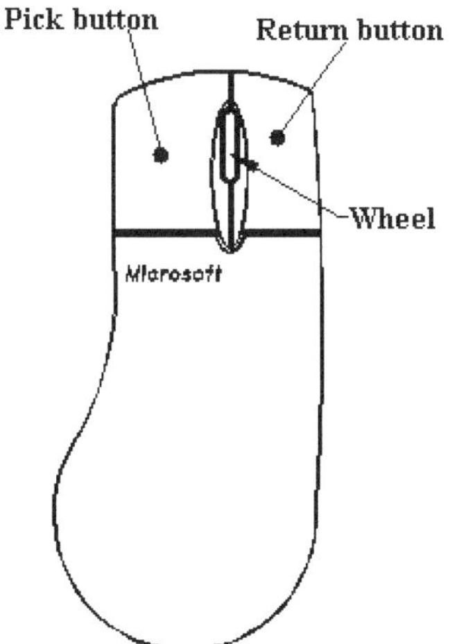

Fig. 1.26 Plan view of a Microsoft Intellimouse

The Microsoft Intellimouse

In particular the Microsoft Intellimouse (Fig. 1.26) can be used with AutoCAD LT 97. This is a two-button mouse with a wheel between the two buttons. The wheel allows zooming and panning, without calling or *entering* tools or commands. Moving the wheel forwards zooms to a larger scale. Moving the wheel backwards zooms to a smaller scale. Holding the wheel down allows the screen to be panned in any direction. See Chapter 2 about zooming and panning.

Terms used throughout this book

LT 97: An abbreviated form of AutoCAD LT 97.

Cursor: Several types of cursor will be seen when using LT 97. Some of these are shown in Fig. 1.27. Cursors can be moved under mouse control. Move the mouse and the cursor currently in action moves as the mouse is moved.

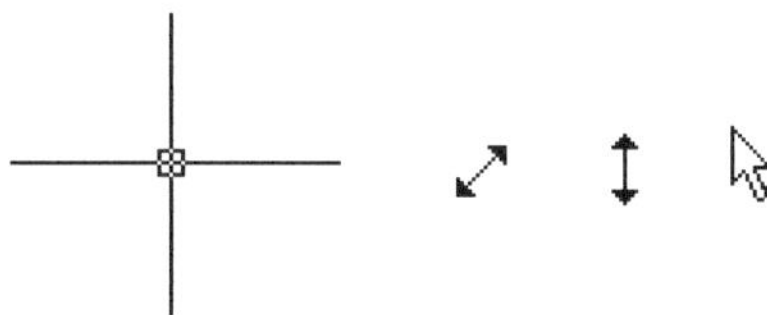

Fig. 1.27 Some of the cursors seen when using LT 97

Left-click: Place the cursor under mouse control onto a feature and press the *Pick* button of the mouse. Shown in this book in italics – *left-click*.

Right-click: Place the cursor under mouse control onto a feature and press the *Return* button of the mouse. Shown in this book in italics – *right-click*.

Double-click: Place the cursor under mouse control onto a feature and press the *Pick* button of the mouse twice in rapid succession. Shown in this book in italics – *double-click*.

Drag: Move the cursor under mouse control, hold down the *Pick* button and move the mouse. The feature moves with the mouse movement. Shown in this book in italics – *drag*.

Select: Move the cursor onto a feature and press the *pick* button of the mouse.

Pick: The same action as select. The two terms are used throughout this book and can be regarded as having the same meaning. Shown in this book in italics – *Pick*.

Pick button: the left-hand button of the mouse.

Pick box: An adjustable square associated with picking features of a construction.

Enter: Type the given word or letters at the keyboard.

Return: Press the **Return** or **Enter** key of the keyboard – shown in this book as *Enter*. Usually, but not always, has the same result as a *right-click,* i.e. pressing the **Return** button of the mouse. Shown in this book in italics – *Return*.

Esc: The **Esc** key of the keyboard. In LT 97 pressing the **Esc** key has the effect of cancelling the current action taking place.

Tab key: The key usually on the left-hand side of the keyboard which carries two arrows.

Tool: The name given to a command in recent releases of AutoCAD.

Icons: A common graphic feature in all Windows applications – a small item of graphics representing a tool or a function of the software in use.

Tool tip: The name of the tool represented by an icon, which appears when the cursor under mouse control is placed onto a tool icon.

Flyout: A number of tool icons have a small arrow in the bottom right-hand corner of the icon. Such icons will produce a flyout when the cursor is placed onto the icon and the *Pick* button of the mouse is held down.

Default: The name given to the settings or parameters of an application as set when the software is first purchased.

Objects: Individual lines, circles etc. as drawn in LT 97. When objects are grouped together as groups or as blocks the whole group will be treated as an object.

Entity: Has the same meaning in LT 97 as has the word object.

Never draw the same thing twice

One of the greatest values of using a Computer Aided Design (CAD) programme such as LT 97 is that by using tools such as **Copy**, **Array**, **Mirror**, **Offset**, **Scale**, **Stretch** the whole, or any part of a drawing when once drawn, need not be drawn again. Also existing drawing held on disk can be added into other drawings, with the aid of the **Insert** tool, without the need to draw the insertion in the existing drawing on screen. This enables the person operating LT 97 to work much faster than when drawing by hand methods.

Questions

1. There are two main methods of starting LT 97 from Windows 95. Can you describe them?
2. What is meant by the term 'Drawing template' when working with LT 97?

3. Can you describe what Paper Space is?
4. What is the purpose of the **Instructions** button in the **Start Up** dialogue box?
5. Can you name the four toolbars which commonly appear on screen when LT 97 is opened?
6. How are the cursor hair lines changed so as to stretch right across the screen from top to bottom and from side to side.
7. How is the Command window made larger?
8. Why is it better to have a Microsoft Intellimouse fitted rather than a standard mouse?
9. What happens on screen when the wheel of the Intellimouse is rotated forward?
10. What is the effect of pressing the **Esc** key of the keyboard when using a tool or a command in LT 97?

CHAPTER 2

Methods of operating LT 97

Toolbars

As stated in Chapter 1, when LT 97 is first opened, four toolbars are usually positioned in the LT 97 window – the **Standard** and **Object Properties** toolbars *docked* at the top of the window, with the **Draw** and **Modify** toolbars *docked* against the left-hand side of the window. Other toolbars can be brought on screen as follows:

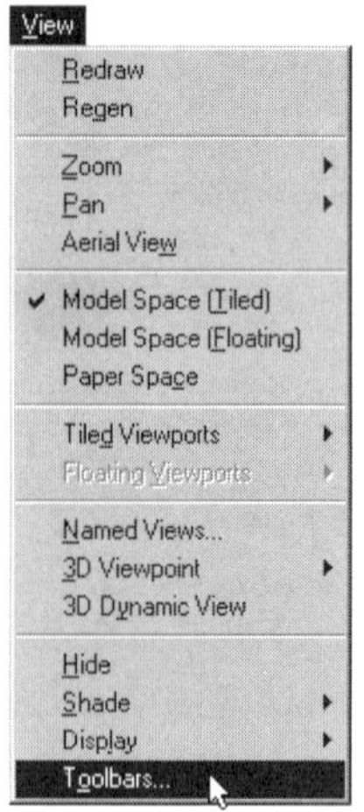

Fig. 2.1 Select **Toolbars...** from the **View** pull-down menu

Method 1

Left-click on **View** in the menu bar. In the pull-down menu, *left-click* on **Toolbars...** (Fig. 2.1). The **Toolbars** dialogue box appears. This contains a list of available toolbars. If the check box to the left of a toolbar name in the list contains an **X** that toolbar is somewhere in the LT 97 window. If the check box is empty, a *left-click* in the check box not only brings the toolbar of that name on screen, but also an **X** appears in the check box, showing the toolbar is in the LT 97 window (Fig. 2.2).

Fig. 2.2 The **Toolbars** dialogue box, with the **Dimension** toolbar selected

Method 2

Right-click in any part of any toolbar on screen, avoiding positioning the cursor over a tool icon. The **Toolbars** dialogue box appears (Fig. 2.3).

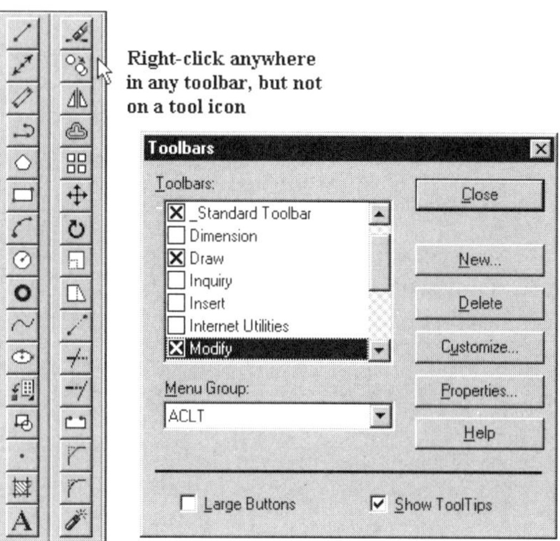

Fig. 2.3 *Right-click* in a toolbar to bring the **Toolbars** dialogue box on screen

The parts of a toolbar

Figure 2.4 shows the names of the parts of a toolbar. Each toolbar contains a number of tool **icons**, a *left-click* on any of which brings the tool represented by the icon into action. The name given to the toolbar appears at the left of the **Title bar**. A *left-click* held for a short time on any icon and the tool's name appears in a **tool tip**.

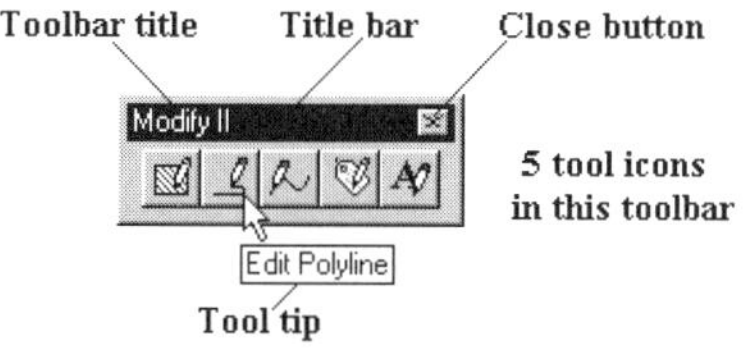

Fig. 2.4 The parts of a toolbar

Creating a new toolbar

If the operator wishes to place those icons of the tools he/she most frequently uses in a toolbar, the following procedure can be used:

1. *Left-click* on the **New...** button in the **Toolbars** dialogue box. The **New Toolbar** box appears. In the **Toolbar Name:** box *enter* the required name for the new toolbar. Figure 2.5 shows the name **My_New_Toolbar** has been *entered*. *Left-click* on the **OK** button

and an empty toolbar appears. The name of the new toolbar also appears in the **Toolbars** dialogue box list.

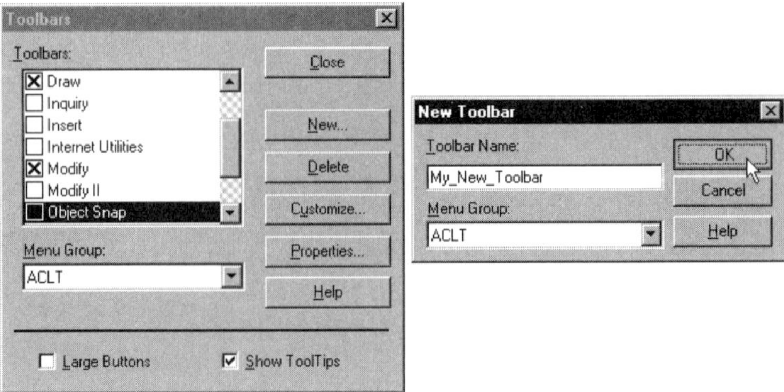

Fig. 2.5 The **New Toolbar** box

2. In the **Toolbars** dialogue box, *left-click* on the **Customize...** button, which brings up the **Customize Toolbar** dialogue box (Fig. 2.6). From the **Categories:** popup list select the toolbar from which a tool icon is to be chosen. All the icons in that toolbar then appear in the dialogue box. Any icon from these can be *dragged* into the new toolbar. Figure 2.6 shows one of the icons being so *dragged*.
3. Figure 2.7 shows the toolbar **My_New_Toolbar** with tool icons which have been selected from the **Draw** and **Modify** toolbars.

Floating toolbars

The upper illustration of Fig. 2.8 shows the **Draw** toolbar, being *dragged* from its position *docked* against the left-hand side of the LT 97 window. This is done by moving the cursor under mouse control onto any part of the **Draw** toolbar not taken up by a tool icon, holding

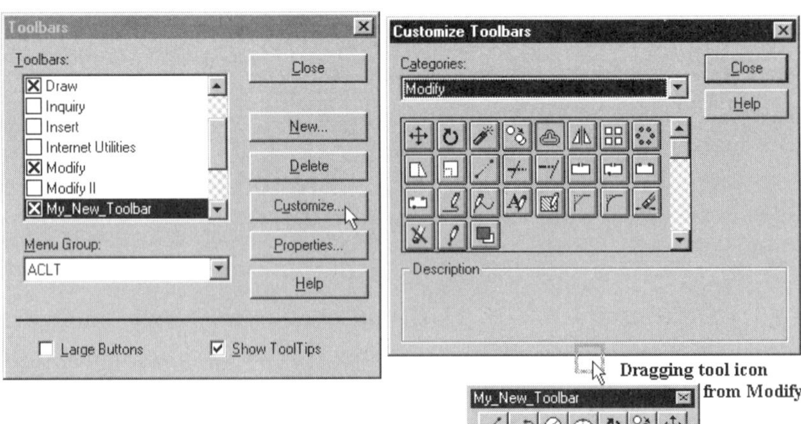

Fig. 2.6 Customising a new toolbar

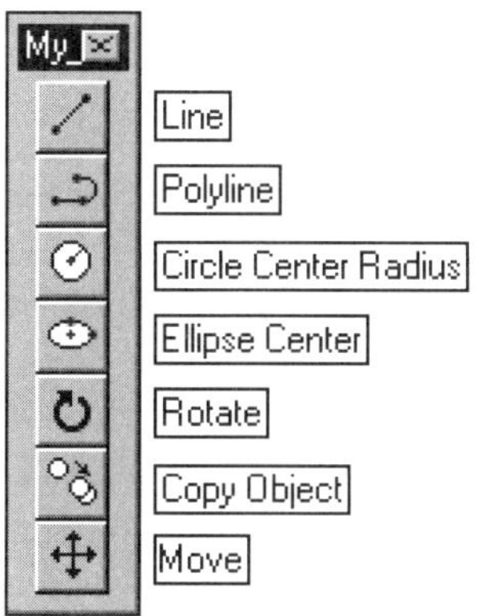

Fig. 2.7 The names of the tools in **My_New_Toolbar**

down the mouse button and moving the then ghosted toolbar away from its *docked* position. Release the mouse button and the toolbar appears. Move the cursor onto any edge of the toolbar and a Windows style cursor appears. This cursor allows the toolbar to be *dragged* to any required shape as shown in the other parts of Fig. 2.8. These different shape toolbars are *floating*. Any toolbar can be *floated* and resized. Several *floating* toolbars can be on screen at any one time.

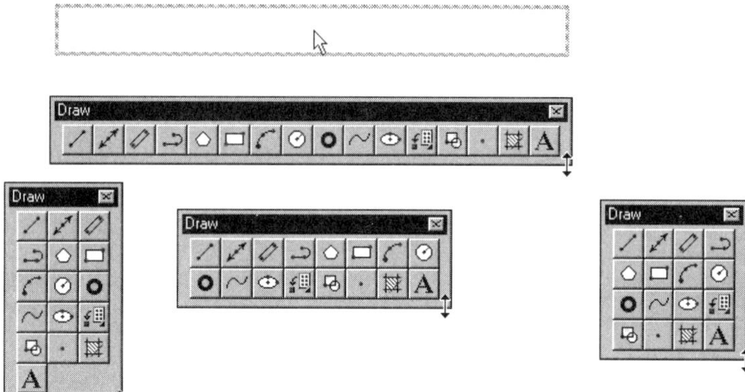

Fig. 2.8 Floating toolbars

Flyouts

If a tiny outward or downward pointing arrow appears with a tool icon, holding a *left-click* on that icon brings a *flyout* from the tool icon containing a number of associated tools. Figure 2.9 shows the **Tracking** tool icon from the **Standard** toolbar at the top of the LT 97 window. As this icon has a small arrow at its bottom right corner, a flyout (Fig. 2.10) will appear when a *left-click* is held over the icon.

Figure 2.10 not only shows the flyout from **Tracking**, but also shows the tool tip of the Object Snap tool in most frequent use.

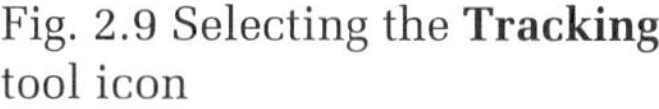

Fig. 2.9 Selecting the **Tracking** tool icon

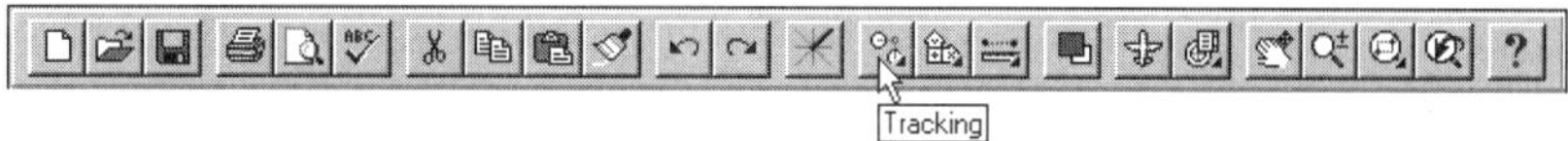

Pull-down menus from the menu bar

All of the menus from the menu bar have been shown in Chapter 1 (Fig. 1.20). Further details about these menus are given here (Fig. 2.11). Note the following:

Commands calling up dialogue boxes: If a command name from a pull-down menu is followed by three fullstops (...), when that command

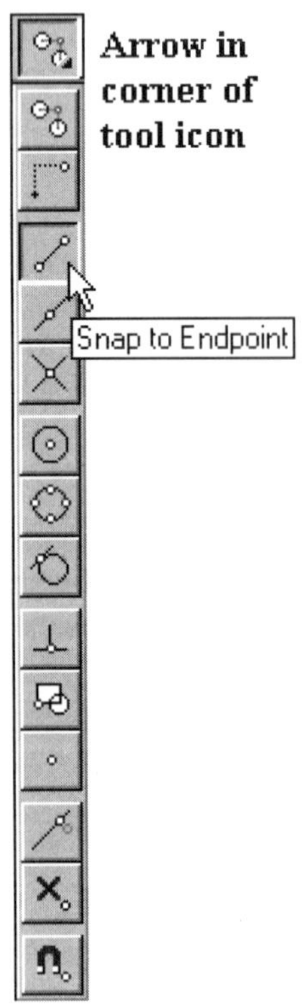

Fig. 2.10 The flyout from the **Tracking** tool icon with the **Snap to Endpoint** tool selected

is selected with a *left-click* on its name, a dialogue box will appear on screen.

Keyboard shortcuts: Some command names are followed on the right-hand side of the pull-down menu with a shortcut such as **Ctrl+N** for **New....** Thus pressing the **Ctrl** key, holding it down and pressing the key **N** will bring up the **Create New Drawing** dialogue box.

Sub-menus: An outward pointing arrow to the right of the menu opposite a command name means that when the name is selected a sub-menu will appear. Figure 2.11 shows the sub-menu which comes to screen when **Drawing Utilities** is selected.

Alt key + menu initial: Pressing the **Alt** key of the keyboard and the initial letter of the required pull-down menu will bring that menu on screen. Thus **Alt+F** brings down the **File** pull-down menu.

Dialogue and message boxes

Figure 2.12 shows the parts of a typical dialogue box, the **Select File** dialogue. Whilst all dialogue boxes do not have all the parts shown in the **Select File** example, Fig. 2.12 does show the essential parts of all dialogue boxes.

Title bar: This not only carries the dialogue box title, but if the cursor under mouse controls is placed in the title bar, the dialogue box can be *dragged* to a new position on screen.

Dialogue box title: This is in the top left-hand corner of the box.

Help ? and Close buttons: *Left-click* on the **?** button, followed by another *left-click* on a part of the dialogue box and a **Help** box appears describing the use of the selected part. In Fig. 2.12 the **?** icon has been placed on the **Open** button followed by a *left-click* with the result that the use of the **Open** button is shown in a **Help** box.

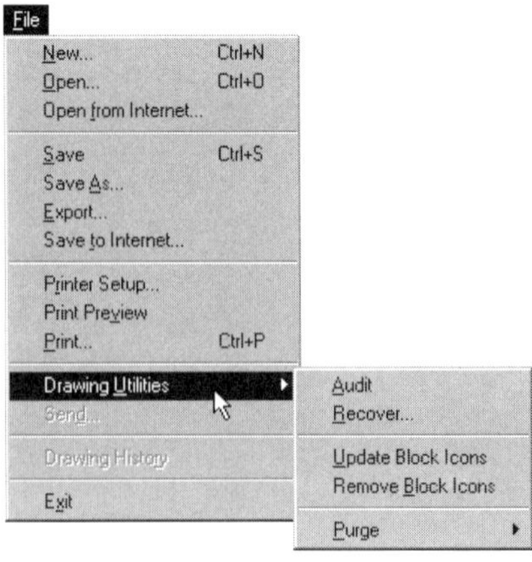

Fig. 2.11 The **File** pull-down menu

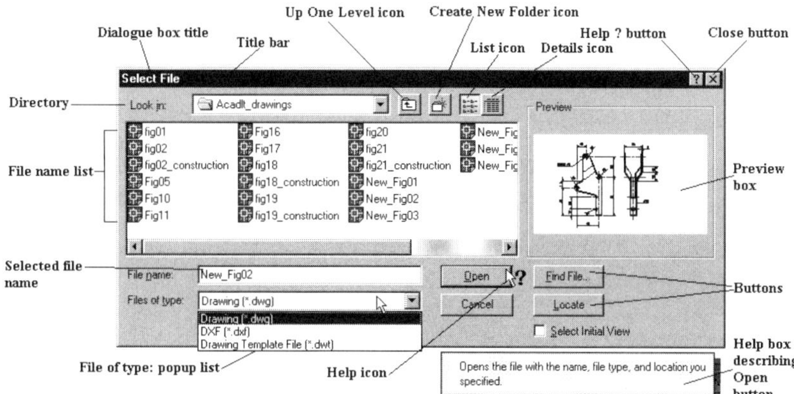

Fig. 2.12 Details of parts of a dialogue box

Directory: A *left-click* in the **Look in:** box brings down a popup list with the names of the disks and directories held on the disks, from which a directory may be chosen.

Tool icons: Four icons to go up a level, create a new folder, list disks or directories and to give details of files are found in a line next to the **Look in:** box.

File name list: Names of all files held in the selected directory are listed here. A *left-click* on a file name and it appears in the **File Name:** box below the File Name list box.

Preview box: This shows a miniature of the drawing in the chosen file.

Type of drawing: *Left-click* in this box and a popup list appears listing the types of files which can be selected from the dialogue box.

Buttons: Four buttons – **Open**, **Find File...**, **Cancel** and **Locate**. Such buttons are common in dialogue boxes. A *left-click* on the **Find File...** buttons brings up the **Browse/Search** dialogue box (Fig. 2.13)

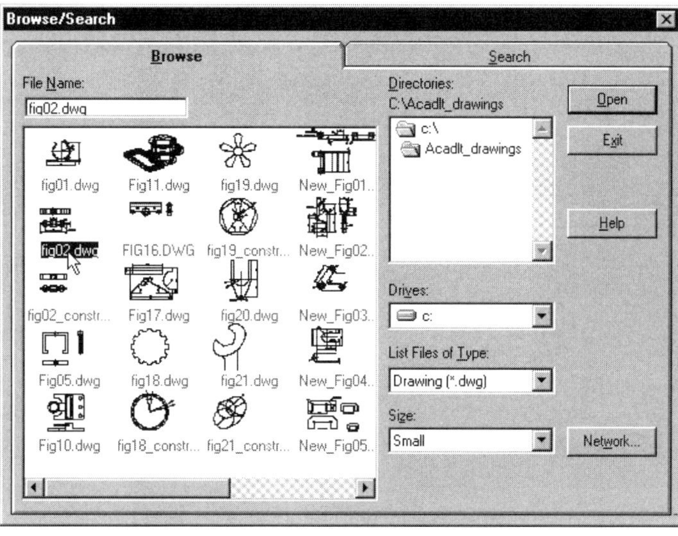

Fig. 2.13 The **Browse/Search** dialogue box

which includes miniatures of the drawings in the selected directory in icon form.

Message boxes

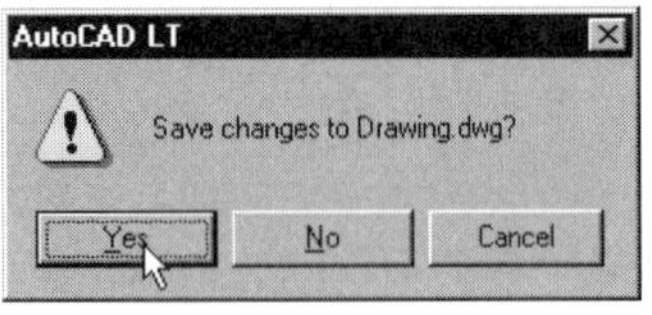

Fig. 2.14 A message box

Figure 2.14 shows a typical message box. This particular message box appears when using the **Open...** command from the **View** pull-down menu if the current drawing has not been previously saved. Other message and warning boxes will be seen as work continues with LT 97. Warning boxes advise the operator when certain operations are not advisable.

Ddcalls

Dialogue boxes can be called to screen by the selection of those commands in pull-down menus which are followed by three fullstops (...). Another method is by calling some of the dialogue boxes from the command line. Dialogue box calls are preceded by **dd** as in the following examples:

ddgrips:	Grips dialogue box.
ddim:	Dimension Styles dialogue box.
ddinsert:	Insert dialogue box.
ddlmodes:	Layer and Linetype Properties dialogue box – layers.
ddltype:	Layer and Linetype Properties dialogue box – linetypes.
ddosnap:	Osnap Settings dialogue box.
ddptype:	Point Style dialogue box.
ddstyle:	Text Style dialogue box.
dducs:	UCS Control dialogue box.
ddunits:	Units Control dialogue box.

Methods of selection of tools (commands)

There are four methods for calling tool (commands) for use when constructing drawings in LT 97. In practice, each operator will decide for him/herself which method it is best to use, or to use one method for calling some tools and different methods for calling others. It depends upon methods of working, but it is usually the method(s) that satisfies the operator as being the fastest to use.

Example 1 – calling the Line tool from the Draw toolbar

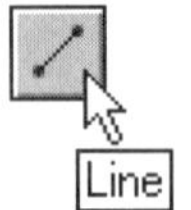

Fig. 2.15 The **Line** tool icon and its tool tip from the **Draw** toolbar

1. Place the cursor under mouse control over the **Line** tool icon in the **Draw** toolbar. Its tool tip appears (Fig. 2.15). A prompt also appears in the Status bar describing the use of the tool (Fig. 2.16).

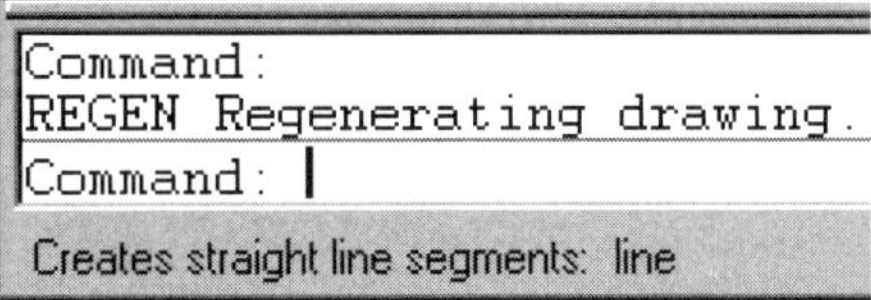

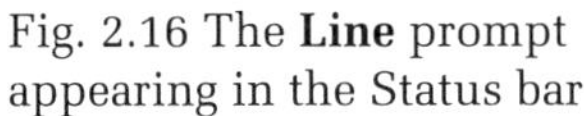

Fig. 2.16 The **Line** prompt appearing in the Status bar

2. *Left-click* and the prompt disappears to be replaced by coordinates giving the position of the cursor at the time. The Command window shows **LINE From point:** (Fig. 2.17).

Fig. 2.17 The **LINE** prompts in the Command window

3. Either move the cursor under mouse control to the coordinate point on screen where the line is to start, followed by a *left-click*, or *enter* the coordinates against the **LINE From point:** prompt, followed by a *right-click*.
4. The prompt in the Command window changes to **To point:**. Either move the cursor under mouse control to the required end of the line and *right-click*, or *enter* the coordinates of the required end of the line.

Example 2 – calling the Line tool from the Draw pull-down menu

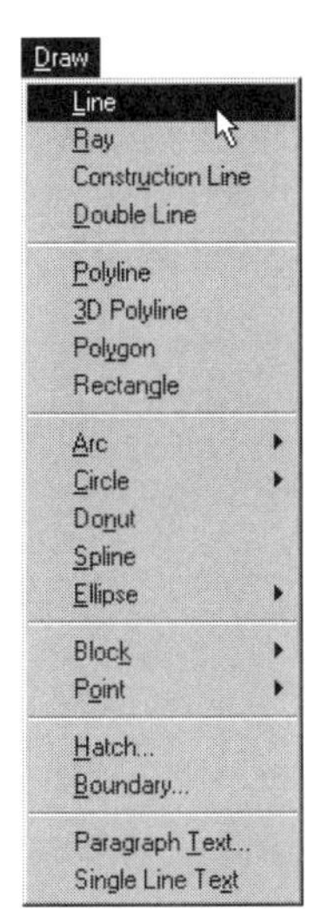

Fig. 2.18 Selecting **Line** from the **Draw** pull-down menu

1. *Left-click* on **Draw** in the menu bar, followed by placing the cursor over the **Line** command (Fig. 2.18). The same prompt as when the **Line** tool icon was selected from the **Draw** toolbar appears in the Status bar.
2. *Left-click* on the **Line** command. The prompts appearing in the Command window only differ from those when the **Line** tool icon is selected by the first line which shows **_line From point** (Fig. 2.19).
3. Draw lines as in the previous example, i.e. either by *entering* coordinates or by selecting points on screen.
4. Note the coordinate figures in the Status bar as the cursor is moved (Fig. 2.19).

Example 3 – entering the tool name in the Command window

1. *Enter* the word **line** in the Command window followed by a *right-click*. Typing letters and/or figures when in LT 97 automatically

enters them at the **Command:** prompt in the Command window (Fig. 2.20).

2. Draw lines as in the previous example – i.e. either by *entering* coordinates or by selecting points on screen.

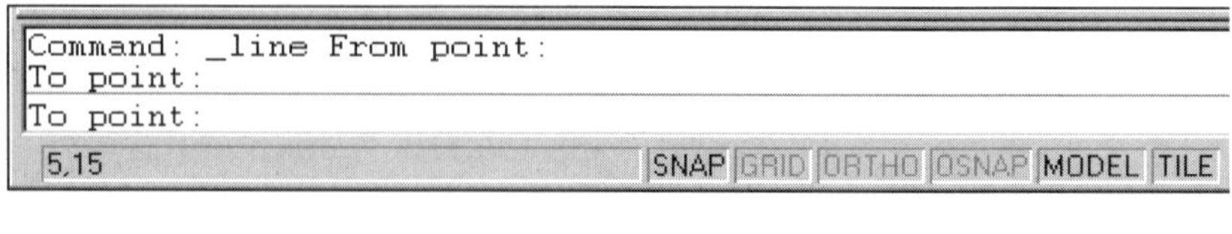

Fig. 2.19 The Command window when **Line** is called from the **Draw** pull-down menu

Command: line
From point:
To point:
295,165
SNAP GRID ORTHO OSNAP MODEL TILE

Fig. 2.20 The Command window when **line** is *entered* at the **Command:** prompt

Example 4 – entering the tool abbreviation in the Command window

1. *Enter* the letter **l** in the Command window followed by a *right-click*.
2. Draw lines as in the previous examples, i.e. either by *entering* coordinates or by selecting points on screen.

Note All tools (commands) have abbreviations allocated to them in LT 97. A list of these in alphabetical order is given in Appendix A (page 247). The abbreviation for **Line** is **l** as shown above in Example 4.

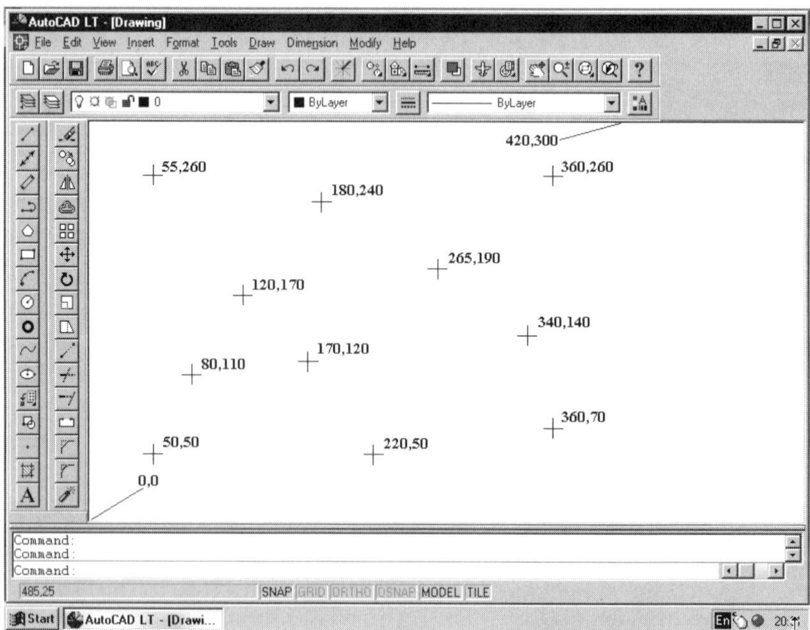

Fig. 2.21 X,Y coordinate points in an AutoCADS LT 97 window

The AutoCAD coordinate system

In the LT 97 window, points in the drawing area of the window are determined by the unit distances horizontally and vertically from an **Origin**. The **Origin** is usually, but not necessarily always, at the bottom left-hand corner of the drawing area and, because it is the origin for all unit distances, it bears the numbers 0,0 – i.e. 0 units horizontally and 0 units vertically.

The units are coordinate units and are stated in LT 97 in terms of X and Y, the X units being those measured along horizontal axes, the Y units those measured along vertical axes. Thus the **Origin** can be referred to as **X,Y = 0,0** or more commonly as x,y=0,0.

The number of X and Y coordinate units in the drawing area is determined by the settings in **Step 5: Area** in the **Advanced Setup** dialogue box (see page 4), or by setting **Limits** as follows:

In the Command window:

Command: *enter* limits *right-click*
ON/OFF/<Lower left corner><0,0>: *right-click*
Upper right corner <12,9>: *enter* 420,300 *right-click*
Command:

Followed by zooming to All (see page 35).

This will set the drawing area to having 420 X units horizontally and 300 Y units vertically.

This method allows any point in the drawing area of an LT 97 window to be determined in terms of x,y coordinate units. The x,y figures for various points in an LT 97 window with Limits set to 420,300 are shown in Fig. 2.21.

Notes

1. X units to the left of the origin (0,0) are measured in negative coordinate units. Thus the point 50 coordinate units to the left of 0,0 is –50,0.
2. Y units below the origin 0,0 are measured in negative coordinate units. Thus the point 50 coordinate units below 0,0 is 0,–50.
3. The point –50,–50 is therefore 50 coordinate units to the left and 50 coordinate units below 0,0.
4. It will be seen later that, when dealing with 3D drawings (Chapter 14), a third coordinate (Z) in a direction perpendicular to the X,Y plane can be introduced into the LT 97 coordinate system.
5. Coordinate units can be taken to represent units of measurement, but take care that **Limits** are set up correctly for this to be possible. For example, in our **Initial.dwt** template, with the upper right-hand corner limits set to 420,300, when a drawing from the window is printed full size, each unit can be taken as representing 1

millimetre. In the USA it is common to set up the top right corner limits to 12,9. In this example, when plotting full scale, each unit can be taken as 1 inch. In this way coordinate units can represent feet, yards, metres, kilometres etc. with a sensible setting of the drawing area limits.

Drawing lines by entering x,y coordinate units

To demonstrate the use of x,y coordinates construct the outline of Fig. 2.22. The upper part of the illustration shows the outline, together with the x,y coordinates *entered* in the Command window to produce the outline. After each coordinate is *entered*, press the *Return* button of the mouse by a *right-click*. Thus the lines of the sequence in the Command window shown in Fig. 2.22 would be *entered* as follows.

1. *Left-click* on the **Line** command in the **Draw** pull-down menu, or *left-click* on **Line** in the **Draw** toolbar. Then in the Command window:

   Command: _line From point: *enter* 80,250 *right-click*
   To point: *enter* 250,250 *right-click*
   And so on until:
   To point : *enter* 80,120 *right-click*
   To point: *enter* c (for Close) *right-click*
   Command:

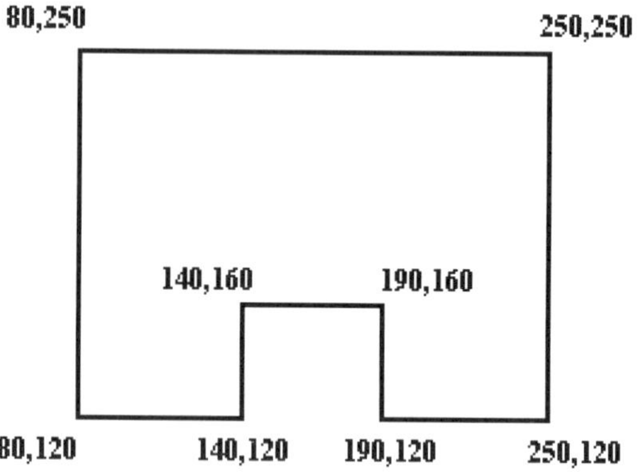


```
Command: _line From point: 80,250
To point: 250,250
To point: 250,120
To point: 190,120
To point: 190,160
To point: 140,160
To point: 140,120
To point: 80,120
To point: c
Command:
```

Fig. 2.22 Drawing a **Line** outline by *entering* coordinate points

Note Sequences such as the above will be frequently seen throughout this book. In these sequences:

Words in **bold** print are the prompts which appear when a tool is chosen or *entered*.
enter means to type at the keyboard. What is typed automatically appears to the right of the prompt being replied to.
right-click means to press the right-hand button of the mouse. The same result can be obtained by pressing the *Return* key of the keyboard, but note it is not always that pressing *Return* has the same result as a *right-click*.

Function key toggles

Using the function keys marked on the keyboard as **F1** to **F10** can speed up working by using these keys to toggle (turn ON or OFF) certain LT 97 functions as follows:

F1 – brings up associative Help. More about Help in Chapter 16.
F2 – toggles the **AutoCAD LT 97 Text Window**, which shows the history of what appears in the Command window.
F3 – brings up the **Osnap Settings** dialogue box.
F4 – toggles a tablet if one is fitted. In this book because a mouse is used as a digitiser, the use of a tablet will not be described.
F5 – toggles between **Top**, **Right** and **Left Isoplanes**. See page 139.
F6 – toggles **Coords**. When on, coordinate numbers show clearly in the Status bar changing with movement of the cursor, showing the location in terms of x,y coordinates of the intersection of the cross hairs of the cursor. When off, the coordinate figures are greyed out and do not change with mouse movement of the cursor cross hair.
F7 – toggles **Grid** points.
F8 – toggles **Ortho**.
F9 – toggles **Snap**.
F10 – second key for toggling a tablet if fitted.

Set variables

The way in which LT 97 functions is largely controlled by settings of set variables. Only a small selection of these will be referred to in this book. Many of the variables are set in dialogue boxes. Many of those we will accept here are the default settings, set when the software package is delivered to the user. Some of the set variables will be shown in Appendix C. To see all the variables:

Command: *enter* setvar *right-click*
Variable name or ?: *enter* **?** *right-click*
Variables (s) to list <*>: *right-click*

And an **AutoCAD LT 97 Text Window** appears showing the first text window of all the set variables and their respective settings. The last line states **Press Enter to continue:**. Repeated pressing of the *Return* key will allow the operator to see all set variables. The first window is shown in Fig. 2.23.

One set variable new to this release of LT is **PICKFIRST**. When this variable is set to **1**, *right-click* menus appear with every selected tool. When set to **0**, the *right-click* menus no longer appear. See page 40.

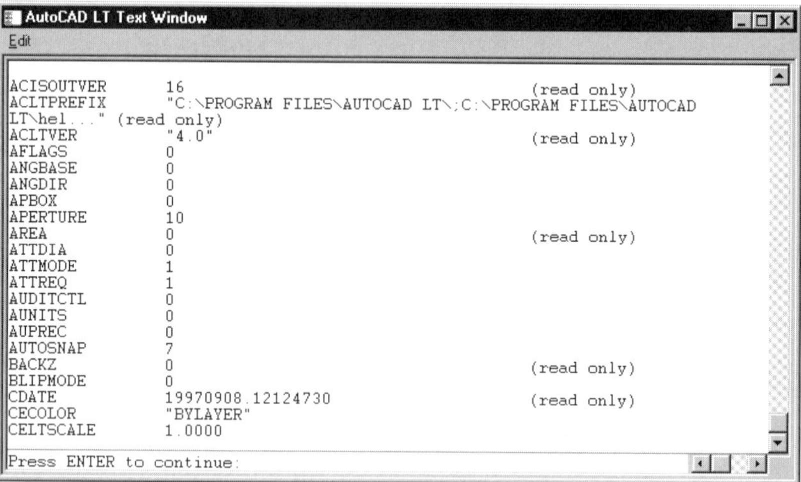

Fig. 2.23 The first of the **AutoCAD LT 97 Text Windows** when setvar is called

Object Snaps (Osnaps)

When the **initial.dwt** template was set up, one of the settings was to set **Snap** to 5 units. This meant that when moving the cursor hairs under mouse control the intersection of the cross hairs snapped from point to point in the drawing area in units of 5 in any direction. When *entering* x,y coordinates in the Command window for the position, e.g. for the ends of lines, these entries ignore the **Snap** setting.

Another form of snap occurs when the **Osnaps** are in operation. With their use, new objects can be started at various points along other objects already in the drawing area. The following Osnaps can be set:

Endpoint: Snap to the endpoint of an object.
Midpoint: Snap to the middle point of an object.

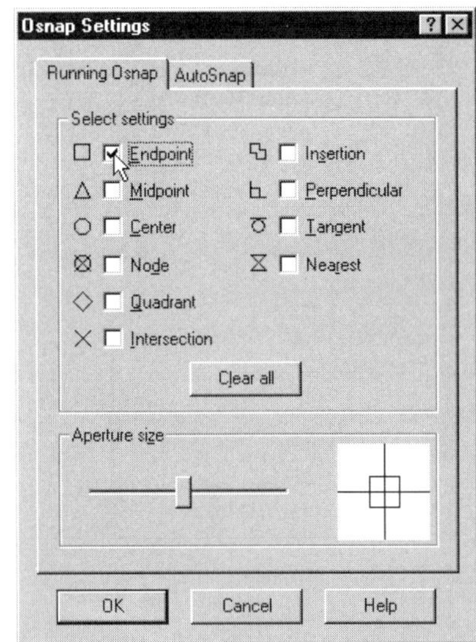

Fig. 2.24 The **Osnap Settings** dialogue box

Center: Snap to the centre of an arc, circle or ellipse.
Node: Snap to a point drawn with the **Point** tool.
Quadrant: Snap to the quadrant point of an arc, circle or ellipse.
Intersection: Snap to the intersecting point of objects on screen – e.g. crossing circles, crossing arcs, lines crossing circle or arc etc.
Insertion: Snap to the insertion point of a block (see Chapter 11).
Perpendicular: Snap so that the object being drawn is perpendicular to the selected object.
Tangent: Snap to the tangent point of an arc, circle or ellipse.
Nearest: Snap to the nearest point on the selected object.

Figure 2.25 gives some examples of the uses of Osnaps. In this illustration the *pick* box is shown on the selected object.

When an Osnap is set, the snap point to which an object becomes attached is the required part of an existing object within the area of the Osnap *pick* box as set in the **Osnaps Settings** dialogue box.

Osnaps can be set in various ways:

Pressing key F3

Press the function key **F3** and the **Osnap Settings** dialogue appears (Fig. 2.24). Any of the Osnaps can be set with a *left-click* in the appropriate check box. If a tick is already in a box, it can be unchecked also with a *left-click* in the box. The size of the *pick* box connected with Osnaps can also be set in this dialogue box, by movement of the slider in the **Aperture Size** area of the box.

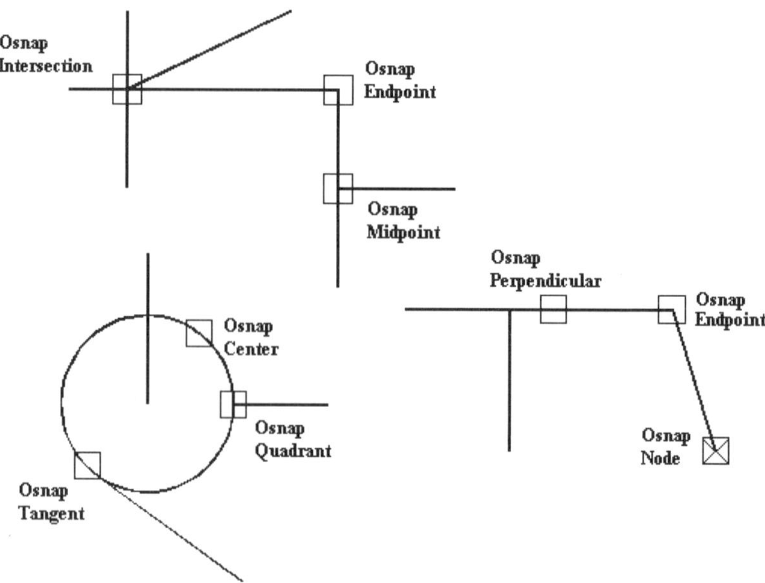

Fig. 2.25 Examples of Osnaps points

Entering ddosnap (or osnap) in the Command window

Command: *enter dd*osnap *right-click*

And the **Osnap Settings** dialogue box appears on screen.

Entering abbreviations as and when required

Enter the following abbreviations for Osnaps in the Command window in response to prompts.

End – for endpoint.
Mid – for midpoint.
Cen – for center.
Nod – for node.
Qua – for quadrant.
Int – for intersection.
Ins – for insertion.
Per – for perpendicular.
Tan – for tangent.

An example of using such abbreviations:

Command: _line From point: *enter* end *right-click*
of *pick* the object on screen
To point: *enter* qua *right-click*
of *pick* near to the quadrant point of the circle to which the line is to be drawn.

And so on.

AutoSnap

Press **F3** to bring up the **Osnap Settings** dialogue box. Then *left-click* on the **AutoSnap** tab at the top of the dialogue box. The **AutoSnap** dialogue box comes up (Fig. 2.26). Set the check boxes against **Marker**, **Magnet** and **Snap Tip** on, set the **Marker** size and colour to your own choice. Then *left-click* on the **Running Osnap** tab and set all the Osnaps on (ticks in their check boxes). See Fig. 2.26.

Now when constructing drawings, when a new object is to snap to another already in the drawing area, AutoSnap pulls the snap onto

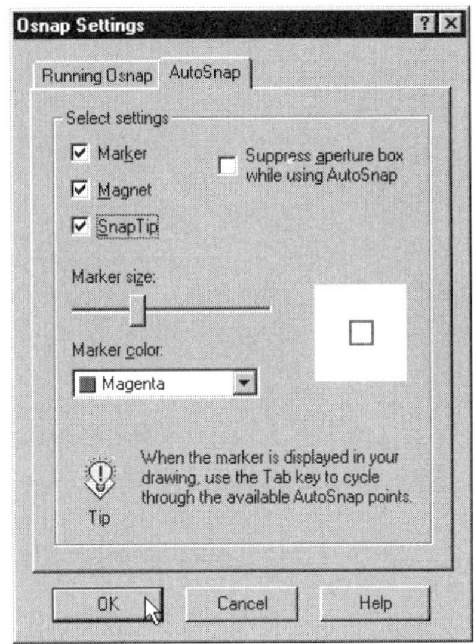

Fig. 2.26 The **AutoSnap** dialogue box

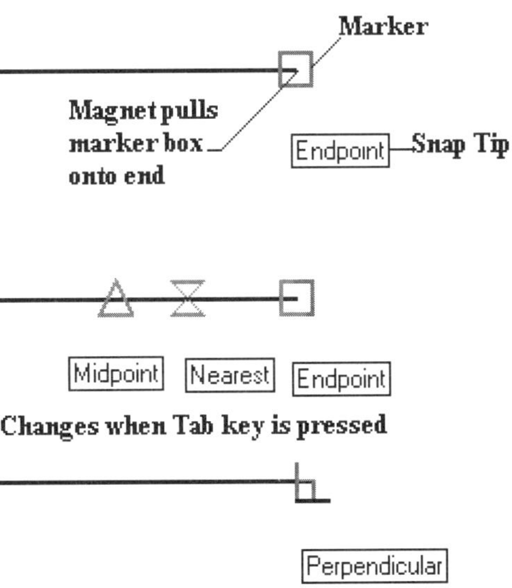

Fig. 2.27 Examples of the **AutoSnap** Marker, Magnet and Snap Tip

the required position with its Magnet, shows its Marker box and its Snap Tip. If, while the Marker and Snap Tip are showing, each time the **Tab** key of the keyboard is pressed, the next AutoSnap point along the object in the drawing area becomes active. See Fig. 2.27.

Figure 2.28 shows other examples of a line being drawn to a circle and the various **AutoSnap** Markers and Snap Tips showing when all Osnaps are active.

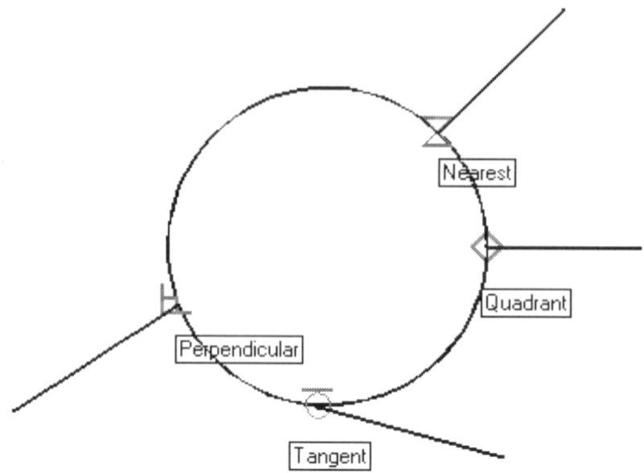

Fig. 2.28 Further examples of **AutoSnap** Markers and Snap Tips

Polar Snap

To set up Polar Snap, at the Command line:

Command: *enter* polar *right-click*

And the **Ortho/Polar Settings** dialogue box appears (Fig. 2.29). In the dialogue box, make sure there is a tick in the **On** check box and a dot

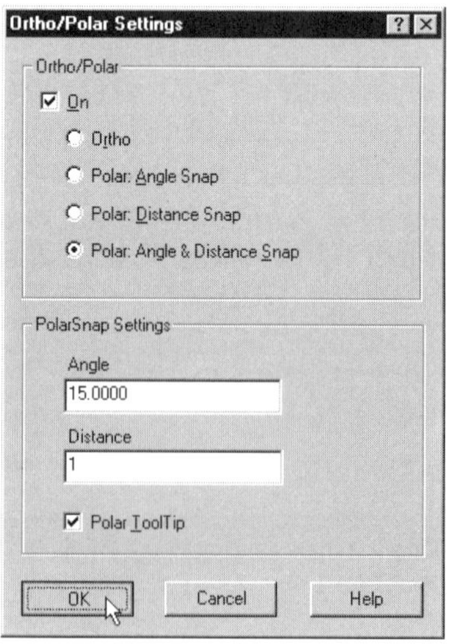

Fig. 2.29 Settings in the **Ortho/Polar Settings** dialogue box

in the **Polar Angle & Distance Snap** check circle. If the tick and dot are not there, *left-click* in the check box and check circle.

Polar Snap only shows the **Angle & Distance Snap** if the **Marker AutoSnap** check box is on in the **AutoSnap** dialogue box. When **Polar Snap** is functioning, objects such as lines and plines can only be drawn at angles as determined by the settings in the **Angle** box of the **Polar Snap Settings** area of the **Ortho/Polar Snap** dialogue box. When they are drawn the **Angle & Distance Snap** shows the angle and distance in relation to the start point of the line or pline. Figure 2.30 shows some typical examples. In Fig. 2.30 the cursor cross hairs have not been included for the sake of clarity.

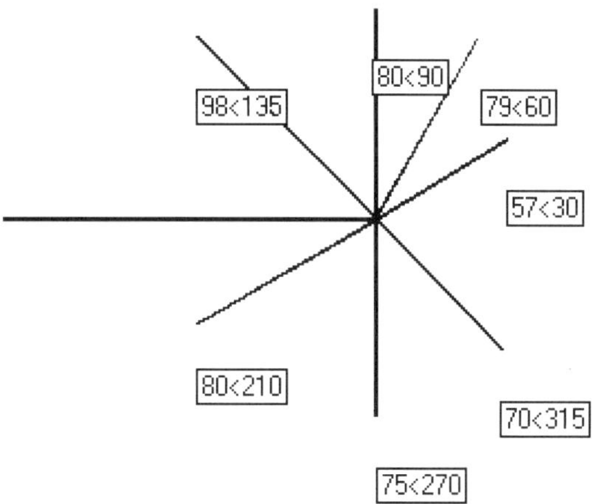

Fig. 2.30 Polar Snaps

Note The default degree angle measurement is counter-clockwise (anticlockwise) from the east. Thus starting with 0 degrees to the right of a start point of an angle measurements are taken anticlockwise back to east. This anticlockwise default angle measurement is shown in Fig. 2.30. It is also shown in Fig. 2.31 in which the angles in 30° intervals from 0° to 330° are shown in the LT 97 default angle measurement method.

Zoom and Pan

The reducing or enlarging parts of a drawing in the drawing area of the LT 97 window (zooming) is an important method employed when inspecting or adding small details to the drawing. Another method frequently employed to see parts of a drawing not within the drawing area is to use panning.

There are a number of ways in which zooms can be initiated:

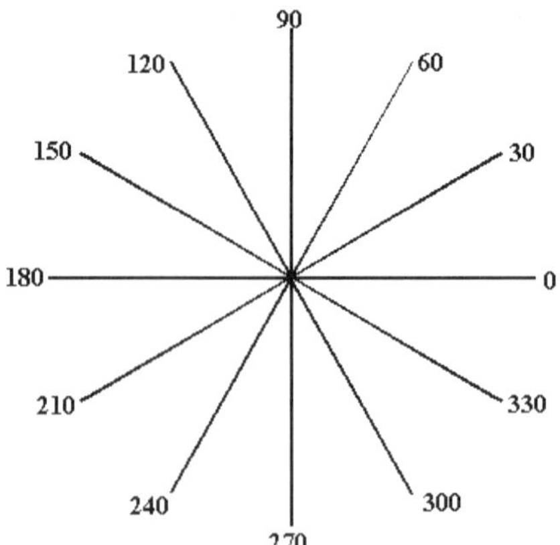

Fig. 2.31 The default angle measurement method of LT 97

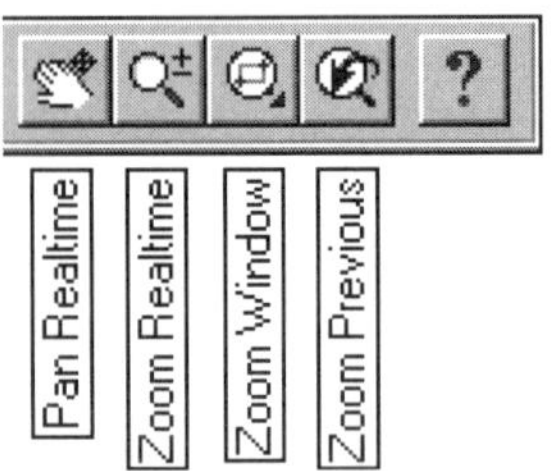

Fig. 2.32 The four **Zoom** and **Pan** icons in the **Standard** toolbar

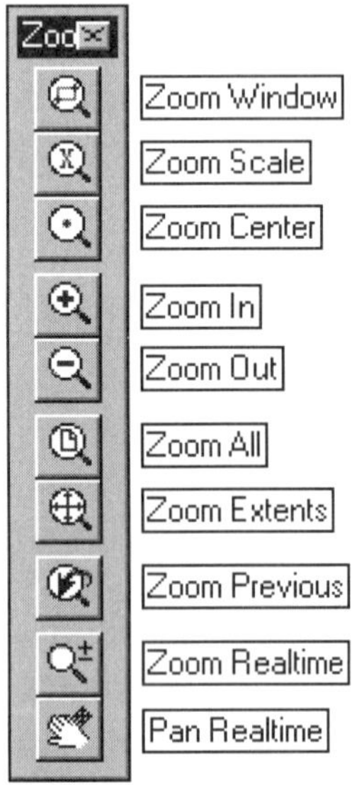

Fig. 2.33 The tools in the **Zoom** toolbar

From the Standard toolbar

Which is usually *docked* in the top of the LT 97 window. The right-hand end of the toolbar contains four tool icons, three of which are **Zoom** tools, the other being the **Pan** tool (Fig. 2.32).

From the Zoom toolbar

The **Zoom** toolbar can, in the same way as other toolbars, be called from the **Toolbars** dialogue box. *Right-click* in any toolbar on screen. The tools in the toolbar are shown in Fig. 2.33.

By entering z in the Command window

Command: *enter* z (for Zoom) *right-click*
All/Center/Extents/Previous/Scale(X/XP)/Window/<Realtime>:

From which series of prompts a zoom can be called by *entering* the initial letter of the required zoom, e.g. w for Window.

Using the central wheel of the Microsoft Intellimouse

Rotating the wheel forward enlarges the drawing in the LT 97 window (**Zoom In**). Rotating the wheel backwards reduces the drawing (**Zoom Out**). Holding the wheel down allows the drawing to be panned in any direction under mouse movement control.

The Zooms

Figures 2.34 to 2.41 illustrate the results of using the variety of zoom tools available. The results are the same no matter which of the methods of calling a zoom is used. The first prompt in the Command window may be either:

> **Command:** **_zoom** or
> **Command: '_zoom or**
> **Command:** *enter* z *right-click*
> **ZOOM**

But the results will be the same.

Zoom All (Fig. 2.34)

Figure 2.34 shows the result of using **Zoom All** on a drawing within the drawing area of LT 97. The drawing area zooms to its limits – in this example in which the top right-hand corner is at x,y = 420,300.

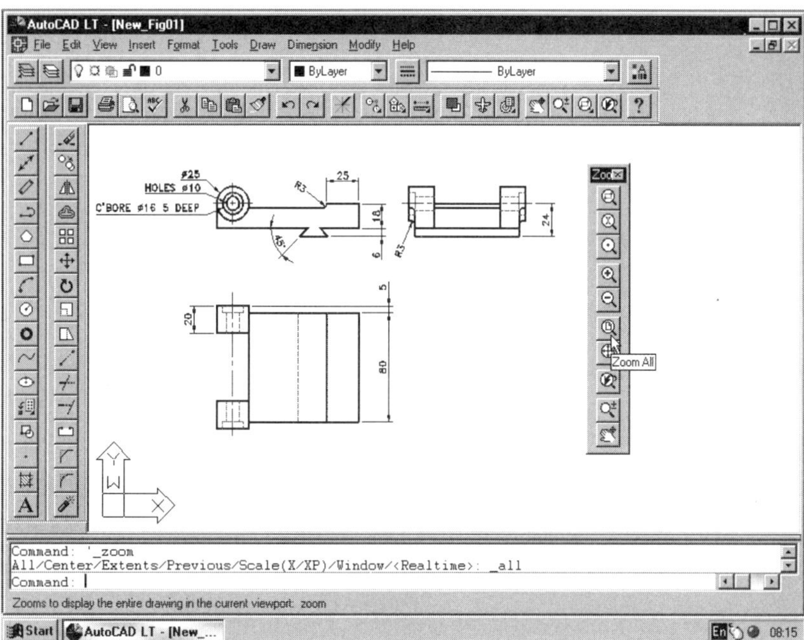

Fig. 2.34 The result of calling **Zoom All**

Zoom Center (Fig. 2.35)

Call **Zoom Center**. The Command line shows:

> **Select Center point:** *pick* the required central point on screen
> **Magnification or Height <297>:** *right-click*

And the drawing regenerates around the central point which has been *picked*. It is advisable to practise with the *entry* of different numbers at this prompt to check on the results.

Note: It is the central point of the drawing area which must be *picked* and not the central part of the drawing.

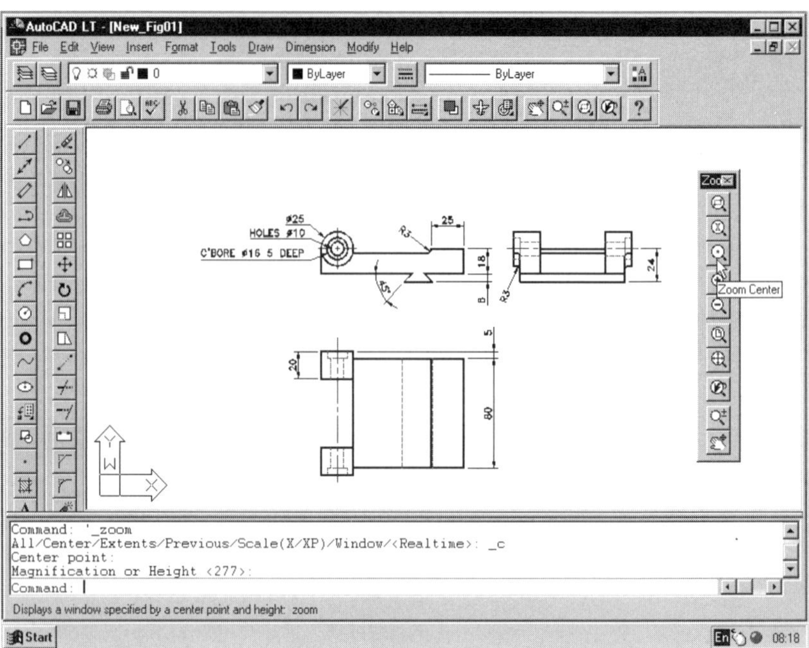

Fig. 2.35 The result of calling **Zoom Center**

Zoom Extents (Fig. 2.36)

Call **Zoom Extents.** The drawing regenerates to fill the drawing area. Parts of the drawing will then be practically touching the borders of the drawing area.

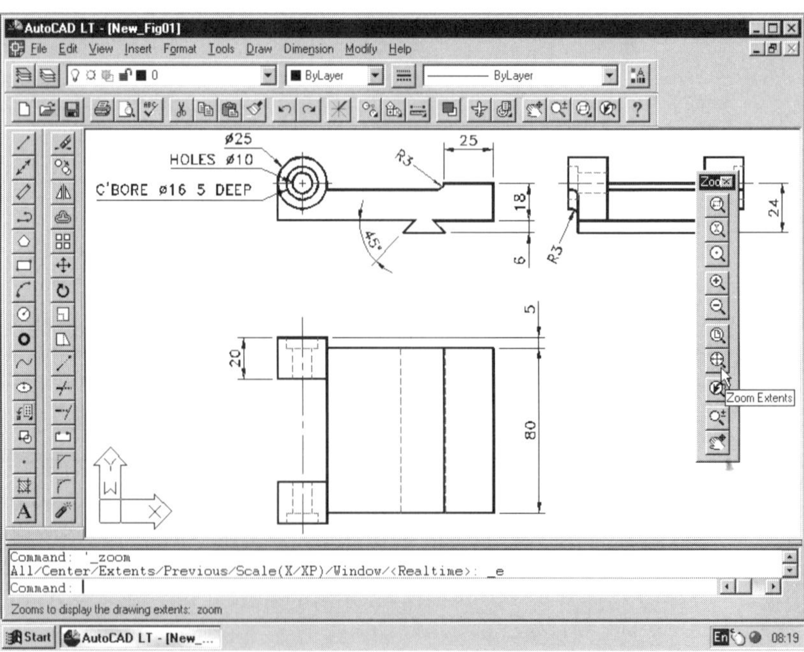

Fig. 2.36 The result of calling **Zoom Extents**

Zoom Window (Fig. 2.37)

Call **Zoom Window**. The Command window shows:

First corner: *pick* **Other corner:** *pick*

And the screen regenerates with that part of the drawing within the selected corner points of the window showing and filling the drawing area. This zoom call is probably the one you will be using most, in order to either examine small areas of a drawing on screen or to construct detailed parts of a drawing.

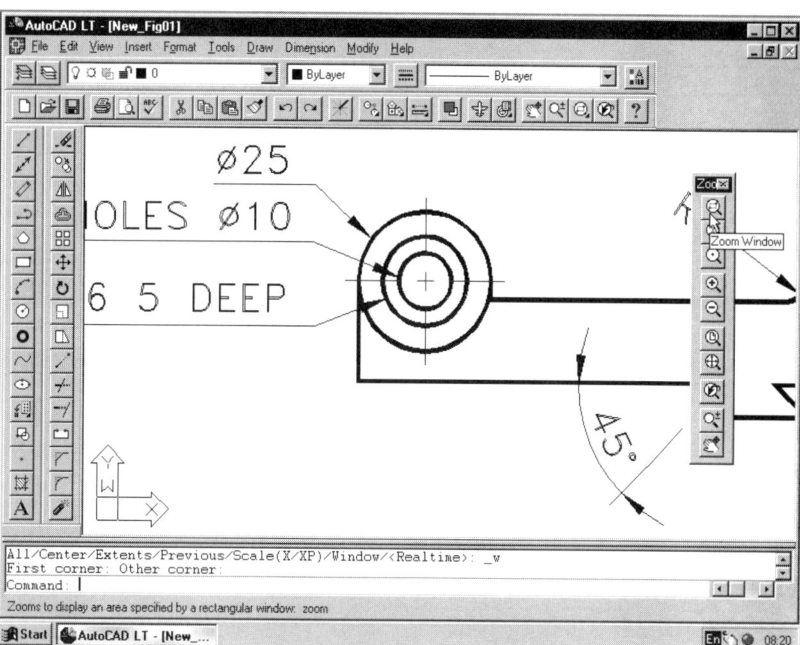

Fig. 2.37 The result of calling **Zoom Window**

Zoom Previous (Fig. 2.38)

Call **Zoom Previous** and the drawing regenerates to the zoom in which the drawing had been placed previously. In the example given (Fig. 2.38) the previous zoom was a **Zoom Extents**.

Zoom Realtime (Fig. 2.39)

Call **Zoom Realtime** and a small zoom icon appears in the window under mouse control. The icon represents a small magnifying glass with a ± symbol on it right. Move the icon upwards under mouse control and the drawing zooms in (gets bigger). Move the icon under mouse control downwards and the drawing zooms out (becomes smaller). To come out of **Zoom Realtime**, *right-click*. This brings a small menu on screen, from which, a *left-click* on **Exit** takes one out

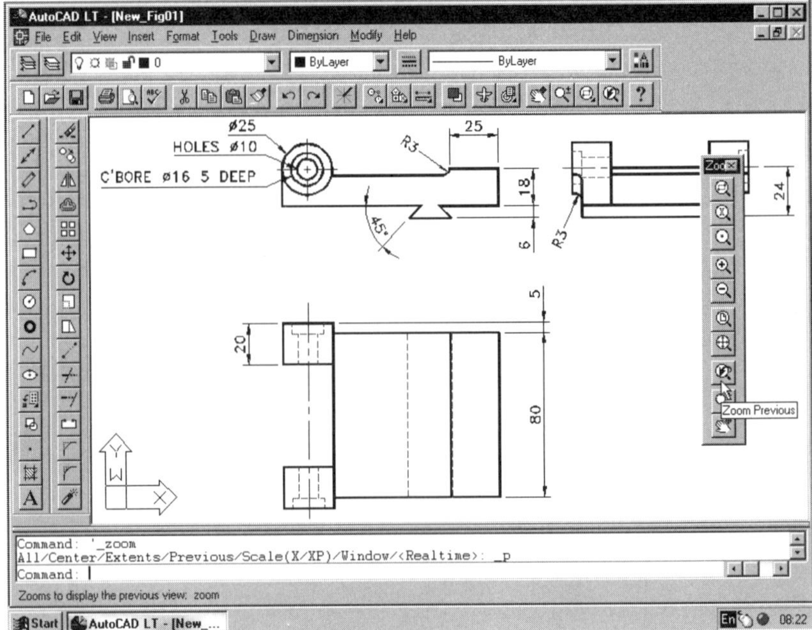

Fig. 2.38 The result of calling **Zoom Previous**

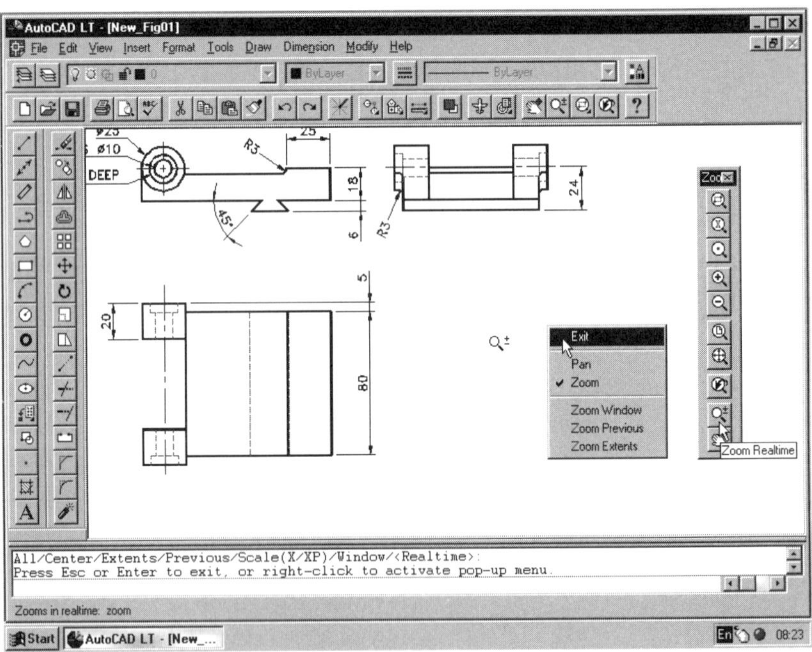

Fig. 2.39 The result of calling **Zoom Realtime**

of the **Realtime Zoom**. The icon and the menu are shown in Fig. 2.39, but in reality they will never appear on screen at the same time.

The Aerial View window (Fig. 2.41)

Select **Aerial View** from the **View** pull-down menu (Fig. 2.40). The **Aerial View** window appears. This is a useful adjunct when using zooms or pans because it shows the results within a thick black rectangle in the drawing area. Figure 2.41 shows the rectangle in the **Aerial View** window of a zoom window in the drawing area of LT 97. A similar black rectangle will show for all zooms and pans. It is advisable to practise zooming and panning with the **Aerial View** window on screen.

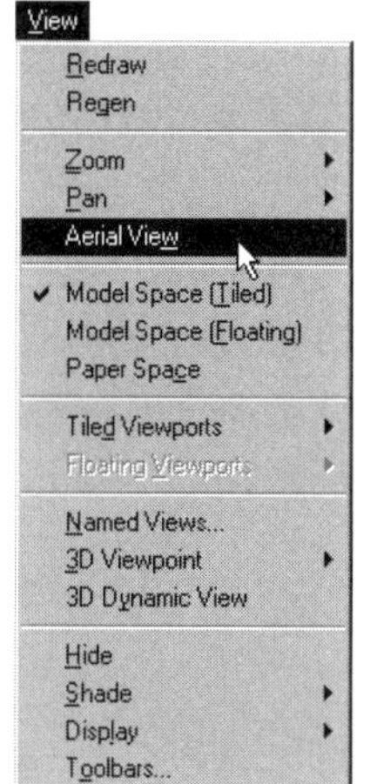

Fig. 2.40 Selecting **Aerial View** from the **View** pull-down menu

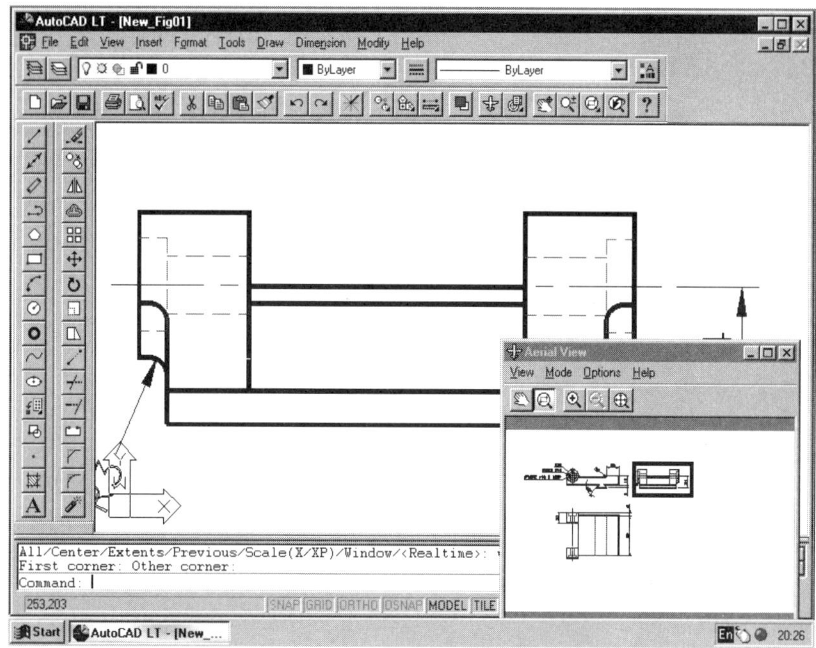

Fig. 2.41 The **Aerial View** window showing the results of a **Zoom Window**

The Pan tool

Call **Pan Realtime** or *enter* p at the Command line. A **Pan** icon appears on screen which can be moved under mouse control (Fig. 2.42). Movement of the icon in any direction moves the whole drawing in that direction. This is known as panning. In the same manner that **Zoom Realtime** is exited, so a *right-click* when the pan icon is on screen, brings up a menu, from which a *left-click* on **Exit** takes the operator out of the panning. See Fig. 2.42.

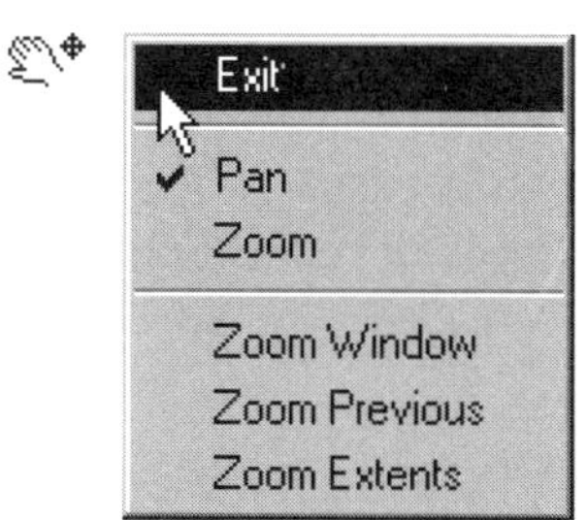

Fig. 2.42 The **Pan** icon and its *right-click* menu

Note Holding down the wheel of the Microsoft Intellimouse also brings a pan icon on screen, which is different in shape to the LT 97 pan icon but operates in a similar manner. Hold down the wheel and the drawing on screen can be panned in the direction in which the mouse is moved.

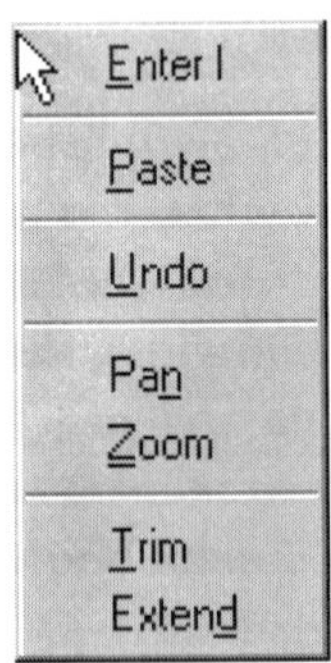

Fig. 2.43 The *right-click* menu when **l** is *entered* at Command line

Fig. 2.44 The *right-click* menu when **Move** is selected from the **Modify** toolbar

Right-click menus

When a tool name or its abbreviation is *entered* at the Command line, followed by a *right-click* a *right-click* menu appears on screen. An example is given in Fig. 2.43 for the menu which appears when **l** is *entered* at the Command line.

If a tool is selected from a toolbar, and if it is immediately called again before another tool is called, the *right-click* which brings back the tool's action brings up a *right-click* menu such as that shown in Fig. 2.44.

Note The set variable PICKFIRST determines whether *right-click* menus show up or not. With PICKFIRST set to **1** *right-click* menus are in action. If set to **0** they are not. At the Command line:

Command: *enter* pickfirst *right-click*
New value for PICKFIRST <1>: *enter* 0 *right-click*
Command:

And the *right-click* menus will no longer show when tools are in action.

Questions

1. How many methods of bringing the **Toolbars** dialogue box on screen are available?
2. How can an operator create his/her own toolbar containing the tools most frequently used?
3. What is meant by the term *floating* toolbar?
4. What is a *flyout*?
5. What is the purpose of the **?** icon which appears at the top right-hand corner of some dialogue boxes?
6. There are four ways in which tools (commands) can be called into action when working in LT 97. Can you describe all four?
7. Can you describe the AutoCAD LT 97 coordinate system?
8. What is a set variable?
9. *Right-click* menus can be displayed when a tool is in action and it has been necessary to *right-click*. How can the operator stop these menus from appearing?
10. What are the differences between an **Osnap**, an **AutoSnap** and a **Polar Snap**.

Exercises

1. Practise calling dialogue boxes on screen, either from a pull-down menu or by using the dd calls. Experiment with settings in the

dialogue boxes you call onto the screen.

2. Draw some lines and then practise using the various **Zoom** calls, noting the results in each case.
3. Set a number of Osnaps from the relevant dialogue box. Also set all the AutoSnap features. Then experiment with Osnaps and AutoSnaps on some lines drawn on screen.
4. Set **PICKFIRST** to **0** and check what happens when tools are being used. Then set it to **1** and check again.

CHAPTER 3

2D drawing tools

Introduction

The four methods of calling **Draw** tools for use in the construction of drawings were described in Chapter 2. The four methods are:

1. Selecting the tool icon from the **Draw** toolbar with a *left-click*.
2. Selecting the tool name from the **Draw** pull-down menu.
3. *Entering* the tool name in the Command window, followed by a *right-click*.
4. *Entering* the tool name abbreviation in the Command window, followed by a *right-click*.

In this chapter drawings constructed with the aid of a number of the **Draw** tools will be described, including their associated prompts which appear in the Command window, together with the operator responses. All four methods of calling the tool will be included in illustrations for each of the tools described.

As an example, the following are the first lines of the prompts appearing in the Command window when the **Polyline** tool is called from the **Draw** toolbar:

Command: _pline
From point: *enter* 100,100 *right-click*
Arc/Close/Halfwidth/Length/Undo/Width/<Endpoint of line>: *enter* w (for Width) *right-click*

In this example:

pline – when a tool is selected from a toolbar its name appears preceded by a bar (). If *entered* from the keyboard, the bar does not appear.
enter – means to type what follows at the keyboard.
right-click – press the right button of the mouse.
Arc/Close/Halfwidth – are the prompts associated with methods of using the tool.

w – the initial letter of the **Width** prompt. To make any prompt effective, *enter* its initial letter, or the parts of the prompt shown in the prompt line in capital letters.

<Endpoint of line>: the default prompt which is automatically accepted if the response is a *right-click*.

The Escape key and the Erase tool

When a mistake has been made, the **Esc** key of the keyboard or the **Erase** tool can be used to rectify the error.

The Esc key of the keyboard

When a wrong tool has been called, pressing the **Esc** key cancels the tool and takes the operator back to **Command:** in the Command window. Also if the operator wishes to escape from a sequence when using a tool's prompts, pressing **Esc** stops further work with that tool and **Command:** appears in the Command window.

The Erase tool (Fig. 3.1)

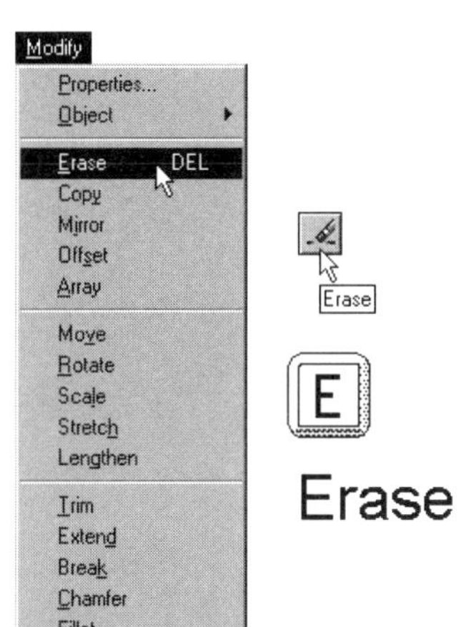

Fig. 3.1 Methods of calling the **Erase** tool

Enter e at the Command line (Fig. 3.1). The Command window shows:

Command: *enter* e *right-click*
Select objects: *pick* the object to be erased
Select objects: *right-click*
Command:

And the object disappears from screen.

If a number of objects are to be erased

Command: *enter* e *right-click*
Select objects: *pick* a point above the top, left-hand corner of the objects
Other corner: *drag* a window down to below the bottom right of the objects and *left-click* **19 found** and the objects ghost
Select objects: *right-click*
Command:

And all the objects **within** the window are erased. If the window is *dragged* from bottom right to top left all objects **crossed** by the lines of the window are erased.

See Fig. 3.2

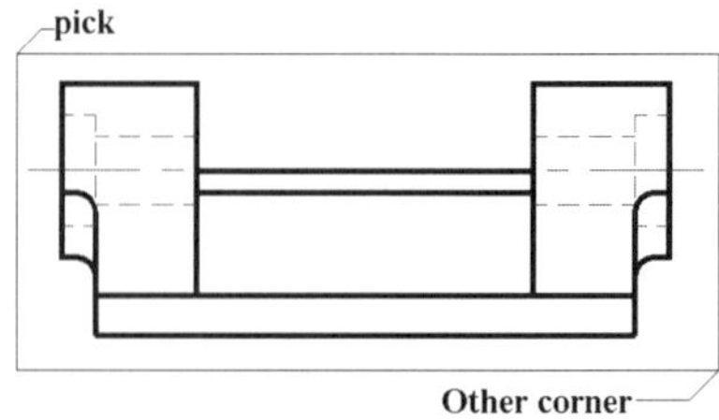

Fig. 3.2 The **Erase** window

Note If a mistake has been made when erasing:

Command: *enter* oops *right-click*
Command:

And the erased object(s) reappear.

Drawing with Draw tools

The Line tool (Fig. 3.3)

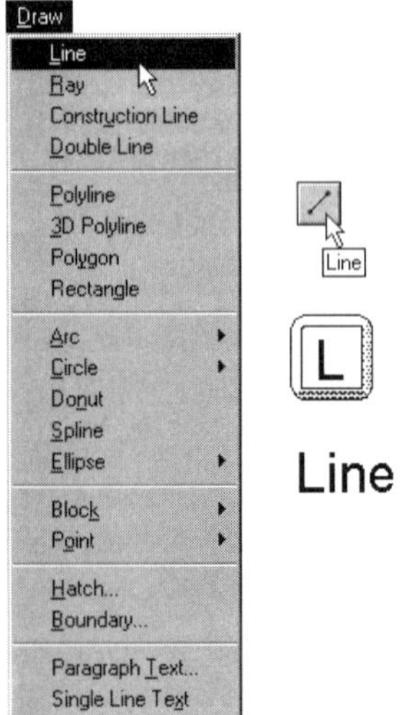

Fig. 3.3 Methods of calling the **Line** tool

Call the **Line** tool from the **Draw** toolbar with a *left-click* on its tool icon (Fig. 3.3) The Command window shows:

Command: _line From point: *enter* 100,220 *right-click*
To point: *enter* 150,220 *right-click*
To point: *enter* 150,180 *right-click*
To point: *enter* 230,180 *right-click*
To point: *enter* 230,220 *right-click*
To point: *enter* 280,220 *right-click*
To point: *enter* 280,100 *right-click*
To point: *enter* 100,100 *right-click*
To point: *enter* c (Close) *right-click*
Command:

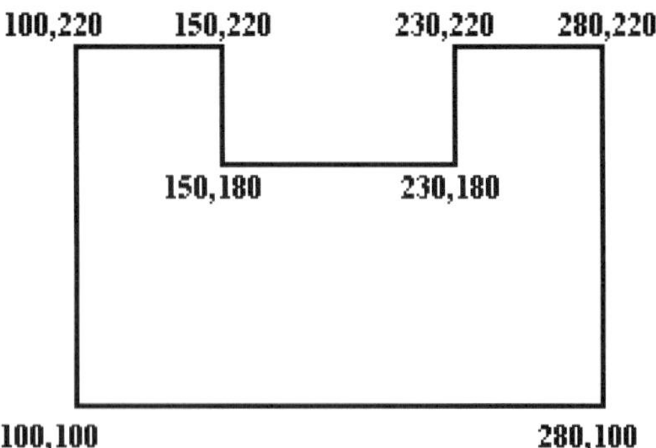

Fig. 3.4 An outline drawn with the aid of the **Line** tool

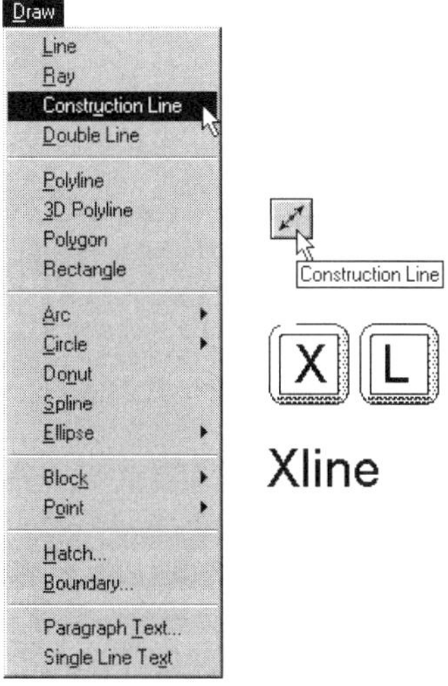

Fig. 3.5 Methods of calling the **Construction Line** tool

The Construction Line tool (Fig. 3.5)

Call the **Construction Line** tool by *entering* xl at the Command line (Fig. 3.5), The Command window shows:

Command: *enter* xl *right-click*
Hor/Ver/Ang/Bisect/Offset/<From point>: *enter* h *right-click*
Through point: *pick* 100,250
Through point: *pick* 100,170
Through point: *pick* 100,90
Through point: *pick* 100,20
Through point: *right-click*
Command: *right-click*
Hor/Ver/Ang/Bisect/Offset/<From point>: *enter* v *right-click*
Through point: *pick* 70,150
Through point: *pick* 160,150
Through point: *pick* 250,150
Through point: *pick* 410,150
Through point: *right-click*
Command:

Notes

1. To *pick* the coordinate point, move the cursor under mouse control until the intersection of the cross hairs shows the coordinate figures in the sequence above in the prompt line.
2. Construction lines are of infinite length passing through the *picked* or *entered* points.
3. Construction lines are of value in setting out guide lines for a drawing. An example is given in Fig. 3.6.

Construction Line example (Fig. 3.6)

1. Reset Units to **Decimal** 2 (Fig. 3.7).

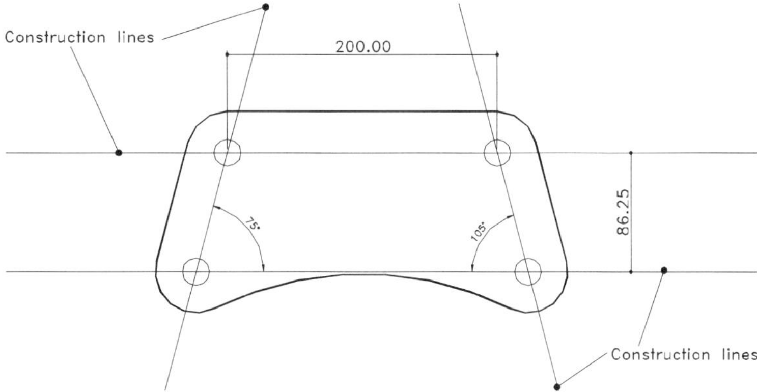

Fig. 3.6 The outline of the **Construction Line** example

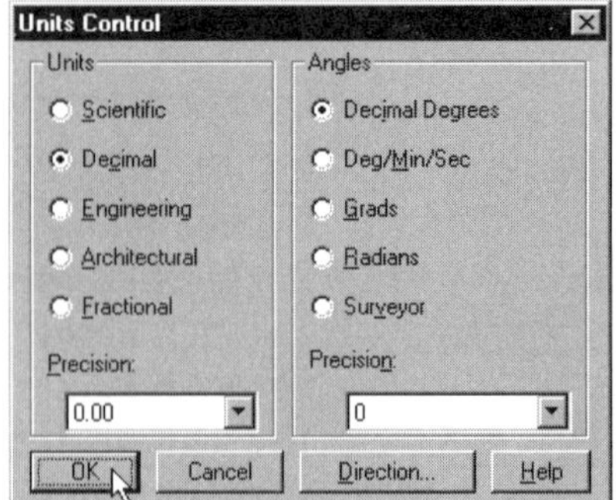

Fig. 3.7 Reset Units to **Decimal** 2

2. Select **Construction Line** from the **Draw** toolbar:

Command: _xline Hor/Ver/Ang/Bisect/Offset/<From point>: *enter* h *right-click*
Through point: *pick* 110,210
Through point: *right-click*
Command: *right-click*
XLINE Hor/Ver/Ang/Bisect/Offset/<From point>: *enter* o *right-click*
Offset distance or Through: *enter* 86.25 *right-click*
Select a line object: *pick* the horizontal construction line
Side to offset: *left-click* on any point below the line
Select a line object: *right-click*
Command: *right-click*
XLINE Hor/Ver/Ang/Bisect/Offset/<From point>: *enter* a *right-click*
Reference/<Enter angle>: *enter* 75 *right-click*
Through point: *pick* 110,190
Through point: *right-click*
Command: *right-click*
XLINE Hor/Ver/Ang/Bisect/Offset/<From point>: *enter* a *right-click*
Reference/<Enter angle>: *enter* 105 *right-click*
Through point: *pick* 300,190
Through point: *right-click*
Command:

This draws four construction lines on which the outline Fig. 3.7 is based.

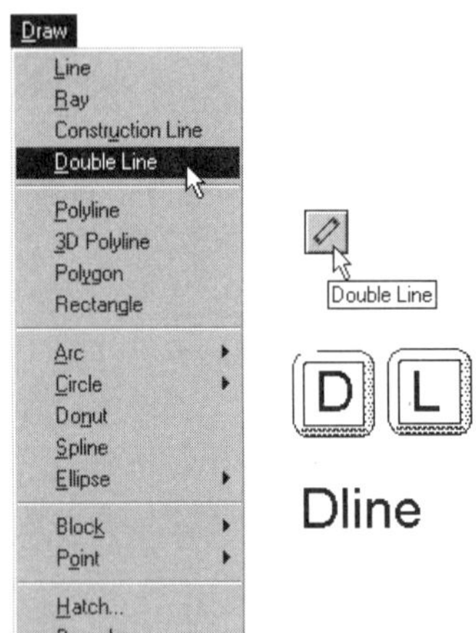

Fig. 3.8 Methods of calling the **Double Line** tool

The Double Line tool (Fig. 3.8)

Select **Double Line** from the **Draw** pull-down menu (Fig. 3.8). The Command window shows:

Command: _dline

Break/Caps/Dragline/Offset/Snap/Undo/Width/<Start point>: *enter* w (Width) *right-click*
New DLINE width <0>: *enter* 20 *right-click*
Break/Caps/Dragline/Offset/Snap/Undo/Width/<start point>: *enter* 40,230 *right-click*
Arc/Break/CAps/CLose/Dragline/Snap/Undo/Width/<nextpoint>: *enter* 270,230 *right-click*
Arc/Break/CAps/CLose/Dragline/Snap/Undo/Width/<nextpoint>: *enter* 270,110 *right-click*
Arc/Break/CAps/CLose/Dragline/Snap/Undo/Width/<nextpoint>: *enter* 40,110 *right-click*
Arc/Break/CAps/CLose/Dragline/Snap/Undo/Width/<nextpoint>: *enter* cl (CLose) *right-click*
Command:

Figure 3.9 shows the results of the above sequence of prompts and responses.

Fig. 3.9 An example of a **Double Line** outline

Figure 3.10 shows the results of some of the responses to the **Double Line** prompts.

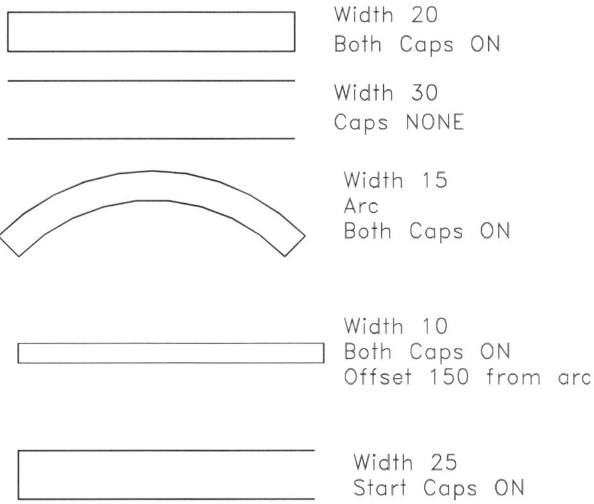

Fig. 3.10 Results of some of responses to **Double Line** prompts

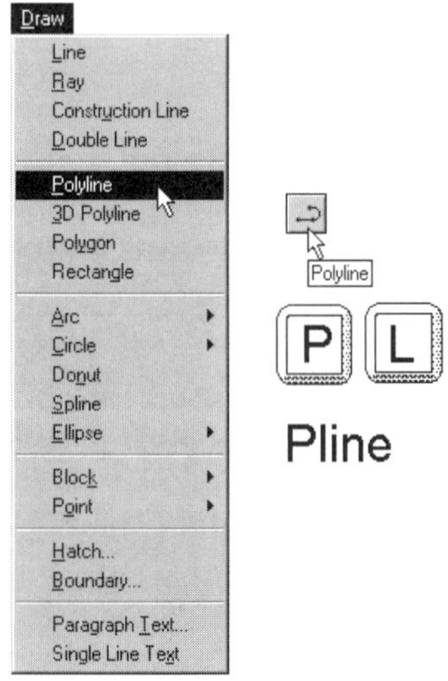

Fig. 3.11 Methods of calling the **Polyline** tool

The Polyline tool (Fig. 3.11)

Select **Polyline** from the **Draw** toolbar (Fig. 3.11). The Command window shows:

Command: _pline
From point: *enter* 25,230 *right-click*
Current line width is 0
Arc/Close/Halfwidth/Length/Undo/Width/<Endpointofline>: *enter* w (Width) *right-click*
Starting width <0> *enter* 1 *right-click*
Ending width <1>: *right-click*
Arc/Close/Halfwidth/Length/Undo/Width/<Endpointofline>: *enter* 200,230 *right-click*
Arc/Close/Halfwidth/Length/Undo/Width/<Endpointofline>: *enter* 200,120 *right-click*

And so on until the outline Fig. 3.12 has been drawn.

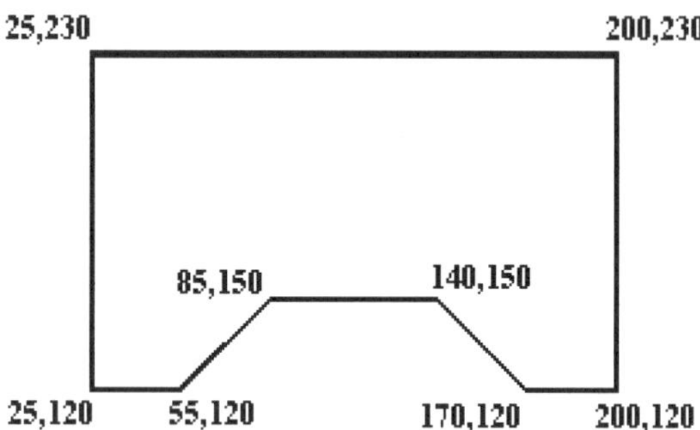

Fig. 3.12 An outline of **Width** 1 drawn with the **Polyline** tool

Figure 3.13 shows some examples of polylines. The prompts and responses for the arc would have been:

Command: _pline
From point: *enter* 10,125 *right-click*
Current line width is 0
Arc/Close/Halfwidth/Length/Undo/Width/<Endpointofline>: *enter* w (Width) *right-click*
Starting width <0> *enter* 2 *right-click*
Ending width <2>: *right-click*
Arc/Close/Halfwidth/Length/Undo/Width/<Endpointofline>: *enter* a (Arc) *right-click*
Angle/CEnter/CLose/Direction/Halfwidth/Line/Radius/Second pt/ Undo/Width/<Endpoint of arc>: *enter* s (Second pt) *right-click*
Second point: *enter* 70,160 *right-click*

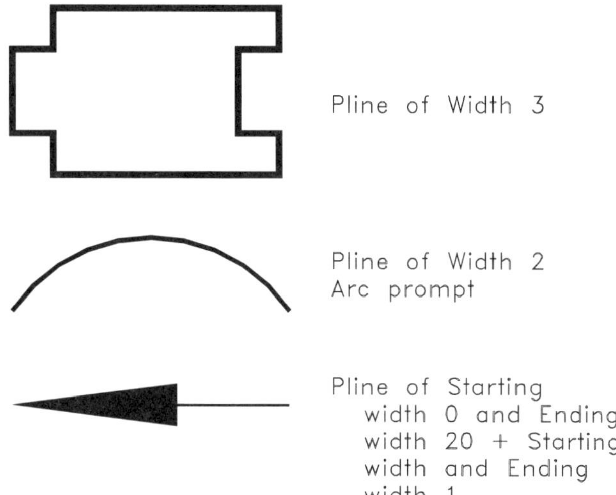

Fig. 3.13 Examples of polylines

End point: *enter* 135,125 *right-click*
<Endpoint of arc>: *right-click*
Command:

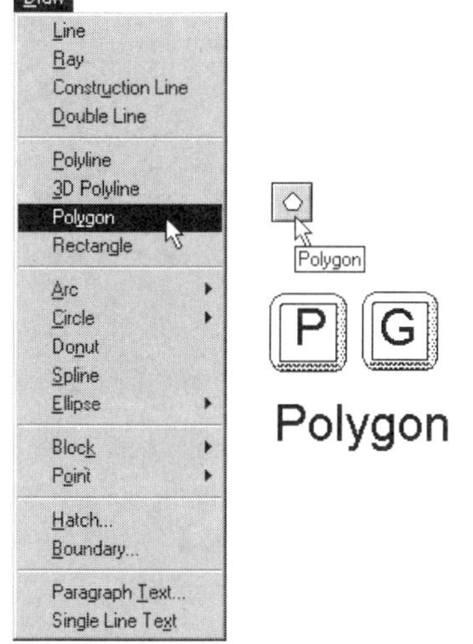

Fig. 3.14 Methods of calling the **Polygon** tool

Note As can be seen from the above examples the prompts of the **Polyline** tool can be rather complex. It is important to practise using the variety of polyline prompts because this tool is among those most likely to be used when constructing drawings in LT 97.

The Polygon tool (Fig. 3.14)

Enter pg at the Command line (Fig. 3.14). The Command window shows:

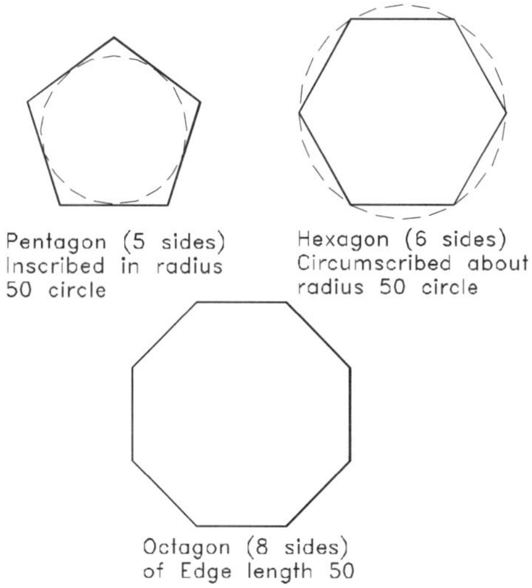

Pentagon (5 sides) Inscribed in radius 50 circle

Hexagon (6 sides) Circumscribed about radius 50 circle

Octagon (8 sides) of Edge length 50

Fig. 3.15 Examples of polygons constructed with the **Polygon** tool

Command: *enter* pg *right-click*
POLYGON Number of sides <4>: *enter* 5 *right-click*
Edge/<Center of polygon>: *enter* 170,180 *right-click*
Inscribed in circle/Circumscribed about circle/(I/C) <I>: *right-click*
Radius of circle: *enter* 50 *right-click*
The pentagon appears on screen, waiting to be *dragged* into position by a rubber band attached to the cursor. It can be fixed in position by *picking* a point on screen.
Command:

Figure 3.15 gives examples of a variety of polygons constructed with the tool.

The Rectangle tool (Fig. 3.16)

Left-click on the **Rectangle** tool in the **Draw** toolbar (Fig. 3.16). The Command window shows:

Command: _rectang
Chamfer/Elevation/Fillet/Thickness/Width/<First corner>: *enter* 20,270 *right-click*
Other corner: *enter* 120,200 *right-click*
Command:

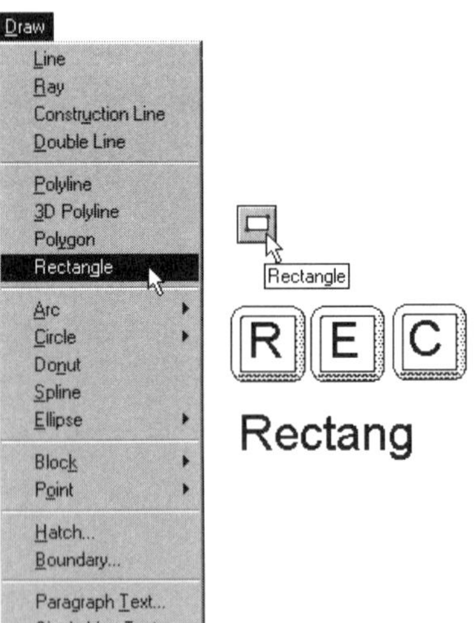

Fig. 3.16 Methods of calling the **Rectangle** tool

The **Elevation** and **Thickness** prompt refer to a rectangular three-dimensional solid which can be constructed as shown in the example shown in Fig. 3.17.

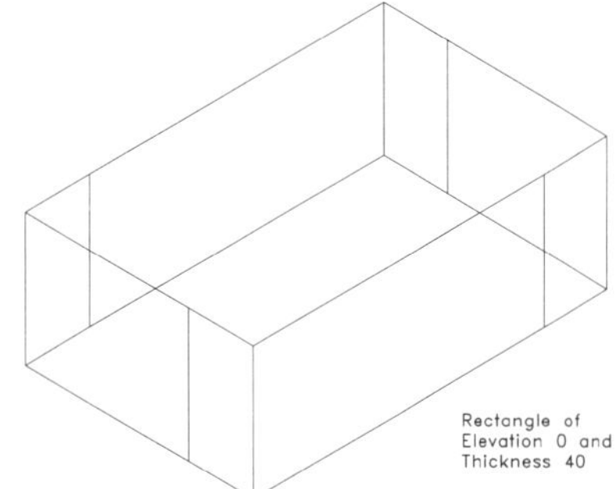

Fig. 3.17 An example of a rectangle constructed with the **Rectangle** tool responding to the **Thickness** prompt

Examples of responses to other prompts from the **Rectangle** tool prompts are shown in Fig. 3.18.

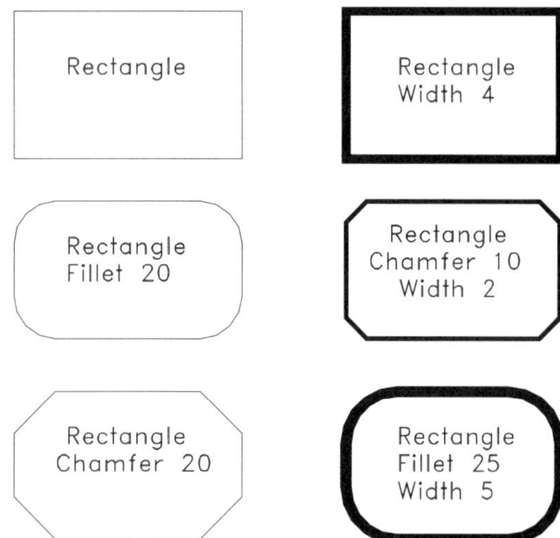

Fig. 3.18 Examples of rectangles using a variety of responses to prompts

The Arc tool (Fig. 3.19)

Left-click on the **Arc** in the **Draw** pull-down menu, followed by a *left-click* on **3 Points** in the sub-menu (Fig. 3.19). The Command window shows:

Command: _arc Center/<Start point>: *enter* 180,160 *right-click*
Second point: *enter* 150,210 *right-click*
End point: *enter* 280,160 *right-click*
Command:

Notes

1. The **Arc** prompts are made up from **Center**, **Start point**, **End point**, **Angle** and **Continue**. As can be seen from the sub-menu of the **Arc**

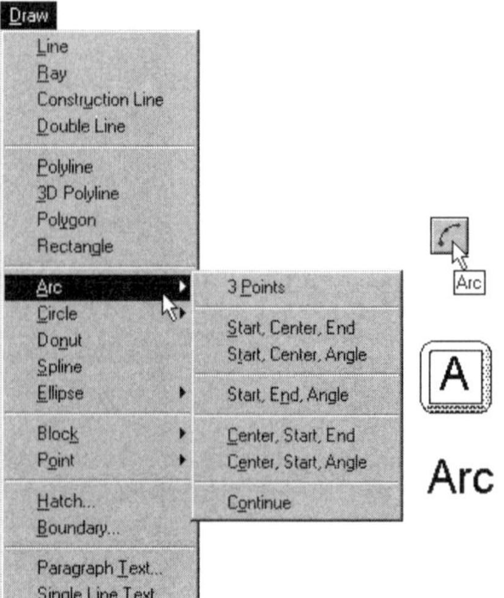

Fig. 3.19 Methods of calling the **Arc** tool

tool in the **Draw** pull-down menu, several combinations of these prompts are available.

2. The prompts can be selected from the Command line by *entering* the initial letters of the required prompt.
3. The default arc angle rotation is anticlockwise (counter clockwise or ccw). This must be taken into account when drawing arcs.

Figure 3.20 shows examples of arcs constructed from a variety of combinations of the available prompts.

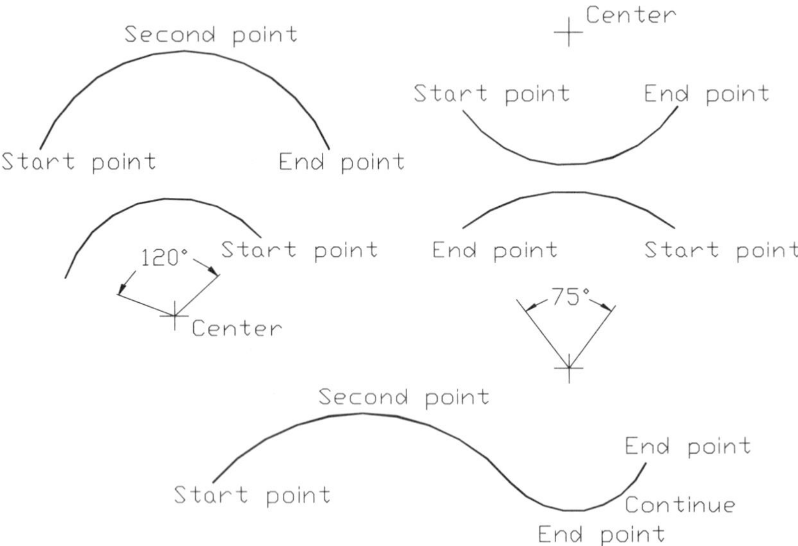

Fig. 3.20 **Arc** tool. Examples of arcs using different prompts

The Circle tool (Fig. 3.21)

Left-click on the **Circle** in the **Draw** pull-down menu, followed by a *left-click* on **Center, Radius** in the sub-menu (Fig. 3.21). The Command window shows:

Command _circle 3P/TTR/<Center point>: *enter* 90,190 *right-click*
Diameter/<Radius>: *enter* 45 *right-click*
Command:

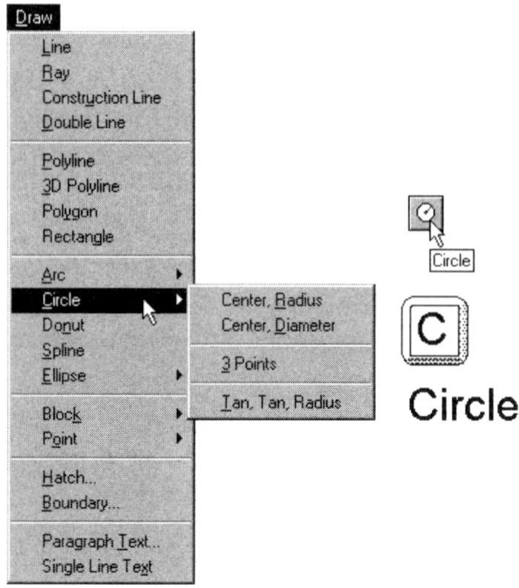

Fig. 3.21 Methods of calling the **Circle** tool

See left-hand drawing of Fig. 3.22.

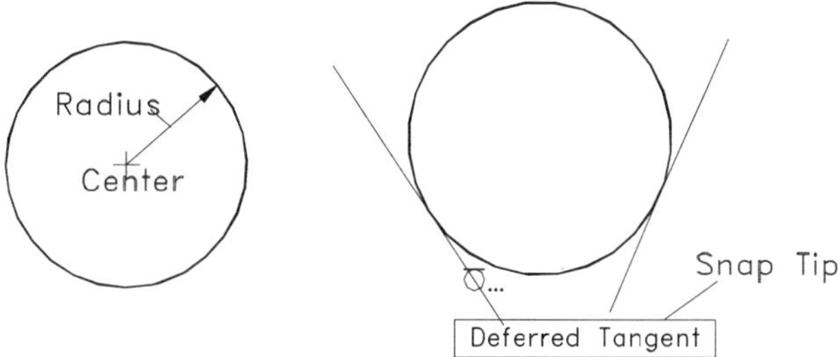

Fig. 3.22 Examples of the use of the **Circle** tool

Using the Tangent, Tangent, Radius (TTR) prompt

Command: _circle 3P/TTR/<Center>: _ttr
Enter Tangent spec: *pick* the object to which the circle is to be tangential

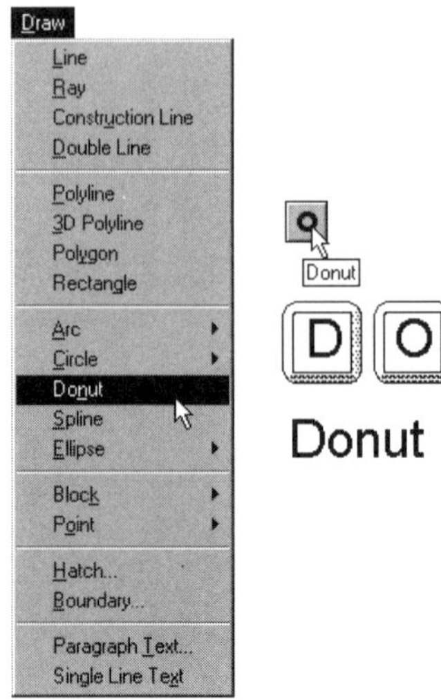

Fig. 3.23 Methods of calling the **Donut** tool

Enter Tangent spec: *pick* the object to which the circle is to be tangential
Enter Second tangent spec: *pick* the second object to which the circle is to be tangential
Radius: *enter* 50 *right-click*
Command:

See right-hand drawing of Fig. 3.22. Note the appearance of the AutoSnap icon and Snap Tip when choosing the objects against which the circle is to be tangential.

The Donut tool (Fig. 3.23)

Left-click on the **Donut** tool in the **Draw** toolbar (Fig. 3.23). The Command window shows:

Command: _donut
Inside diameter <1>: *enter* 0 *right-click*
Outside diameter <1>: *enter* 10 *right-click*
Center of doughnut: *enter* 40,230 *right-click*
Center of doughnut: *enter* 90,230 *right-click*
and so on until:
Center of doughnut: *enter* 140,180 *right-click*
Center of doughnut: *right-click*
Command:

The results of this series of placing donuts is shown in the left-hand drawing of Fig. 3.24. That illustration also shows other donuts of differing inside and outside diameters.

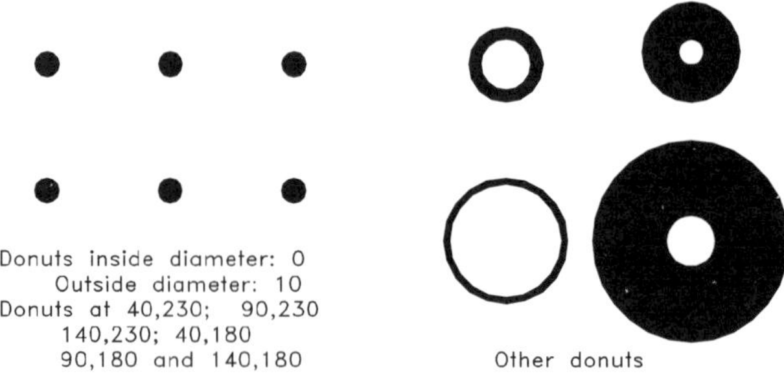

Fig. 3.24 Examples of donuts

The Ellipse tool (Fig. 3.25)

Left-click on the **Ellipse** tool in the **Draw** pull-down menu, followed by another *left-click* on **Center** in the **Ellipse** sub-menu (Fig. 3.25). The Command window shows:

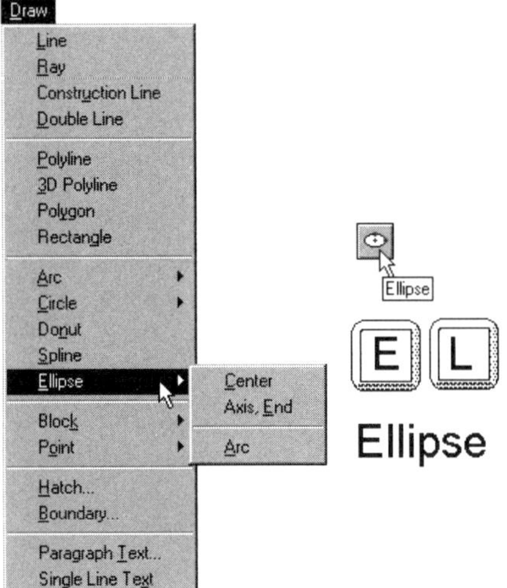

Fig. 3.25 Methods of calling the **Ellipse** tool

Command: _ellipse
Arc/Center/<Axis endpoint 1>: _c
Center of ellipse: *enter* 100,230 *right-click*
Axis endpoint: *enter* 10,230 *right-click*
Other axis distance: *enter* 100,260 *right-click*
Command:

See left-hand drawing of Fig. 3.26.

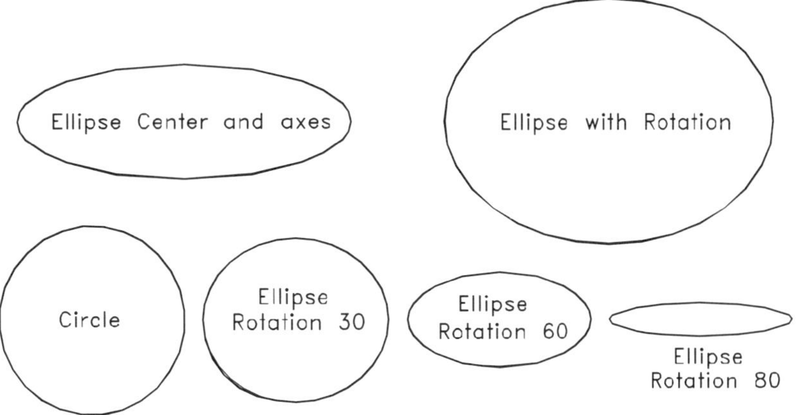

Fig. 3.26 Various ellipses constructed with the **Ellipse** tool

The following shows the use of the **Rotation** prompt.

Command: _ellipse
Arc/Center/<Axis endpoint 1>: _c
Center of ellipse: *enter* 320,230 *right-click*
Axis endpoint: *enter* 240,230 *right-click*

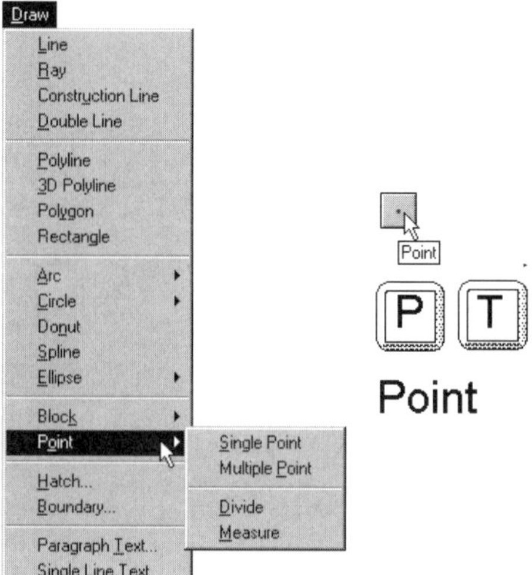

Fig. 3.27 Methods of calling the **Point** tool

<Other axis distance> Rotation: *enter* r *right-click*
Rotation around major axis: *enter* 45 *right-click*
Command:

See right-hand drawing of Fig. 3.26.

Looking at a circle as it is rotated around an horizontal axis (its major axis) shows as an ellipse. Its vertical axis (minor axis) size depends upon the angle of rotation. The greater the angle the smaller the minor axis.

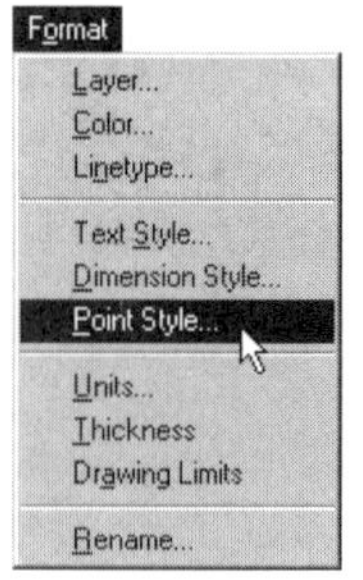

Fig. 3.28 Select **Point...** from the **Format** pull-down menu

The Point tool (Fig. 3.27)

Left-click on **Point** in the **Draw** pull-down menu, followed by another on **Single Point** in the sub menu. The Command window shows:

Command: _point POINT *enter* 100,195 *right-click*
Command:

And a point appears at that coordinate. Points can be varied by first selecting **Point...** from the **Format** pull-down menu (Fig. 3.28), which brings up the **Point Style** dialogue box Fig. 3.29). An alternative method of bringing the dialogue box on screen is to *enter* ddptype at the Command line. From the dialogue box, the type of point shape and its size relative to the screen or in units can also be set.

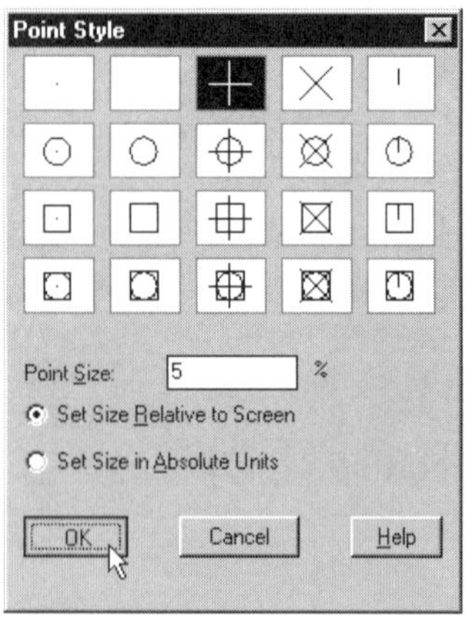

Fig. 3.29 The **Point Style** dialogue box

Saving drawings to disk

When saving a drawing as file data to disk, it is usually saved with the file extension ***.dwg**. Other file extensions are used for saving

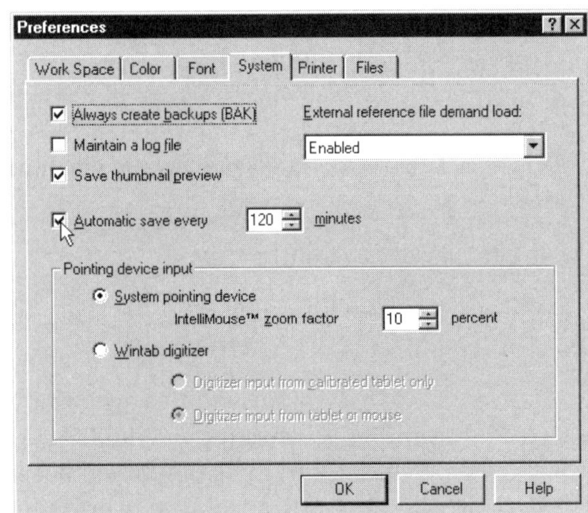

Fig. 3.30 Setting **Automatic Save**

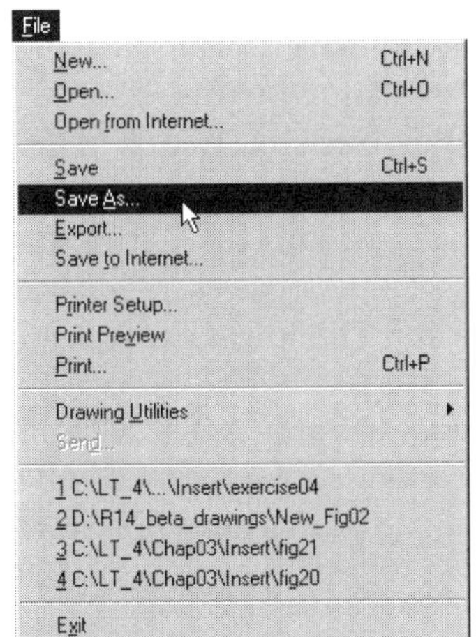

Fig. 3.31 Select **Save As...** from the **File** pull-down menu

drawings for a variety of purposes. These will be dealt with later in this book.

When constructing a drawing, it is advisable to save at regular intervals, say at about every 15 minutes. Then if something goes wrong with the computer – a software or hardware 'crash' or a failure of the electricity supply – then at least part of the construction will be saved prior to the crash. Automatic Save can be set in the **Preferences** dialogue box as shown in Fig. 3.30 if desired.

The Save Drawing As dialogue box

When the operator wishes to save his/her drawing, *left-click* on **Save As...** in the **File** pull-down menu (Fig. 3.31) or on the **Save** tool icon in the **Standard** toolbar (Fig. 3.32). The **Save Drawing As** dialogue box appears (Fig. 3.33). In the dialogue box:

Fig. 3.32 The **Save** tool icon from the **Standard** toolbar

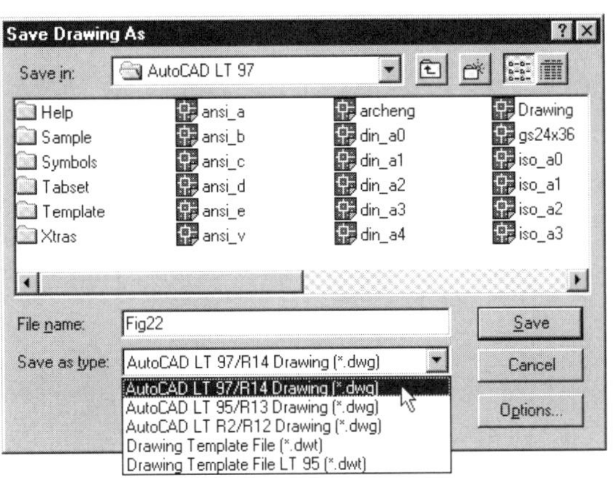

Fig. 3.33 The **Save Drawing As** dialogue box

1. In the **Save in:** box select the directory in which the drawing file is to be saved.
2. Select the type of file to be saved from the **Save as type:** popup list.
3. *Enter* the drawing file name in the **File name:** box .
4. *Left-click* on the **OK** button of the dialogue box.

And the file will be saved to the name *entered* with the extension, usually ***.dwg**.

Questions

1. Can you describe the use of the **Esc** key of the keyboard when working in AutoCAD LT 97?
2. Why is the **Erase** tool important?
3. If an object is erased in error how can the object be made to reappear?
4. What is the purpose of the **Construction Line** tool?
5. The **Polyline Tool** is probably used more extensively when working in LT 97 that any other tool. Can you explain why this is so?
6. Any size arrow can be drawn with the **Polyline** tool. Which of the **Polyline** prompts is used to construct an arrow?
7. Three types of polygon can be constructed with the aid of the **Polygon** tool. Can you name them?
8. What are the purposes of the **Elevation** and **Thickness** prompts of the **Rectangle** tool?
9. In which direction is an arc formed when working in LT 97? Can the direction be changed? If so how?
10. Many different types of **point** can be included in a drawing. How are they chosen?

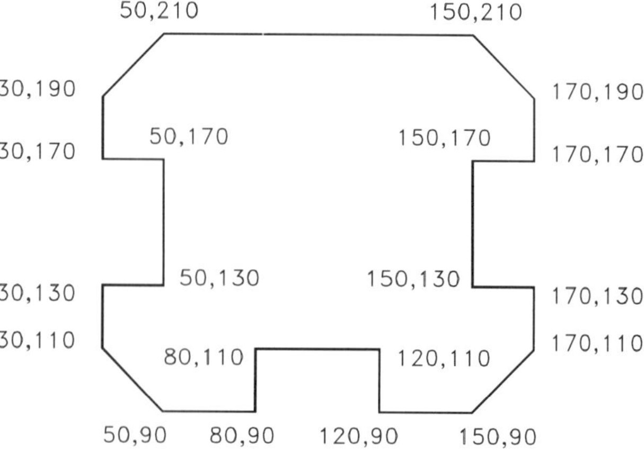

Fig. 3.34 Exercise 1

Exercises

1. Construct the outline given in Fig. 3.34 with the aid of the **Line** tool.
2. Construct the drawing given in Fig. 3.35 using the **Construction Line** tool, the **Line** tool and the **Circle** tool.

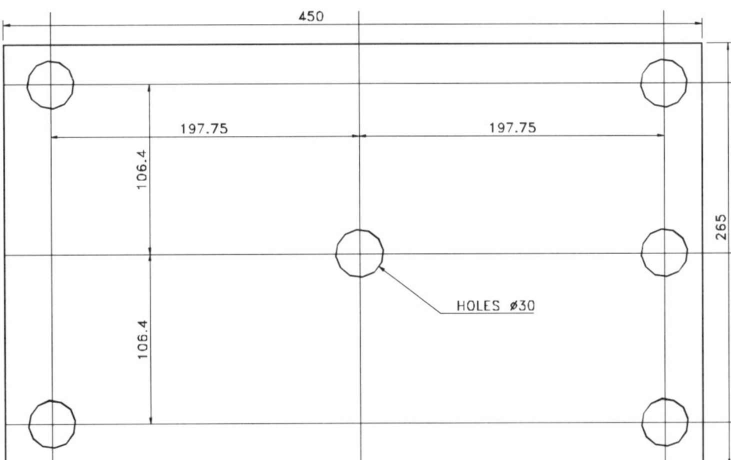

Fig. 3.35 Exercise 2

3. Figure 3.36 is a drawing of a metal plate. It has been drawn with the aid of the **Polyline** tool with **Width** set to 2.

   Construct the outline to the coordinates given with the drawing.

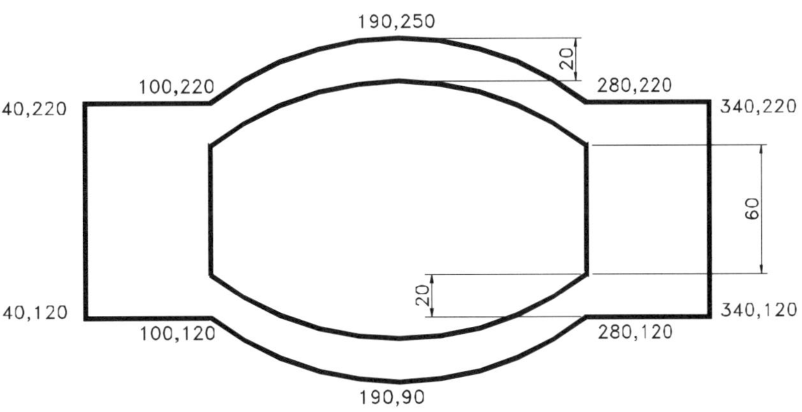

Fig. 3.36 Exercise 3

4. The four outlines of Fig. 3.37 were all drawn with the aid of the **Rectangle** tool. Construct the outlines to the information given with Fig. 3.37.
5. Construct the double line figures of Fig. 3.38 with the aid of the **Dline** tool working to the information given with the illustration.

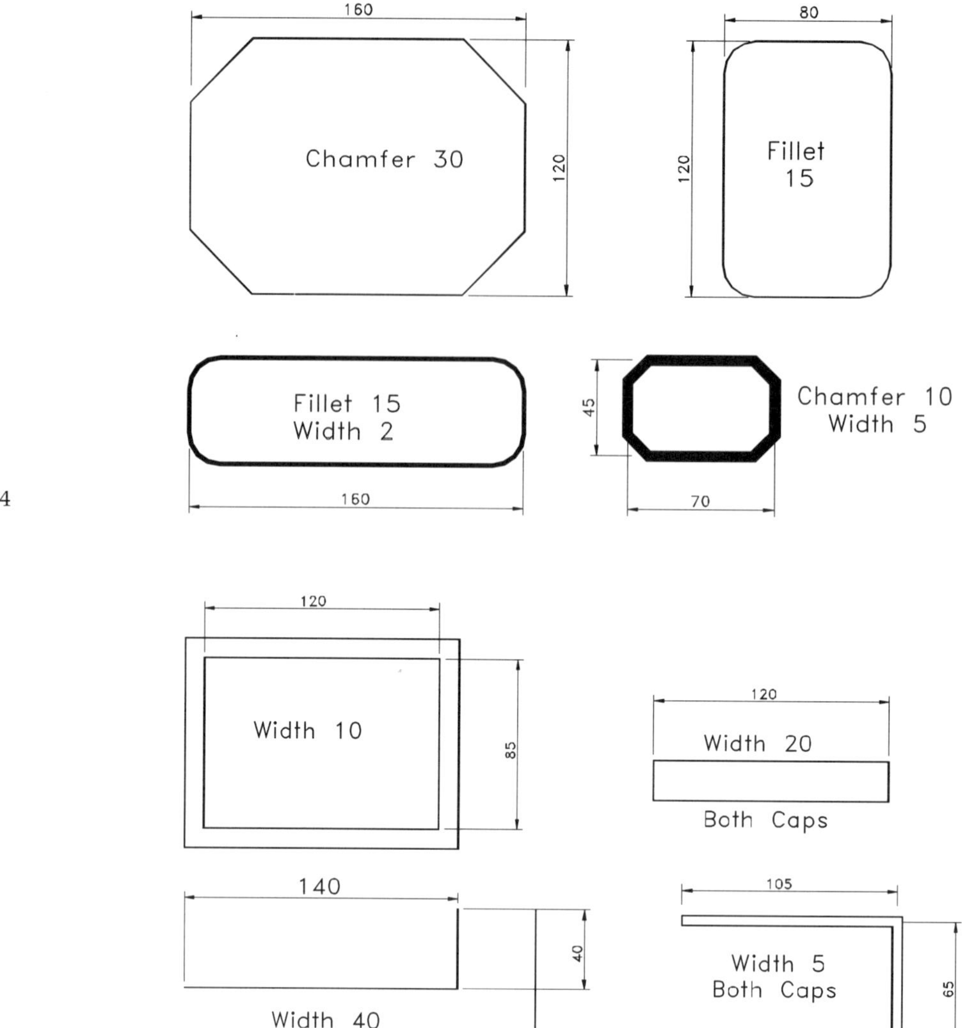

Fig. 3.37 Exercise 4

Fig. 3.38 Exercise 5

6. Figure 3.39 shows a steel plate in which four circular holes and an elliptical hole have been cut. Construct the outline of the plate with its holes.
7. Figure 3.40 shows a number of polygons constructed with the aid of the **Polygon** tool. Construct the given polygons to the information given with Fig. 3.40.
8. Construct the ellipses given in Fig. 3.41 working to any convenient sizes, but using the prompts given with each of the ellipses.
9. Figure 3.42 shows several arrows constructed with the aid of the **Polyline** tool. Construct the given arrows to the dimensions given. Dimensions not shown should be estimated.

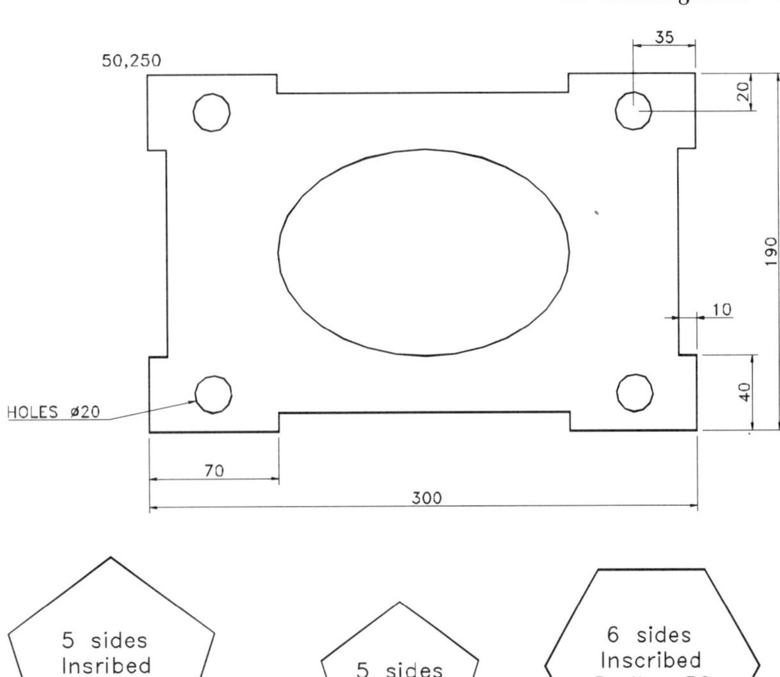

Fig. 3.39 Exercise 6

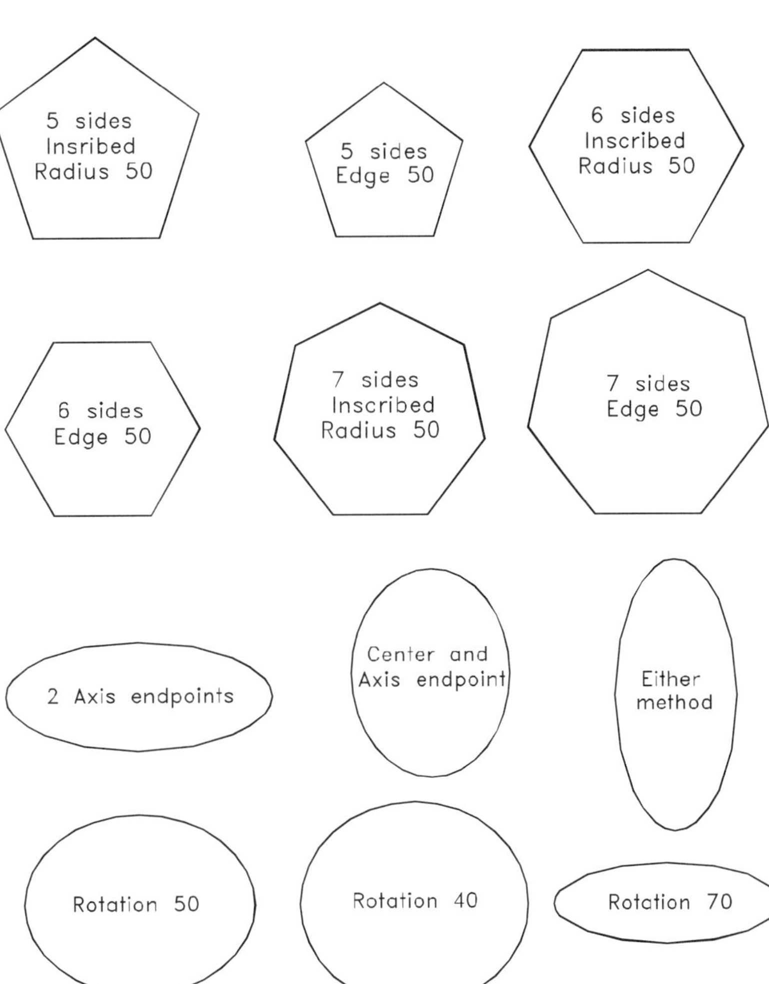

Fig. 3.40 Exercise 7

Fig. 3.41 Exercise 8

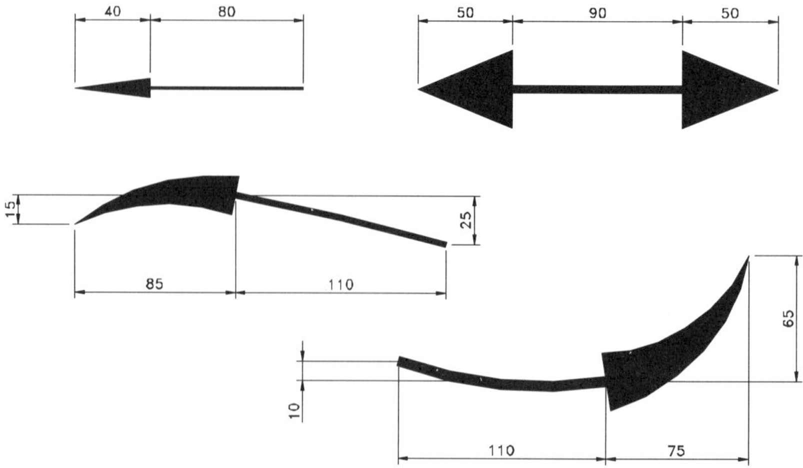

Fig. 3.42 Exercise 9

CHAPTER 4

Accurate drawing with Draw tools

Introduction

There are two methods by which text can be included with a drawing – using **Multiline Text** (Paragraph Text) or **Single Line Text**. **Multiline Text** requires the text to be placed in the **Multiline Text Editor** before it is placed on screen. **Single Line Text** is *entered* from the Command line.

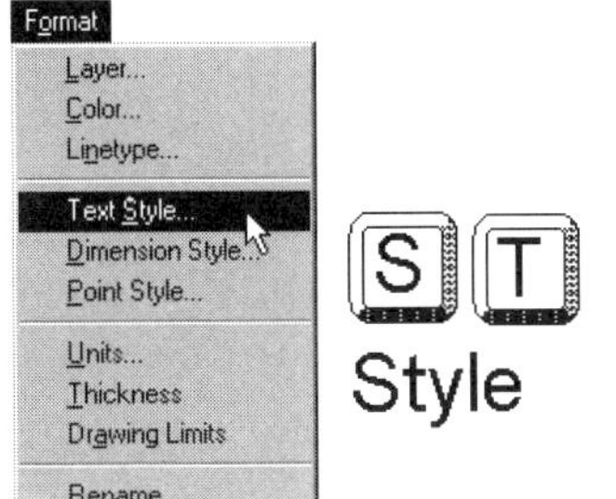

Fig. 4.1 Methods of calling the **Text Style** dialogue box on screen

Setting Text styles

At the Command line *enter* st (Fig. 4.1) The **Text Style** dialogue box appears (Fig. 4.2). Figure 4.2 shows the popup list appearing with a *left-click* in the **Font Name:** box. Scrolling the popup list will show all the AutoCAD SHX fonts and all the Windows 95 True Type fonts (TT). Fonts can be loaded into the current drawing from this list as follows:

1. *Left-click* on the **New...** button. The **New Text Style** box appears (Fig. 4.3). The name **Style 1** automatically appears in the **Style**

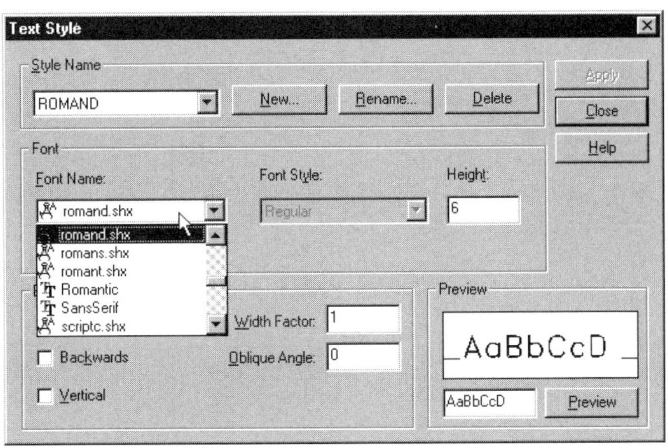

Fig. 4.2 The **Text Style** dialogue box

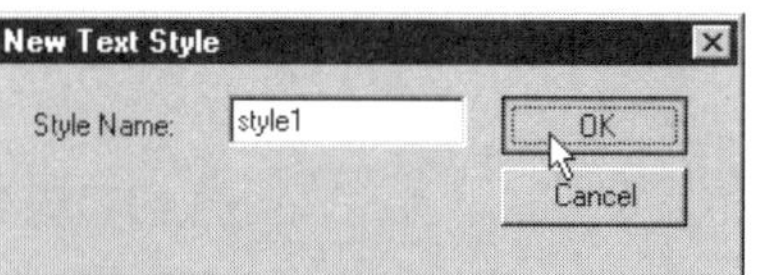

Fig. 4.3 The **New Text Style** box

Name: box. This name can be changed to a required new font style name by *entering* the style name over **Style1**. *Left-click* **OK**. The name **STYLE1** (or the *entered* font name) appears in the parent dialogue box.

2. Select the required font from the **Font Name:** popup list. *Left-click* on the **Rename...** button. The **Rename Text Style** box appears carrying a name such as **Style2**. *Enter* over this name the required font name, followed by a *left-click* on the **OK** button of the box. The new name appears in the **Style Name:** box of the **Text Style** dialogue box.

Fig. 4.4 The **Rename Text Style** box

3. Repeat items 1 and 2 above until all the required fonts are loaded. Figure 4.5 shows the popup list from the **Style Name:** box listing the names of the fonts loaded into the current drawing.

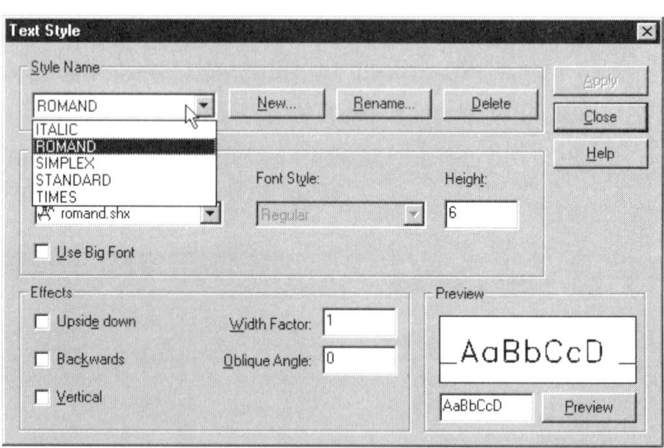

Fig. 4.5 The **Style Name:** popup list of the **Text Style** dialogue box

4. Select a style from the popup list with a *left-click* on its name. The font name appears in the **Font Name:** box. From the popup list appearing with a *left-click* in the **Font Style** box, select **Bold**.
5. In the **Height:** box *enter* the required height. If it is this particular font at this height that is required in the drawing, *left-click* on the

Apply button, followed by another on the **Close** button. It is this font at this height which will become the current text style for adding text in a drawing on screen. See Fig. 4.6.

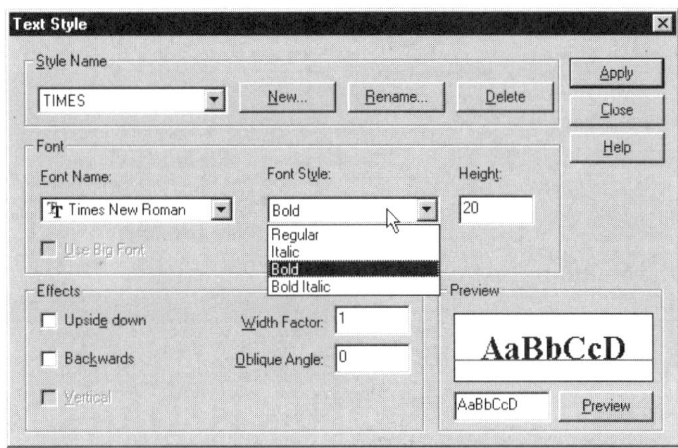

Fig. 4.6 Selecting a font and applying it as the current font style

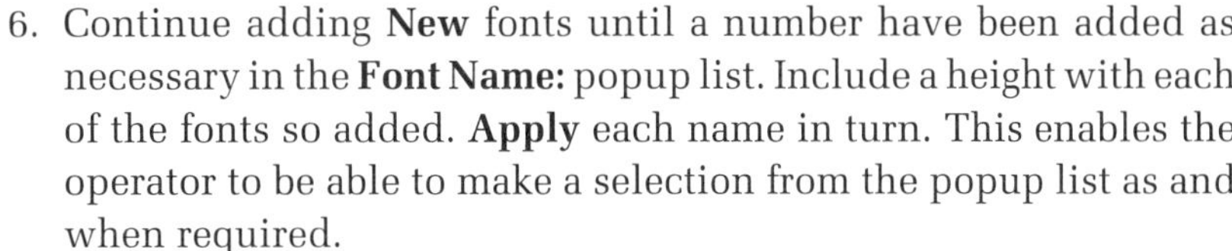

6. Continue adding **New** fonts until a number have been added as necessary in the **Font Name:** popup list. Include a height with each of the fonts so added. **Apply** each name in turn. This enables the operator to be able to make a selection from the popup list as and when required.

Note It is the Windows TT fonts which can be made to appear in **bold**, *italic* and/or <u>underlined</u> form. AutoCAD SHX fonts can only be set up to appear in the form in which the font was originally created.

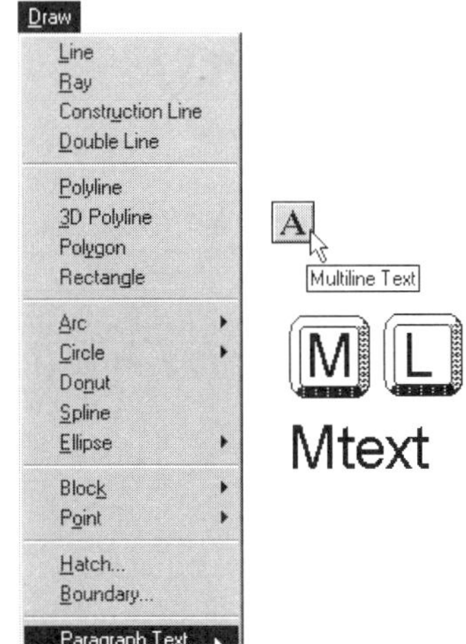

Fig. 4.7 Methods of calling the **Multiline Text** tool

Multiline Text (Fig. 4.7)

Left-click on the **Multiline Text** tool in the **Draw** toolbar (Fig. 4.7). The Command window shows:

Command: _mtext Current text style: TIMES height 20
Specify first corner: either *pick* a point on screen or *enter* coordinates and *right-click*.
Specify opposite corner or (Height/Justify/Rotation/Style/Width):
Unless any of the prompts associated with the above are required and if the current text style is suitable either *pick* a point on screen or *enter* coordinates and *right-click* (Fig. 4.8).
The **Multiline Text Editor** box appears on screen (Fig. 4.9).

In the text editor enter the required text and *left-click* on the **OK** button of the editor box. The text appears on screen within the area defined by the window selected by *picking* or by the *entering* of coordinates. Figure 4.10 shows three examples of the text *entered* in

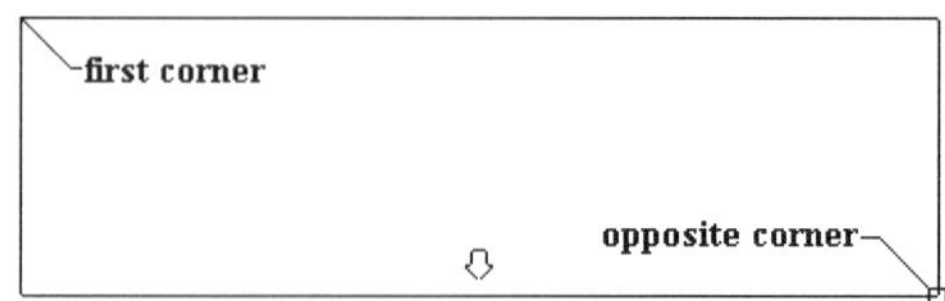

Fig. 4.8 The box appearing on screen for **Multiple Text**

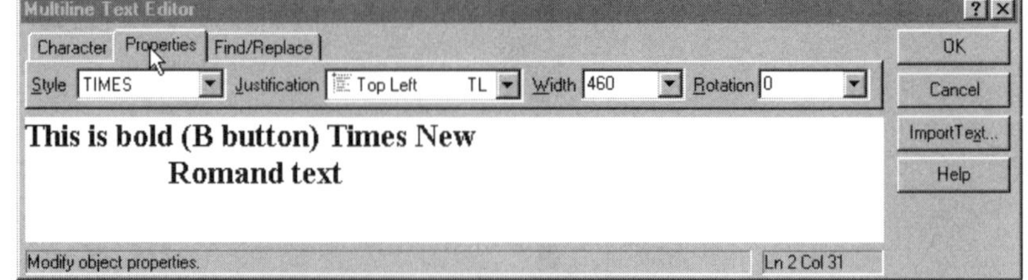

Fig. 4.9 The **Multiline Text Editor** box

This is Times New Roman text.
It is a Windows TT font.

This is bold (B button) Times New Roman text

This is bold, italic Times New Roman text (B and I buttons)

Fig. 4.10 Text from the **Multiline Text Editor** on screen

the **Multiline Text Editor** as it would appear on screen. In these three examples the current text style has been used.

AutoCAD LT 97 includes a large number of different fonts, from which a small example is given in Fig. 4.12. A full list of all fonts available in LT 97 is given in Fig. 4.13 on page 68.

The Multiline Text Editor

The **Multiline Text Editor** is a complex dialogue box, within which other dialogues can be seen by *left-clicks* on the **Character**, **Properties** and **Find/Replace** tabs at the top of the dialogue box. Figure 4.12 shows the popup lists associated with the **Character** and **Properties** parts of the **Multiline Text Editor**.

Fig. 4.11 Examples of Windows TT fonts and AutoCAD ***.shx** fonts

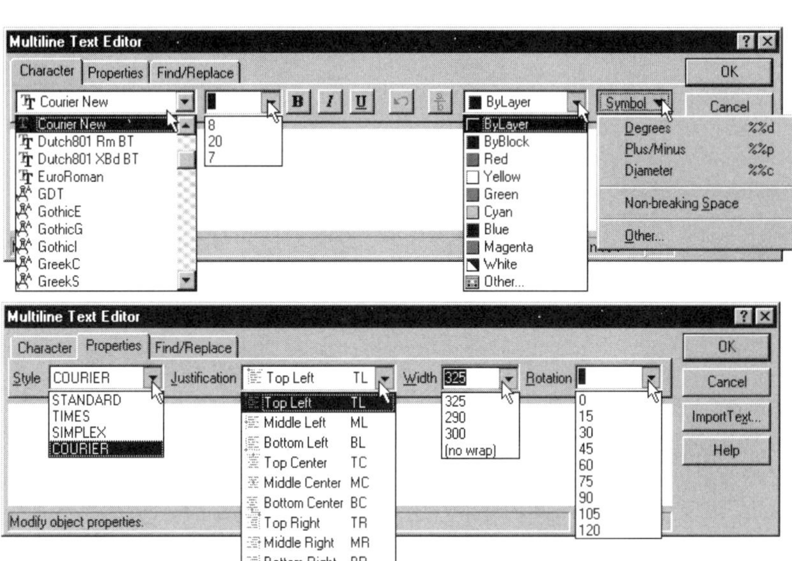

Fig. 4.12 The popup lists of the **Multiline Text Editor**

In addition to the possibilities available using these popup lists, text can be imported from other applications, providing the text is in ASCI format (usually in files with the extension ***.txt**) with the use of the **Import Text...** button.

Single line text

At the Command line *enter* dt and *right-click* (see Fig. 4.14). The Command window then shows:

Command: *enter* dt *right-click*
DTEXT Justify/Style/<Start point>: either *pick* a point or *enter* the coordinates of the required point and *right-click*
Rotation angle <0>: *right-click* (to accept 0)

Fig. 4.13 A full list of fonts available in LT 97

Text: *enter* the required text and then press the **Return** key (not a *right-click*)

The text appears in the Command window and also on screen commencing at the **Start point**. The text will be in the current style.

The other prompts of the Dtext tool

Command: *enter* t *right-click*
DTEXT Justify/Style/<Start point>: *enter* j *right-click*
Align/Fit/Center/Middle/Right/TL/TC/TR/ML/MC/MR/BL/BC/BR: *enter* the initials of the required justification *right-click*

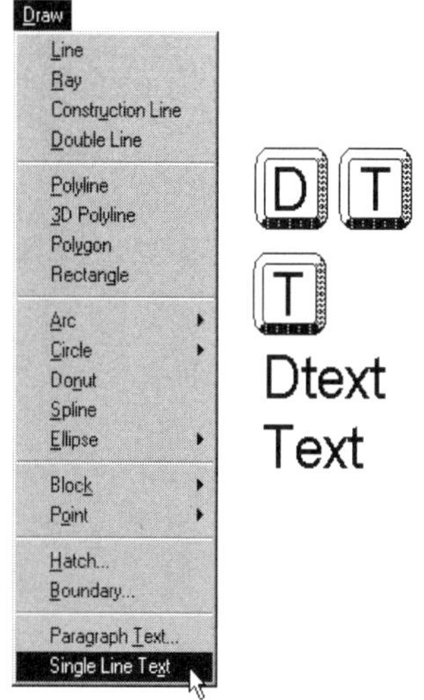

Fig. 4.14 Methods of calling **Single Line Text**

Top/left point: *pick* require point (or *enter* coordinates)
Rotation Angle <0>: *right-click*
Text: *enter* the required text and then press the **Return** key
Text: another line of text can now be *entered*. If only one line of text press **Return**
Command:

Figure 4.16 shows the results of some of the justifications.

If the response to first line of the dtext sequence is s (Style):

Command: *enter* dtext *right-click*
DTEXT Justify/Style/<Start point>: *enter* s *right-click*
Style name (or ?) <SIMPLEX>: *enter* **?** *right-click*
Text style(s) to list <*>: *right-click*

And an **AutoCAD LT 97** text window appears listing text styles previously loaded, together with their **Height**, **Width** and **Obliquing Angle** parameters.

If the required text style is known and previously has been loaded, *entering* the name against the prompt **Style name (or ?) <SIMPLEX>:** will make that text style current.

Fig. 4.15 Methods of calling **Spelling**

Checking text

Spell check

If text has been placed on screen which includes spelling errors the spelling can be checked and rectified by calling the **Check Spelling** dialogue box (Fig. 4.17). To call the **Spelling** tool (Fig. 4.15), in the Command window:

Command: *enter* sp *right-click*
Select object: *pick* the line of misspelt text

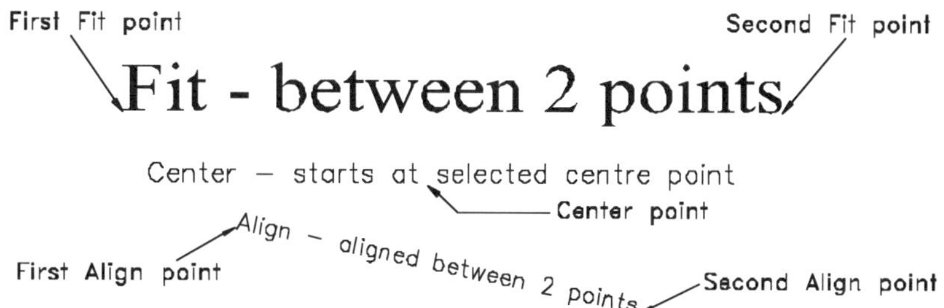

Fig. 4.16 Some text Justifications

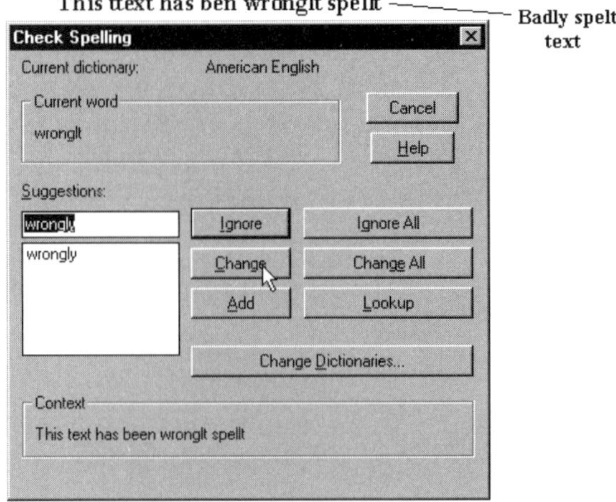

Fig. 4.17 The **Check Spelling** dialogue box

The **Check Spelling** dialogue box appears with a suggested respelling of the first misspelt word. *Left-click* on **Change** to the suggested word and the next misspelt word appears for changing. This goes on until all wrongly spelt words have been checked and changed. If the suggested spelling is not as wished, the operator's own spelling can be *entered* in its place. When completed, the dialogue box automatically disappears and an AutoCAD LT 97 Message box appears stating that the spelling check is complete. *Left-click* on the **OK** button of the message box.

Modifying text

If text on screen is to be changed, select **Object/Text...** from the **Modify** pull-down menu (Fig. 4.18) and *pick* the text to be modified. The **Multiline Text Editor** appears with the selected text showing in the editor. Modifications can be carried out as wished to the text in the editor.

Accurate drawing

By entering absolute coordinate positions

The method of *entering* coordinates at the Command line when constructing drawings has already been described in Chapter 3.

By entering coordinates relative to the last point

If an @ is *entered* before x,y coordinates as a response when constructing a drawing, the next x,y point will be relative to the last

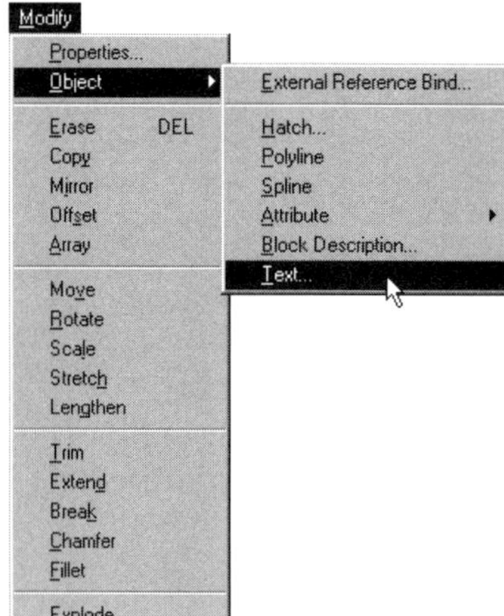

Fig. 4.18 Selecting **Object/ Text...** from the **Modify** pull-down menu

point selected. Figure 4.19 is a simple example of using the method of *entering* of relative coordinates. To construct this simple example:

Left-click on the **Line** tool icon in the **Draw** toolbar
Command: _line From point: *enter* 30,225 *right-click*
To point: *enter* @160,0 *right-click*
To point: *enter* @0,-100 *right-click*
To point: *enter* @-160,0 *right-click*
To point: *enter* @c (for Close) *right-click*
Command:

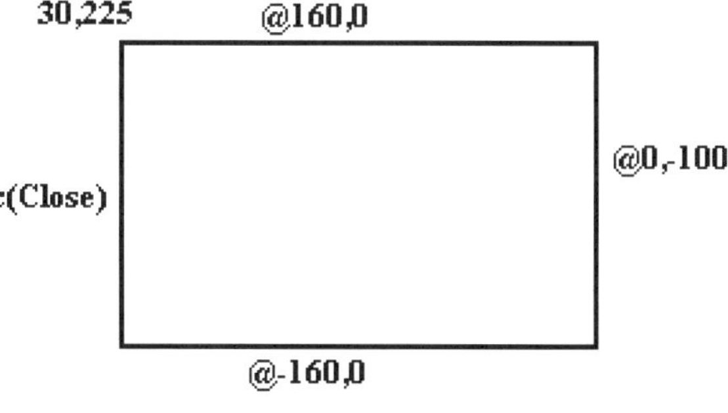

Fig. 4.19 An example of drawing using the relative coordinate method

Notes

1. +ve **X** figures are horizontally to the right.
2. –ve **X** figures are horizontally to the left.
3. +ve **Y** figures are vertically upwards.
4. –ve **Y** figures are vertically downwards.

Relative coordinate entry involving angles

If an angle is to be included with a relative coordinate *entry*, the < sign should precede angle degrees number, remembering angles are by default measured from the east ccw (counter clockwise) with the east position being 0°. Figure 4.20 is a simple example. As the outline was constructed, the Command line showed:

Command: _line From point: *enter* 65,225
To point: *enter* @150,0 *right-click*
To point: *enter* @100<315 *right-click*
To point: *enter* @–150,0 *right-click*
To point: *enter* @30<135 *right-click*
To point: *enter* @30,0 *right-click*
To point: *enter* @40<135 *right-click*
To point: *enter* @–30,0 *right-click*
To point: *enter* c (for Close) *right-click*
Command:

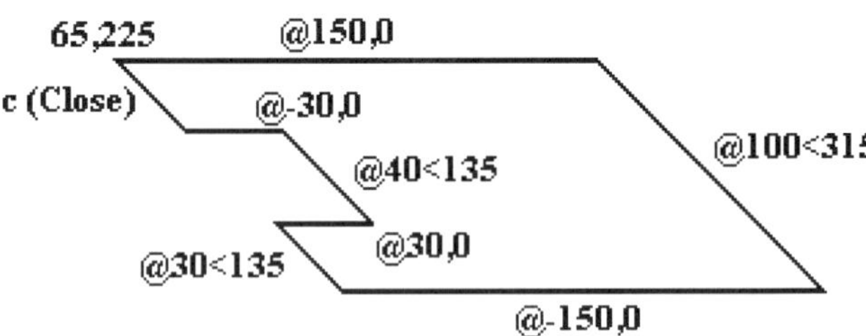

Fig. 4.20 An example of drawing using the relative coordinate method involving angles

Direct distance entry

As an example of direct distance entry, call the **Line** tool. At the Command line:

Command: _line From point: *pick* a point on screen
To Point: *drag* the rubber band from the *picked* point horizontally to the right. *Enter* 80 *right-click*
To Point: *drag* the rubber band vertically downwards. *Enter* 120 *right-click*
To Point: *drag* the rubber band from the *picked* point horizontally to the left. *Enter* 80 *right-click*
To Point: *drag* the rubber band from the *picked* point horizontally to the right. *Enter* 80 *right-click*
To Point: *enter* c (Close) *right-click*
Command:

The top left-hand drawing of Fig. 4.21 shows the resulting line rectangle. The other drawings of Fig. 4.21 show direct distance entry when using the **Polyline** tool, the **Polygon** tool, the **Arc** tool and the **Ellipse** tool.

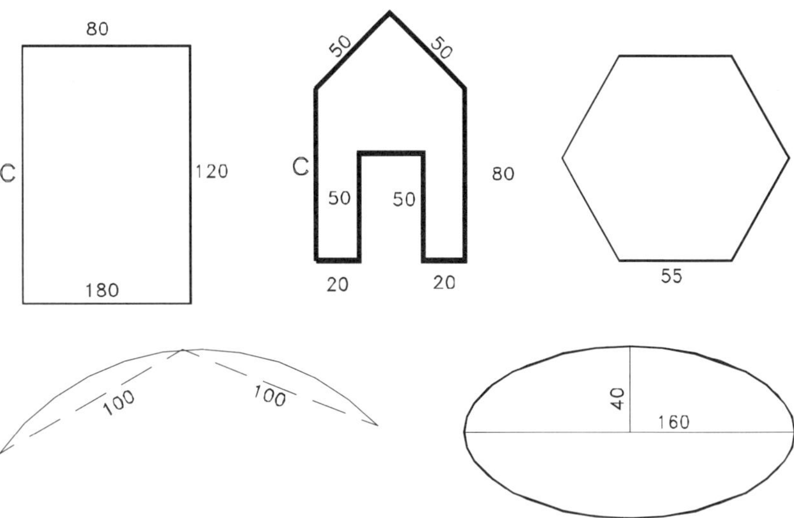

Fig. 4.21 Examples of direct distance entry

Note If an outline which includes lines at an angle to each other is being constructed using the direct distance entry method, it is advisable to have **Polar Snap** set on. This will allow angular lines to be constructed at the correct angles to other parts of the outline. Depending upon the angle to be drawn, the **Angle** setting can be varied from the default of 15 degrees.

Using Ortho

Ortho can be set either by pressing the **F8** key, which toggles **Ortho** on/off, or with a *double-click* on the **ORTHO** button in the Status bar at the bottom of the LT 97 window, which also toggles **Ortho** on/off. When **Ortho** is set on, constructions are restrained to move only in the horizontal or vertical directions – along either the **X** or **Y** axes. This restriction is of particular value when constructing orthographic projections (Chapter 9) or when placing **Construction Lines** in the LT 97 window in the horizontal or vertical positions.

Questions

1. If six text styles are set within the **Text Style** dialogue box, how can one of them be selected for current use?
2. How can the operator see all the fonts available in LT 97?

3. If bold, italic underlined text is required in a drawing, what type of font must be used for the text style?
4. What are the differences between placing text in a drawing using the **Multiline Text** tool compared with using the **Dtext** tool?
5. How can badly spelt words added to a drawing be corrected for spelling?
6. If errors are made in the wording of text in a drawing, which tool can be used to correct the text?
7. What is the difference between constructing outlines using the **absolute coordinate entry** method compared with using the **relative coordinate entry** method?
8. Can you describe construction of an outline using the **direct distance entry** method?
9. What is the value of setting **Ortho** on?
10. Another method of ensuring accurate drawing is to use the **Grid** and/or **Snap** settings. Are there disadvantages to this method?

Exercises

1. Make an accurate drawing of the drawing shown in Fig. 4.22. Do not attempt including any of the dimensions.

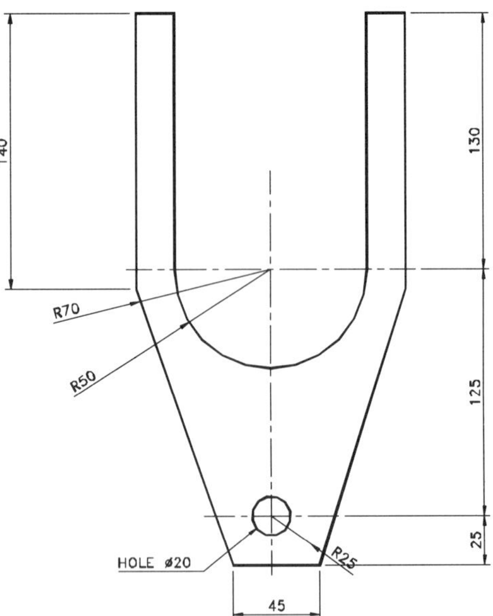

Fig. 4.22 Exercise 1

2. Make an accurate copy of the drawing shown in Fig. 4.23. Do not include any dimensions.

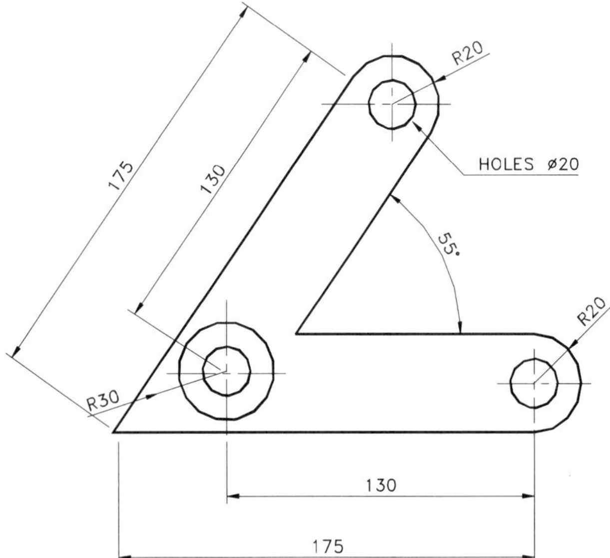

Fig. 4.23 Exercise 2

3. Figure 4.24 is the outline of a compartment from a tool box. Make an accurate copy of the outline without including any of its dimensions.

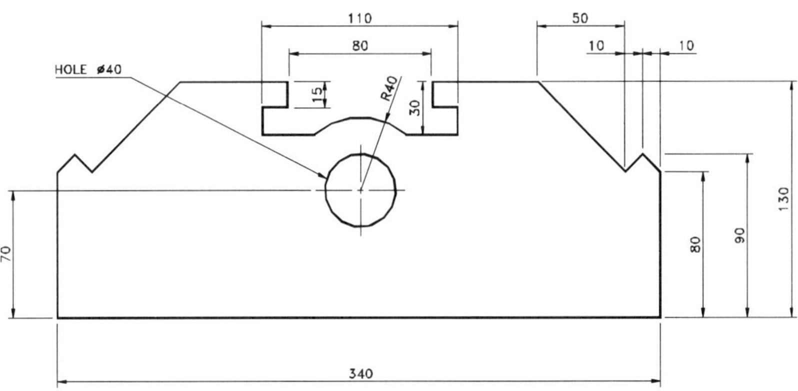

Fig. 4.24 Exercise 3

4. Figure 4.25 is a two-view orthographic projection of a clip. Construct an accurate drawing of the two views.
5. Figure 4.26 is the outline of a sheet of plywood from an instrument case. Construct an accurate drawing of the outline, without including any of the dimensions.
6. Figure 4.27 is an outline drawing of an icon for a telephone symbol. Make an accurate, full size copy of the outlines without including any dimensions.
7. Copy the given drawing Fig. 4.28 to any suitable size.

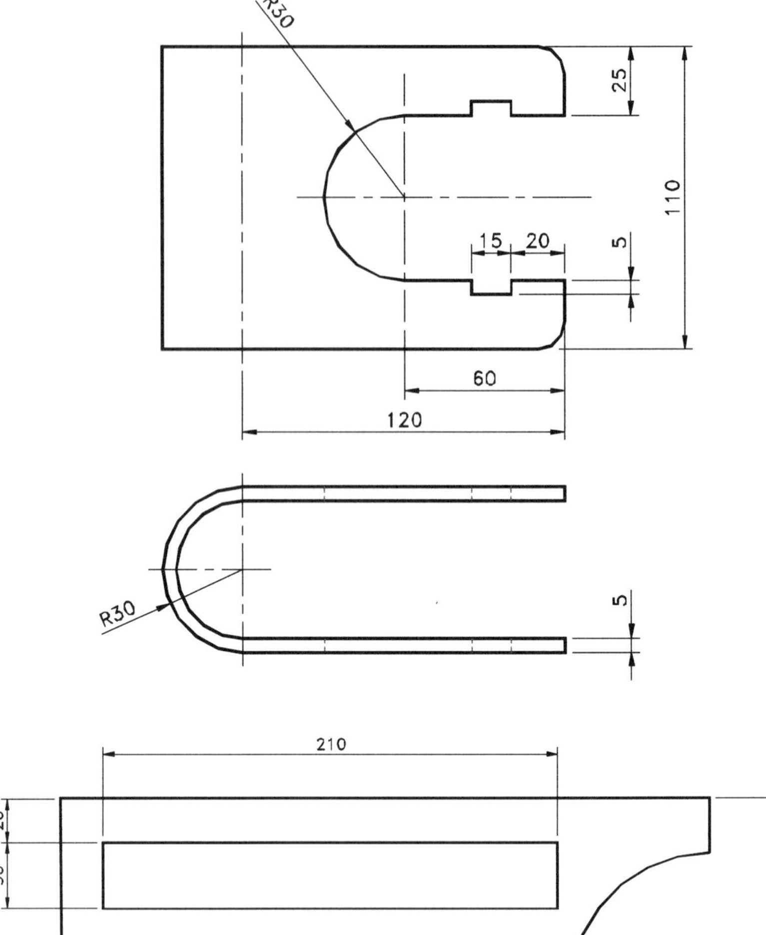

Fig. 4.25 Exercise 4

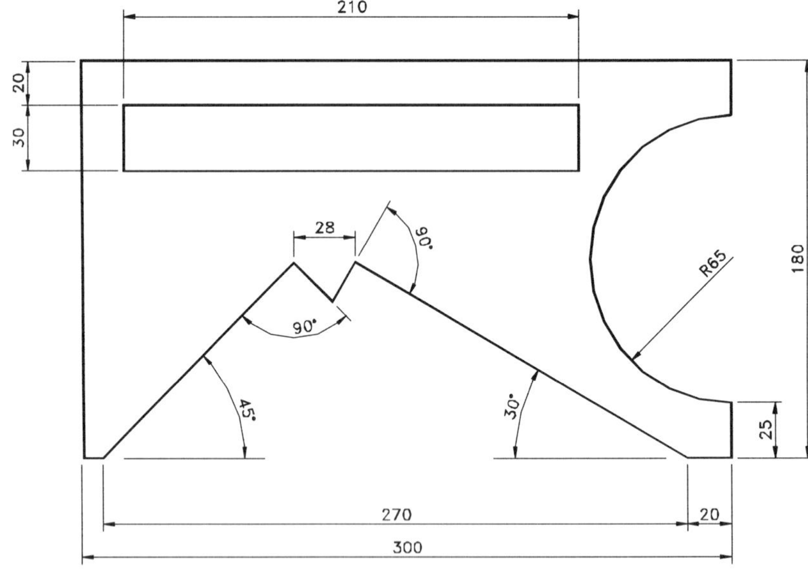

Fig. 4.26 Exercise 5

8. Copy the given drawing Fig. 4.29 to any suitable size and using any suitable text style.

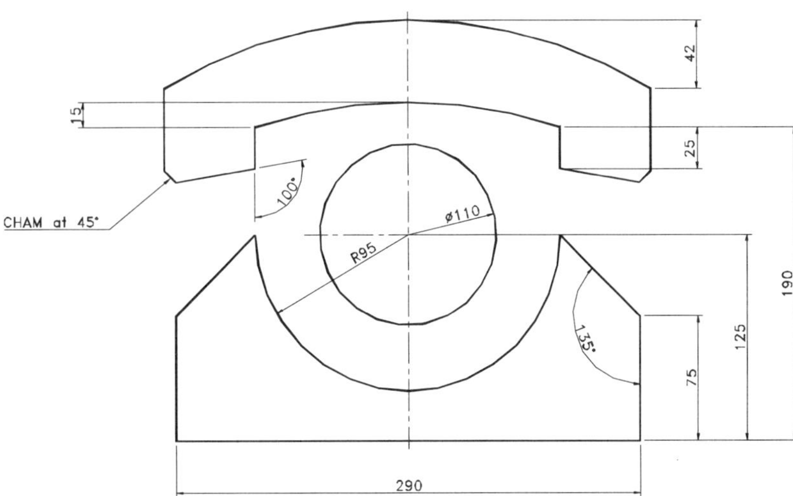

Fig. 4.27 Exercise 6

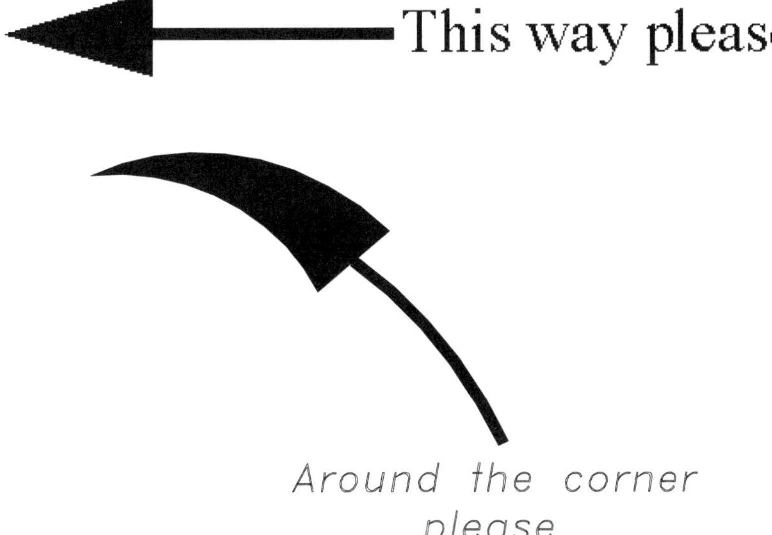

Fig. 4.28 Exercise 7

Fig. 4.29 Exercise 8

9. Figure 4.30 shows two donuts connected by a pline of width 10. Copies have been made and each rotated at angles of 30°. In all 12 copies were made, although only 6 are shown in Fig. 4.30. Construct a drawing including all 12 copies.
10. Figure 4.31 gives the dimensions for the minute hand of a clock, together with an hour hand slightly shorter in height. Make a copy to suitable dimensions of the clock face with its hour and minute hand and the hours figures.

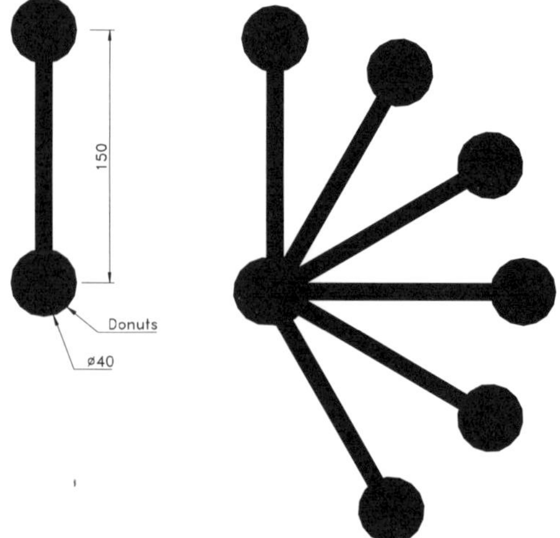

Fig. 4.30 Exercise 9

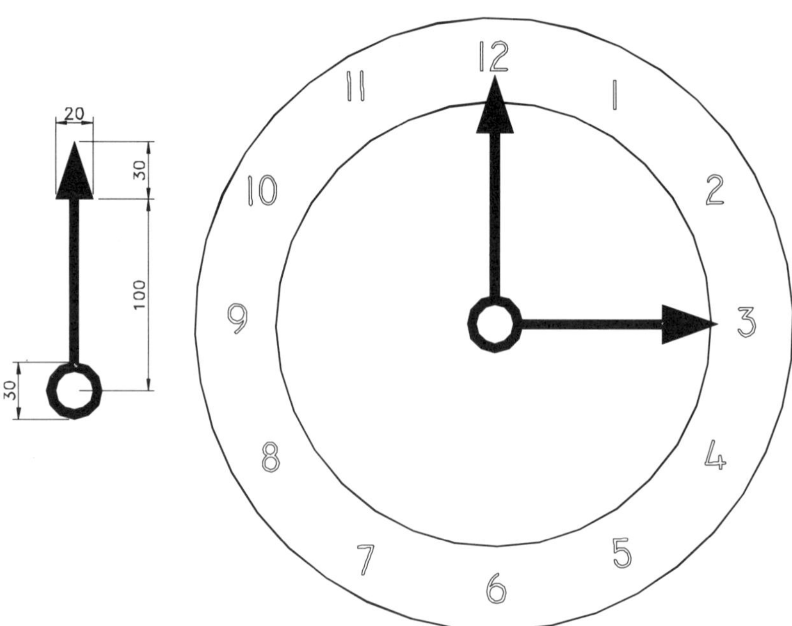

Fig. 4.31 Exercise 10

CHAPTER 5

Layers and Layer Management

Introduction

Constructing drawings on layers is a common concept when using most CAD software programs. The layer systems of LT 97 are quite complex, but easy to use.

The idea of layers can be regarded as being similar to the use of tracings when constructing technical drawings using hand methods. In the same way as different features can be drawn on tracing paper or tracing cloth over a master drawing, so features can be constructed on layers when working with a CAD system. Figure 5.1 shows a Gear Change Bracket in two views drawn with the aid of LT 97. The drawing was constructed on a number of layers. A diagrammatic view of the layers is suggested in Fig. 5.2.

The value of layers is that, in the same way as tracings can be removed or placed over a master drawing as required, layers can be turned on (visible) or turned off (invisible) as required. Layers in CAD can also be frozen or locked. These terms will be explained later in this chapter.

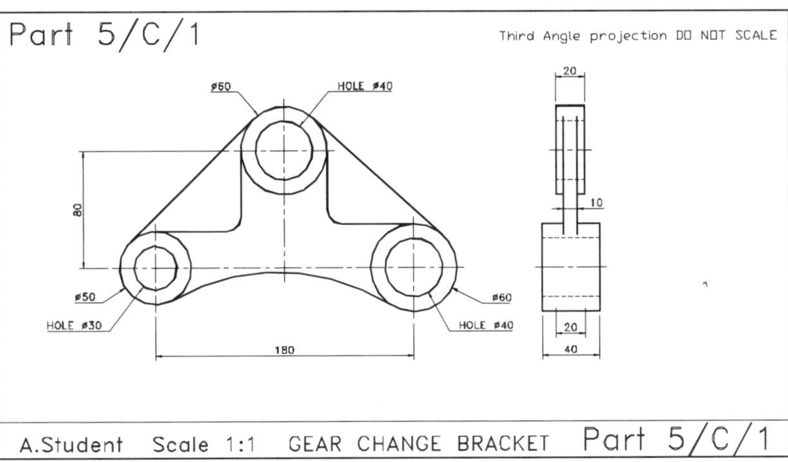

Fig. 5.1 An engineering drawing constructed on a number of layers

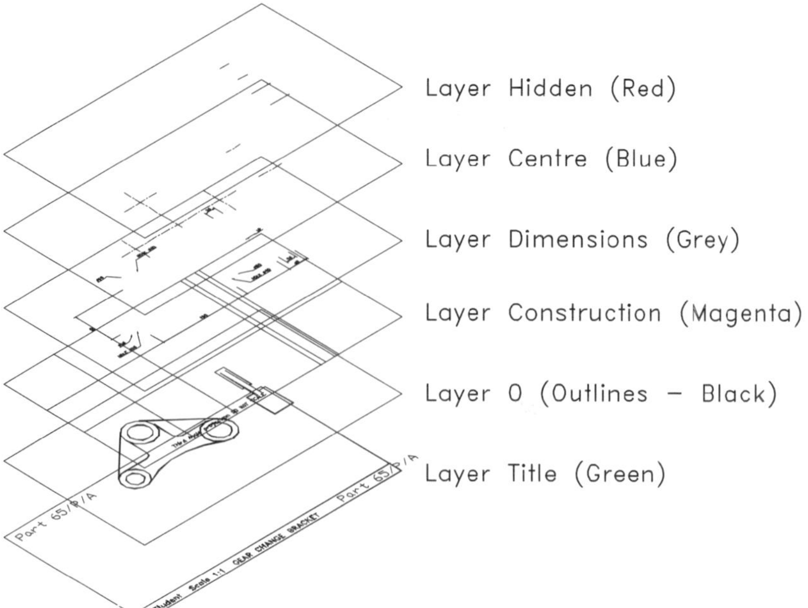

Fig. 5.2 Layers in CAD are similar to tracings in hand drawing

The Layer tools and controls

As can be seen from Fig. 5.2, the drawing Fig. 5.1 was constructed on six layers:

The outline drawing on Layer **0**, the default layer – colour black
Title and border lines on layer **Title** – colour green
Construction lines on layer **Construction** – colour magenta
Dimensions on layer **Dimensions** – colour grey
Centre lines on layer **Centre** – colour blue
Hidden detail lines on layer **Hidden** – colour red

The layer control tools are held in the **Object Properties** toolbar which is usually *docked* just below the **Standard** toolbar at the top of the LT 97 window. Figure 5.3 shows the toolbar *dragged* from its *docked* position.

Fig. 5.3 The **Object Properties** toolbar *dragged* from its normal position

The various layer tools of the **Objects Properties** toolbar are shown in Fig. 5.4, with the popup lists from the various boxes in the toolbar showing.

The Layer and Linetype Properties dialogue box

Left-click on the **Layers** tool icon (Fig. 5.4) and the **Layer and Linetype Properties** dialogue box (Fig. 5.5) appears. In Fig. 5.5 the **Details...** button has been *clicked* to bring up an extension to the dialogue box showing the properties of the selected layer – in this example, of the layer **Centre**. In the dialogue box, the layers for the template file **ay.dwt** are shown. This template is reasonably suitable for simple mechanical engineering drawings. It must, however, be remembered that some drawing may have dozens, sometimes even hundreds of layers, depending upon the complexity of the drawing.

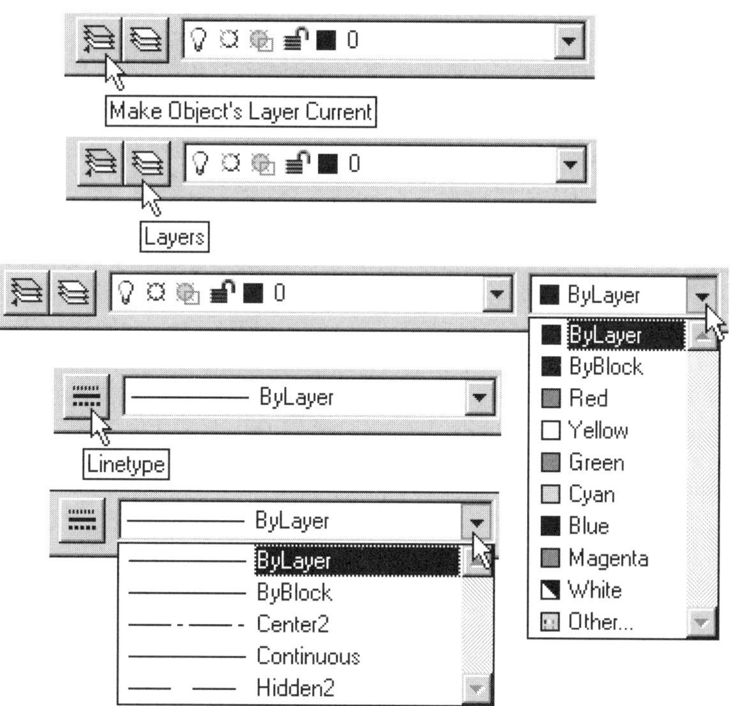

Fig. 5.4 The layer tools and popup lists of the **Object Properties** toolbar

To set a new layer

1. *Left-click* on the **New...** button of the **Layer & Linetype** dialogue box (Fig. 5.6). The name **Layer1** appears in the **name** list of the dialogue box.
2. *Left-click* on the **Details>>** button and the dialogue box lengthens to show details of **Layer1**. *Enter* another name over **Layer1** if desired – in the example Fig. 5.7 the name has been changed to **Fittings**.
3. From the **Color:** and **Linetype:** popup lists (Fig. 5.8) select a colour and a linetype for the new layer. The new colour and linetype name automatically appears in the main dialogue.

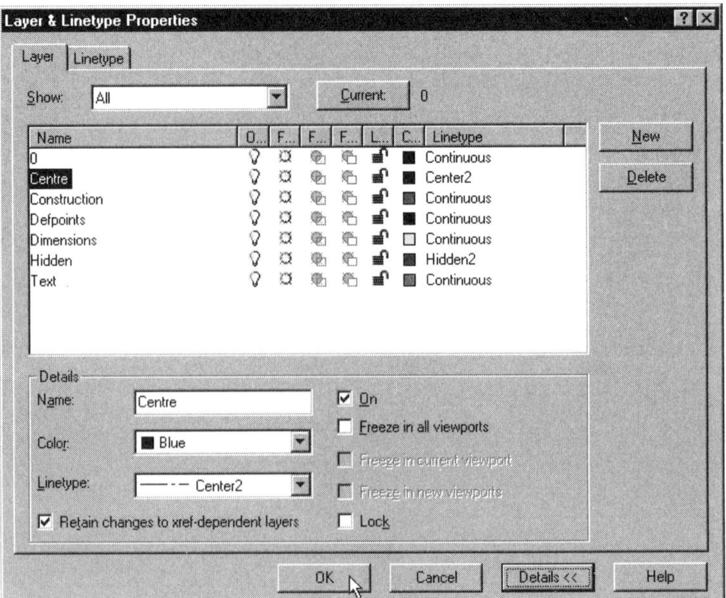

Fig. 5.5 The **Layer and Linetype Properties** dialogue box

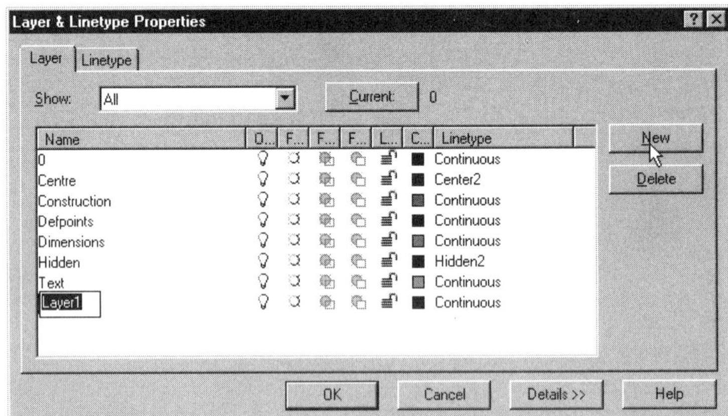

Fig. 5.6 *Left-click* on the **New...** button of the dialogue box

4. If the linetype is not as required, *left-click* within the name of the linetype of the layer. The **Select Linetype** dialogue box appears. *Left-click* on the **Load** button and the **Load or Reload Linetype** dialogue box (Fig. 5.9) appears, from which a new linetype can be selected.
5. In a similar manner, by *left-clicking* in a colour box of a linetype, a **Select Color** dialogue box appears from which a new colour can be chosen.

The Layer Control icons

A *left-click* in the **Layer Control** box or on its downward-pointing arrow brings up a popup list which contains not only the names of

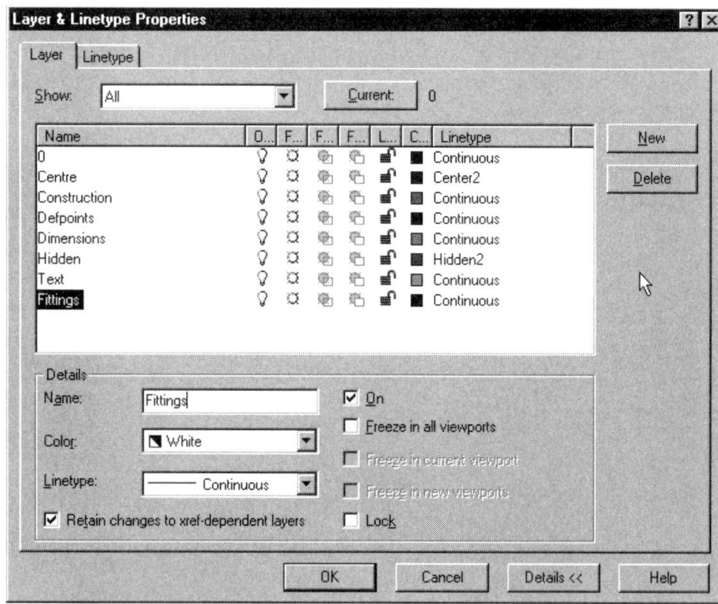

Fig. 5.7 Setting up a new layer

Fig. 5.8 Setting **Color:** and **Linetype:** for the new layer

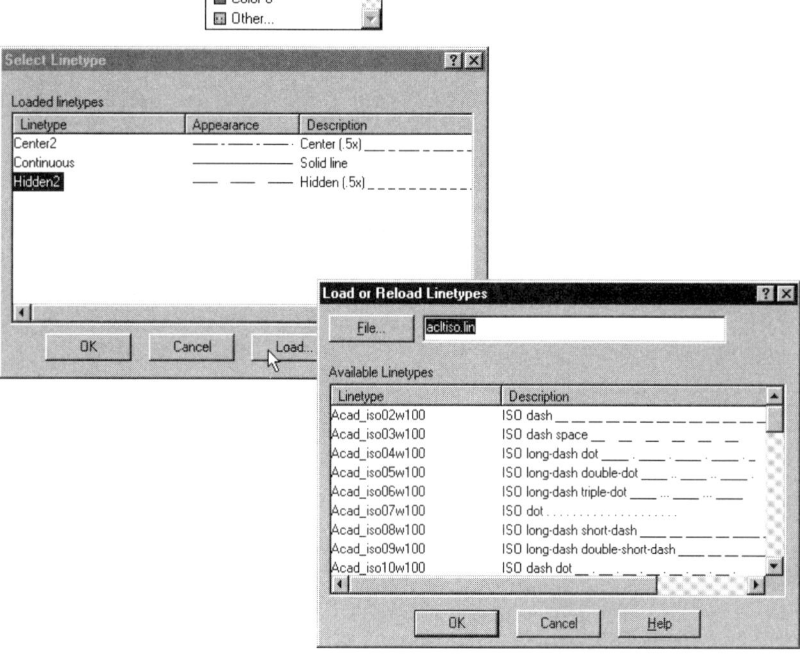

Fig. 5.9 The **Select Linetype** and **Load or Reload Linetype** dialogue boxes

the layers which have been set, but also a number of icons against each layer name (Fig. 5.10).

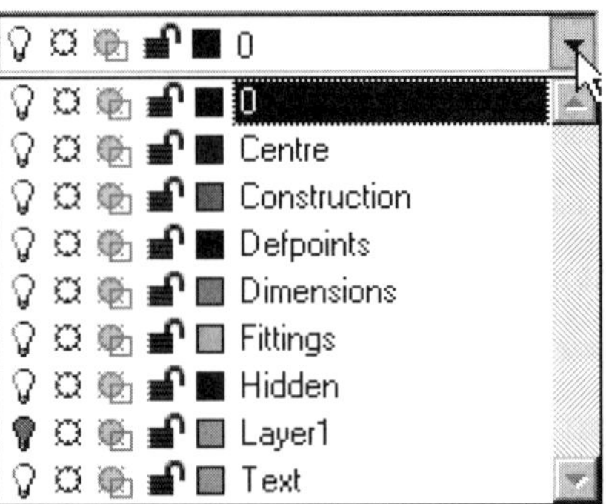

Fig. 5.10 The **Layer Control** popup list

Figure 5.11 shows the tool tips associated with each of the icons in the popup list. *Left-clicks* on the icons have the following actions:

On/Off icon: A *left-click* on the icon when it is 'lit' turns off the layer. Repeat the *click* and the layer is back on.

Freeze/Thaw in all viewports: Freezes layers in all viewports (see Chapter 14) and renders the layer invisible. Thawing unfreezes a layer which has been frozen.

Freeze/Thaw in current viewport: Freezes or thaws only in the current viewport (see Chapter 14).

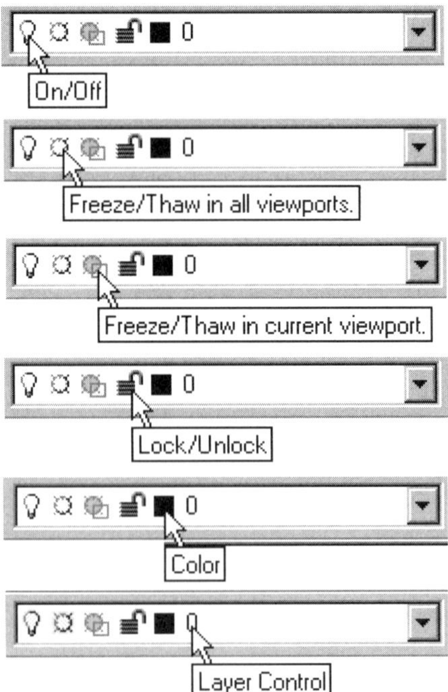

Fig. 5.11 The icons in the **Layer Control** box

Lock/Unlock: A *left-click* on an open lock icon closes it and the layer is locked. When a layer is locked, constructions can be added on the layer, but no modification can take place of any construction already on the layer – e.g. an already drawn line cannot be erased.

Color: The colour boxes show the colours assigned to each layer.

Layer Control: This tool tip shows, no matter where the cursor is placed, except on an icon.

Note Changes in layer parameters by *clicking* on an icon can only take place within the popup list. *Clicking* on an icon in the layer showing in the **Layer Control** box will have no effect, except to bring up the popup list.

An example of a drawing constructed on layers

Figure 5.12 shows the completed drawing, which was constructed on six layers. Figure 5.13 shows the **Layer Control** popup list with the layer names. Plate V shows the completed drawing in colour with all layers ON. To construct the drawing:

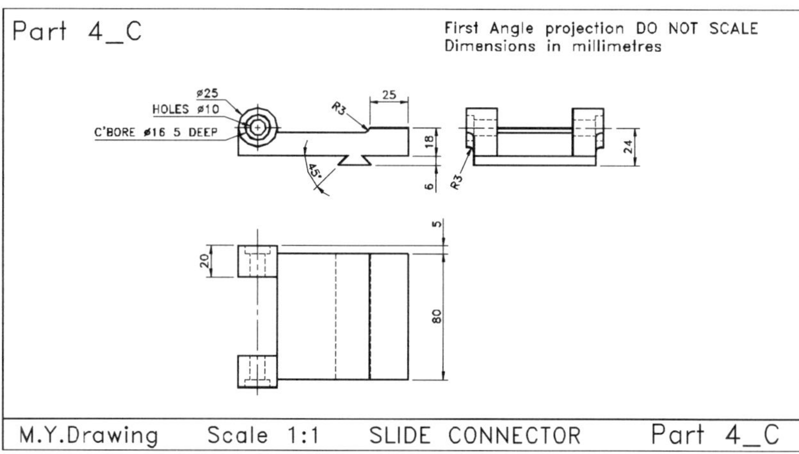

Fig. 5.12 The completed example drawing

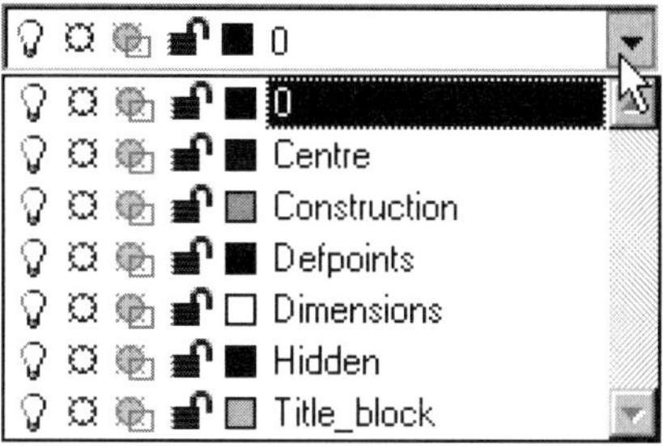

Fig. 5.13 An example of the **Layer Control** popup list

1. *Left-click* on **New** in the **File** pull-down menu, followed by opening the **ay.dwt** template.
2. Set the layer **Construction** as the current layer – in the **Layer & Linetype** dialogue box, *left-click* on the layer name, followed by another *left-click* on the **Current** button (top centre of dialogue box).
3. Draw construction lines on which the three outlines for the views are to be based – Fig. 5.14.

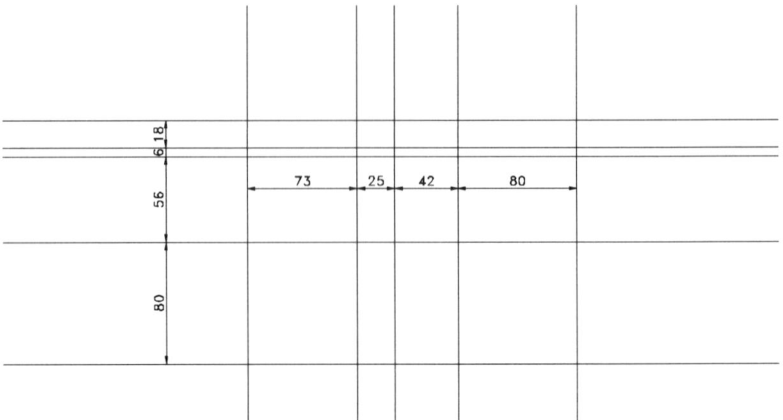

Fig. 5.14 An example of construction lines on Layer **Construction**

4. Turn Layer **0** on. On Layer **0** construct the three views using the construction lines for guidance (Fig. 5.15).

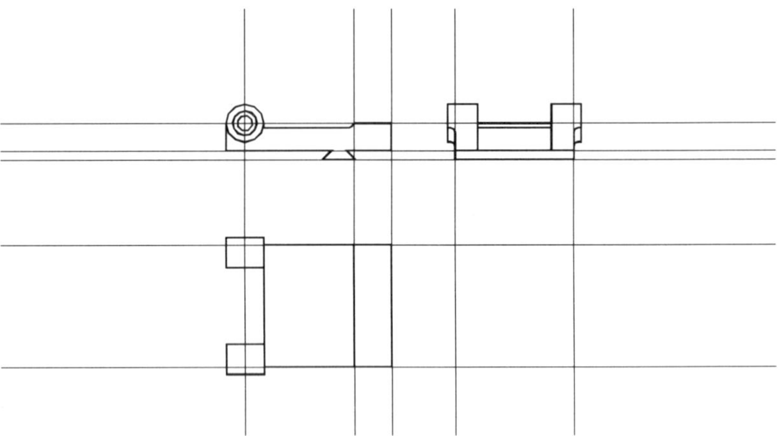

Fig. 5.15 An example of outlines drawn on Layer **0**

5. Turn Layer **Construction** off. Make Layer **Centre** current. Add centre lines to the drawing (Fig. 5.16).
6. Make Layer **Hidden** current. Add hidden detail lines (Fig. 5.17).

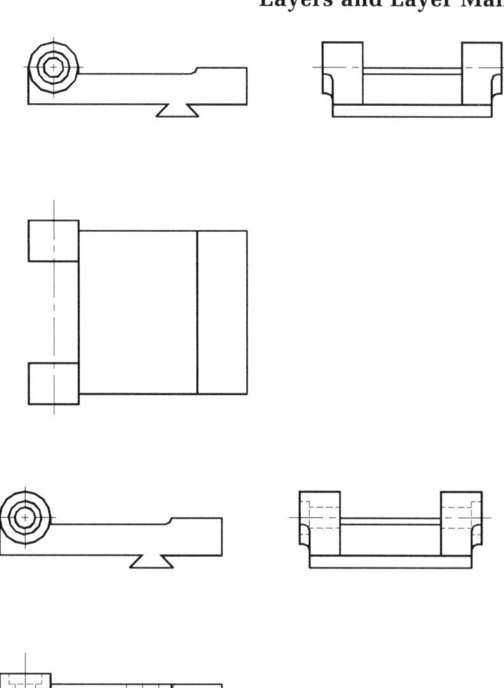

Fig. 5.16 An example of adding centre lines on Layer **Centre**

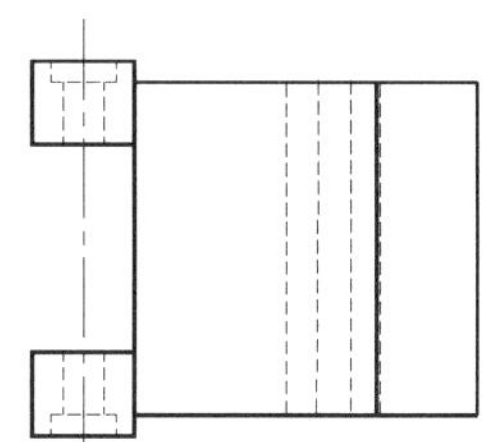

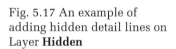

Fig. 5.17 An example of adding hidden detail lines on Layer **Hidden**

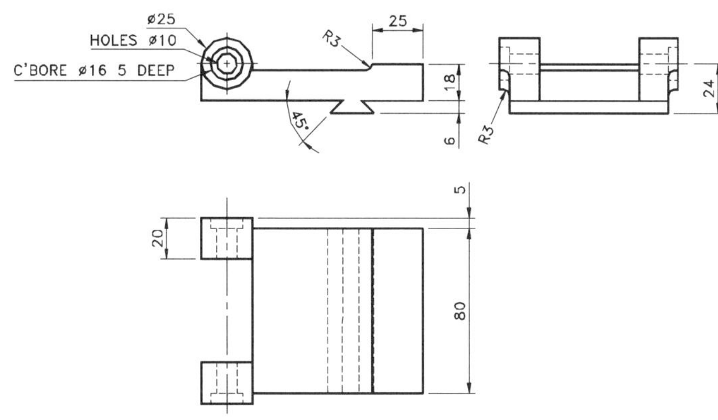

Fig. 5.18 An example of adding dimensions on Layer **Dimensions**

7. Make Layer **Dimensions** current. Add dimensions – see Chapter 10 (Fig. 5.18).
8. Make Layer **Title_block** current. Add the title and all text to the drawing (Fig. 5.12 on page 85).

Note If the following is *entered* at the Command line, the **Layer & Linetype** dialogue box comes to screen.

Command: *enter* la *right-click*

Exercises

Construct the two drawings given in Figures 5.19 and 5.20 below on the layer set shown in this chapter. Do not include the dimensions, until you have worked through Chapter 10. If your drawings are saved to file, dimensions can be added at that stage.

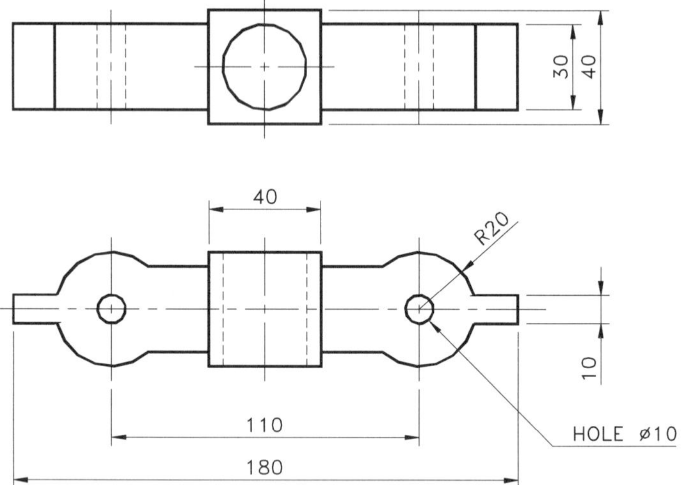

Fig. 5.19 First exercise

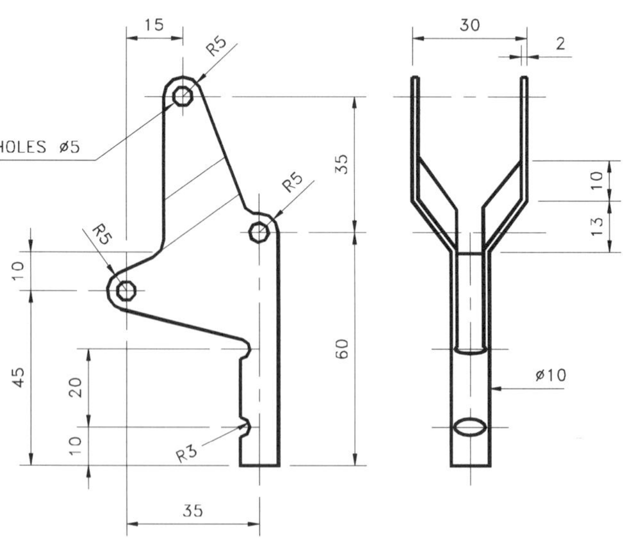

Fig. 5.20 Second exercise

CHAPTER 6

Some Modify tools

Introduction

As its name implies, the **Modify** toolbar carries those tools for modifying (editing) drawings constructed in LT 97. The toolbar is by default *docked* against the **Draw** toolbar on the left-hand side of the LT 97 window. Figure 6.1 shows the tooltips from each of the tools in the toolbar. In this chapter descriptions of the uses for the tools will be given in a series of drawing examples.

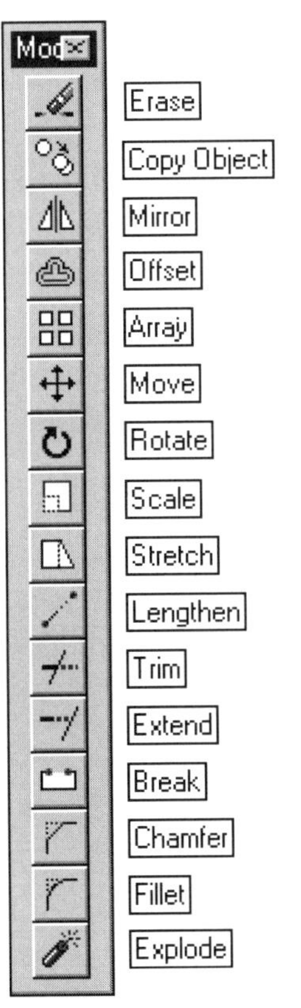

Fig. 6.1 The tools in the **Modify** toolbar

The Modify tools

The Erase tool

Probably the quickest way of calling the **Erase** tool is to *enter* e at the Command line, followed by a *right-click* (Fig. 6.2). The Command window shows:

For a single object (left of Fig. 6.3)

Command: *enter* e *right-click*
ERASE
Select objects: *pick* the object to be erased
Select objects: *right-click* **1 found**
Command:

Objects within a window (central of Fig. 6.3)

Command: *enter* e *right-click*
ERASE
Select objects: *enter* w (Window) *right-click*
First corner: *pick* **Other corner:** *pick* **8 found**
Select objects: *right-click*
Command:

Using a crossing window (right of Fig. 6.3)

Command: *enter* e *right-click*

ERASE
Select objects: *enter* c (crossing) *right-click*
First corner: *pick* **Other corner:** *pick* **6 found**
Select objects: *right-click*
Command:

Note In addition a crossing window effect is achieved by a *picking* a window starting at a **First corner:** to the bottom right of the objects to be erased, with the **Other corner:** to the top left.

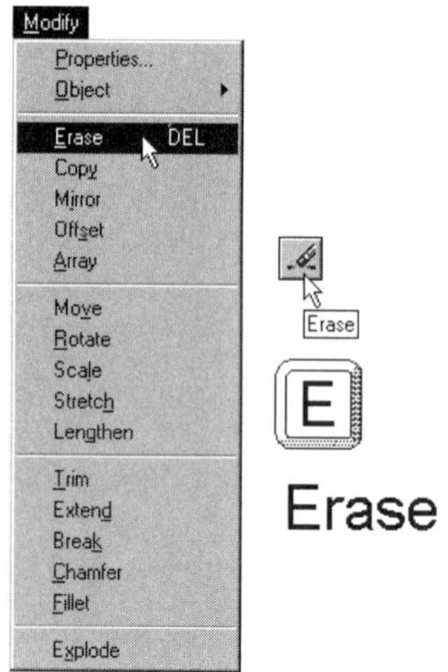

Fig. 6.2 Methods of calling the **Erase** tool

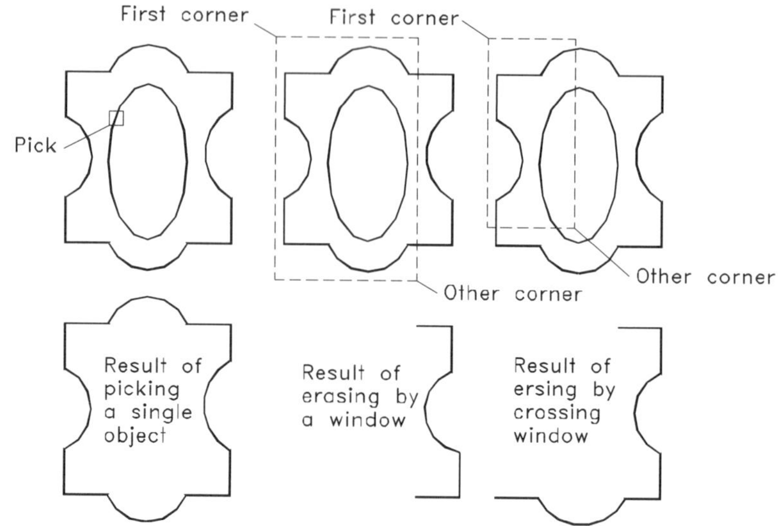

Fig. 6.3 Three methods of erasing objects

The Copy Object tool

Left-click on the **Copy Object** tool icon in the **Modify** toolbar (Fig. 6.4). The Command window shows:

For a single object (upper Fig. 6.5)

Command: _copy
Select objects: *pick* the object (the object is a polyline) **1 found**
Select objects: *right-click*
<Base point or displacement>Multiple: *pick* a point on the object
Second point of displacement: *pick* the required point
Command:

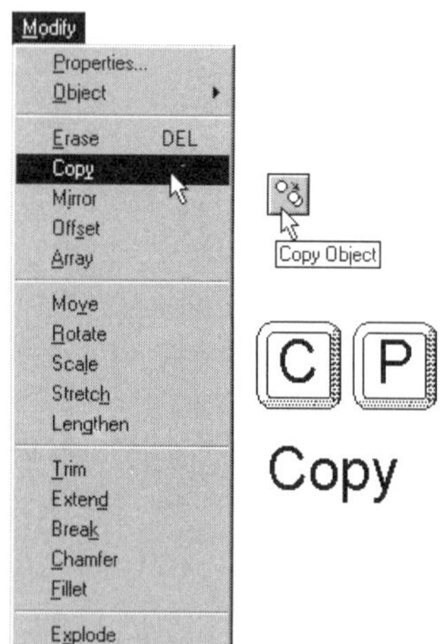

Fig. 6.4 Methods of calling the **Copy Object** tool

Copying an object several times (bottom of Fig. 6.5)

Command: _copy
Select objects: *pick*
Select objects: *right-click*
<Base point or displacement>Multiple: *enter* m *right-click*

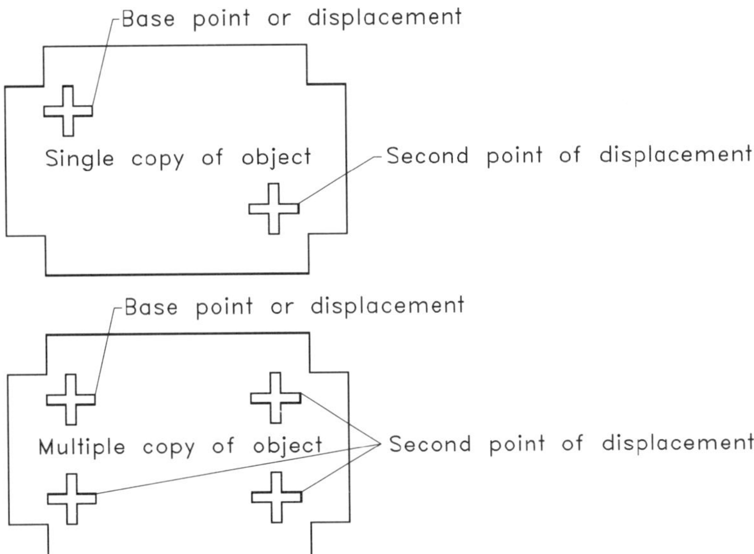

Fig. 6.5 Single and Multiple copies using the **Copy Object** tool

Base point: *pick*
Second point of displacement: *pick* the required point
Second point of displacement: *pick* the second point
Second point of displacement: *pick* the third point
Second point of displacement: *right-click*
Command:

Notes

1. Objects can be selected within a window or a crossing window.
2. Points of displacement can be *entered* as x,y coordinates in place of a *picked* point.
3. Note the **or** in **Base point or displacement**. If a coordinate entry is given the base point will be from that x,y point.

The Mirror tool

Left-click on the **Mirror** tool icon in the **Modify** toolbar (Fig. 6.6). The Command window shows:

Fig. 6.6 Methods of calling the **Mirror** tool

Command: _mirror
Select objects: *enter* w *right-click*
First corner: *pick* **Other corner:** *pick* **18 found**
Select objects: *right-click*
First point on mirror line: *pick* or *enter* coordinates *right-click*
Second point: *pick* or *enter* coordinates *right-click*
Delete old objects <N>: *right-click*
Command:

Figure 6.7 shows some examples of the use of **Mirror**. In particular, note that when text is mirrored, the way in which the mirroring acts depends upon the setting of the set variable MIRRTEXT. To set the variable:

Command: *enter* mirrtext *right-click*
New value for MIRRTEXT <!>: *enter* 0 (or 1 as required) *right-click*
Command:

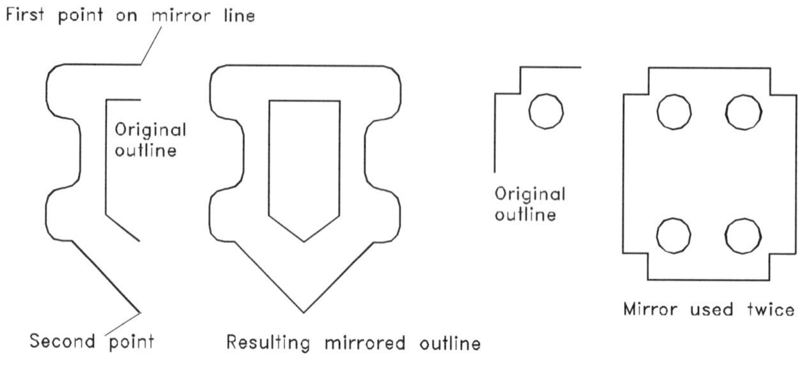

Fig. 6.7 Examples of the use of the **Mirror** tool

The Offset tool

Left-click on the **Offset** tool icon in the **Modify** pull-down menu (Fig. 6.8). The Command window shows:

Command: _offset
Offset distance or Through<Through>: *enter* 12 *right-click*
Select object to offset: *pick*
Side to offset: *pick*
Select object to offset: *right-click*
Command:

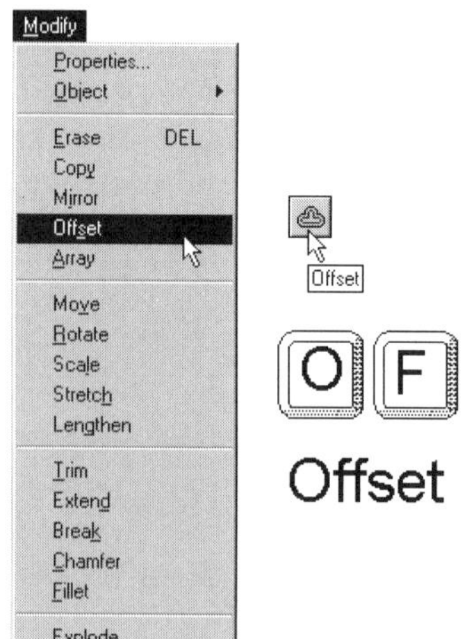

Fig. 6.8 Methods of calling the **Offset** tool

Notes

1. At the prompt **Offset distance or Through<Through>:** either a figure for the offset distance in units can be *entered*, or two points the required **Through** distance apart can be *picked* on the screen.
2. Figure 6.9 gives examples of the use of the **Offset** tool on a variety of objects
3. Only single objects can be offset. This means that joined plines, which are single objects, can be offset. See Fig. 6.10.

Fig. 6.9 Examples of the use of the **Offset** tool

Fig. 6.10 Examples of the use of the **Offset** tool on a joined pline outline

The Array tool

Rectangular Array

Left-click on **Array** in the **Modify** pull-down menu (Fig. 6.11). The Command window shows:

Command: _array
ARRAY
Select objects: *pick* a corner top left **Other corner:** *drag* the window *bottom right* and *pick*
Select objects: *right-click*
Rectangular or polar Array (<R>/P): *right-click*
Number of rows (---) <1>: *enter* 4 *right-click*

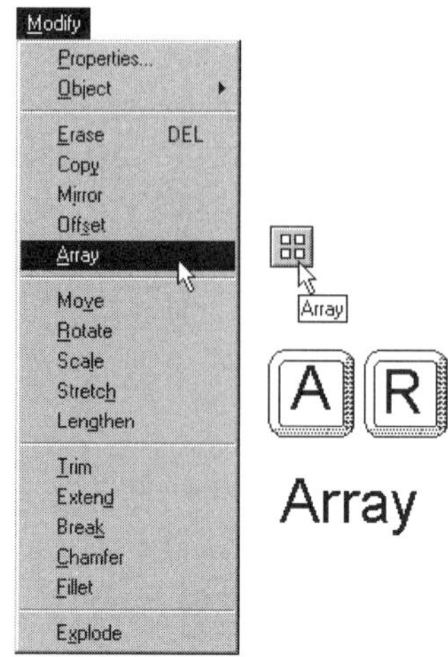

Fig. 6.11 Methods of calling the **Array** tool

Number of columns (| | |) <1>: *enter* 5 *right-click*
Unit cell or distance between rows (---): *enter* –60 *right-click*
Distance between columns (| | |): *enter* 50 *right-click*
Command:

Note the – (minus) 60 response to **distance between rows**.

Figure 6.12 shows the result of the above sequence.

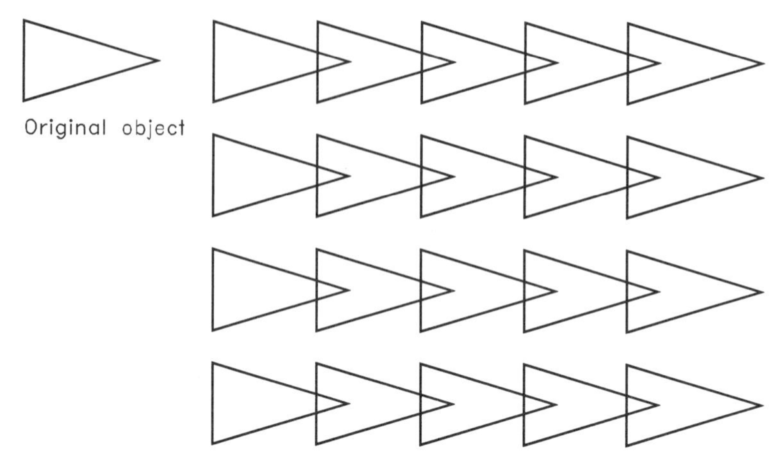

Fig. 6.12 Example of the use of **Rectangular Array**

Polar Array

Command: _array
ARRAY
Select objects: *pick* a corner top left **Other corner:** *drag* the window *bottom right* and *pick*
Select objects: *right-click*
Rectangular or polar Array (<R>/P): *enter* p *right-click*
Base/<Specify center point of array>: *pick* or *enter* coordinates
Number of items: *enter* 12 *right-click*
Angle to fill (+=ccw, -=cw) <360>: *right-click*
Rotate objects as they are copied <Y>: *right-click*
Command:

Figure 6.13 shows three examples of the use of the tool **Polar Array**.

The Move tool

Left-click on the **Move** tool icon in the **Modify** toolbar (Fig. 6.14). The Command window shows:

Command: _move
Select objects: *pick* (or window objects as necessary) **1 found**
Select objects: *right-click*

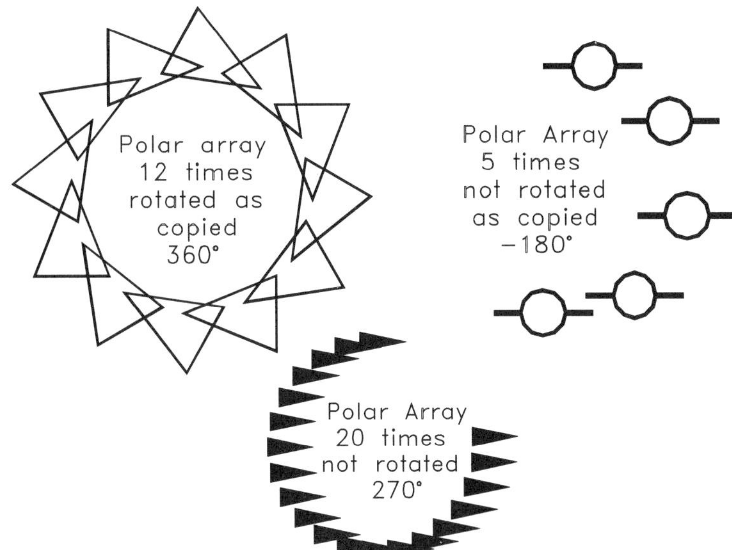

Fig. 6.13 Examples of the use of **Polar Array**

Base point or displacement: *pick* or *enter* coordinates
Second point of displacement: *pick* or *enter* coordinates
Command:

Figure 6.15 gives an example of the use of **Move** on a single object (a polyline).

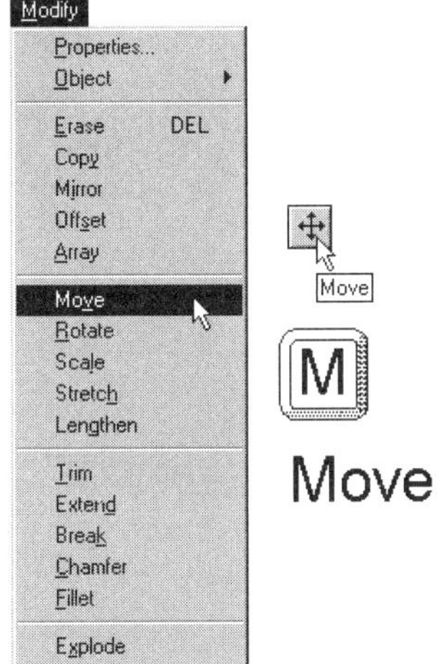

Fig. 6.14 Methods of calling the **Move** tool

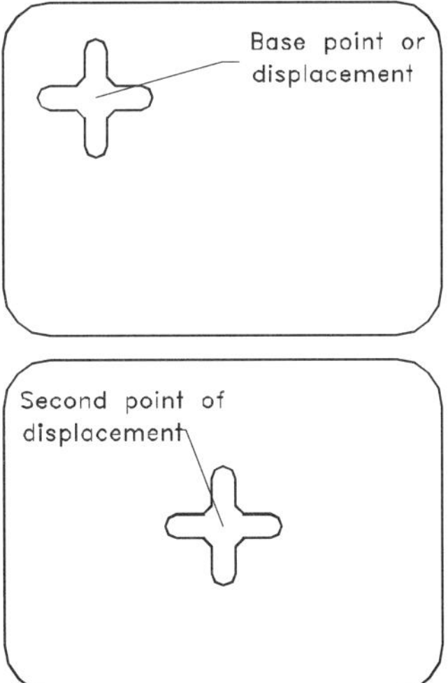

Fig. 6.15 An example of the use of **Move**

The Rotate tool

Enter ro at the Command line (Fig. 6.16). The Command window shows:

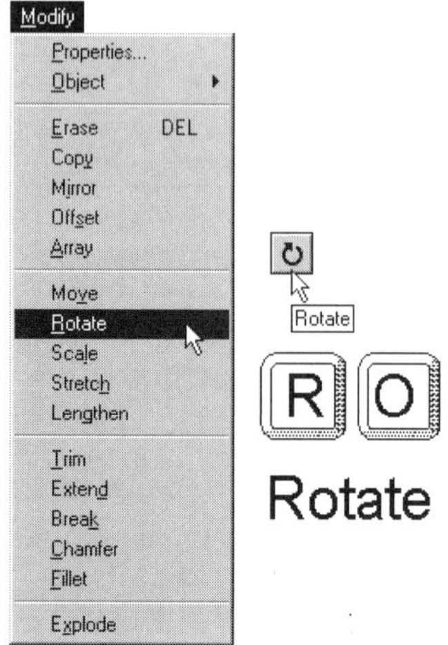

Fig. 6.16 Methods of calling the **Rotate** tool

Command: *enter* ro *right-click*
Select objects: *pick* or window objects to be rotated **1 found**
Select objects: *right-click*
Base point: *pick* or *enter* coordinates
<Rotation angle>/Reference: *enter* 45
Command:

Figure 6.17 shows examples of rotating a windowed group of objects made up of plines and a donut using the **Rotation angle** prompt.

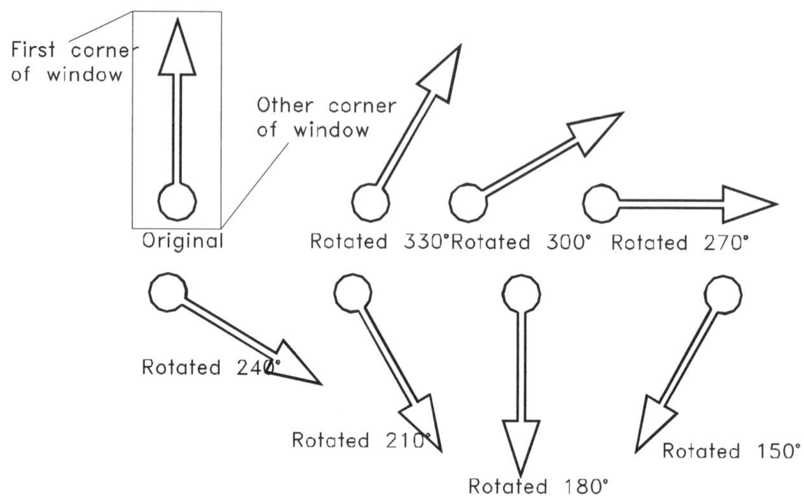

Fig. 6.17 Examples of the use of **Rotate**

With the Reference prompt of Rotate (Fig. 6.18)

Command: *enter* ro *right-click*
Select objects: window objects to be rotated *right-click* **1 found**

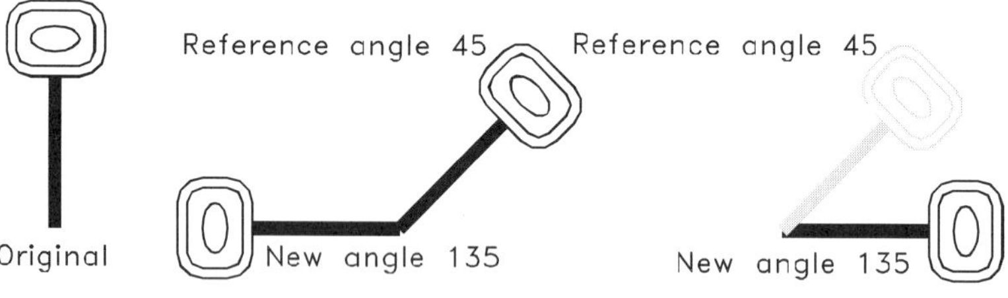

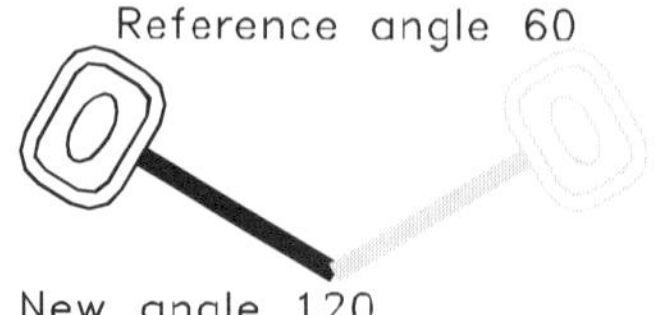

Fig. 6.18 Examples of using **Rotate** with the **Reference** prompt

Select objects: *right-click*
Base point: *pick* or *enter* coordinates
<Rotation angle>/Reference: *enter* r *right-click*
Reference angle <0>: *enter* 45 *right-click*
A ghosted copy of the objects appears at the given angle
New angle: *enter* 135 *right-click*
Command:

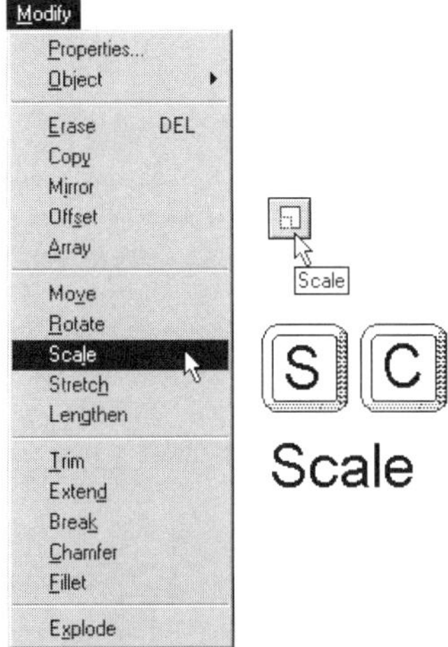

Fig. 6.19 Methods of calling the **Scale** tool

The Scale tool

Left-click on the **Scale** tool in the **Modify** toolbar (Fig. 6.19). The Command window shows:

Command: _scale
Select objects: window the objects **6 found**
Select objects: *right-click*
Base point: *pick* or *enter* coordinates and *right-click*
<Scale factor>: Reference <1>: *enter* 1.5 *right-click*
Command:

Figure 6.20 gives examples of scaling a drawing to different scales with the aid of the **Scale** tool.

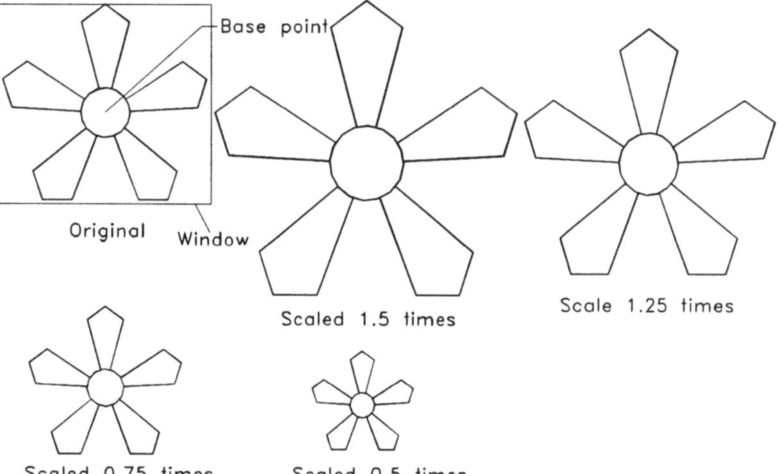

Fig. 6.20 Examples of the use of **Scale**

If a response to the **Reference** prompt is given:

Command: _scale
Select objects: window the objects **6 found**
Select objects: *right-click*
Base point: *pick* or *enter* coordinates and *right-click*
<Scale factor>: Reference: *enter* r *right-click*
Reference length <1>: *right-click* (accept the figure 1)

New length: *enter 1.5 right-click*
Command:

And the objects are scaled to 1.5 times of the original objects.

The Stretch tool

Left-click on the **Stretch** tool in the **Modify** toolbar (Fig. 6.21). The Command window shows:

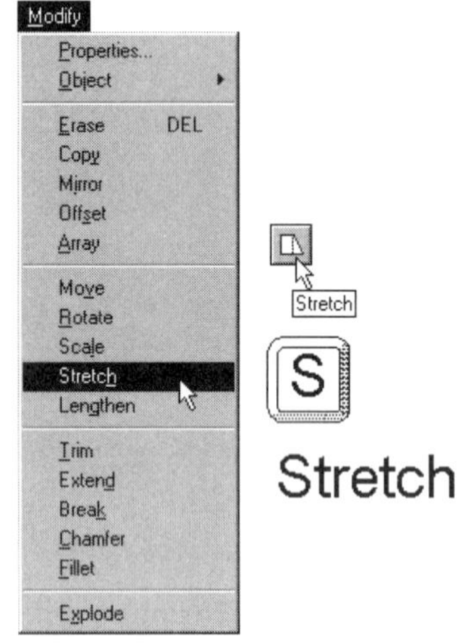

Fig. 6.21 Methods of calling the **Stretch** tool

Command: _stretch
Select objects by crossing window or crossing-polygon
Select objects: *enter* c (crossing) *right-click*
First corner: *pick* **Other corner:** *pick* **found**
Select objects: *right-click*
Base point or displacement: *pick* or *enter* coordinates and *right-click*
Second point of displacement: *pick* or *enter* coordinates and *right-click*
Command:

Figure 6.22 shows some examples of the use of the **Stretch** tool.

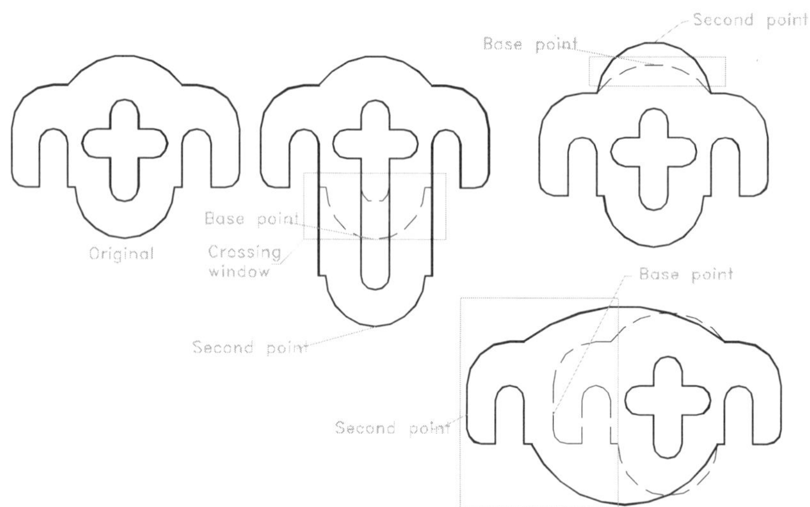

Fig. 6.22 Examples of the use of **Stretch**

The Lengthen tool

Left-click on the **Lengthen** tool in the **Modify** toolbar (Fig. 6.23). The Command window shows:

Command: _lengthen
DElta/Percent/Total/DYnamic/<Select object>: *enter* de *right-click*

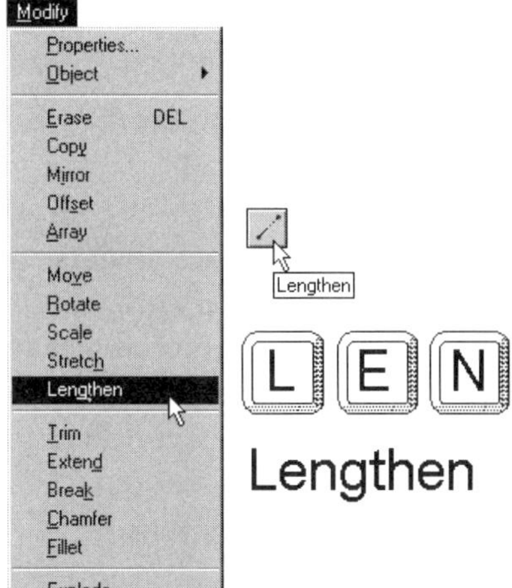

Fig. 6.23 Methods of calling the **Lengthen** tool

Angle/<Enter delta length <0>: *enter* 45 *right-click*
Select object top change>/Undo: *pick* the object
Select object top change>/Undo: *right-click*
Command:

Figure 6.24 shows the results of responses to the three prompts **DElta**, **Percent** and **Dynamic** on a line, a pline, an arc and an elliptical arc. In the case of the **DYnamic** prompt, the length of the object is *dragged* to its new length.

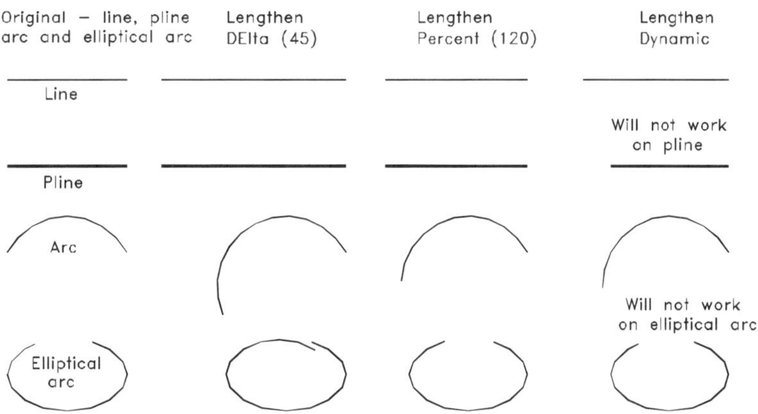

Fig. 6.24 Examples of the use of the **Lengthen** tool

Note The **Lengthen** tool will not function when the **DYnamic** prompt is in action on either a pline or an elliptical arc.

The Trim tool

Trim is a tool that will probably be frequently used to trim objects back to an edge. Methods of calling the tool are shown in Fig. 6.25.

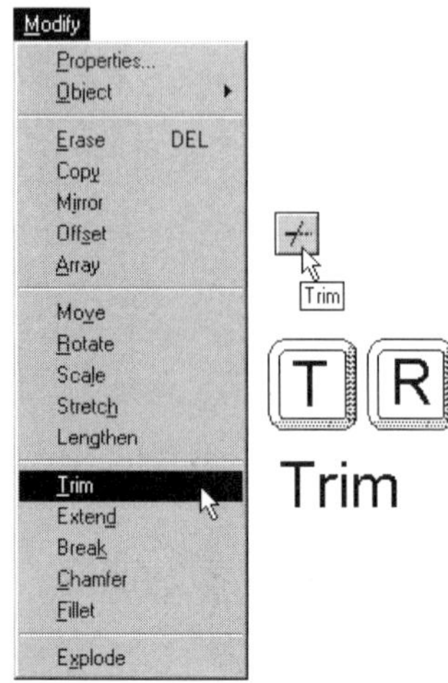

Fig. 6.25 Methods of calling the **Trim** tool

As an example *enter* tr at the Command line. The Command window will then show:

Command: *enter* tr *right-click*
TRIM
Select cutting edges: (Projmode = UCS, Edgemode = No extend)
Select objects: *pick* the cutting edge **1 found**
Select objects: *right-click*
<Select object to trim>/Projmode/Edge/Undo: *pick*
<Select object to trim>/Projmode/Edge/Undo: *pick*
<Select object to trim>/Projmode/Edge/Undo: *pick*
<Select object to trim>/Projmode/Edge/Undo: *right-click*
Command:

Figure 6.26 is an example of an outline constructed from two circles and two lines (Drawing 1 of Fig. 6.26). The two lines have been trimmed to the circles (Drawing 2 of Fig. 6.26) and have been arrayed eight times around the centre of the two circles (Drawing 3 of Fig. 6.26). Repeated trimming produces the resulting completed outline (Drawing 4 of Fig. 6.26).

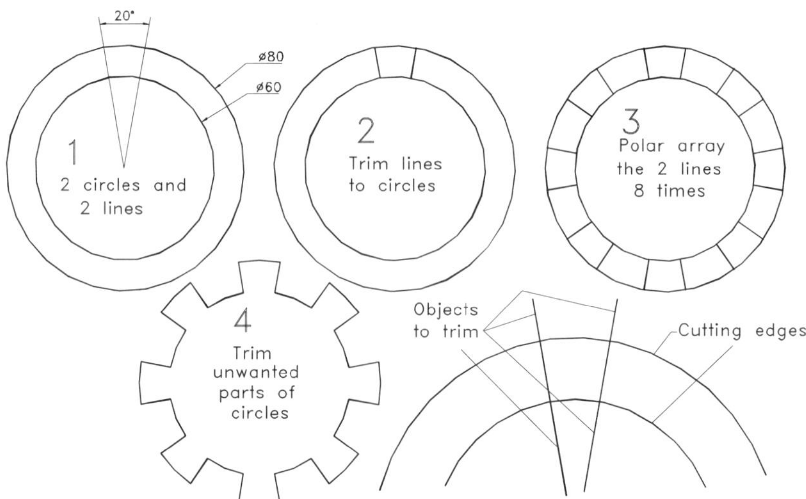

Fig. 6.26 First example of using the **Trim** tool

Figure 6.27 is another example of the use of **Trim**. Multiple trimming can be achieved with the use of a fence – when the fence crosses a line that line is trimmed back to the cutting edge. The Command window for this second example would show:

Command: *enter* tr *right-click*
TRIM
Select cutting edges: (Projmode = UCS, Edgemode = No extend)

Select objects: *pick* the cutting edge **1 found**
Select objects: *right-click*
<Select object to trim>/Projmode/Edge/Undo: *enter* f (fence) *right-click*
First fence point: *pick*
Undo/<Endpoint of line>: *pick*
Undo/<Endpoint of line>: *right-click*
<Select object to trim>/Projmode/Edge/Undo: *right-click*
Command:

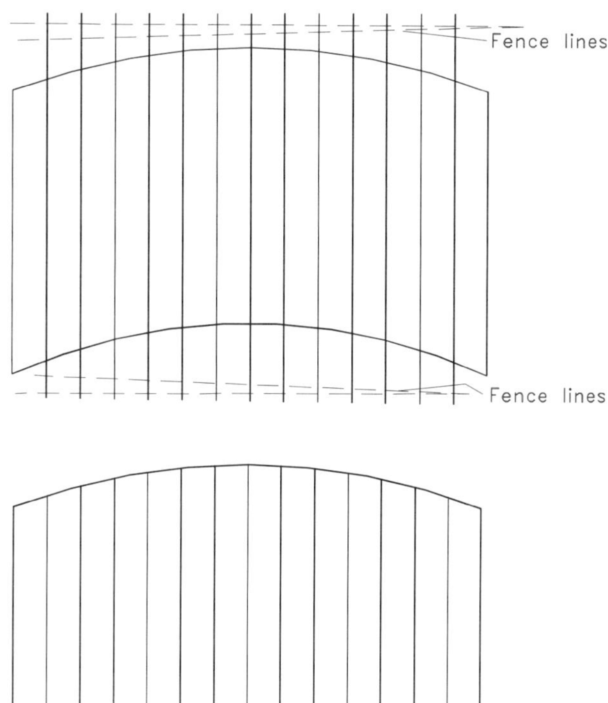

Fig. 6.27 Second example of using the **Trim** tool

The Extend tool

Left-click on the **Extend** tool in the **Modify** toolbar. For a single object to be extended, the Command window shows:

Command: _extend
Select boundary edges: (Projmode = UCS, Edgemode = No extend)
Select objects: *pick* **1 found**
Select objects: *right-click*
<Select object to extend>/Project/Edge/Undo: *pick*

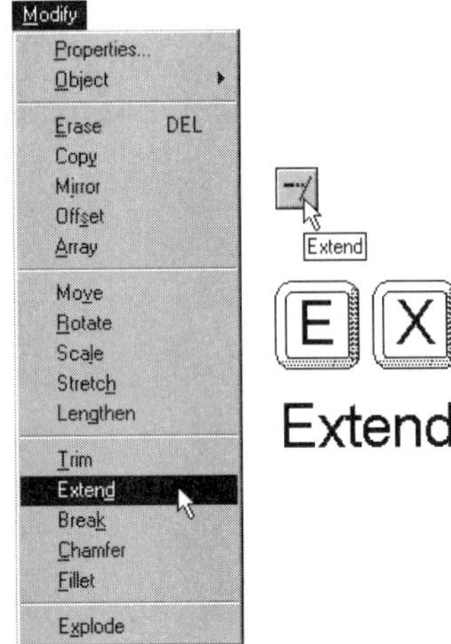

Fig. 6.28 Methods of calling the **Extend** tool

<Select object to extend>/Project/Edge/Undo: *right-click*
Command:

Figure 6.29 shows examples of the extension of lines, plines, arcs and elliptical arcs.

When the **Edge** response is used:

<Select object to extend>/Project/Edge/Undo: *enter* e (for Edge) *right-click*
Extend/No extend/<No extend>: *enter* e (for Extend) *right-click*

The object being extended will extend to an imaginary point in line with the boundary edge. Figure 6.30 shows examples of the use of the **Edge** prompt.

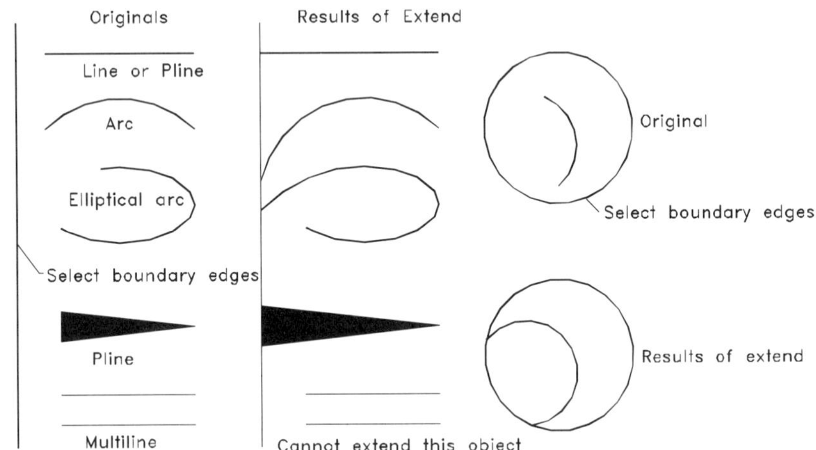

Fig. 6.29 Examples of the use of the **Extend** tool

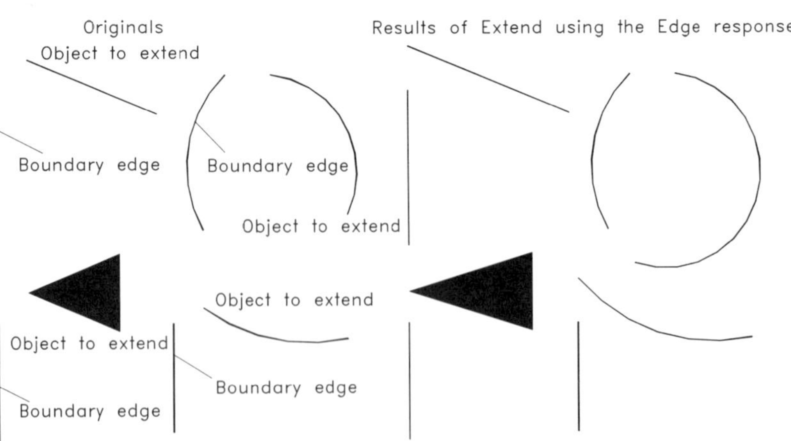

Fig. 6.30 Examples of the use of the **Extend** tool with the **Edge** prompt

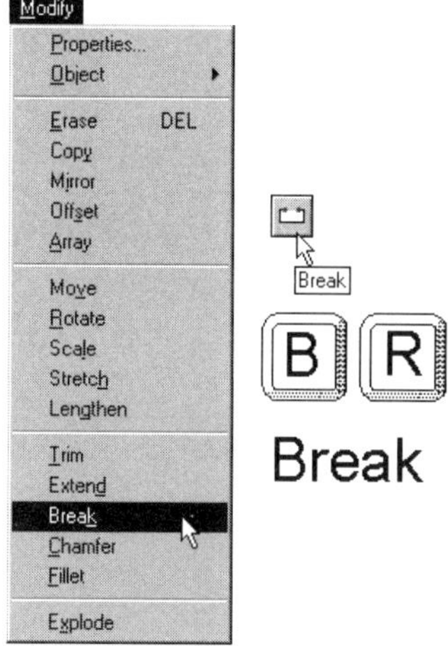

Fig. 6.31 Methods of calling the **Break** tool

The Break tool

Enter br at the Command line and the Command window shows:

Command: *enter* br *right-click*
BREAK Select object: *pick* the object
Enter second point (or F for first point): *pick*
Command:

Or:

Command: *enter* br *right-click*
BREAK Select object: *pick* the object
Enter second point (or F for first point): *enter* f *right-click*
Enter first point: *pick*
Enter second point: *pick*
Command:

Figure 6.32 shows the results of using both methods.

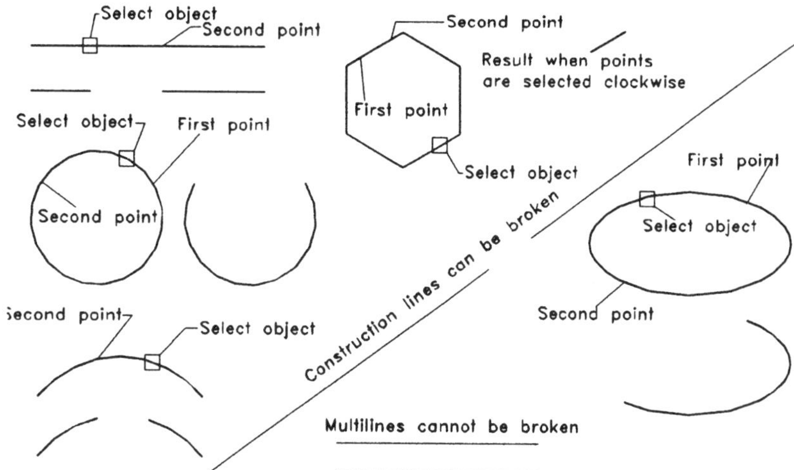

Fig. 6.32 Examples of the use of the **Break** tool

Note When selecting **Break** points on circles, arcs or polygons, the selection must be taken counter-clockwise (anticlockwise) to obtain the expected breaking.

The Chamfer tool

Figure 6.33 shows the four methods of calling the tool. In the following example, the method of selection from the **Modify** pull-down menu was chosen.

Command: _chamfer
(TRIM mode) Current chamfer Dist1 = 10, Dist2 = 10
Polyline/Distance/Angle/Trim/Method/<Select first line>: *pick*

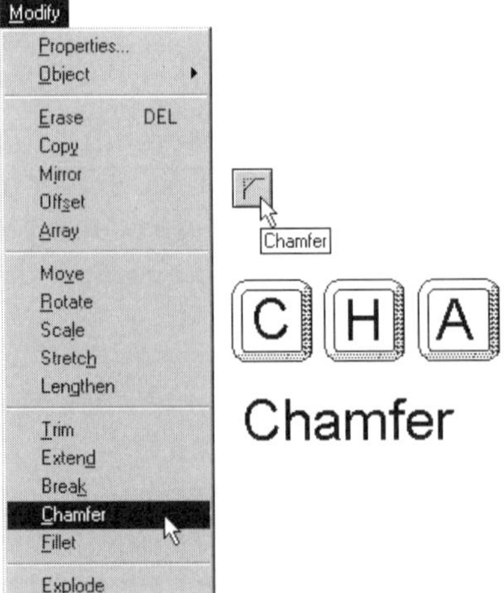

Fig. 6.33 Methods of calling the **Chamfer** tool

> **Select second line:** *pick*
> **Command:**

For the **Polyline** prompt sequence (Fig. 6.34):

> **Polyline/Distance/Angle/Trim/Method/<Select first line>:** *enter* p (for Polyline) *right-click*
> **Select 2D polyline:** *pick*
> **4 lines were chamfered**
> **Command:**

For the **Trim** prompt sequence (Fig. 6.34):

> **Polyline/Distance/Angle/Trim/Method/<Select first line>:** *enter* t (for Trim) *right-click*
> **Trim/No trim/<Trim>:** *enter* n (for No trim) *right-click*

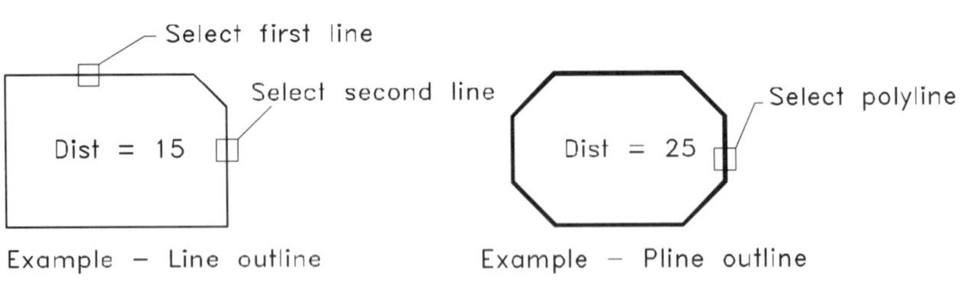

Fig. 6.34 Examples of the use of the **Chamfer** tool

Polyline/Distance/Angle/Trim/Method/<Select first line>: *pick*
Select second line: *pick*

For the **Angle** prompt sequence (Fig. 6.34):

Polyline/Distance/Angle/Trim/Method/<Select first line>: *enter* a (for Angle) *right-click*
Enter chamfer distance on the first line <10>: *enter 20* right-click
Enter chamfer angle from the first line: *enter* 60 *right-click*

The Fillet tool

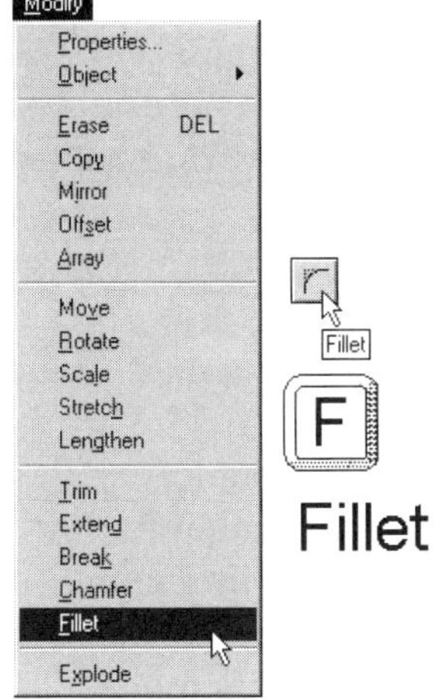

Fig. 6.35 Methods of calling the **Fillet** tool

The sequence of operations involved in using the **Fillet** tool follow closely on those of the **Chamfer** tool, except that only one radius has to be set, where two distances or a distance and an angle have to be set when using **Chamfer**.

Left-click on **Fillet** in the **Modify** toolbar. The Command window then shows:

Command: _fillet
(TRIM mode) Current fillet radius = 10
Polyline/Radius/Trim/<Select first object: *enter* r *right-click*
Enter fillet radius <10>: *enter* 15 *right-click*
Command: *right-click*
Polyline/Radius/Trim/<Select first object: *pick*
Select second object: *right-click*
Command:

The above is the sequence for the top left outline of Fig. 6.36. The response to prompt sequences for the other three outlines shown in Fig. 6.36 follows similar routines to those given for the **Chamfer** tool.

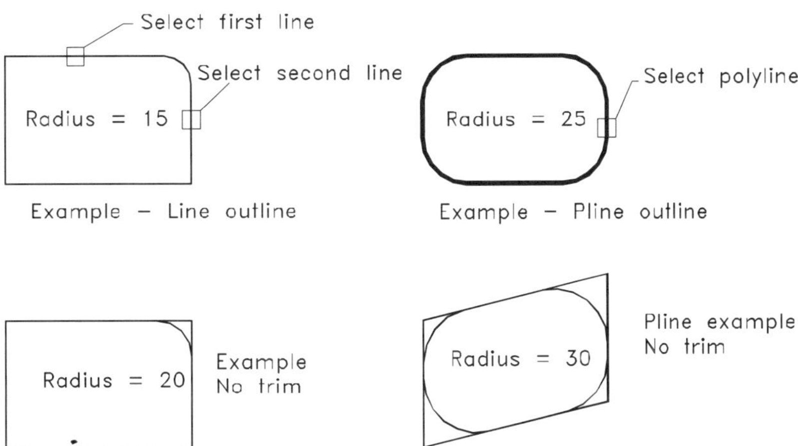

Fig. 6.36 Examples of the use of the **Fillet** tool

The Explode tool

The uses for this tool will be given in Chapter 11 in connection with the insertion and treatment of blocks.

Questions

1. What is the difference in the results between using an **Erase** window from top left to bottom right compared with a window from bottom right to top left?
2. What is the purpose of the set variable MIRRTEXT?
3. There are two methods of setting the distance by which an offset of an object can be performed. Can you describe them?
4. When using **Array** in its rectangular form, it is often necessary to *enter* a negative number in response to the prompt **Unit cell or distance between rows (---):** Why is this so?
5. When using the polar form of **Array**, in which direction should the array be expected to develop?
6. What happens if a negative number is given in response to the **Rotate** prompt **<Rotation angle>/Reference:**?
7. Can a fence be used in connection with the **Stretch** tool?
8. Can a multiline be lengthened with the aid of **Lengthen**?
9. What is the purpose of the **No trim** mode of the **Trim** Command line sequence?
10. Can a construction line be acted upon by the **Modify** tools?

Exercises

The following include revision exercises of the use of tools described in previous chapters, as well as exercises using the tools described in this chapter.

1. The right-hand drawing of Fig. 6.37 shows an enlarged drawing with dimensions of a plastic clip. Start by drawing the constructions shown in the left-hand drawing of Fig. 6.37. Then set **Snap** to 5 and use the tools **Line**, **Circle** with **TTR**; **Offset**; **Trim**; with **Osnaps** as necessary to complete the outline (right-hand drawing of Fig. 6.37).
2. Figure 6.38. The upper pair of drawings show the construction for the two-view orthographic projection (see Chapter 9) in the lower pair of drawings.

   Set **Snap** to **5**. Use **Line**, **Circle**, **Rectangle**, **Trim** and construct the two-view projection. Do not include any dimensions.
3. Figure 6.39. The left-hand drawing shows the construction needed to produce the right-hand drawing.

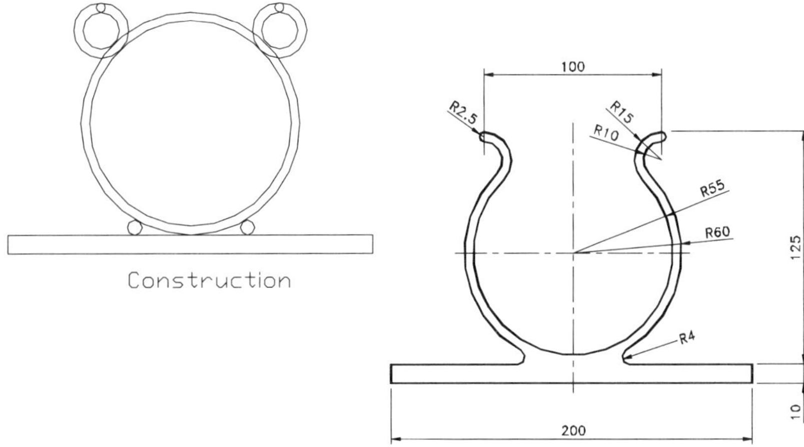

Fig. 6.37 Exercise 1

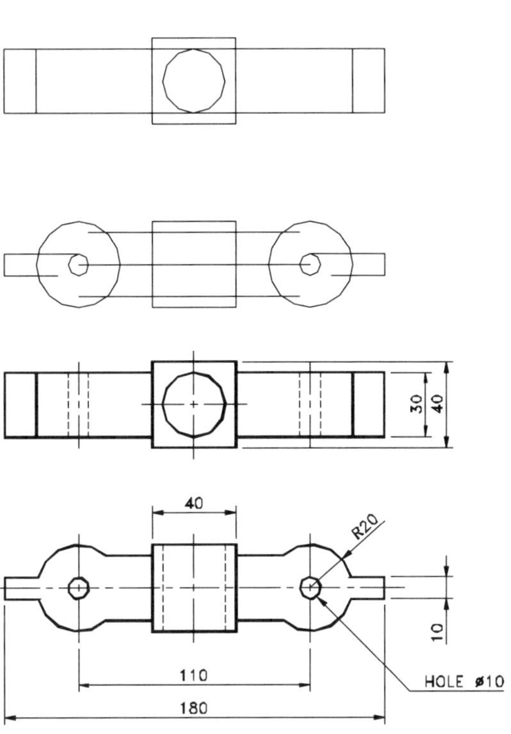

Fig. 6.38 Exercise 2

Set **Osnap** to **5**. Use the tools **Circle**, **Line**, **Polygon**, **Rotate**, **Copy (Multiple)**, **Trim**, **Osnaps** and **Erase**.

Note that instead of drawing polygons and multiple copying, **Array (Polar)** could have been used, but for this exercise use **Copy**.

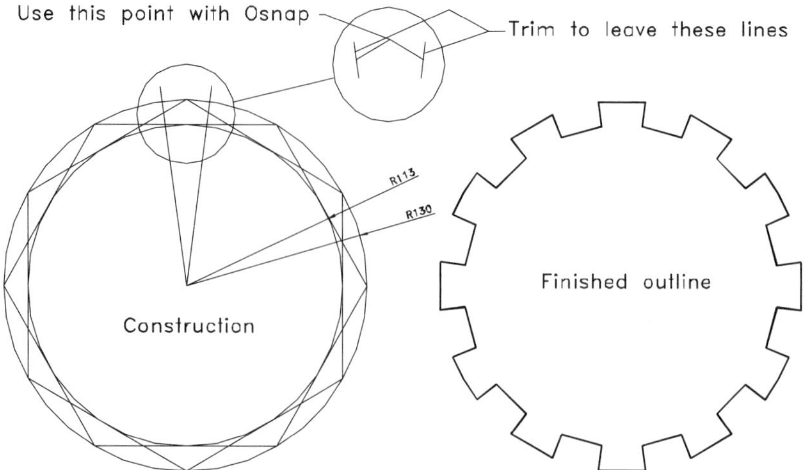

Fig. 6.39 Exercise 3

4. Figure 6.40. The left-hand drawing shows the construction behind the right-hand drawing.

   Set **Snap** to **5**. Use the tools **Circle**, **Line**, **Polygon**, **Array (Polar)**, **Trim** and construct the right-hand drawing.

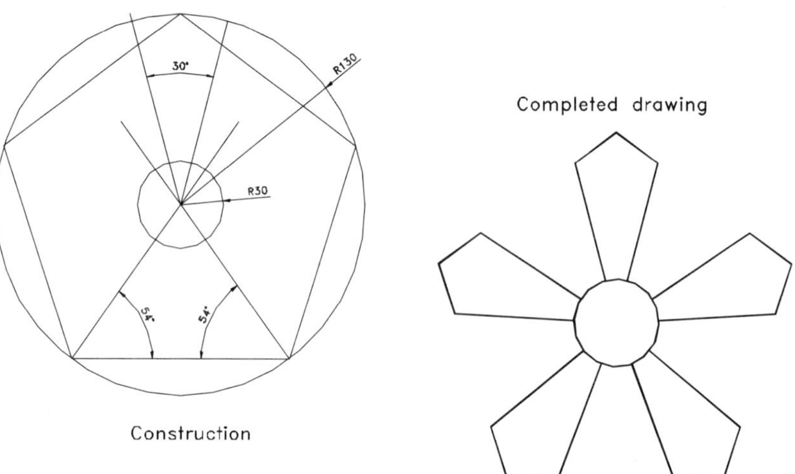

Fig. 6.40 Exercise 4

5. Figure 6.41 The left-hand drawing shows the basic construction for the right-hand drawing.

   Set **Snap** to **5**. Use the tools **Polygon**, **Circle**, **Osnaps**, **Trim**, **Offset** (for handle), **Circle with TTR**. Construct the drawing.

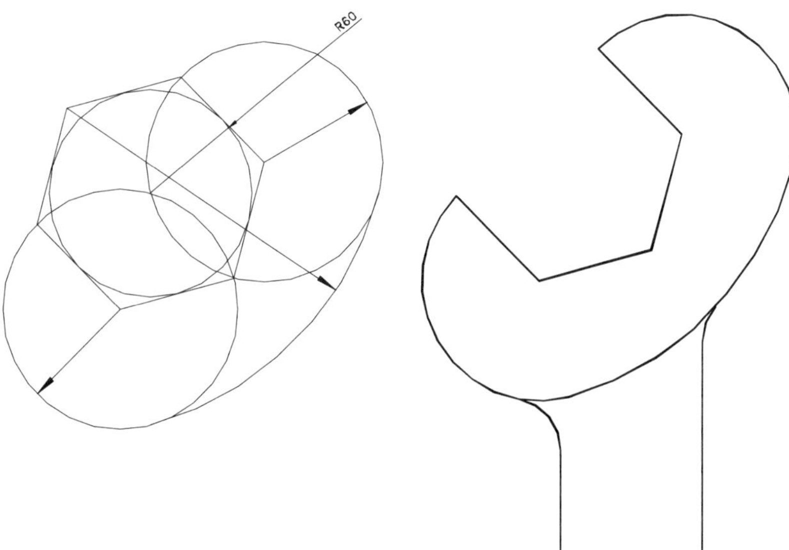

Fig. 6.41 Exercise 5

6. Figure 6.42 shows a view of a clamp and its screw. Figure 6.43 shows the basic construction for the screw thread.

   Construct the outline as given in Fig. 6.43. Use **Mirror** to mirror the thread across the centre line of the drawing. Add other details to the drawing to sizes considered suitable and complete the drawing Fig. 6.42.

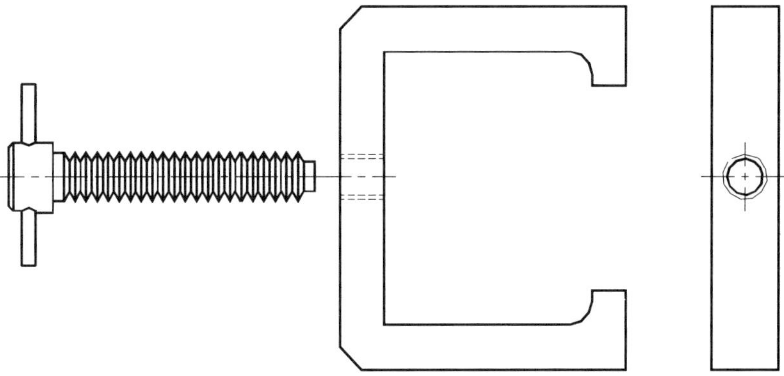

Fig. 6.42 Exercise 6

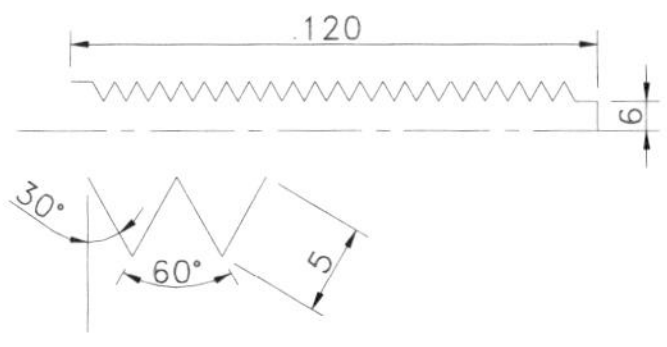

Fig. 6.43 Construction for the screw thread of Exercise 6

7. Figure 6.44 gives details of the basic construction for the exercise as shown in Fig. 6.45.

   Construct the gear tooth as shown in Fig. 6.44 and using the **Trim** and **Erase** tools, trim and erase the excess constructions from the gear tooth. Then add details as shown in Fig. 6.46 and use the **Array (Polar)** tool to complete the exercise.

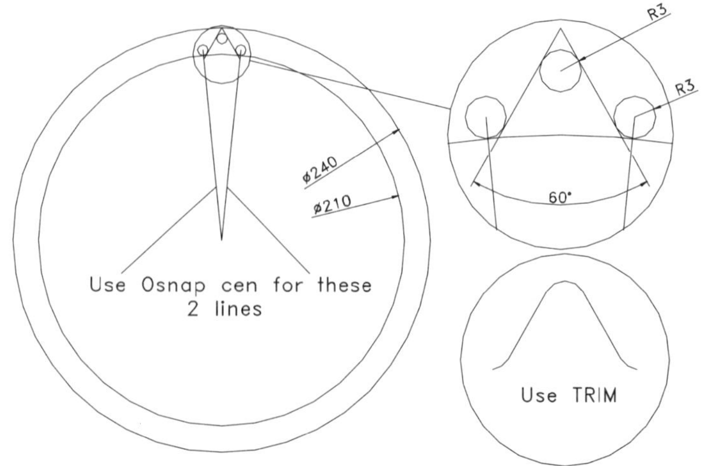

Fig. 6.44 Construction for Exercise 7

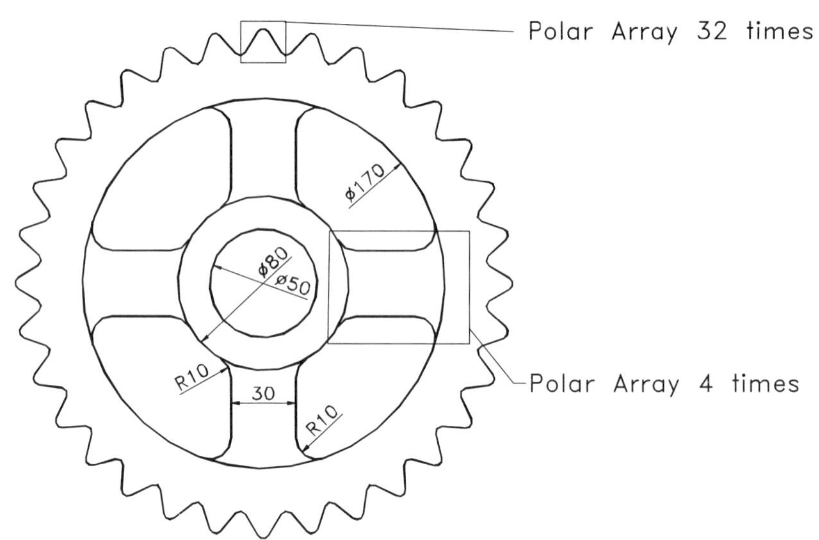

Fig. 6.45 Exercise 7

8. Construct the outline given in Fig. 6.47.

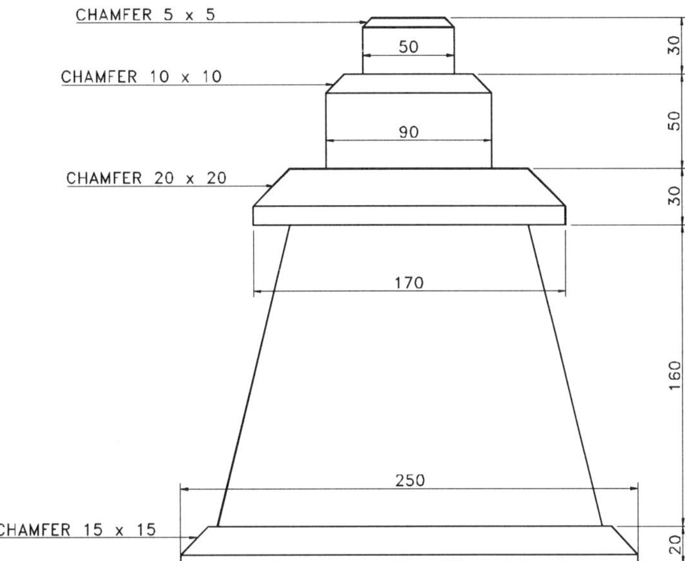

Fig. 6.46 Exercise 8

CHAPTER 7

Some tools from Modify and Inquiry

Introduction

As shown in Chapter 6, the **Modify** pull-down menu contains the same tools as are contained in the **Modify** toolbar. There are,

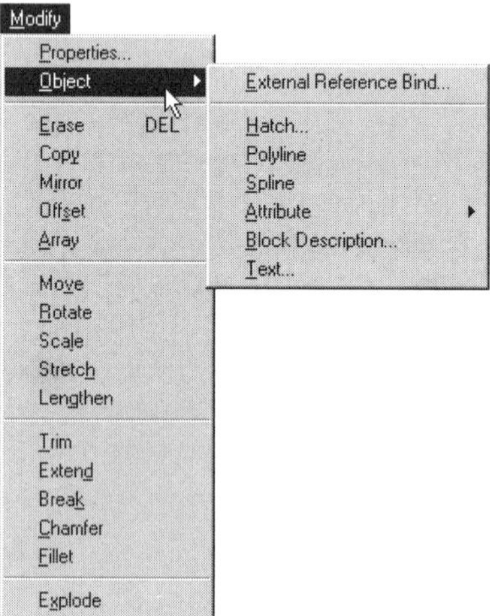

Fig. 7.1 The **Modify** pull-down menu showing the **Object** sub-menu

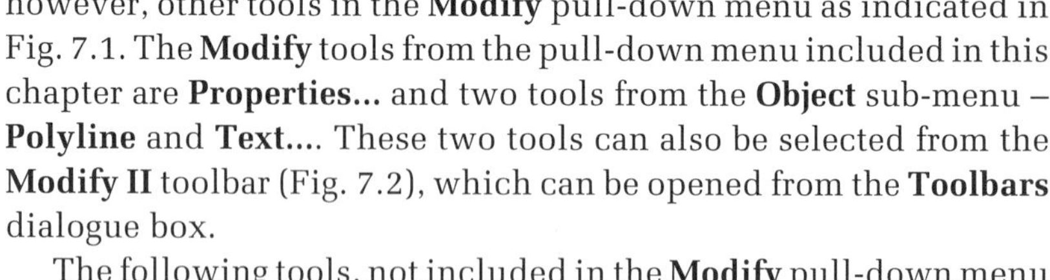

however, other tools in the **Modify** pull-down menu as indicated in Fig. 7.1. The **Modify** tools from the pull-down menu included in this chapter are **Properties...** and two tools from the **Object** sub-menu – **Polyline** and **Text....** These two tools can also be selected from the **Modify II** toolbar (Fig. 7.2), which can be opened from the **Toolbars** dialogue box.

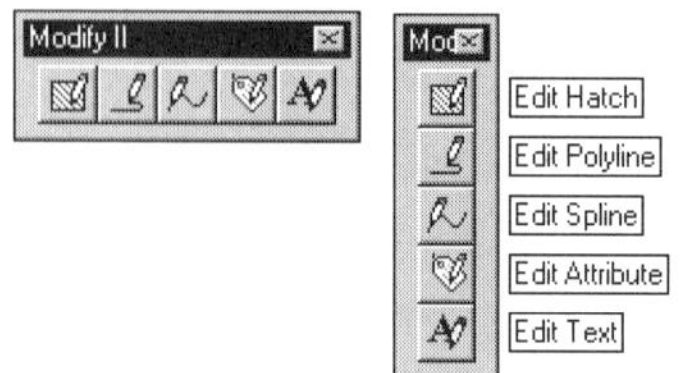

Fig. 7.2 The **Modify II** toolbar

The following tools, not included in the **Modify** pull-down menu or the **Modify** toolbar, but which are described in this chapter are **Divide** and **Measure** from the **Point** sub-menu of the **Draw** pull-down menu or from a flyout from the **Standard** toolbar and **Area** and **Distance** from the **Inquiry** toolbar. **Distance** and **Area** can also be

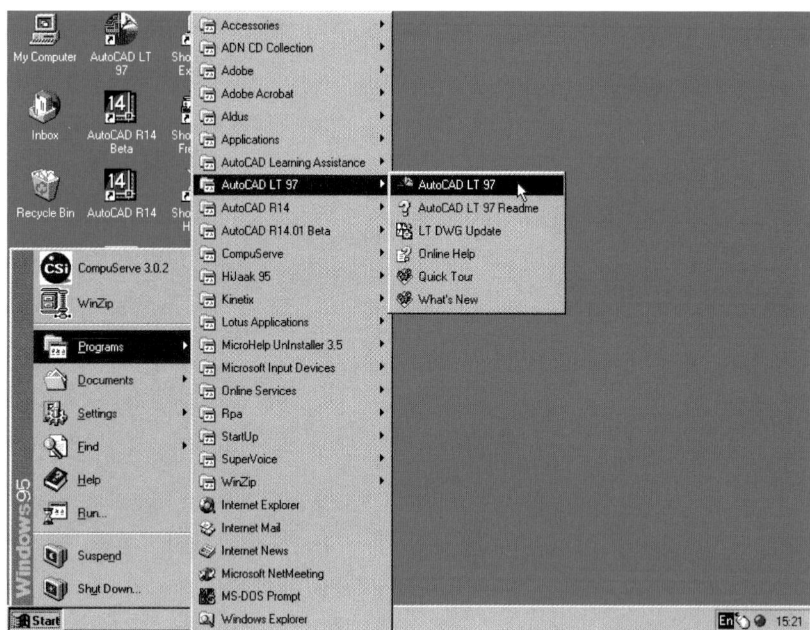

Plate I The Windows 95 **Start** menu showing **AutoCAD LT 97** selected

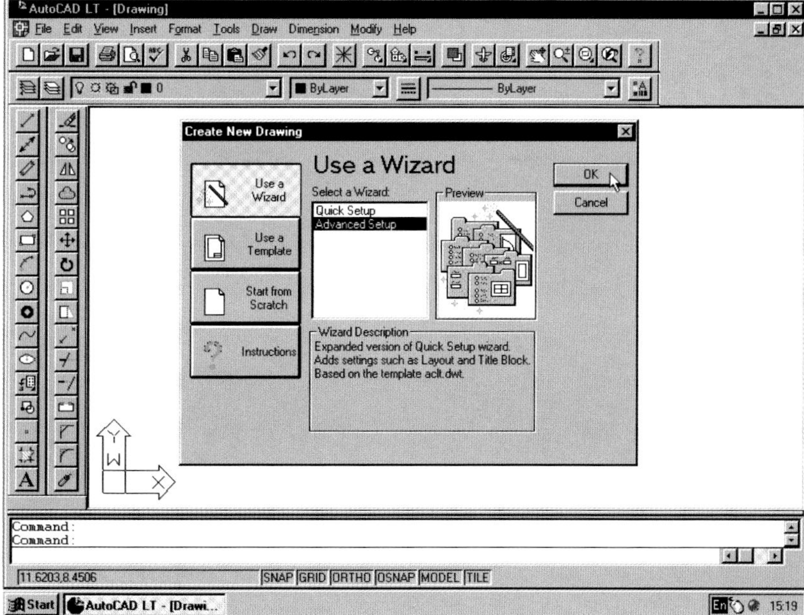

Plate II The AutoCAD LT 97 start up dialogue box with **Advanced Setup** selected

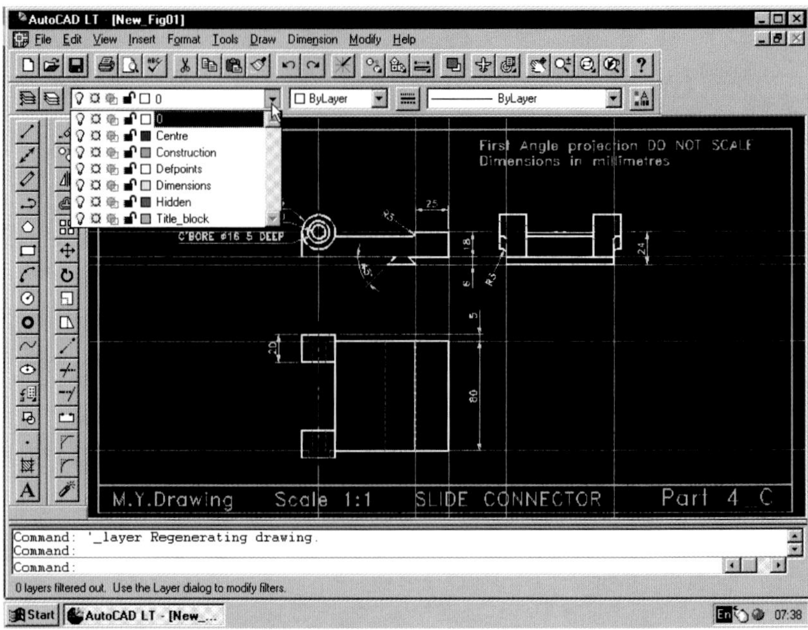

Plate III A three-view orthographic projection on a black background

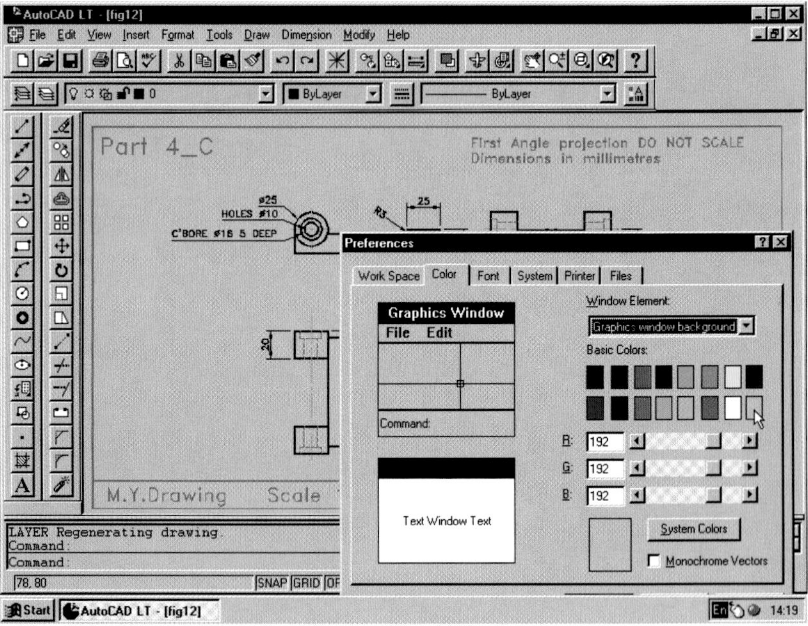

Plate IV The same three views shown in Plate III with both the graphics and command window background set to gray

Plate V A front view of a house with the **Layer Control** popup list showing the different layers in the drawing

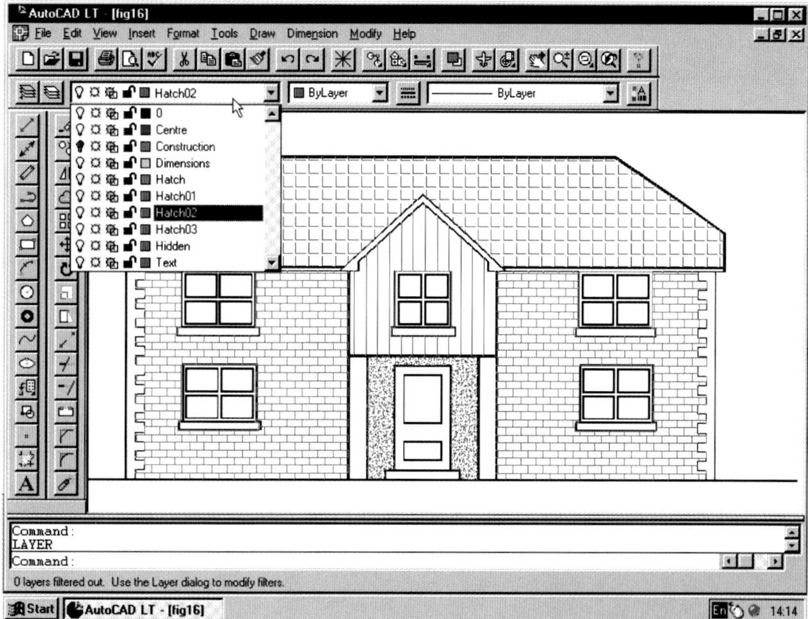

Plate VI The same front view shown in Plate V with the **Aerial View** window on screen

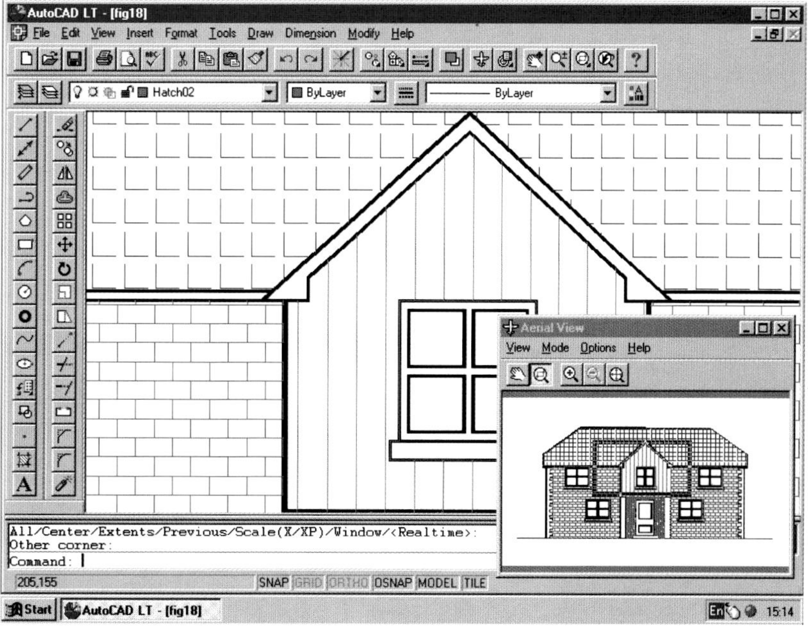

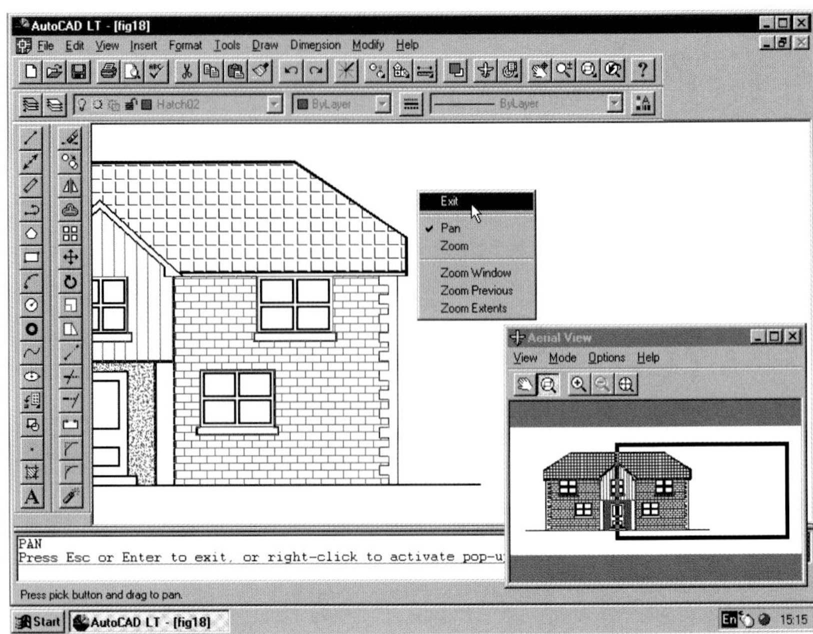

Plate VII Another view of Plate V after the **Pan** tool has been used

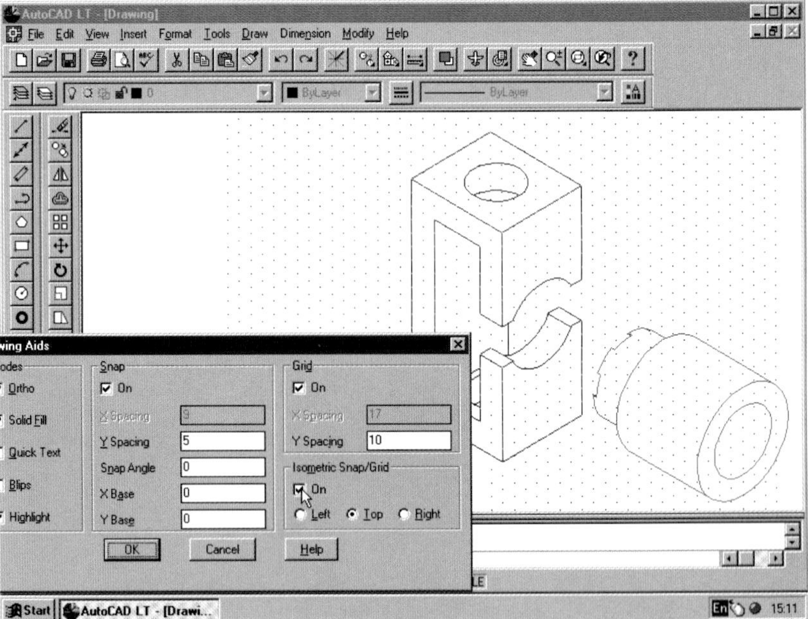

Plate VIII An isometric drawing with the **Drawing Aids** dialogue box on screen

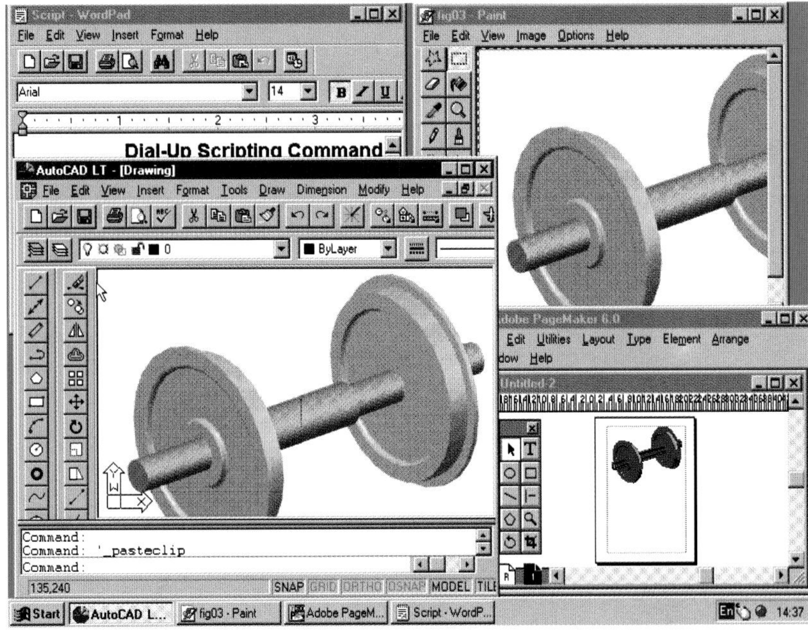

Plate IX Four applications running simultaneously in Windows 95

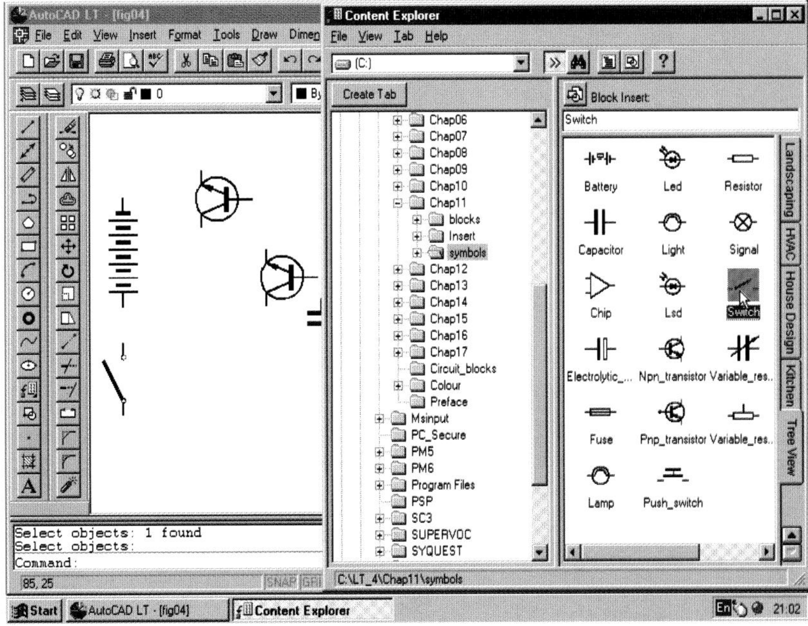

Plate X The **Content Explorer** on screen

Plate XI Nine different hatch patterns selected from the **Boundary Hatch** dialogue box

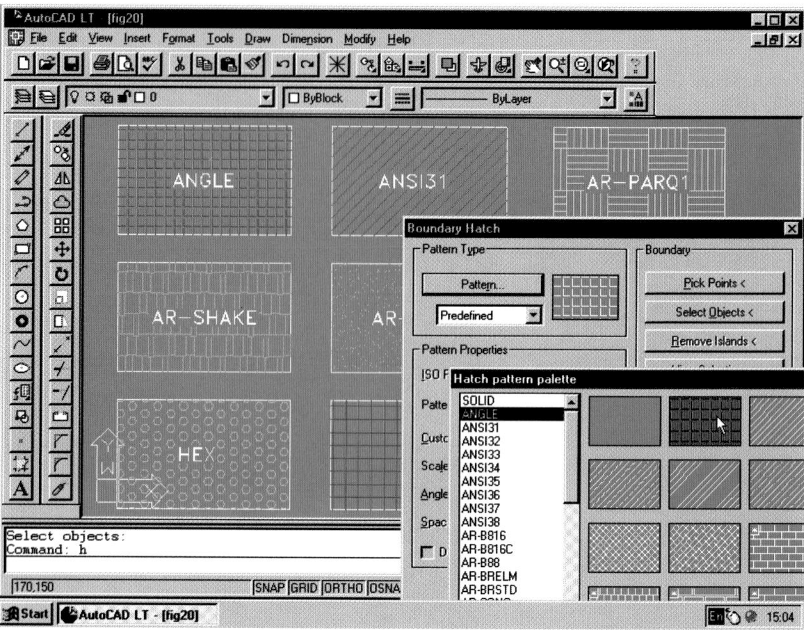

Plate XII A rendered 3D solid model from AutoCAD Release 14, captured as a bitmap and displayed in the Windows 95 **Paint** program; the bitmap has been selected for copying to LT 97

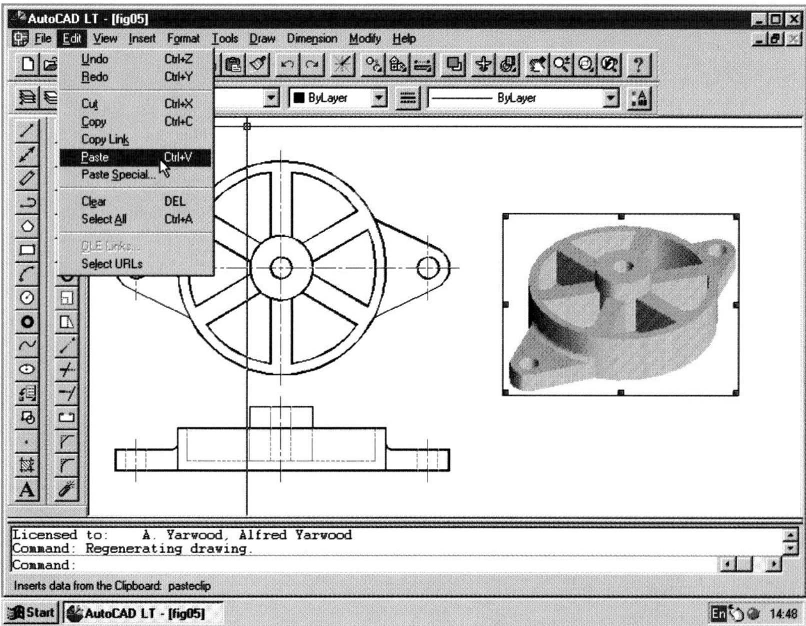

Plate XIII The bitmap from Plate XII inserted in a 2D two-view orthographic projection in LT 97

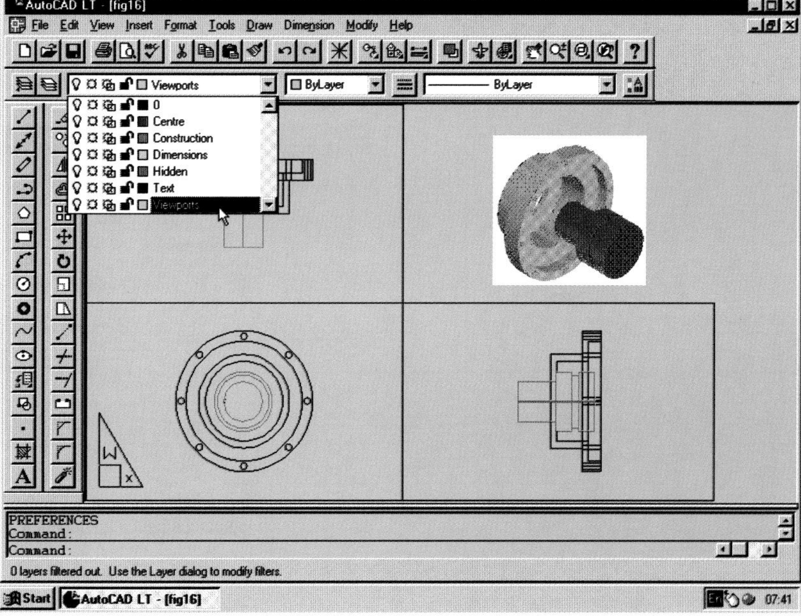

Plate XIV A 'paper space' screen in which one viewport has been deleted and replaced with an inserted bitmap

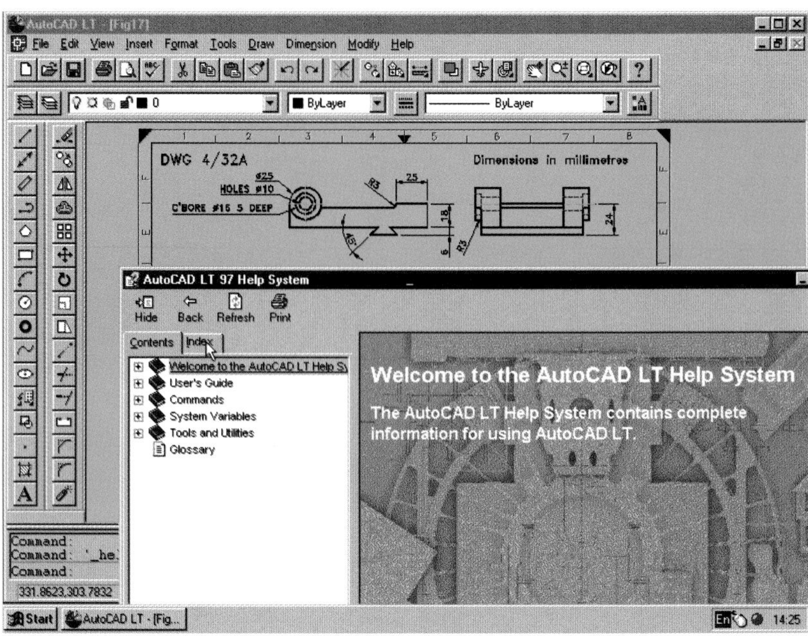

Plate XV The LT 97 **Help** screen when it is first loaded

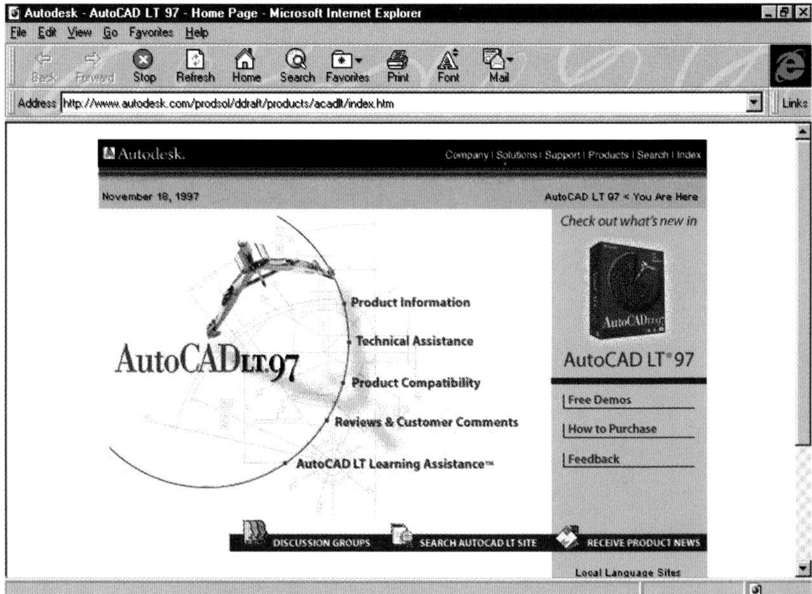

Plate XVI The **AutoCAD LT 97** Internet **home page**

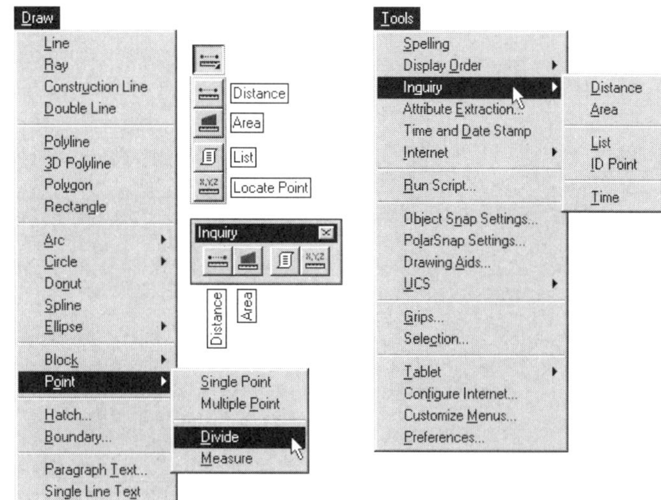

Fig. 7.3 Methods of selecting **Distance**, **Area**, **Divide** and **Measure**

called from the **Inquiry** sub-menu of the **Tools** pull-down menu. See Fig. 7.3.

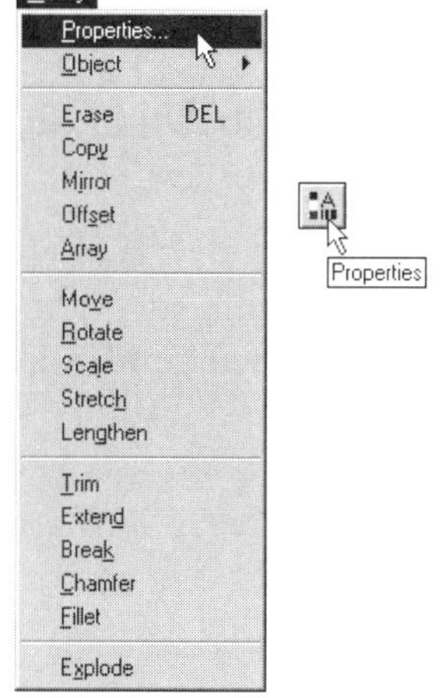

Fig. 7.4 Methods of calling the **Properties** tool

The Properties tool

Left-click either on **Properties** in the **Modify** pull-down menu, or on the **Properties** tool icon in the **Object Properties** toolbar (Fig. 7.4). The Command window then shows:

Command:
Select objects: *pick* an object
Select objects: *right-click*

And the **Modify Line** (or **Polyline** or **Circle** etc.) dialogue box appears as in Fig. 7.5.

In the dialogue box, not only can the object's layer, colour and/or linetype be changed, but so also can the position of the object,

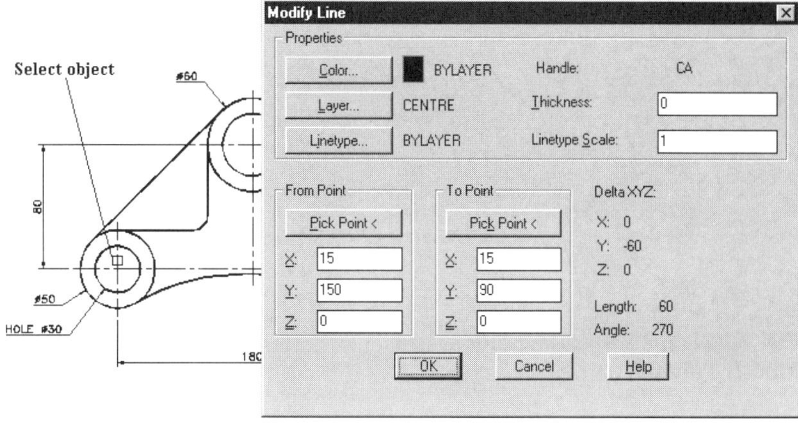

Fig. 7.5 The **Modify Line** dialogue box

either by the *picking* of new points for its ends, or its centre, radius etc., or by *entering* new coordinates for the positions and/or sizes of the object.

If an area of a drawing is windowed in response to the **Select objects** prompt of the **Properties** tool, the **Change Properties** dialogue box appears as in Fig. 7.6. As can be seen from the dialogue box, amendments can be made to the various properties of all the objects within the window. This means the window must be selected with care.

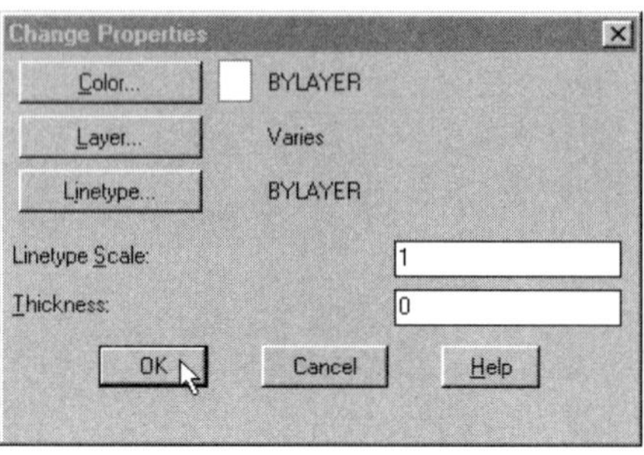

Fig. 7.6 The **Change Properties** dialogue box

The Modify Polyline tool

Call the **Modify Polyline** tool by one of the methods shown in Fig. 7.7. The Command window shows:

Command: *enter* pe *right-click*
PEDIT Select polyline: *pick* the polyline to be modified
Close/Join/Width/Edit vertex/Fit/Spline/Decurve/Ltype gen/Undo/eXit/<X>:

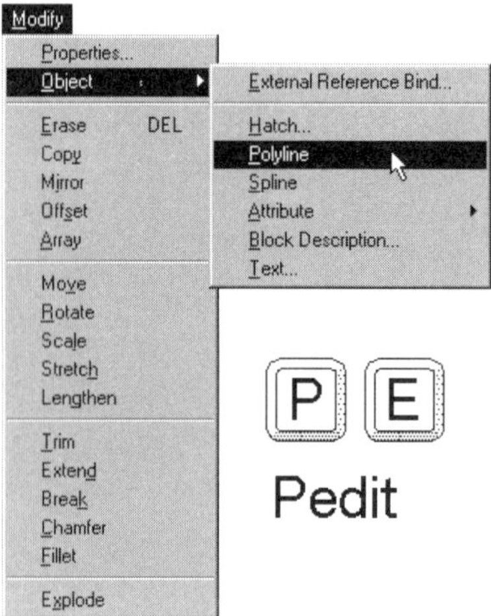

Fig. 7.7 Methods of calling the **Modify Polyline** tool

Figure 7.8 shows the results of making different responses to the prompts of the tool. These are as follows:

Close

Close/Join/Width/Edit vertex/Fit/Spline/Decurve/Ltype gen/Undo/ eXit/<X>: *enter* c *right-click*

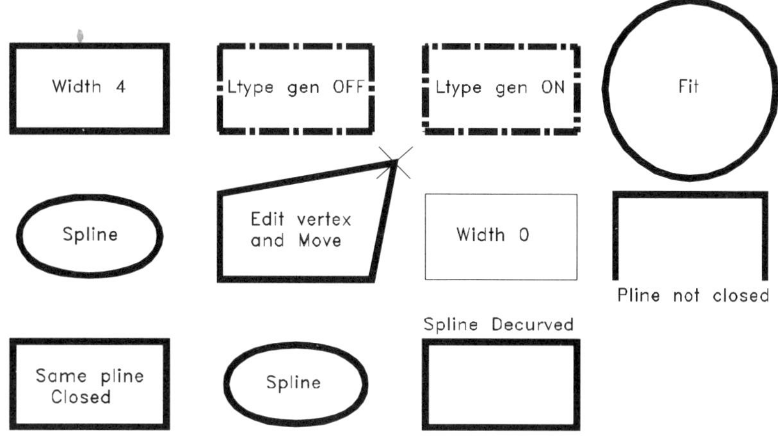

Fig. 7.8 Examples of the use of the **Modify Polyline** tool

And if there are any gaps in an outline composed of plines, the outline closes to form a single pline.

Join

Close/Join/Width/Edit vertex/Fit/Spline/Decurve/Ltype gen/Undo/ eXit/<X>: *enter* j *right-click*

And either window the parts to be joined or pick them individually.

Width

Close/Join/Width/Edit vertex/Fit/Spline/Decurve/Ltype gen/Undo/ eXit/<X>: *enter* w *right-click*
Enter new width for all segments: *enter* 4 *right-click*
Close/Join/Width/Edit vertex/Fit/Spline/Decurve/Ltype gen/Undo/ eXit/<X>:

If the object selected is a **Line**, the prompt asks:

The object selected is not a polyline
Do you wish to turn it into one? <Y>:

Edit vertex

Close/Join/Width/Edit vertex/Fit/Spline/Decurve/Ltype gen/Undo/ eXit/<X>: *enter* j *right-click*

And either window the parts to be joined or pick them individually.

Close/Join/Width/Edit vertex/Fit/Spline/Decurve/Ltype gen/Undo/ eXit/<X>: *enter e right-click*

A cross appears at the first point chosen for an outline made up from plines and the prompt becomes:

Next/Previous/Break/Insert/<Move/Regen/Straighten/Tangent/ Width/eXit <X>: *enter* m *right-click*

And depending upon the response, the vertex at which the diagonal cross is situated can be moved, another vertex inserted and so on. In Fig. 7.8 one of the examples shows a vertex having been moved.

Fit

Close/Join/Width/Edit vertex/Fit/Spline/Decurve/Ltype gen/Undo/ eXit/<X>: *enter* f *right-click*

And an arc forms between each vertex. Figure 7.8 includes an example.

Spline

Close/Join/Width/Edit vertex/Fit/Spline/Decurve/Ltype gen/Undo/ eXit/<X>: *enter* s *right-click*

And a spline forms between each vertex of the polyline. See Fig. 7.8.

Decurve

Close/Join/Width/Edit vertex/Fit/Spline/Decurve/Ltype gen/Undo/ eXit/<X>: *enter* d *right-click*

And a fitted or splined polyline reverts to its original shape.

Ltype gen

Close/Join/Width/Edit vertex/Fit/Spline/Decurve/Ltype gen/Undo/ eXit/<X>: *enter* l *right-click*
Full PLINE linetype or ON/OFF <Off>:

In Fig. 7.8 when **ON** the line continues all around an outline without making any allowance for vertices. When **OFF** the linetype starts and ends at the vertices. In Fig. 7.8 the polyline is a centre line.

Undo

Undoes the last part of a pline which has been constructed. Repeated use of **Undo** will eventually undo all a pline outline while it is being constructed.

eXit

Enter an x and the **Modify Polyline** sequence of prompts ends to revert to **Command:**

Note It is obvious from the above that the actions of the **Modify Polyline** tool are quite complex.

The Modify Text tool

Call **ddedit** by one of the methods given in Fig. 7.9. The Command window shows:

Command: _ddedit
<Select an annotation object>/Undo: *pick* a line of text

The **Edit Text** dialogue appears (Fig. 7.10) with the selected line of text in its **Text:** box. The text can be edited with the **Delete** key, by inserting new letters etc. When the text has been edited, *left-click* on the **OK** button and the edited text appears in place of the selected text.

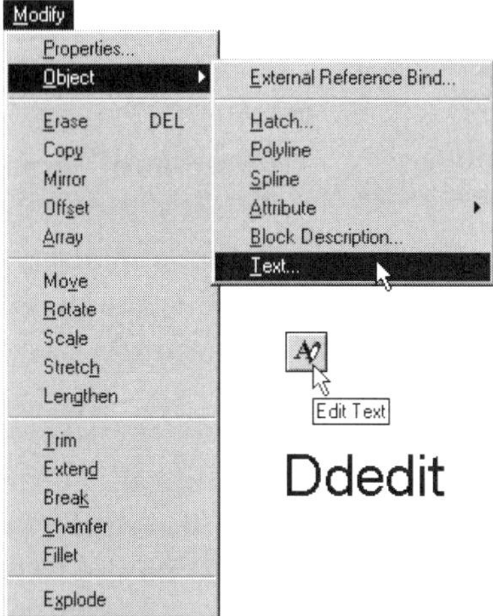

Fig. 7.9 Methods of calling **ddedit**

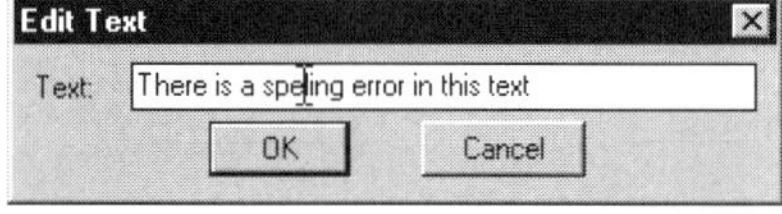

Fig. 7.10 The **Edit Text** dialogue box

The Distance tool

Left-click on the **Distance** tool icon in the **Standard** toolbar at the top of the LT 97 window (Fig. 7.11). The Command window shows:

Command: _dist First point: *pick* a point **Second point:** *pick* another point
Distance=218, Angle in XY Plane=335, Angle from XY Plane=0
Delta X = 197, Delta Y = -93, Delta Z = 0
Command:

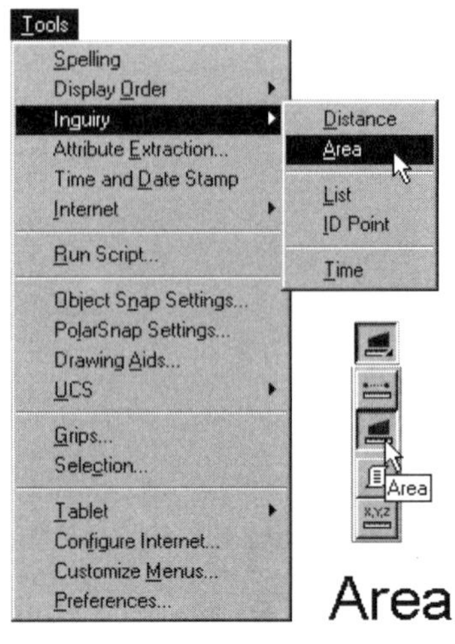

Fig. 7.11 Methods of calling the **Distance** tool

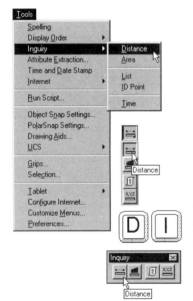

The **Delta X** figure shows the distance along the X axis from the **First point**. **Delta Y** shows the distance along the Y axis from the **First point**.

The Area tool

Left-click on the **Area** tool from the **Inquiry** toolbar (Fig. 7.12). The Command window shows:

Command: _area
<First point>/Object/Add/Subtract: *pick* point
Next point: *pick*
Next point: *pick*
Next point: *pick*
Next point: *right-click*
Area = 2016, Perimeter = 342
Command:

Or:

Command: _area
<First point>/Object/Add/Subtract: *enter* o (Object) *right-click*
Select objects: *pick*
Area = 33826, Perimeter = 749
Command:

Or:

Command: _area
<First point>/Object/Add/Subtract: *enter* a (Add) *right-click*
(ADD mode) Select objects: *pick*
Area = 33826, Perimeter = 749
(ADD mode) Select objects: *pick* second object
Area = 2173, Perimeter = 189
Total area = 35999
(ADD mode) Select objects: *right-click*
Command:

Fig. 7.12 Methods of calling the **Area** tool

The Divide tool

This tool divides an object into an equal number of segments. If the **Block** prompt is used, a block is placed at the ends of each segment. The block must be incorporated in the drawing data of the object being divided. A block is formed as follows:

First construct the required block. In this example the block is a pair of plines forming a simple diagonal cross.

Left-click on the **Make Block** tool icon in the **Draw** toolbar (Fig. 7.13). The **Create Block** dialogue box appears (Fig. 7.14). Make

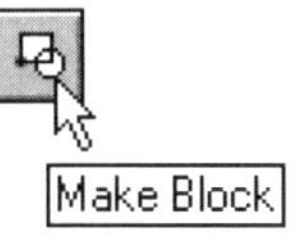

Fig. 7.13 Select the **Make Block** tool from the **Draw** toolbar

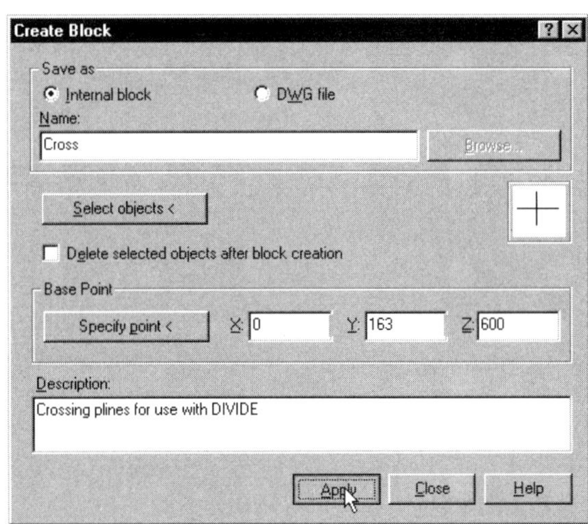

Fig. 7.14 The **Create Block** dialogue box

entries in the dialogue box as shown in Fig. 7.14, *left-click* on the **Select objects** button, window the cross drawn on screen. The dialogue box reappears. *Left-click* on the **Apply** button. The cross disappears from screen, but can be recalled by *entering* oops at the Command line.

Having made the block, call the **Divide** tool (Fig. 7.15). The Command line shows:

Command: _divide
Select object to divide: *pick*
<Number of segments>/Block: *enter* b (Block) *right-click*
Block name to insert: *enter* cross *right-click*
Align block with object? <Y>: *right-click*
Number of segments: *enter* 7 *right-click*
Command:

Examples are given in Fig. 7.16.

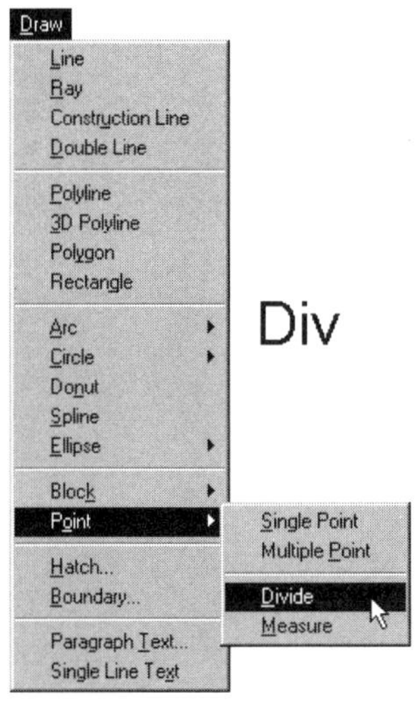

Fig. 7.15 Methods of calling the **Divide** tool

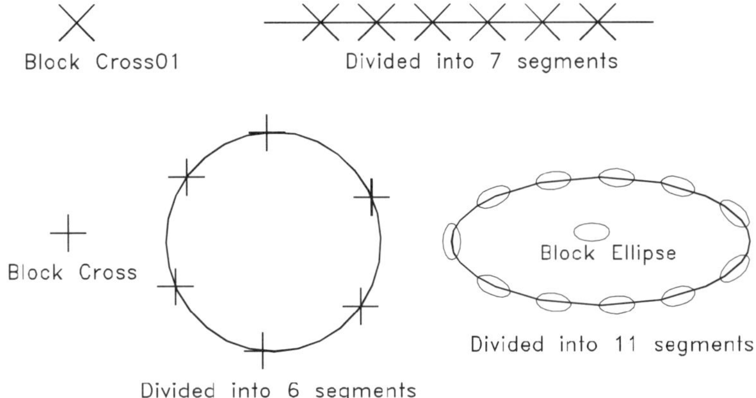

Fig. 7.16 Examples of using the **Divide** tool

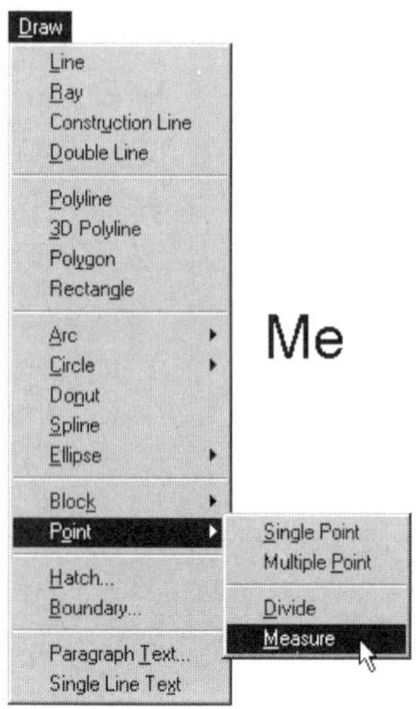

Fig. 7.17 Methods of calling the **Measure** tool

The Measure tool

This tool divides an object into a number of measured segments, as distinct from the **Divide** tool which divides an object into equal segments. *Enter* me at the Command line (Fig. 7.17). The Command window then shows:

Command: *enter* me *right-click*
MEASURE
Select object to measure: *pick*
<Segment length>/Block: *enter* b *right-click*
Block name to insert: *enter* ellipse *right-click*
Align block with object? <Y>: *right-click*
Segment length: *enter* 54 *right-click*
Command:

Figure 7.18 shows several examples of the use of the **Measure** tool.

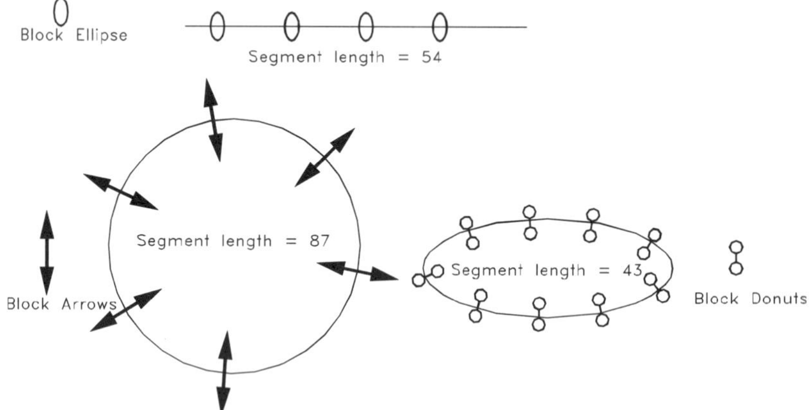

Fig. 7.18 Examples of the use of the **Measure** tool

Questions

1. What are the differences in the results of using the **Divide** tool compared with using the **Measure** tool?
2. Can you list the changes to a polyline which can be made with the aid of the **Modify Polyline** tool?
3. Can the width of a polyline be changed with the aid of the **Properties** tool?
4. Which tool can be used to measure the length of a line on screen?
5. How can the perimeter of an outline be measured?

Exercises

1. With the aid of the **Divide** tool construct the drawings given in Fig. 7.19. The sizes of the blocks are left to your own judgement.

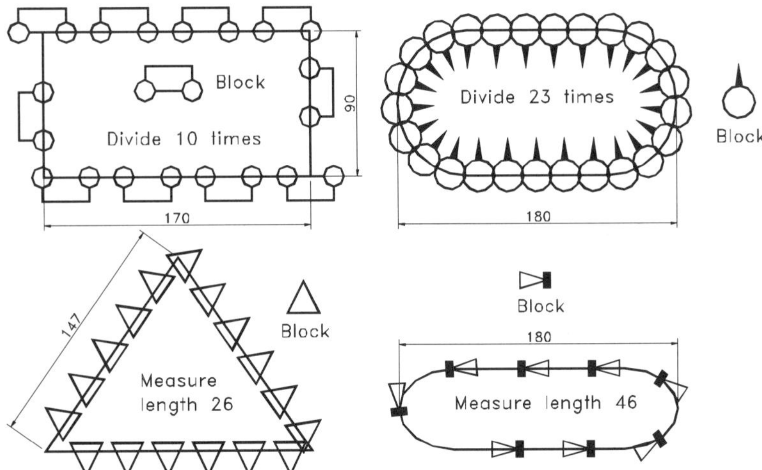

Fig. 7.19 Exercise 1

2. Figure 7.20. Copy the outlines 1 to 6 given in Fig. 7.20. Use the **Modify Polyline** to make the following changes to the outlines:

   Drawing 1: Construct the rectangle with a pline of width 0 and change it to one of width 2.

   Drawing 2: Construct the circle using the **Polyline** tool with the arc prompt. After constructing a semicircle, the **CL** response will close the semicircle to a circle.

   Drawing 3: Construct the arc as shown to Width 0 and change it to Width 3.

   Drawing 4: Construct the given polyline with a pline of width 0 and change it to one of width 5.

   Drawing 5: Copy the given pline and close it using **Modify Polyline**.

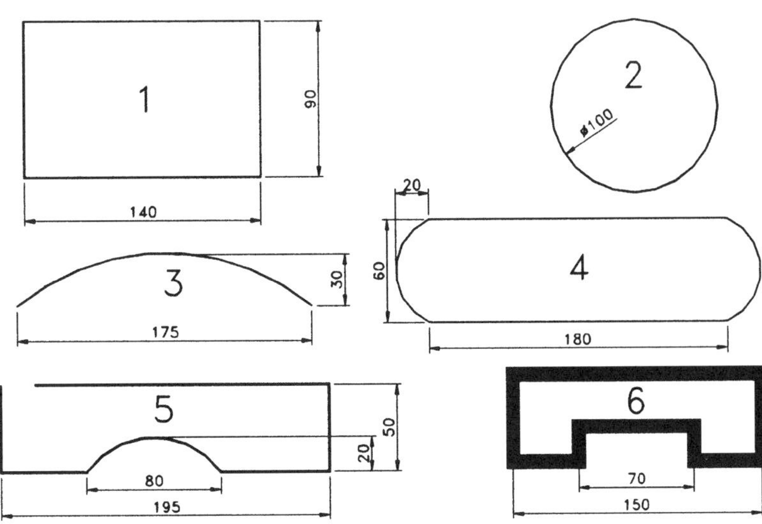

Fig. 7.20 Exercise 2

Drawing 6: Copy the given polyline which is of width 8 and use the Fit prompt of **Modify Polyline** on the outline.

3. Set the Romand font to a height of 15, copy the misspelt text as given in Fig. 7.21. Then using the **Edit Text** tool correct the spelling.

This text is Romand (ann SHX Font) at a heihgt of 15 uniots. It contains speling errors which can be edit by entering ddeddit at the Commsnd line.
The text can also be edited with tthe aid of the Spelling tool fron the Standard tooolbar.

Fig. 7.21 Exercise 3

4. Copy the three drawings of Fig. 7.22. Use your own judgement concerning the sizes of the blocks in the drawings. Use the **Measure** tool to place the blocks at the distances as shown.

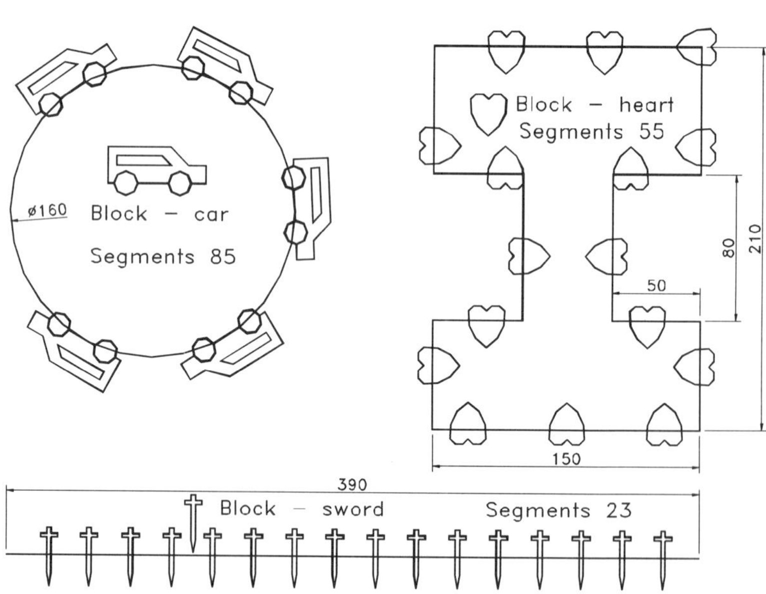

Fig. 7.22 Exercise 4

CHAPTER 8

Hatching

Introduction

Hatching, or the filling of areas within drawing outlines with line patterns, is carried out under the control of the **Hatch** tool in conjunction with the **Boundary Hatch** dialogue box. The pattern and its parameters are set and areas to be hatched can be selected from this dialogue box

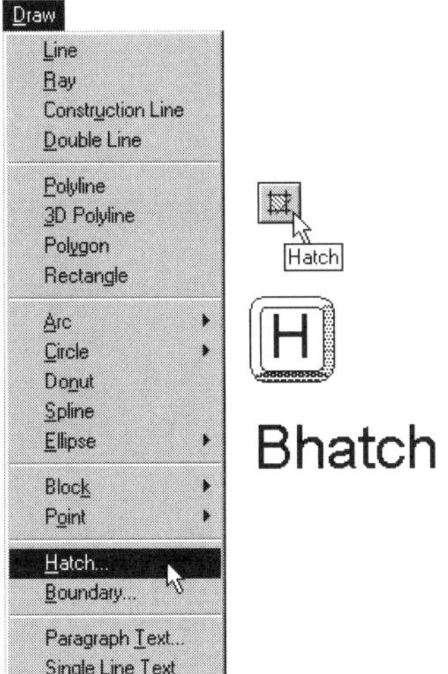

Fig. 8.1 Methods of calling the **Hatch** tool

The Hatch tool

To call the **Hatch** tool, either *left-click* on the **Hatch** tool icon in the **Draw** toolbar, *left-click* on **Hatch...** in the **Draw** pull-down menu, *enter* h at the Command line, or *enter* bhatch at the Command line (Fig. 8.1). No matter which of these options is chosen for calling hatch, the **Boundary Hatch** dialogue box (Fig. 8.2) appears.

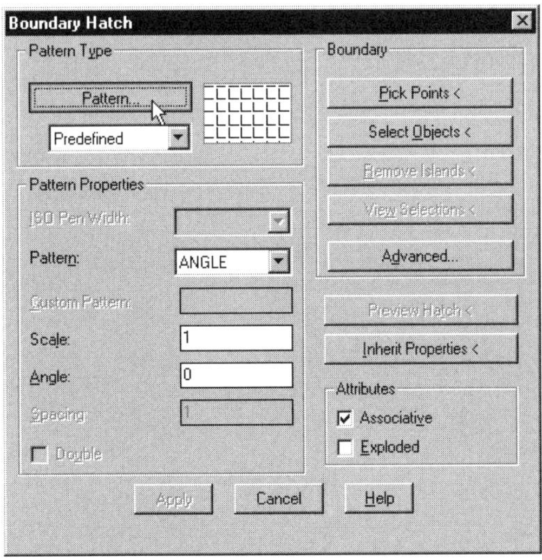

Fig. 8.2 The **Boundary Hatch** dialogue box

Note The **Boundary Hatch** dialogue box does not come to screen if hatch is *entered* at the Command line. When hatch is *entered*, responses to determine the hatching of an area within a drawing must be made from prompts *entered* at the Command line.

The Boundary Hatch dialogue box

The dialogue box contains a number of buttons, some of which call further dialogue boxes to screen. There are also a number of boxes into which settings may be *entered* or which produce popup lists with a *left-click* in their area or on the downward pointing arrow to the right of the popup list box.

The **Pattern...** button: A *left-click* on this button causes one of the **Hatch pattern palette**s, the first of which is shown in Fig. 8.3, to

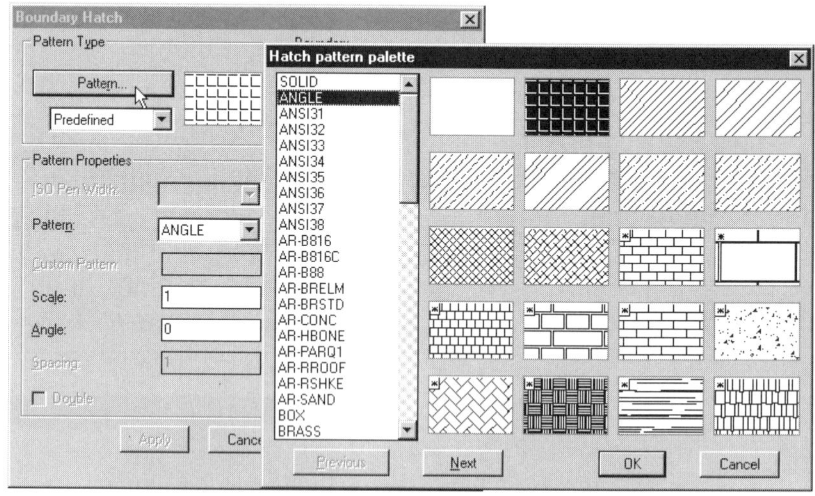

Fig. 8.3 The first of the **Hatch pattern palettes**

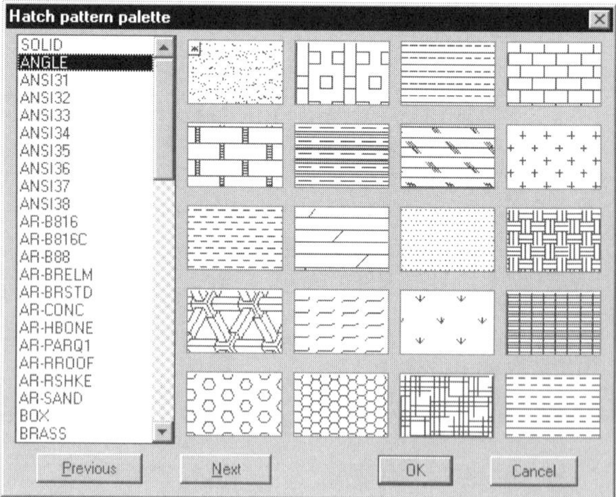

Fig. 8.4 The second of the **Hatch pattern palettes**

appear. A *left-click* on the **Next** button of the palette brings up another palette (Fig. 8.4). The next is shown in Fig. 8.5. In all there are four of these palettes in the standard default LT 97 **Hatch Boundary** dialogue box.

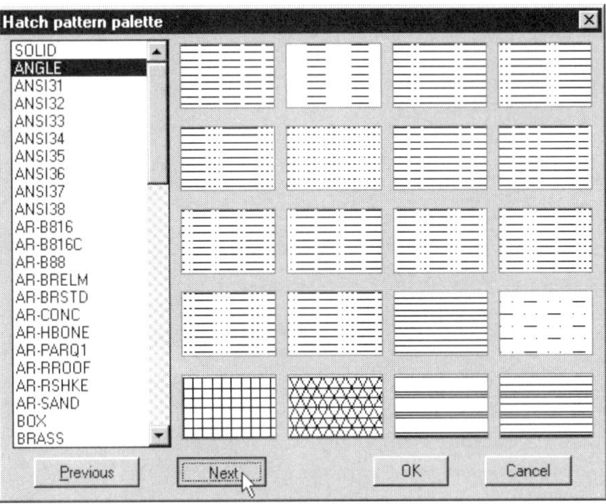

Fig. 8.5 The third of the **Hatch pattern palettes**

The **Predefined** box: A *left-click* on the arrow of this box brings down a popup list from which the operator can select a pattern which has been previously constructed and defined by the operator or which is a custom pattern from a library of patterns. As far as we are concerned in this book, only **Predefined** patterns will be used.

The Pattern Properties area of the dialogue box

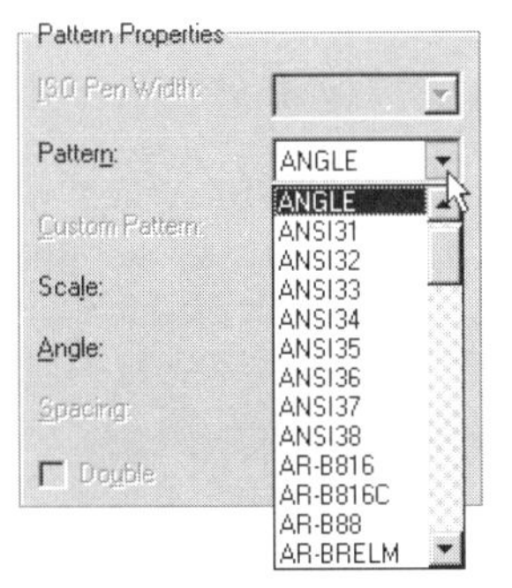

Fig. 8.6 The **Pattern:** popup list

In this part of the dialogue box, the boxes which concern us here are the **Pattern:** box and its popup list, the **Scale:** box and the **Angle:** box in which settings can be *entered*.

The **Pattern:** box: A *left-click* on the down pointing button at the right-hand end of the box brings down a scrollable popup list, from which a pattern can be selected (Fig. 8.6). The list contains the same patterns as can be seen in the **Hatch pattern palettes**.

The **Scale:** box: Figures for the scale of the chosen pattern are *entered* in this box.

The **Angle:** box: Figures for the angle at which the pattern are to be loaded are *entered* in this box.

The Boundary area of the dialogue box

In Fig. 8.2 only four of the buttons of the **Boundary** area of the dialogue box are available. The others are greyed-out. The others become available after either points or objects have been selected.

The **Pick Points** < button: *Left-click* on this button and the dialogue box disappears to allow the operator to *pick* points within a boundary which is to be hatched.

The **Select Objects** < button: *Left-click* on this button and the dialogue box disappears allowing the operator to *pick* objects surrounding an area to be hatched.

The **Advanced...** button: *Left-click* and the **Advanced Options** dialogue box appears (Fig. 8.7) appears. Note in particular the various option available in this dialogue box under the **Style:** popup list within the **Boundary Style** area of the dialogue box.

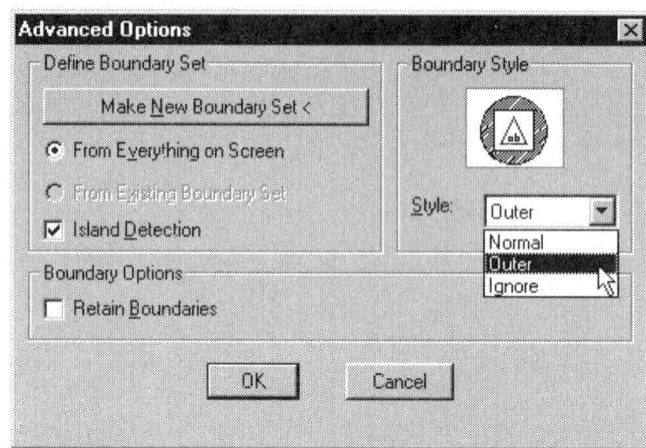

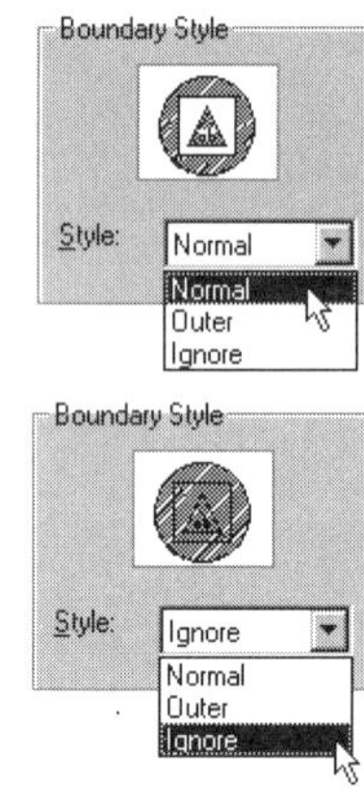

Fig. 8.7 The **Advanced Options** dialogue box

The **Inherit Properties** < button: Using this button allows the operator to select a hatch pattern already within a drawing. The details of the pattern and its settings then appear in the dialogue box.

The Attributes area of the dialogue box (Fig. 8.8)

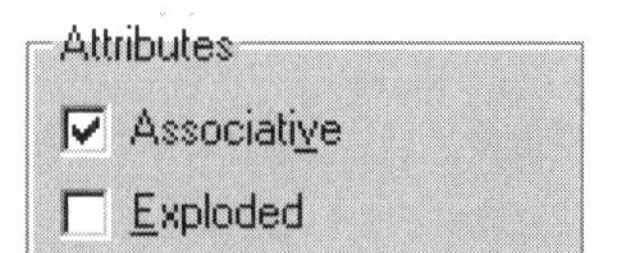

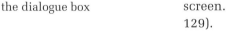

Fig. 8.8 The **Attributes** area of the dialogue box

Within this area the hatching being applied within a boundary can be made to be **Associative** or can be **Exploded**. Hatch patterns appear on screen as blocks – i.e. as single objects. If the **Explode** check box is ticked, the pattern is exploded into its separate objects. There may well be reasons for the operator to wish for the pattern to be exploded, allowing him/her to modify the pattern once it is on screen. More about **Associative** hatching later in this chapter (page 129).

Hatching an area within a drawing

Figure 8.9 shows an outline within which three circles have been drawn. The easiest method of hatching either the area other than the circles or the circles only is as follows:

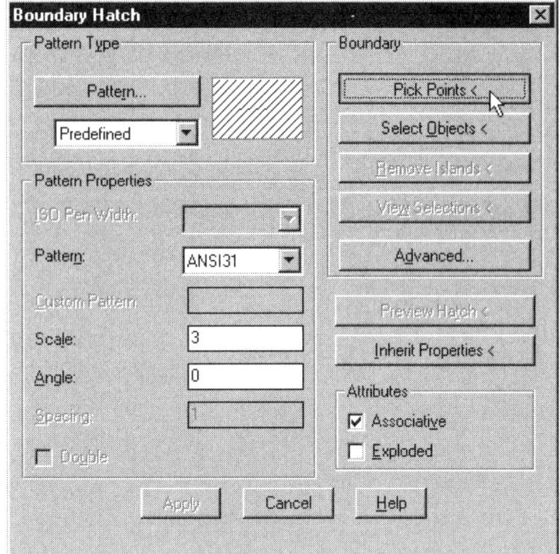

Fig. 8.9 The settings in the **Boundary Hatch** dialogue box for the two examples given in Fig. 8.10

1. **Command:** *left-click* on the **Hatch** tool icon. The **Boundary Hatch** dialogue box appears.
2. From the **Hatch pattern palettes** or from the **Pattern**: popup list select the required hatch pattern. In the examples shown in Fig. 8.10 the selected pattern is **ANSI31**.
3. *Enter* the required **Scale:** and **Angle:** figures. In the example given in Fig. 8.9 the **Scale:** is 3 and the **Angle:** 0. See Fig. 8.10
4. *Left-click* on the **Pick Points <** button. The dialogue box disappears.
5. *Pick* points within the areas to be hatched as indicated in Fig. 8.9, followed by a *right-click*. The dialogue box reappears.
6. In the dialogue box, *left-click* on the **Preview Hatch <** button, which is now no longer greyed out.

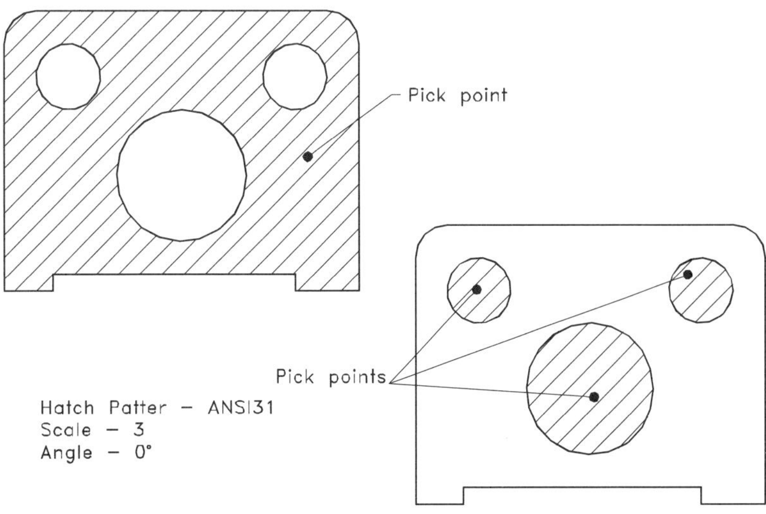

Fig. 8.10 Two examples of *picking* points within boundaries to be hatched

Fig. 8.11 The **Boundary Hatch** message box

7. The drawing reappears with the **Boundary Hatch** message box showing (Fig. 8.11). Examine the hatching and *left-click* on the **Continue** button of the message box and the dialogue box reappears.
8. If the hatching has been successful as to **Pattern**, **Scale** and **Angle** *left-click* on the **Apply** button of the dialogue box. The dialogue box disappears and the hatching is complete.

Note If the hatching is correct as to pattern, scale and angle, but incorrect as to the areas of the outlines which have been hatched, *left-click* on the **Advanced...** button and check whether the correct settings have been made in the **Boundary Style** of the **Advanced Options** dialogue box.

Figure 8.12 shows four examples of boundaries with different hatch patterns to various scales and angles in which the **Pick Point <** method has been used.

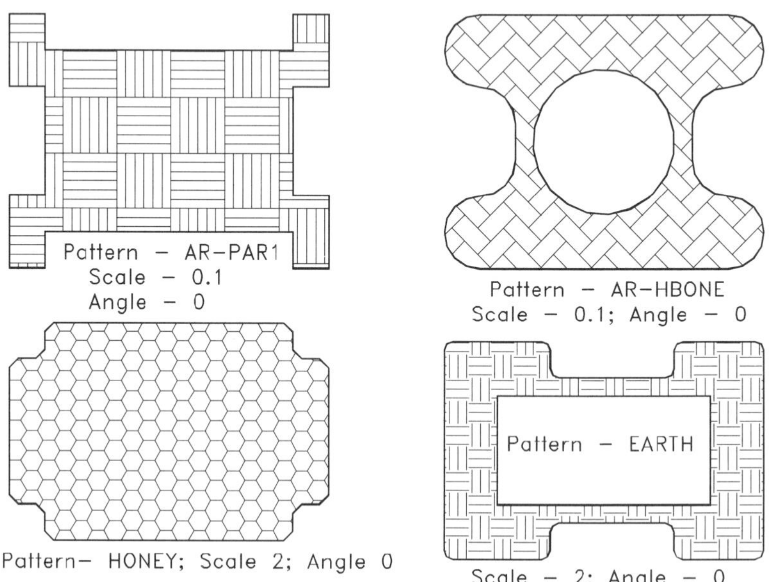

Fig. 8.12 Examples of four different hatching patterns

What happens if a boundary is not closed

Figure 8.13 shows the results of faulty hatching of areas within boundaries which are not completely closed. No matter how small a gap exists within the outline of an area to be hatched, when a point is *picked* within that boundary, the message box Fig. 8.14 shows. A *left-click* on the **OK** button of the message box followed by a *right-click* brings back the **Boundary Hatch** dialogue box.

Note When this happens it is sometimes possible to gain good hatching by using the **Select Objects <** button, followed by *picking*

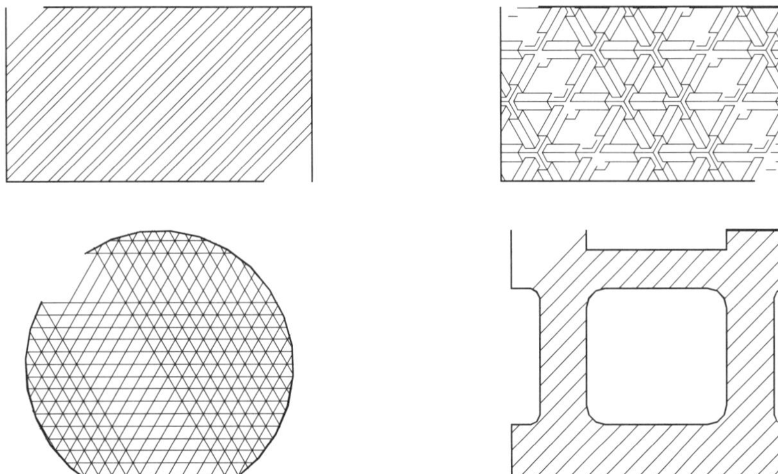

Fig. 8.13 Examples of hatching within boundaries which are not closed.

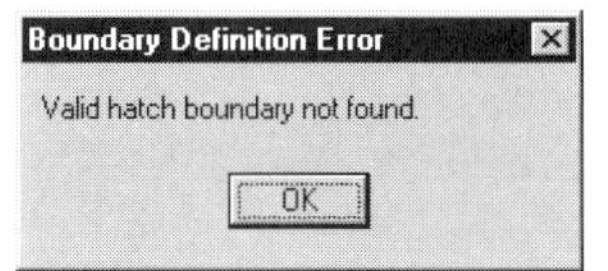

Fig. 8.14 The **Boundary Definition** message box

each of the objects surrounding the required area and which form the boundary of the hatching. This has been in connection with the boundaries shown in Fig. 8.13, but as can be seen, the hatching contains gaps where the boundaries are not fully closed.

Associative hatching

If the **Associative** check box in the **Boundary Hatch** dialogue box contains a tick, meaning that **Associative** hatching is set on, when a boundary within a hatch pattern is moved, the hatching associated with the boundary adjusts to accommodate the move. The effect of such a move is shown in Fig. 8.15. The **Move** must take place within a move window which surrounds the boundary of the moved part as well as its contents. Another example is given in Fig. 8.18 on page 131.

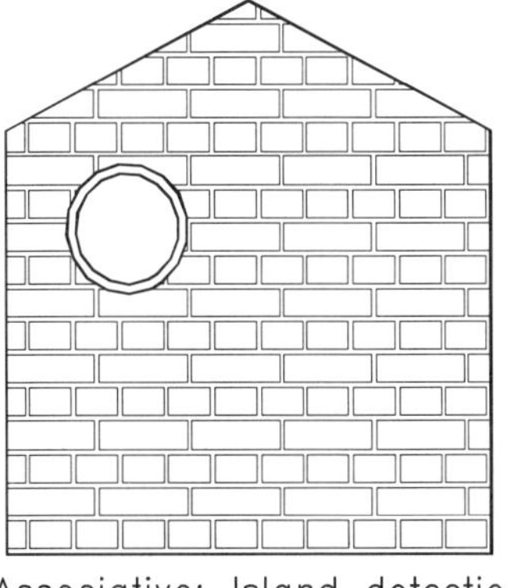

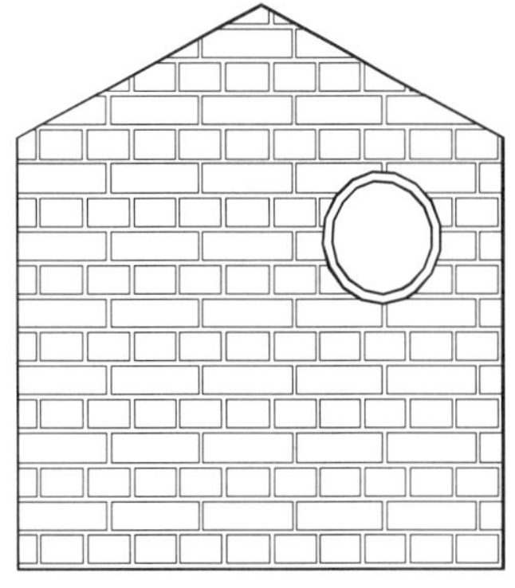

Fig. 8.15 An example of using **Associative** hatching

Examples of hatching

First example (Fig. 8.16)

The hatch patterns employed in this example are:

Roof: Pattern ANGLE; Scale 1; Angle 0.
Walls: Pattern AR-B816; Scale 0.3; Angle 0.
Upper part of porch: Pattern ANSI31; Scale 2; Angle 45.
Wall near doorway: Pattern AR-CONC; Scale 0.4; Angle 0.

Fig. 8.16 An example of hatching in a building drawing – the front view of a house

There are two methods which can be used to avoid hatching the windows. The first is to set the **Boundary Style** in the **Advanced Options** dialogue box to **Outer**. The second, illustrated in Fig. 8.17, is to make a new layer **Hatch**, make it the current layer and draw lines around the windows. Then hatch with the **Boundary Style** set to **Normal** and *pick* the area to be hatched. When the hatching is complete, turn the layer **Hatch** off.

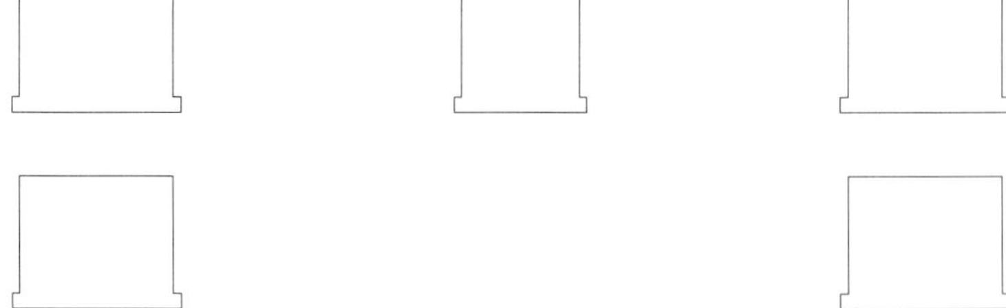

Fig. 8.17 The window outlines on layer **Hatch**

Figure 8.18 is another example of the use of setting **Associative** hatching on in the **Boundary Hatch** dialogue box in order to allow parts of a drawing to be moved and hatching to automatically adjust to the move.

Fig. 8.18 Another example of part of a drawing moved with **Associative** hatching set on

Other engineering drawing examples (Fig. 8.19)

Figure 8.19 contains seven drawings showing different techniques for the hatching of sectional views in engineering drawings. In general the most commonly used hatch pattern for this purpose is **ANSI31**, although many of the **ANSI** hatch patterns differentiate between materials used in manufacturing. To check these:

Command: *enter* hatch *right-click*
Enter pattern name or [?/Solid/User defined] *enter* ? *right-click*
Pattern(s) to list <*>: *right-click*

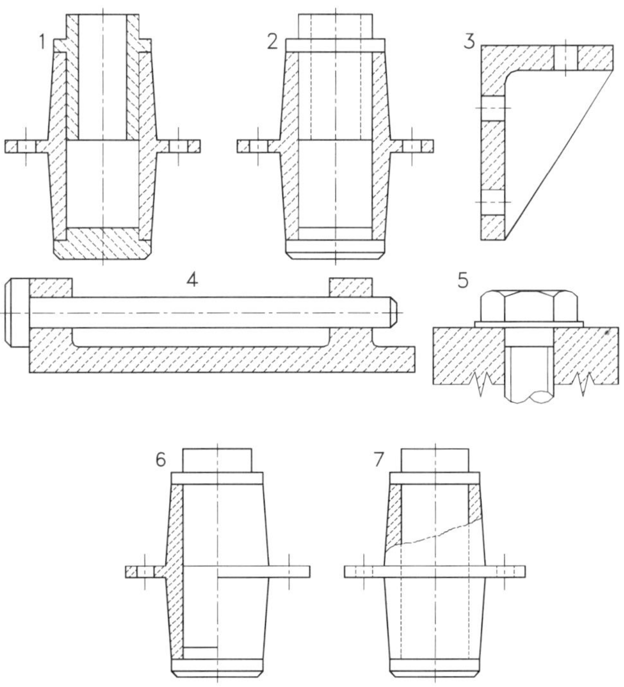

Fig. 8.19 Further examples of the use of hatching in engineering drawings

And the **AutoCAD LT Text Window** appears (Fig. 8.20) which shows the materials represented by the hatch patterns.

Drawing 1: Shows a normal section taken centrally through the component. Note the hatching at opposite angles in adjacent hatched parts.

Drawing 2: Shows the normally accepted method of hatching a component which includes circular parts. The circular parts are shown by outside views.

Drawing 3: Shows the normally accepted method of hatching a web or rib when the hatched surface passes through such features. The web or rib is shown by an outside view.

Drawing 4: Shows the normally accepted method of section hatching when a spindle is part of the section. The spindle is shown by an outside view.

Drawing 5: The normally accepted methods of showing a bolt and washer included in a sectional view. Such parts are shown by outside views.

Drawing 6: A half-section. When both sides of a view will be identical, only half the view needs to be hatched.

Drawing 7: A part section. The sectioned part of the drawing is distinct from the unsectioned part by a sketched line.

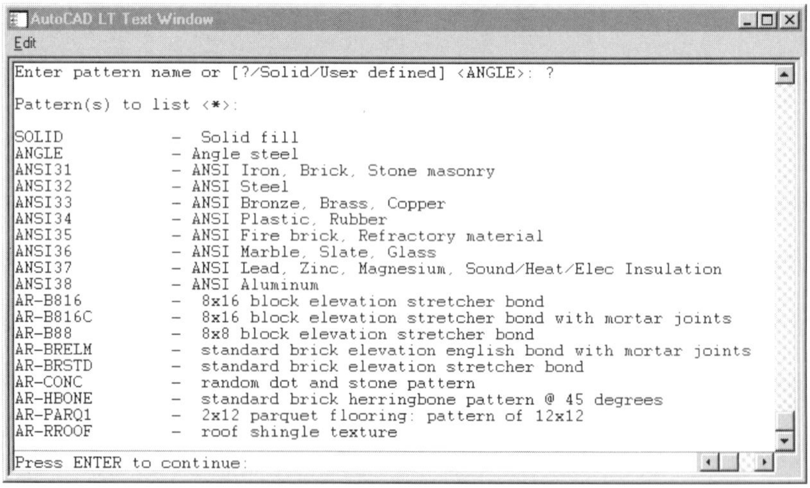

AutoCAD LT Text Window

Edit

```
Enter pattern name or [?/Solid/User defined] <ANGLE>: ?

Pattern(s) to list <*>:

SOLID          -  Solid fill
ANGLE          - Angle steel
ANSI31         - ANSI Iron, Brick, Stone masonry
ANSI32         - ANSI Steel
ANSI33         - ANSI Bronze, Brass, Copper
ANSI34         - ANSI Plastic, Rubber
ANSI35         - ANSI Fire brick, Refractory material
ANSI36         - ANSI Marble, Slate, Glass
ANSI37         - ANSI Lead, Zinc, Magnesium, Sound/Heat/Elec Insulation
ANSI38         - ANSI Aluminum
AR-B816        -  8x16 block elevation stretcher bond
AR-B816C       -  8x16 block elevation stretcher bond with mortar joints
AR-B88         -  8x8 block elevation stretcher bond
AR-BRELM       -  standard brick elevation english bond with mortar joints
AR-BRSTD       -  standard brick elevation stretcher bond
AR-CONC        -  random dot and stone pattern
AR-HBONE       -  standard brick herringbone pattern @ 45 degrees
AR-PARQ1       -  2x12 parquet flooring: pattern of 12x12
AR-RROOF       -  roof shingle texture

Press ENTER to continue:
```

Fig. 8.20 The **AutoCAD LT Text Window** describing the hatch patterns

Text within hatched areas

When text is placed within an area which is to be hatched, an invisible boundary which surrounds text prevents the hatching from crossing or coming right up against the text. Two examples are given in Fig. 8.21.

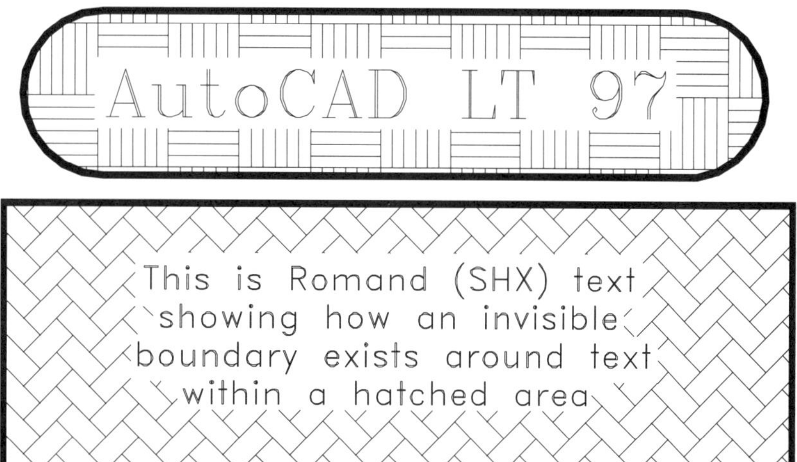

Fig. 8.21 Two examples of text within hatched areas

Other examples of hatching

Example 1 (Fig. 8.22)

Figure 8.22 shows the word (or initials) CAD (Computer Aided Design), which has not been drawn with the aid of a text tool, but has been drawn as separate outlines. The inside of each letter has been hatched with the hatch patter **Solid**. The area around the initials CAD has been hatched with the pattern **ANSI31** applied at a scale of 4 and an angle of 135°. Because the text has been constructed, no invisible border surrounds the text, thus the lines of the hatch pattern ANSI31 go through the text.

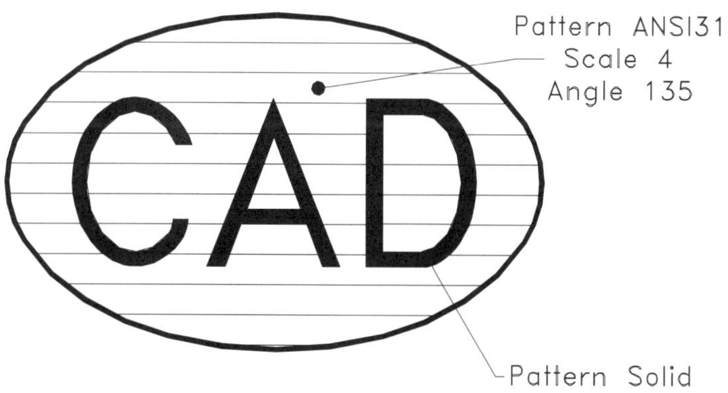

Fig. 8.22 Example 1

Example 2 (upper drawing of Fig. 8.23)

Both the arrow and the word EXIT were drawn with plines of width 2. The arrow is hatched with Pattern **ANSI37** at an Angle **0**. The word EXIT is hatched with Pattern **Solid**.

Example 3 (lower drawing of Fig. 8.23)

A half-scale drawing of the front view of a house from Fig. 8.18 is placed within a pline rectangle, which itself is within another pline rectangle. The text is in **italic.shx** of height 10. The surrounding hatching is Pattern **Honey** at a Scale of **1**.

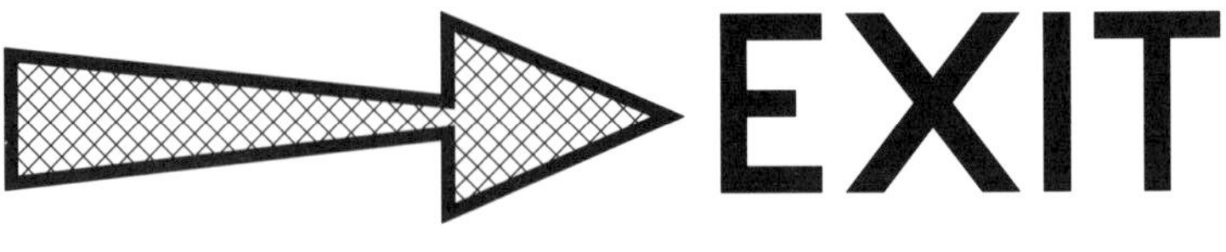

Fig. 8.23 Examples 2 and 3

Example 4 (Fig. 8.24)

1. This pattern started with a pair of arcs forming a 'petal'.
2. These were polar arrayed around a central circle six times.
3. Excess parts of the resulting 'flower' were trimmed away.

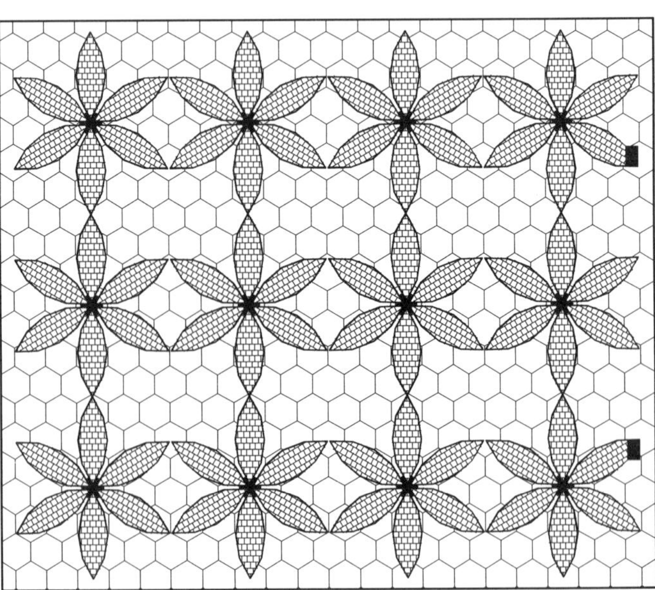

Fig. 8.24 Example 4

4. The 'petals' were then hatched using Pattern **AR-B88** at Scale **0.4** and Angles **0**, **30** and **330**. The central trimmed circle was hatched with the Pattern **Solid**.
5. The resulting 'flower' was rectangular arrayed into three rows and four columns.
6. A pline rectangle of width 2 was drawn around the array.
7. The area between the patterns was hatched using pattern **Honey** at Angle **0** and with the **Boundary Style** of **Advanced Options** set to **Outer**.

Questions

1. Why is it not always advisable to *enter* hatch at the Command line when wishing to hatch an area of a drawing?
2. There are two ways in which a hatch pattern can be selected from the **Boundary Hatch** dialogue box. Can you name them?
3. Why is it important that when hatching, it is advisable to check the **Advanced Options** first?
4. What advantage is there in having the **Associative** check box of the **Boundary Hatch** dialogue box set on (tick in box)?
5. When would you wish to have the **Explode** check box from the **Boundary Hatch** dialogue box set on?
6. Why must a boundary of an area being hatched be completely closed?
7. When text within a drawing is hatched what do you expect to see?
8. When the word **hatch** is *entered* at the Command line, what methods are used to hatch an area within a drawing?
9. Some of the hatch patterns are used to represent materials when used to hatch an area of a drawing. How can the name of the material which the hatch pattern represents be checked?
10. What is meant by a half section in an engineering drawing?

Exercises

1. Figure 8.25 shows the name **AutoCAD LT 97** within two boundaries constructed from plines, with the space between the boundaries hatched. Using any suitable hatch pattern and working to sizes of your own choice construct a similar drawing.
2. Figure 8.26 is an addition to Fig. 8.25, using the same font for text and the same pattern for hatching. Construct a similar drawing to that shown in Fig. 8.26.
3. Figure 8.27 shows a pattern made up from squares and rectangles within a pline boundary. Some of the squares and rectangles

Fig. 8.25 Exercise 1

Fig. 8.26 Exercise 2

making the pattern have been hatched. Working to dimensions of your own choice construct a similar drawing to the one shown.

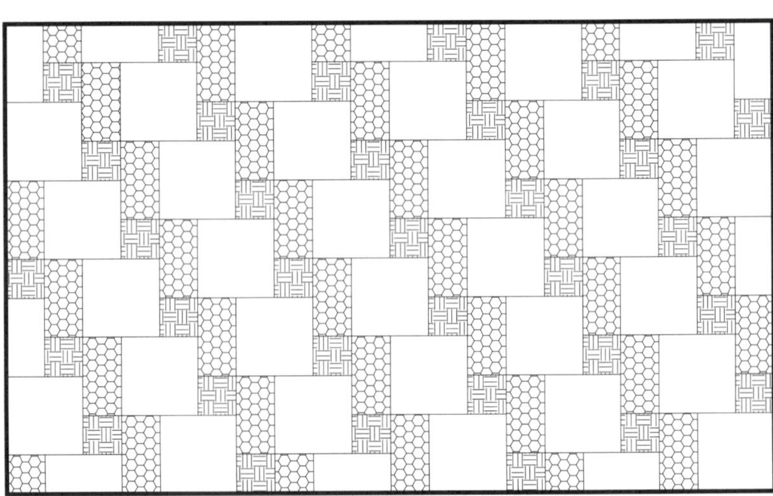
Fig. 8.27 Exercise 3

4. Working to the dimensions given with the two sectional views of Fig. 8.28 copy the two drawings. There is no need to include the dimensions.
5. Figure 8.29 is a front view of a bungalow with various parts hatched in a variety of hatch patterns. Working to sizes of your own choice make a fair copy of the drawing.

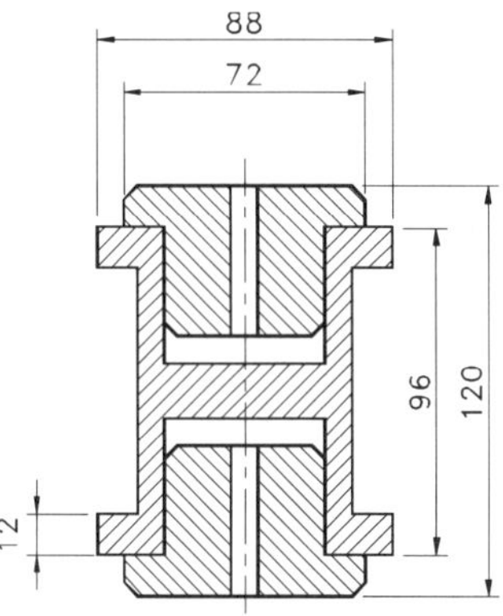

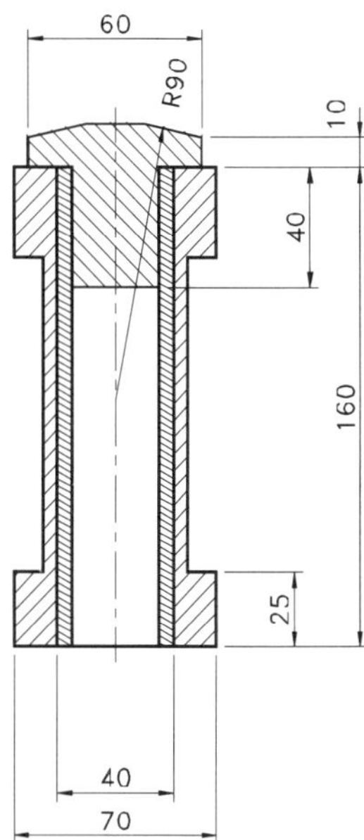

Fig. 8.28 Exercise 4

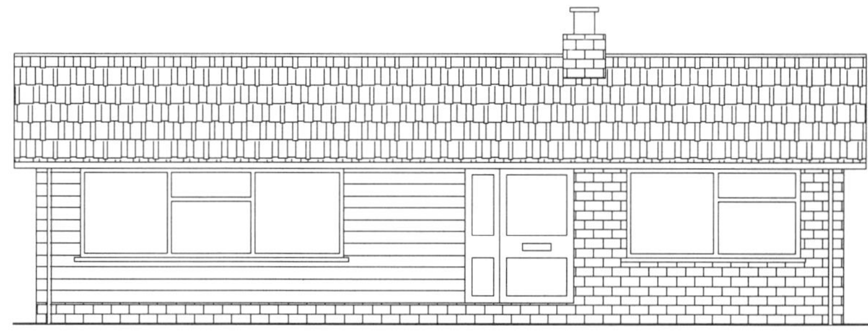

Fig. 8.29 Exercise 5

6. Figure 8.30 shows a pattern enclosed within a hatched frame. Working to sizes of your own choice construct a similar drawing; use **Array** to form the pattern of the drawing. The centres of each part of the pattern have been hatched with the hatch pattern **Solid**.

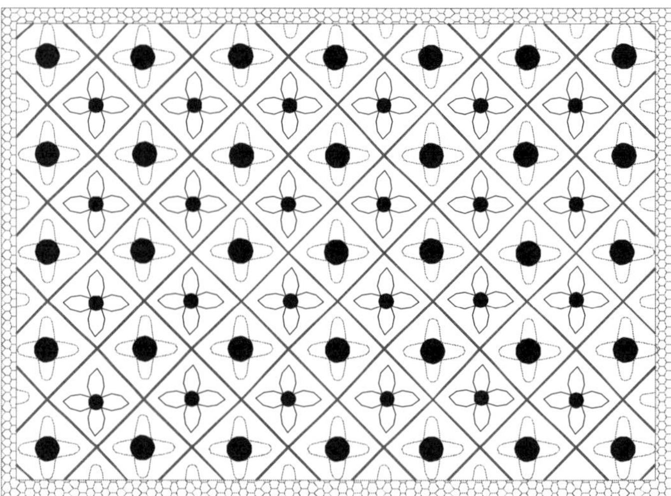

Fig. 8.30 Exercise 6

CHAPTER 9

Engineering technical drawings

Isometric drawing

AutoCAD LT 97 includes tools for the construction of the 2D pictorial form of drawing commonly known as isometric drawing. The pictorial views produced in isometric drawing are based upon three axes – a vertical axis (90°) and axes at angles of 30° and 150° as indicated in Fig. 9.1. The construction of isometric drawings is possible with the aid of two systems – setting **Snap** to **Isometric** and the setting of **Isoplanes**.

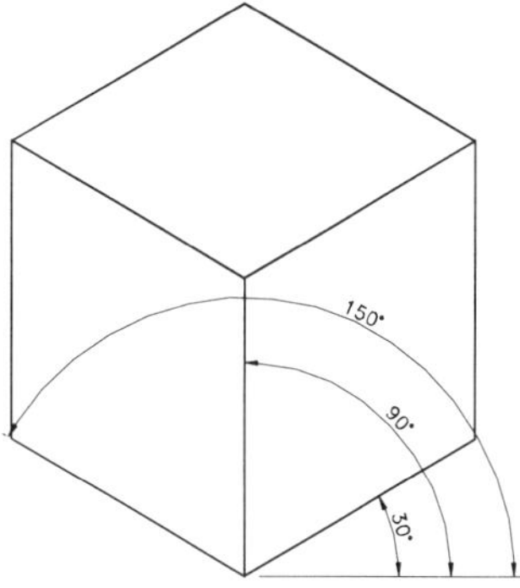

Fig. 9.1 The three axes of isometric drawing

To set **Snap** to the **Isometric** setting. At the Command line:

Command: *enter* sn (for snap) *right-click*
Snap spacing/or ON/OFF/Aspect/Rotate/Style <5>: *enter* s (for Style) *right-click*
Standard/Isometric <S>: *enter* i (for Isometric) *right-click*
Vertical spacing <5>: *right-click*
Command:

The cursor hair lines change as shown in Fig. 9.2.

To set the **Isoplanes** either press key **F5** or press **Ctrl+E**. These two key shortcuts toggle the isoplanes between **Isoplane Top**, **Isoplane Right** and **Isoplane Left**. As the isoplanes are toggled the

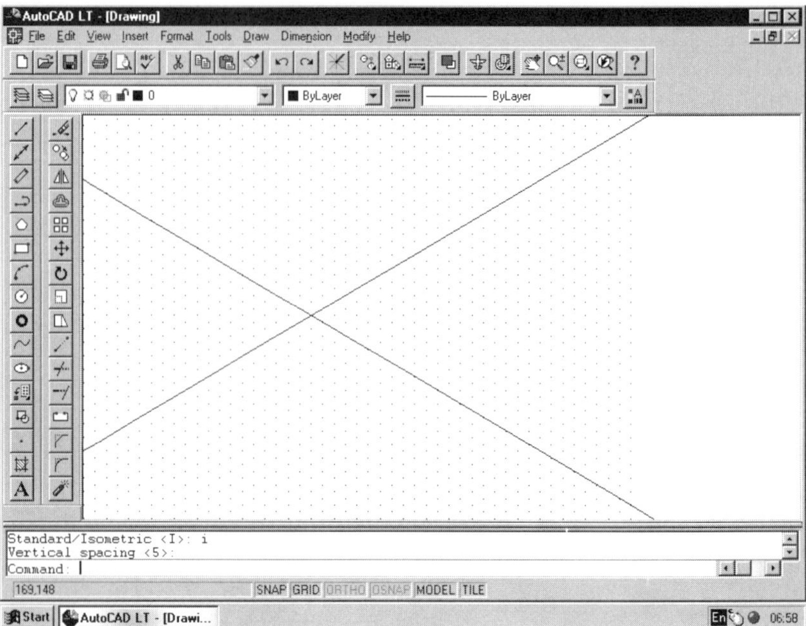

Fig. 9.2 The LT 97 window after **Isometric Snap** has been set

cursor hairlines change to accommodate the new isoplane. Figure 9.3 shows three isometric 'squares' in the isoplane positions.

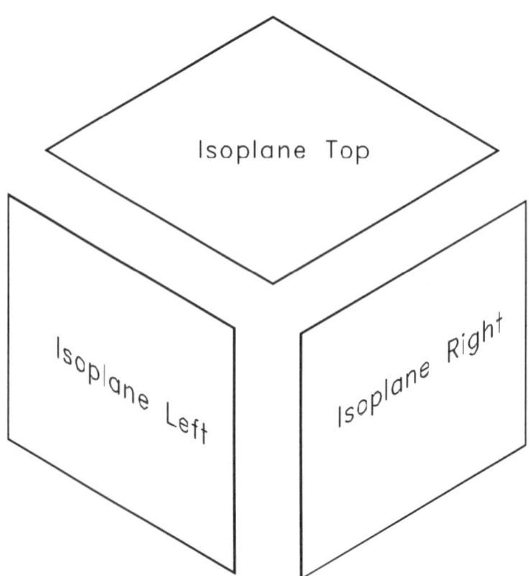

Fig. 9.3 The three **Isoplane** positions

The Drawing Aids dialogue box

Isometric snap and isoplanes can also be set from the **Drawing Aids** dialogue box. To call the dialogue box on screen, either *left-click* on **Drawing Aids...** in the **Tools** pull-down menu or:

Command: *enter* ddrmodes *right-click*

Fig. 9.4 Calling the **Drawing Aids** dialogue box

And the **Drawing Aids** dialogue box appears. As can be seen from Fig. 9.5, in the **Isometric/Snap/Grid** area of the dialogue box, **Isometric** can be set on (tick in check box) and the **Isoplanes** can be set to **Left**, **Top** or **Right**.

Other keyboard shortcuts

To remind the reader of other keyboard shortcuts which are of value when constructing isometric drawings, **F7** toggles **Grid** on/off; **F8** toggles **Ortho** on/off; **F9** toggles **Snap** on/off. These shortcuts are in addition to the use of **F5** or **Ctrl+E** to toggle through the **Isoplanes**.

Another shortcut which may prove of value is **Ctrl+D** to toggle between **Coords** showing as absolute figures, showing relative figures or not showing.

Isometric ellipses

Ellipses aligned along the isometric axes are of importance when constructing isometric drawings. To ensure accuracy in the alignment, use the **Isocircle** prompt from the **Ellipse** command sequence:

Command: *enter* el *right-click*
Arc/Center/Isocircle/<Axis endpoint 1>: *enter* i *right-click*
Center of circle: either *pick* or *enter* coordinates and *right-click*
<Circle radius>/Diameter: *enter* the radius figures *right-click*
Command:

Figure 9.6 shows the isocircles aligned to the three isoplanes. Note these are isometric ellipses correctly aligned along the isometric drawing axes.

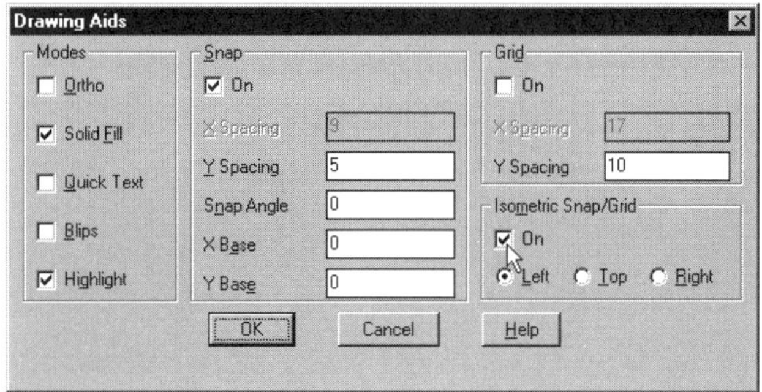

Fig. 9.5 The **Drawing Aids** dialogue box

Warning note

Isometric drawing gives the appearance of being three-dimensional (3D). It must be understood however that it is a two-dimensional

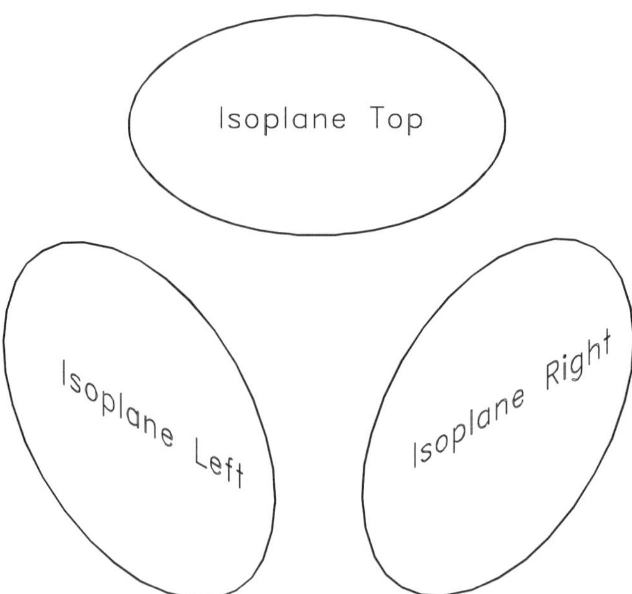

Fig. 9.6 The three isocircles aligned on the isoplanes

(2D) method of pictorial drawing. Some details about 3D drawings and the facilities in LT 97 for 3D work are included in Chapter 14.

Examples of isometric drawings

Example 1 (Fig. 9.7)

1. Set **Snap** to **Style/Isometric** with **Spacing** of **5**.
2. **Ctrl+E** to set **Isoplane Top**.
3. **F8** to set **ORTHO** on.

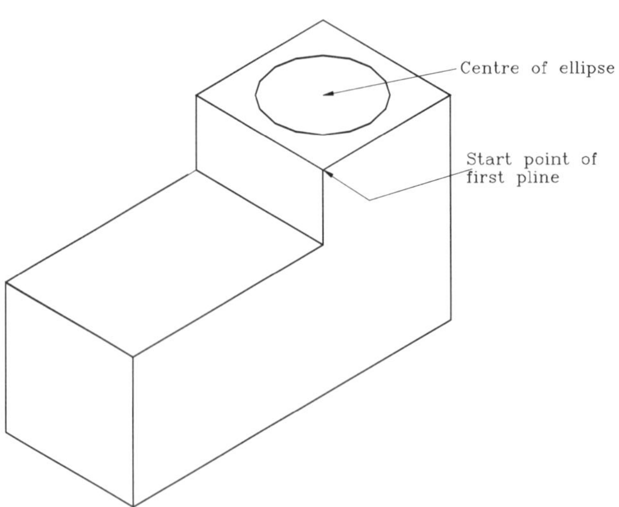

Fig. 9.7 Example 1

4. Call the **Polyline** tool:

   Command: _pline
   From point: *pick* point 251,185
   Arc/Close/Halfwidth/Length/Undo/Width/<endpoint of line>:
   Move cursor along 30° and *enter* 80 *right-click*
   Arc/Close/Halfwidth/Length/Undo/Width/<endpoint of line>:
   Move cursor along 150° axes and *enter* 80 *right-click*

   Continue thus to construct the top isometric square (really a rhombus).
5. **Ctrl+E** to set **Isoplane Right**.
6. Draw plines 120 along vertical axis and 200 along 30° axis and continue to complete right-hand side of drawing.
7. **Ctrl+E** to set **Isoplane Left**.
8. Draw plines to draw front face of drawing.
9. **Ctrl+E** to set **Isoplane Top**.
10. Draw plines to complete the outline.
11. Call the **Ellipse** tool:

   Command: _ellipse
   Arc/Center/Isocircle/<Axis endpoint 1>: *enter* i *right-click*
   Center of circle: *pick* point 251,225
   <Circle radius>/Diameter: *enter* 30 *right-click*
   Command:

Example 2 (Fig. 9.8)

1. Set **Snap** to **Style/Isometric** with **Spacing** of **5**.
2. **Ctrl+E** to set **Isoplane Top**.
3. **F8** to set **ORTHO** on.

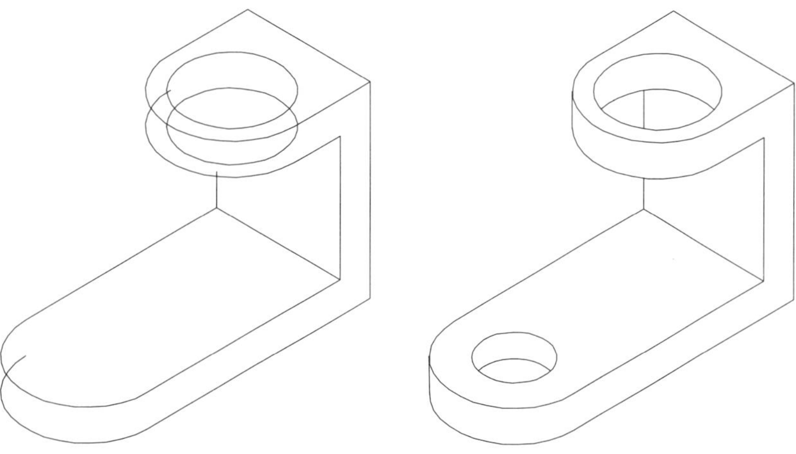

Fig. 9.8 Example 2

4. Call the **Polyline** tool:

 Command: _pline
 From point: *pick* point 165,245
 Arc/Close/Halfwidth/Length/Undo/Width/<endpoint of line>: Move cursor along 30° and *enter* 50 *right-click*
 Arc/Close/Halfwidth/Length/Undo/Width/<endpoint of line>: Move cursor along 150° axes and *enter* 80 *right-click*
 Arc/Close/Halfwidth/Length/Undo/Width/<endpoint of line>: Move cursor along 30° and *enter* 50 *right-click*
 Arc/Close/Halfwidth/Length/Undo/Width/<endpoint of line>: *right-click*
 Command:

5. Call the **Ellipse** tool:

 Command: _ellipse
 Command: _ellipse
 Arc/Center/Isocircle/<Axis endpoint 1>: *enter* i *right-click*
 Center of circle: *pick* point 199,225
 <Circle radius>/Diameter: *enter* 30 *right-click*
 Command:

6. Call the **Trim** tool and trim the ellipse to a half ellipse.
7. Call the **Copy** tool and copy the semi-ellipse vertically down 20 units.
8. Call the **Ellipse** tool and, using the same centre as previously, draw an isocircle of radius 30.
9. Call **Copy** and copy the ellipse of radius 30 vertically down 20 units.
10. In a similar manner draw the half ellipses and isocircles at the front bottom of the component being drawn.
11. Complete the outlines as shown in the left-hand drawing of Fig. 9.8.
12. Draw plines between the left-hand edges of the half ellipses with the aid of the **Osnap nearest**.
13. With **Trim** complete the drawing as shown in the right-hand drawing of Fig. 9.8.

Note At any time during a construction, even in the middle of a tool's option sequences **Ctrl+E** can be used to toggle the **Isoplanes**.

Example 3 (Fig. 9.9)

Figure 9.9 shows the two stages in the construction of the right-hand isometric drawing. The left-hand drawing shows the initial stages in the construction. The right-hand drawing shows the finished result.

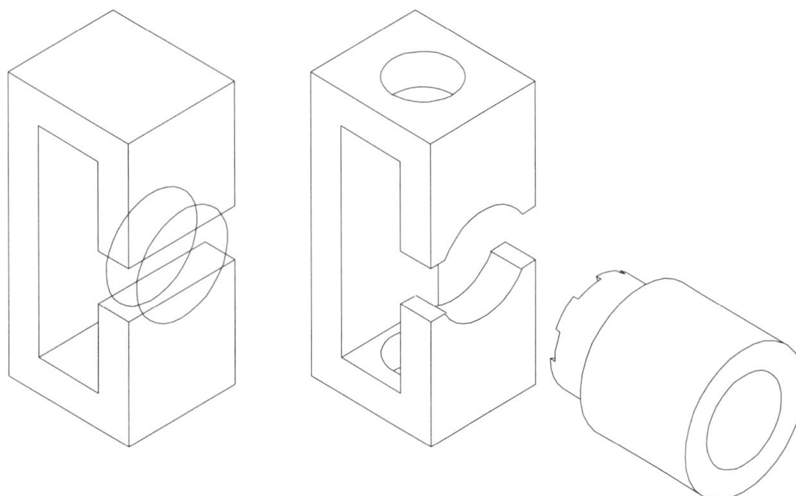

Fig. 9.9 Example 3

Orthographic projection

Orthographic projection is one of the most widely used methods of technical drawing. This method relies upon looking at the object being drawn from front, from above, from left, from right, or from any other viewing position. What is seen is imagined as being projected via parallel rays onto planes parallel to the face being viewed, or perpendicular to the viewing direction.

Figure 9.10 shows the basis of orthographic projection:

1. The object to be drawn is imagined as being looked at from the front and what is seen is projected without observing perspective, onto a vertical plane – this produces what is known as a **FRONT VIEW**.

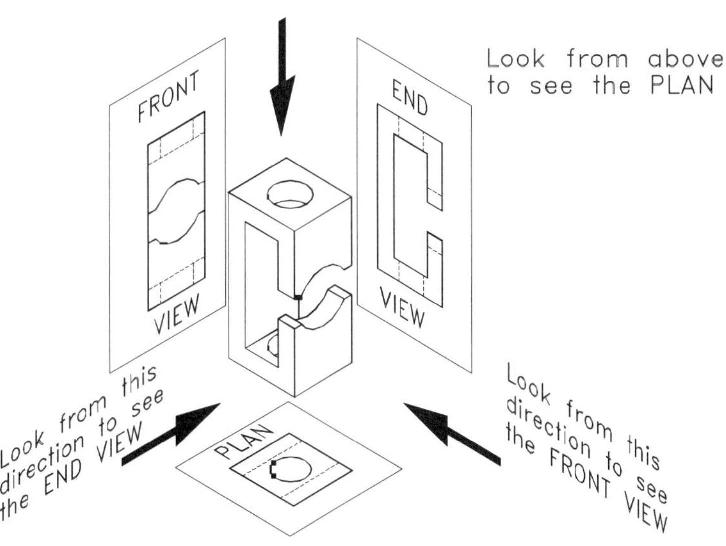

Fig. 9.10 The basis of orthographic projection

2. The object is then viewed from one side and what is seen projected onto another vertical plane – this produces an **END VIEW**.
3. The object is then viewed from above and what is seen projected on top of a horizontal plane – this produces what is known as a **PLAN**.

The three views so obtained are then all placed side by side onto a 2D plane (a flat surface). This is what is known as the orthographic projection (Fig. 9.11).

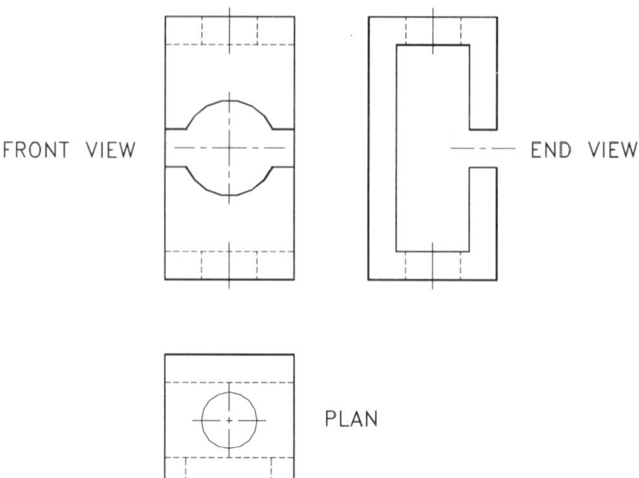

Fig. 9.11 The three planes placed on a single 2D plane in First angle projection

Notes

1. Any number of views can be obtained in this way – from either side, from the rear, from below, from any angle.
2. In general there are two major forms of orthographic projection – **FIRST ANGLE** (as shown in the drawing of Fig. 9.11) and **THIRD ANGLE** (Fig. 9.12).

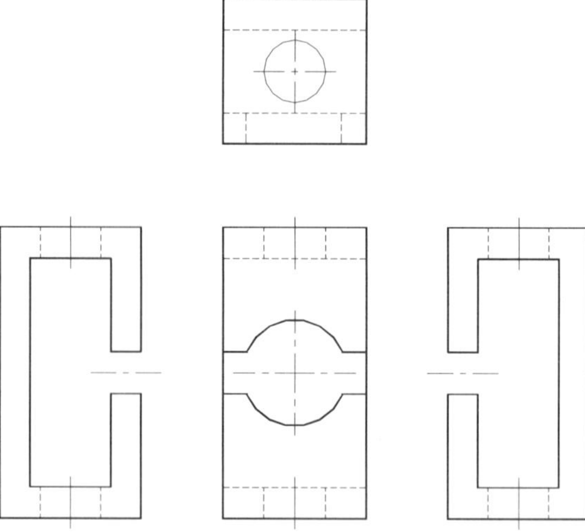

Fig. 9.12 Third angle projection

3. The basis of third angle projection is different from that of first angle. In third angle projection the imaginary planes are placed between the viewer and the object and what is seen is, as it were, drawn onto the planes between the viewer and the object.
4. In general the names of the views are not included in an orthographic projection, unless it is considered such labels will make the drawing easier to interpret.

Some rules for orthographic projection

1. In first angle projection end views and plans face outwards from the front view.
2. In third angle projection end views and plans face inwards towards the front view.
3. Orthographic projections can consist of a mixture of first and third projections, but if this practice is observed, labels should be placed with views to indicate the directions of viewing.
4. Centre lines are normally drawn through all circular parts in all three directions.
5. Lines in the views which cannot be seen from the outside are indicated by hidden lines.
6. Where necessary, in order to make the meaning of a drawing clear, sectional views may be included with orthographic views. See Fig. 9.13.

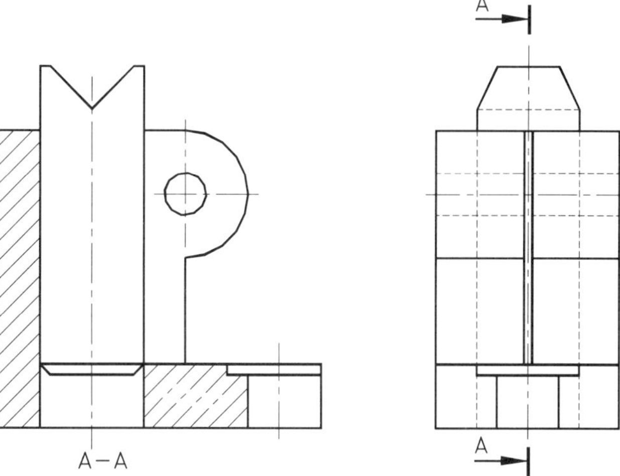

Fig. 9.13 An orthographic projection which includes a sectional view

Lines in engineering drawings

Types of lines

Figure 9.14 shows the types of line commonly associated with engineering drawings.

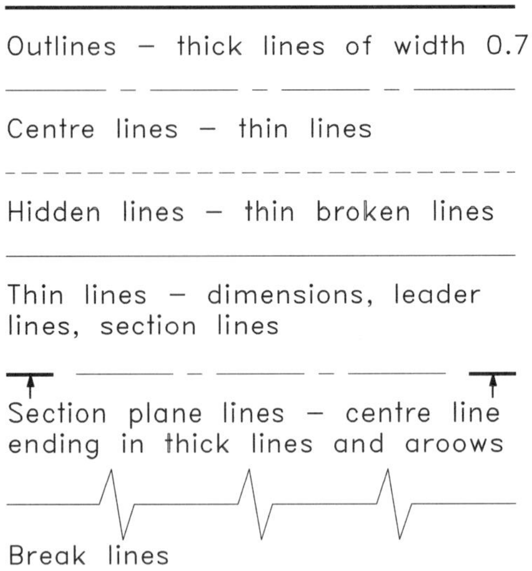

Outlines – thick lines of width 0.7

Centre lines – thin lines

Hidden lines – thin broken lines

Thin lines – dimensions, leader lines, section lines

Section plane lines – centre line ending in thick lines and aroows

Break lines

Fig. 9.14 Types of lines used in engineering drawings

Engineering drawings produced by CAD software systems are often drawn without taking the thickness of outlines into account. In the following description of types of lines employed in engineering drawings, it is suggested that outlines should be drawn thicker than other lines in such drawings. The thickness (or width) of lines is easily controlled by using the **Polyline** (pline) tool for the construction of outlines.

As suggested earlier in this book (page 82) types of line in LT 97 can be set in the **Layer and Linetype** dialogue box. The type of line can also be changed with the aid of the **Properties** tool from the **Object Properties** toolbar by associating a chosen object with the type of line placed on a layer. Figure 9.15 shows the changing of a line into a hidden detail line in the **Modify Line** dialogue box, called as follows:

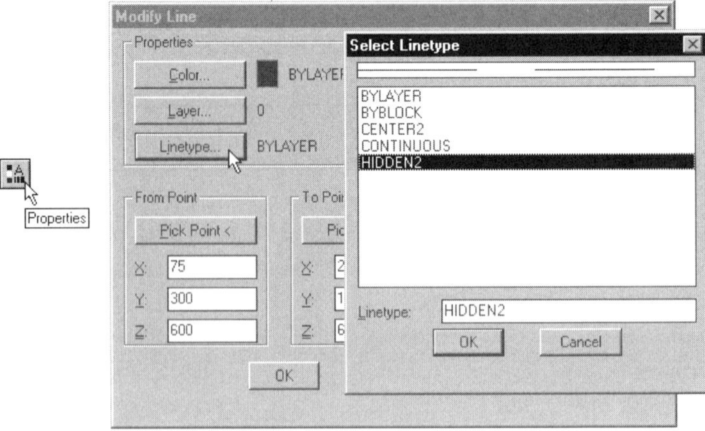

Fig. 9.15 The **Modify Line** dialogue box, called with the **Properties** tool

Select the **Properties** tool from the **Object Properties** toolbar. The Command window then shows:

Command: *pick* the **Properties** tool icon
Select objects: *pick* a line **1 found**
Select objects: *right-click*

The **Modify Line** dialogue box appears on screen (Fig. 9.15)
In the dialogue box, *left-click* on the **Linetype...** button.
The **Select Linetype** box appears, from which the required linetype can be selected. *Left-click* on the **OK** buttons of both dialogue boxes and the line changes to the chosen linetype.

Changing linetype scale

If the scale of a line such as a hidden detail line or a centre line is not suitable, its scale can be changed as follows:

Command: *enter* ltscale *right-click*
New scale factor <1.0000>: *enter* required scale figure
Regenerating drawing
Command:

And the scale of all lines in the drawing will change. It is advisable to experiment with **ltscale** to see the results of linetype scaling.

Drawing sheet layout

Drawings to which those in colleges and in industry work are often referred to as 'working drawings'. These are usually based upon orthographic projection. Depending on the reason for which the drawings are being constructed, different forms of drawing layout

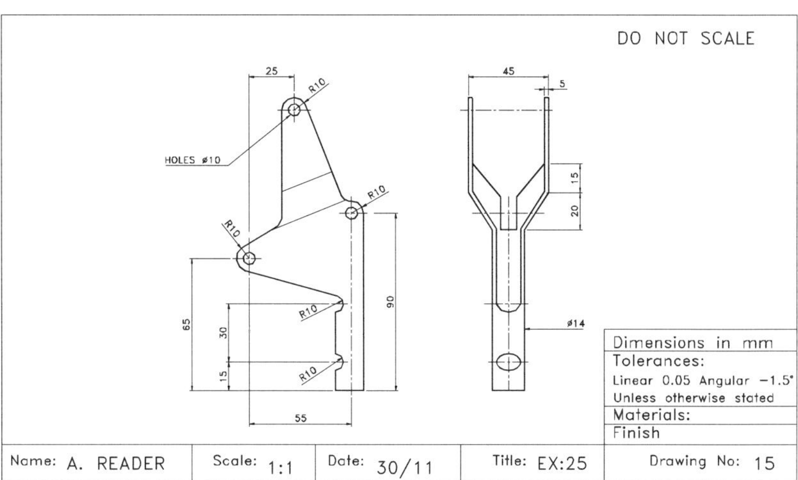

Fig. 9.16 A form of drawing layout

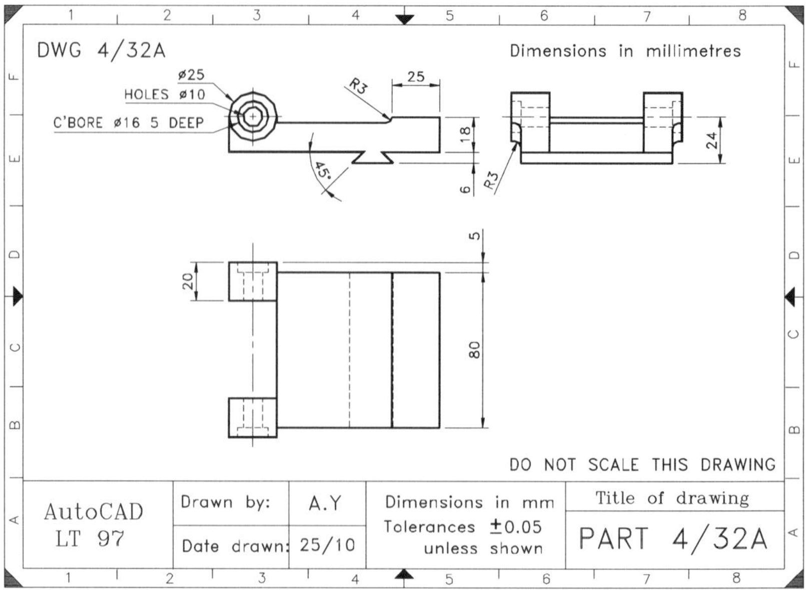

Fig. 9.17 Another form of drawing layout

may be employed. Two examples are given – Fig. 9.16, which would be a suitable layout for students constructing drawings in response to exercises and Fig. 9.17, a more sophisticated form of layout suitable for drawings from a small engineering firm.

Notes

1. A border or margins around the drawing area.
2. A title block varied according to requirements.
3. Information within the title block and elsewhere in the drawing sheet area.
4. Tidy layout of the views.

Questions

1. What is the difference between an isometric drawing and a 3D model drawing?
2. How are isoplanes changed?
3. The **Ellipse** tool is used to place ellipses in isometric drawings. But ellipses are not usually placed on screen in an isometric angle. How is an isometric ellipse drawn?
4. Is there a limit to the number of views which can be included with an orthographic projection?
5. It will have been noted that in this chapter isometric **drawing** has been the term used for pictorial drawing, but orthographic **projection** has been used for orthographic drawings. Why refer to one form of drawing as **drawing** and to the other as **projection**?

6. What is the major difference between a first angle orthographic projection and a third angle orthographic projection?
7. What is the purpose of centre lines in an engineering drawing?
8. If it is necessary to change a line on screen to another type of line, which tool is used for the purpose?
9. How is the scale of a line changed?
10. In this book different linetypes have been set for certain layers. Can you describe and name the layers in the **initial.dwt** template used throughout this book?

Exercises

The drawings in the illustrations on which the exercises below are based include dimensions. The adding of dimensions to drawings is described in the next chapter. When answering the exercises below, do not include any of the dimensions. It is, however, a good idea to save answers to a floppy disk. Then they can be loaded back into a computer in order to add dimensions after working through the descriptions in the next chapter.

1. Figure 9.18 is a 'rendering' of a 3D (three-dimensional) model of the part shown in the end view of Fig. 9.19. The total depth of the part is 100 mm.

   Working to the dimensions given in Fig. 9.19 construct a three-view orthographic projection of the part. Work in first angle projection.

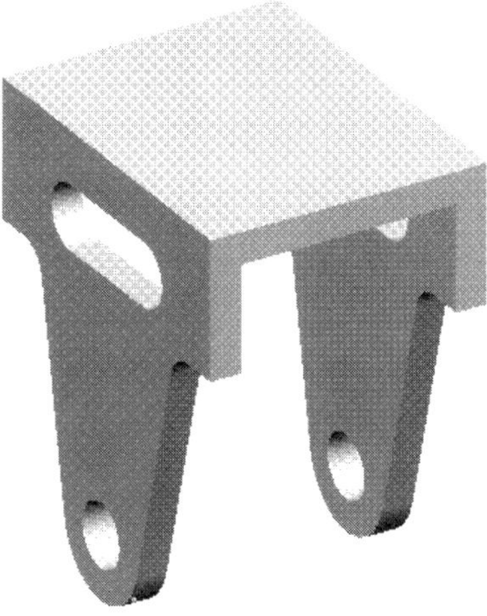

Fig. 9.18 Exercise 1 – a rendering

2. Figure 9.20 is a rendering of the part shown in a front view in Fig. 9.21. The total depth from front to back of the part is 150 mm.

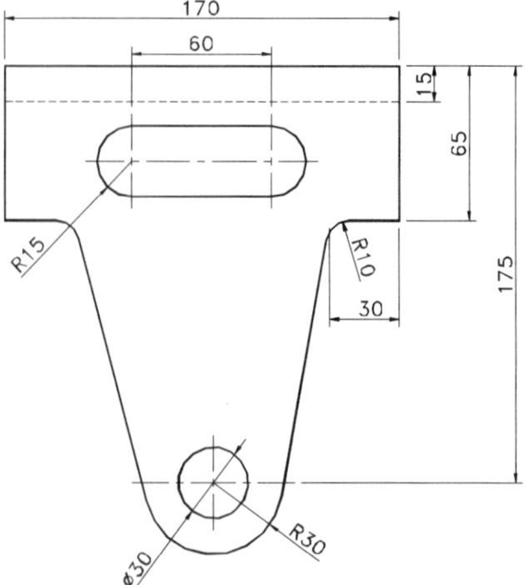

Fig. 9.19 Exercise 1

Working to the sizes given in Fig. 9.21 construct a three-view third angle orthographic projection of the part.

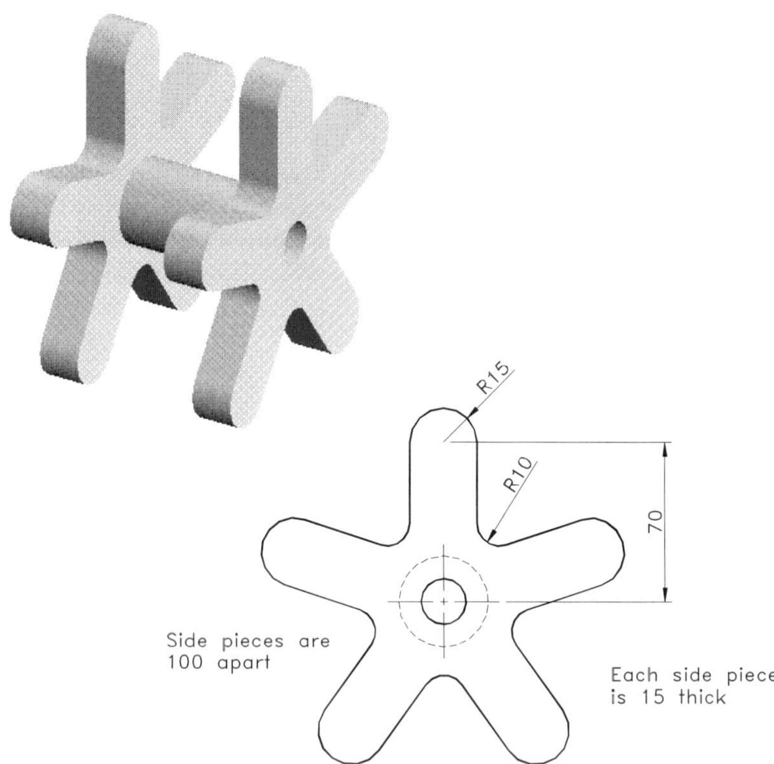

Fig. 9.20 Exercise 2 – a rendering

Fig. 9.21 Exercise 2

3. Figure 9.22 is a rendering of the part shown in a two-view first angle orthographic projection.

Working to the dimensions given in Fig. 9.22 construct a three-view third angle orthographic projection of the part.

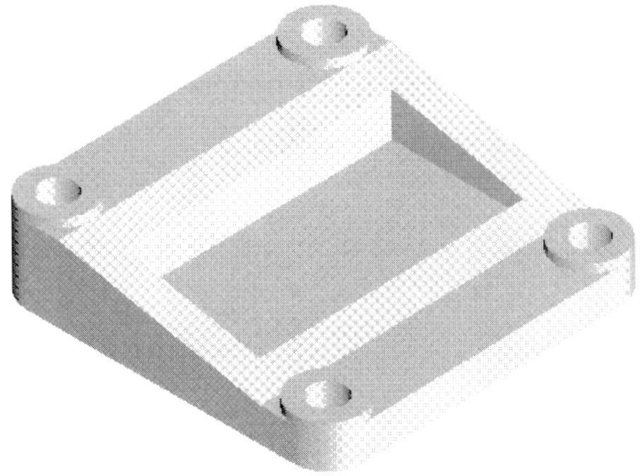

Fig. 9.22 Exercise 3 – a rendering

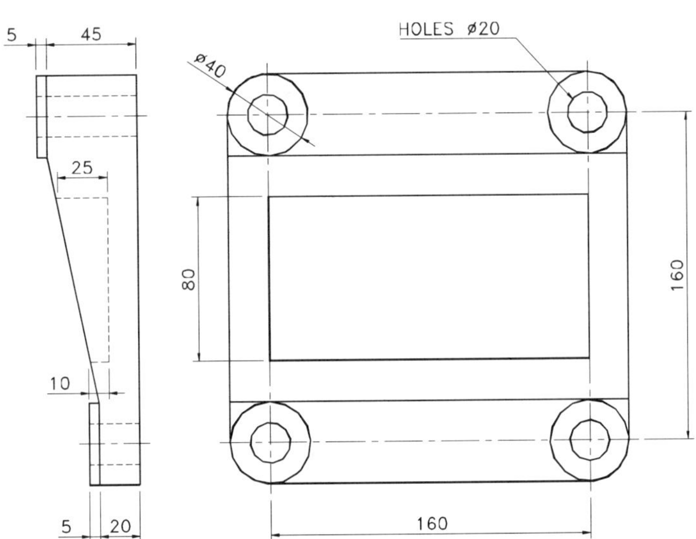

Fig. 9.23 Exercise 3

4. Figure 9.24 is a rendering of the part, details of which are given in a front view Fig. 9.25.

   Working to the details given in Fig. 9.25, construct a three-view first angle orthographic projection of the part.
5. Figure 9.26 is a three-view third angle projection of a part. Working to the sizes given in the projection, construct an isometric drawing of the part.
6. Figure 9.27 is a three-view first angle orthographic projection of a component. Working to the dimensions given with Fig. 9.27 construct an isometric drawing of the part.

Fig. 9.24 Exercise 4 – a rendering

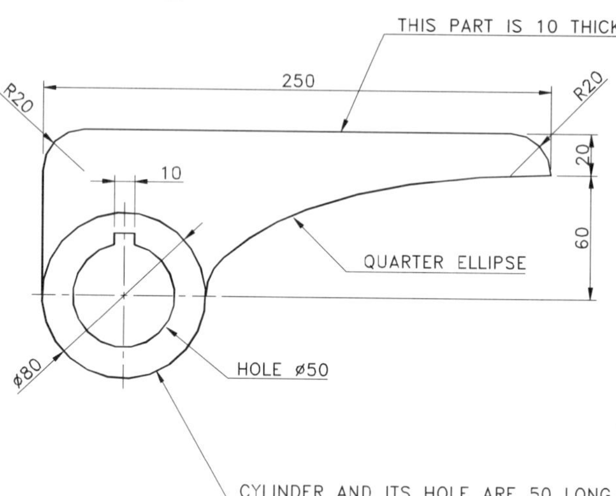

Fig. 9.25 Exercise 4

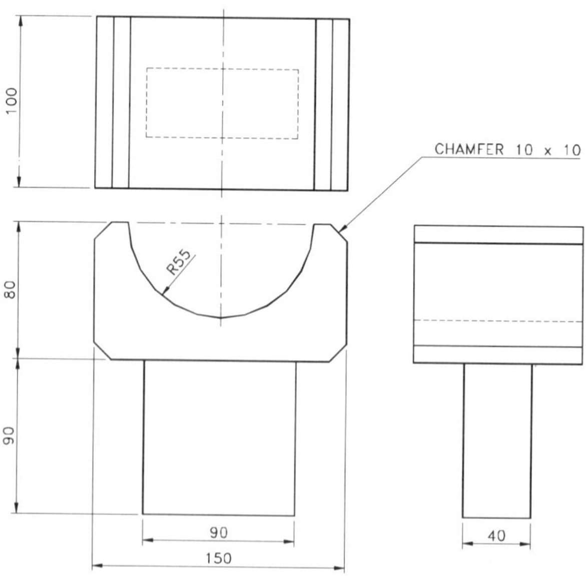

Fig. 9.26 Exercise 5

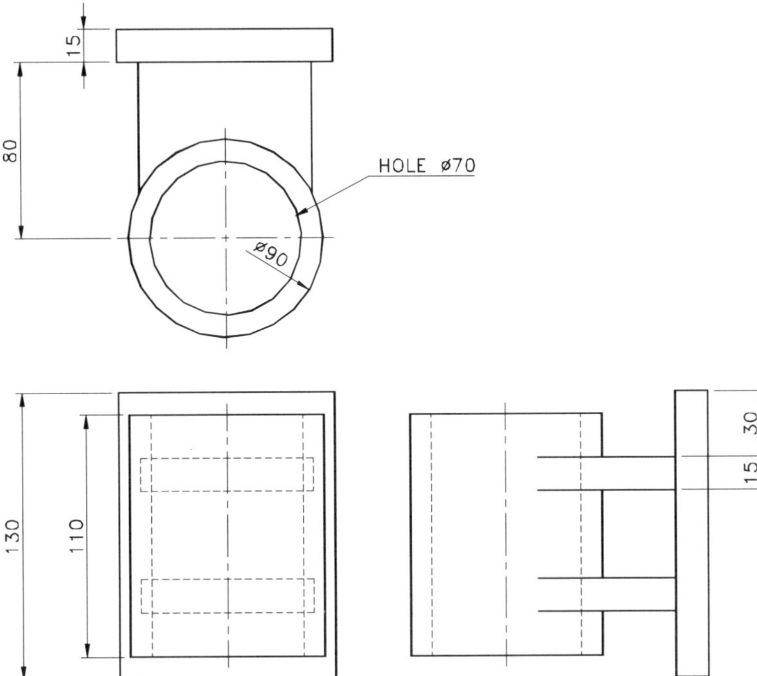

Fig. 9.27 Exercise 6

7. Figure 9.28 is a three-view orthographic projection of a box on a stand. Construct an isometric drawing of the box and its stand to the given dimensions.

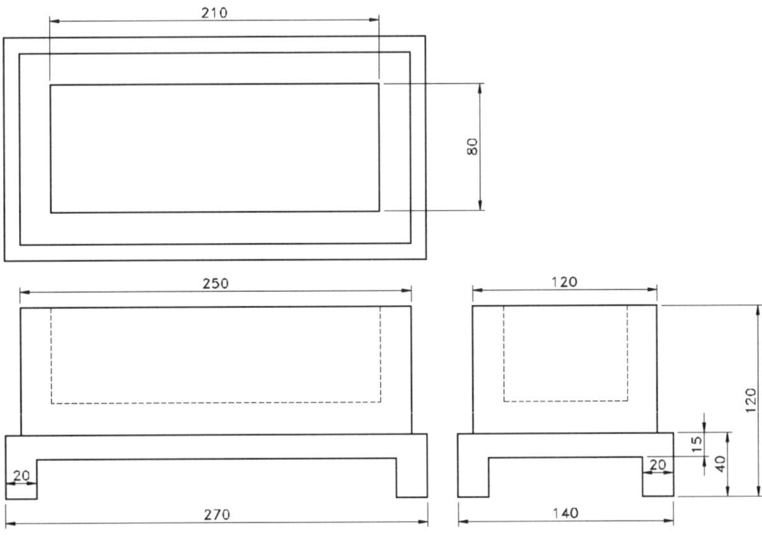

Fig. 9.28 Exercise 7

CHAPTER 10

Dimensioning

Introduction

The inclusion of dimensions in drawings is an important part of the work of a CAD operator. LT 97 has a complex set of dimensioning tools. In general, there are two methods available for adding dimensions to drawings:

1. By selecting the appropriate dimensioning tool from the **Dimension** toolbar as indicated in Fig. 10.1. The toolbar is called to screen as indicated in Fig. 10.2.
2. From the *entering* of abbreviations at the Command line.

The operator will choose which of the two methods he/she finds most appropriate to his/her methods of working.

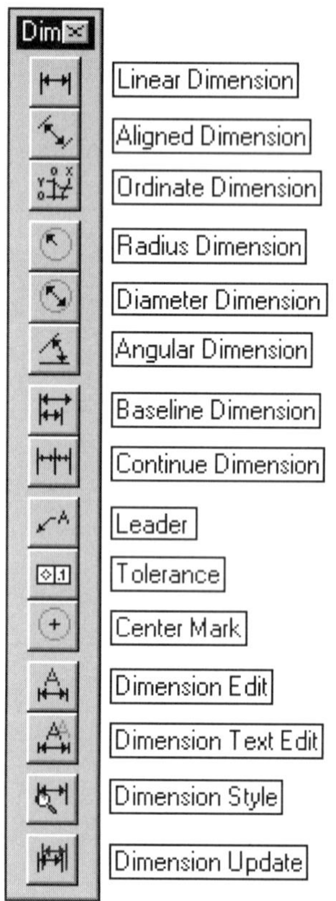

Fig. 10.1 The **Dimension** toolbar showing names of tools

Setting dimensioning style

Before including a dimension in a drawing, it is advisable to set the dimension style. Either select the **Dimension Style** tool from the **Dimension** toolbar, or select **Dimension Style...** from the **Format**

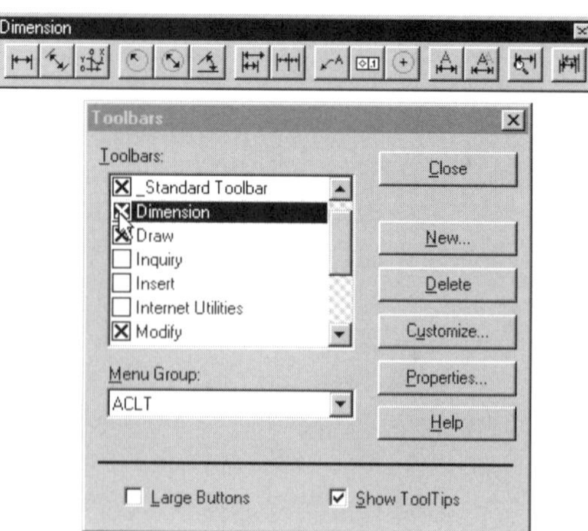

Fig. 10.2 Calling the **Dimension** toolbar to screen

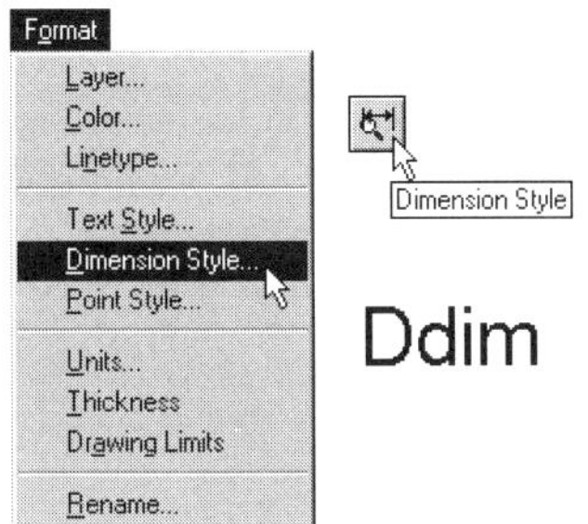

Fig. 10.3 Calling the **Dimension Styles** dialogue box

pull-down menu, or *enter* ddim at the Command line. See Fig. 10.3. No matter which of these methods is used, the **Dimension Styles** dialogue box comes on screen (Fig. 10.4).

The following sequence shows how to set up a dimension style suitable for the **initial.dwt** template:

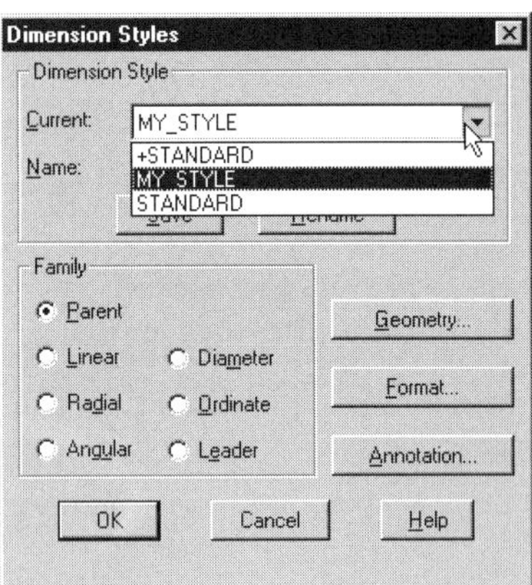

Fig. 10.4 The **Dimension Styles** dialogue box

1. In the dialogue box, *left-click* on the **Rename** button and *enter* a name for the dimensions style. In Fig. 10.4, the name **MY_STYLE** has been *entered*.
2. *Left-click* on the **Geometry...** button, which brings up the **Geometry** dialogue box (Fig. 10.5).
3. In the **Arrowheads** area of the dialogue box, from both the **1st** and **2nd** arrowhead popup lists select **Closed Filled** followed by *entering* **5** in the **Size:** box.
4. In the **Center** area, *left-click* in the **None:** check circle so that no centre mark appears in circles and/or arcs when a dimension is placed.
5. In the **Extension Line** area, *enter* **3** in both the **Extension:** and **Origin:** boxes.
6. Turn off the check circle for **Scale to Paper Space**.
7. In the **Scale** area, *enter* **1** in the **Overall Scale:** box.
8. *Left-click* on the **OK** button of the **Geometry** box.
9. *Left-click* on the **Format...** button in the main dialogue box.
10. Make settings in the **Format** box as shown in Fig. 10.6.
11. *Left-click* on the **OK** button of the dialogue box.
12. In the main dialogue box, *left-click* on the **Annotation...** button.
13. In the **Annotation** dialogue box, in the **Style** popup list, select **ROMAND** and set **Height:** to **5** and **Gap:** to **1.5** as shown in Fig. 10.7.
14. *Left-click* on the **Units...** button in the **Primary Units** area of the box and set **Units** to **Decimal** and **Precision** to **0**.

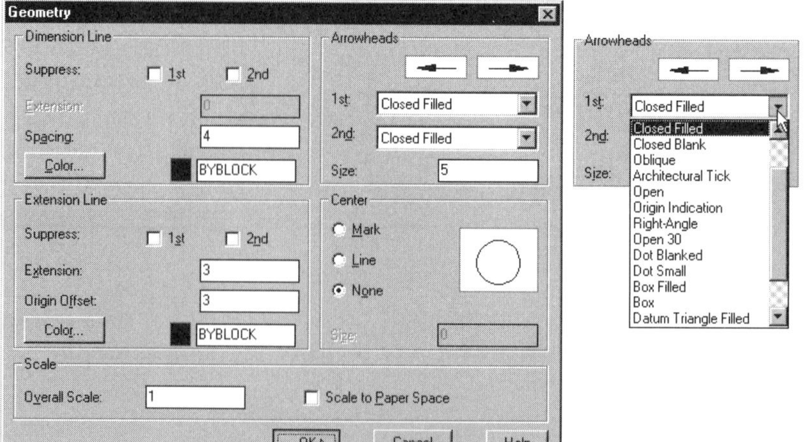

Fig. 10.5 Settings in the **Geometry** dialogue box

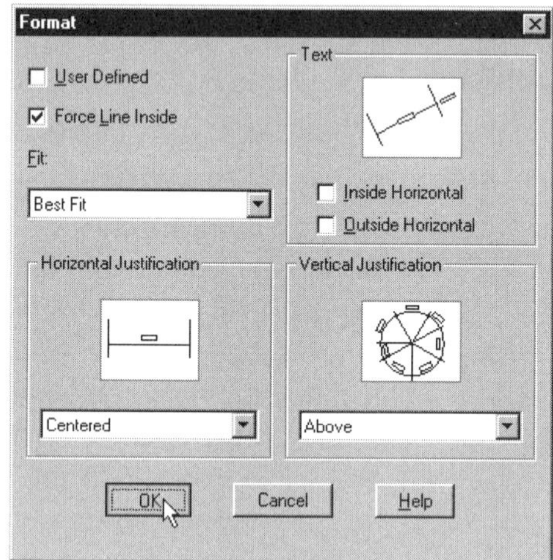

Fig. 10.6 Settings in the **Format** dialogue box

15. In the **Angles** area of the box, set **Decimal Degrees** and **Precision:** to **0** as shown in Fig. 10.7.
16. Make sure **Tolerance** is set to **Method: None**.
17. *Left-click* on the **OK** button of the **Annotation** box and again in the **Dimensions Style** box. The dimension style **MY_STYLE** has now been set.

Notes

1. The text styles available in the **Annotation** box are those previously set in the **Text Style** dialogue box (see page 63).
2. Once the dimension style has been set, it can then be saved to the template **initial.dwt**.
3. It is advisable to practise varying the settings in the **Dimension Style** boxes in order to become fully acquainted with the results of different settings.

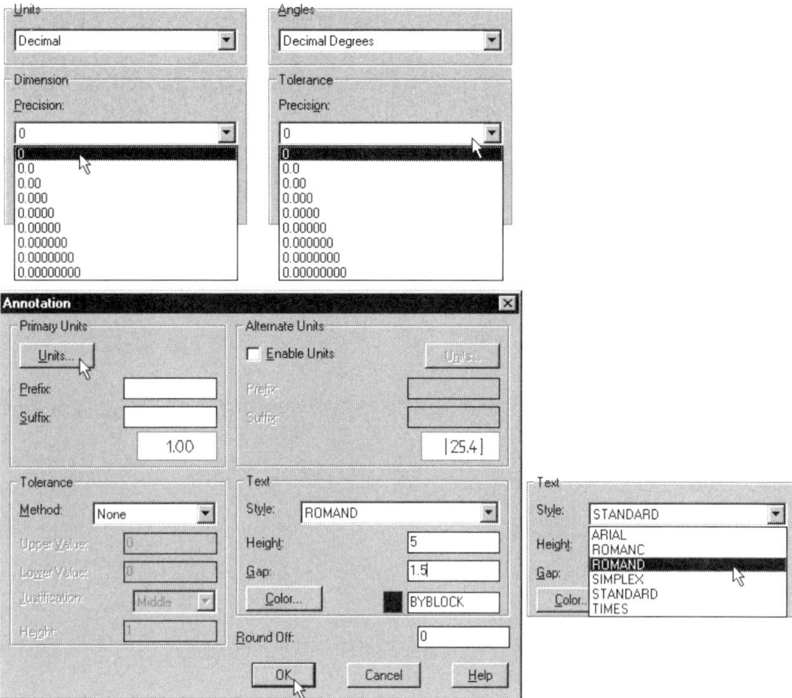

Fig. 10.7 Settings in the **Annotation** dialogue box

4. *Entering* e or pressing the **Esc** key of the keyboard finishes a **DIM** sequence and the Command line reverts to **Command:**

The two methods of dimensioning

Entering commands at the Command line

There are a large number of different forms of dimension possible working from the Command line, but they all take a form of prompts similar to the following two examples.

The first is an example of dimensioning by selection of the object to carry the dimension (upper part of Fig. 10.8). The second by selection of the ends of the objects to carry the dimension (lower part of Fig. 10.8).

Example 1

Command: *enter* d (or dim) *right-click*
DIM
Dim: *enter* hor *right-click*
First extension line origin or press ENTER to select: *right-click*
Select object to dimension: *pick*
Dimension line location (Text/Angle): *pick*

Dimension text <190>: *right-click*
Dim: *enter* ve *right-click*
First extension line origin or press ENTER to select: *right-click*
Select object to dimension: *pick*
Dimension line location (Text/Angle): *pick*
Dimension text <90>: *right-click*

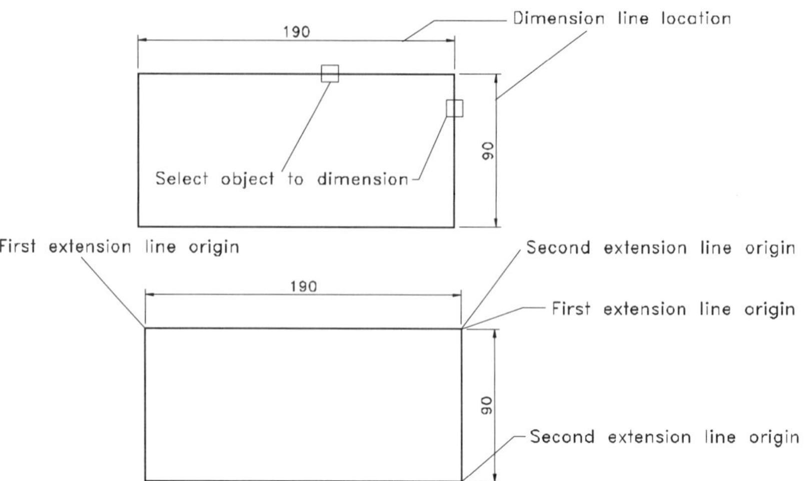

Fig. 10.8 Examples of horizontal and vertical dimensions

Example 2

Dim: *enter* hor *right-click*
First extension line origin or press ENTER to select: *pick*
Second extension line origin: *pick*
Dimension line location (Text/Angle): *pick*
Dimension text <190>: *right-click*
Dim: *enter* ve *right-click*
First extension line origin: *pick*
Second extension line origin: *pick*
Dimension line location (Text/Angle): *pick*
Dimension text <90>: *right-click*
Dim:

Abbreviations for dimensioning

From the above two examples it can be seen that the abbreviation **hor** stands for horizontal and **ve** for vertical. Other abbreviations are:

al aligned.
an angular.
ba baseline.

cen centre mark – only if set in the **Geometry** dialogue box.
co continue.
d diameter.
l leader.
or ordinate.
ra radius.
st style.

Examples of these forms of dimensioning are given in Fig. 10.9

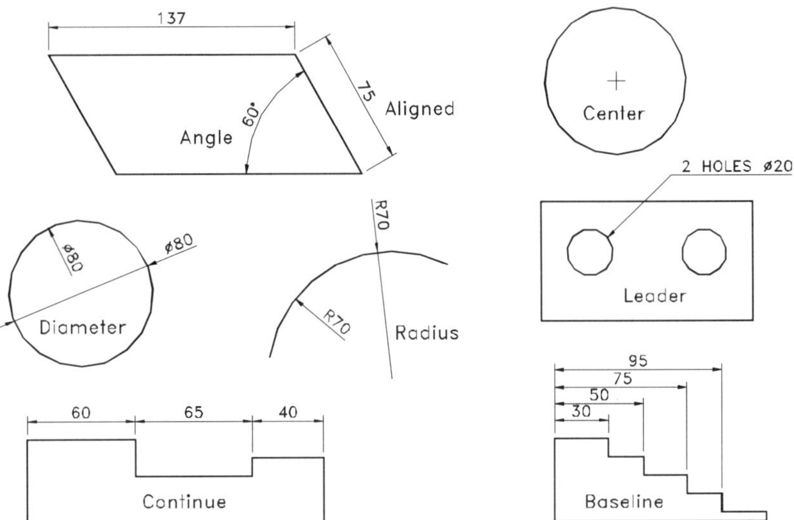

Fig. 10.9 Examples of different forms of dimensioning

Note: In the case of diameter and radii dimensioning, the dimension lines and figures may be placed inside or outside the object being dimensioned, depending upon where the operator chooses to place them in response to the **Dimension line location (Text/Angle):** prompt.

Calling a dimension tool from the toolbar

When *entering* d (or dim) at the Command line, the dimensioning sequence is continuous – once one dimension had been placed, the **Dim:** prompt is repeated without having to call the tool again. When dimensioning with the aid of tools from the **Dimension** toolbar, as each dimension is added, so the tool will need to be called again. As an example, *left-click* on the **Linear Dimension** tool icon (Fig. 10.10). The Command line shows:

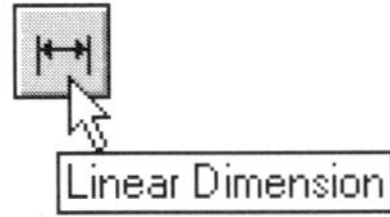

Fig. 10.10 Selecting the **Linear Dimension** tool

Command: _dimlinear
First extension line origin or press ENTER to select: *right-click*
Select object to dimension: *pick*

Dimension line location (Mtext/Text/Angle/Horizontal/Vertical/ Rotated): *pick*
Dimension text <190>: *right-click*
Command:

Notes

1. Unless a *right-click* confirms that linear dimensioning is to proceed, another tool must be selected.
2. As with *entering* d (or dim), objects can be selected for linear dimensioning. As an example, if an arc is selected its length and not its radius is dimensioned (see Fig. 10.11).

Examples of using the Dimensions tools

In these examples, the **Dimension Style** as set above is used throughout.

Example 1 – linear dimensions (Fig. 10.11)

Left-click on the **Linear Dimension** tool in the **Dimension** toolbar. The Command line shows:

Command: _dimlinear
First extension line origin or press ENTER to select: *right-click*
Select object to dimension: *pick* the upper line (Fig. 10.11)
Dimension line location (Mtext/Text/Angle/Horizontal/Vertical/ Rotated): *enter* m (Mtext) *right-click*

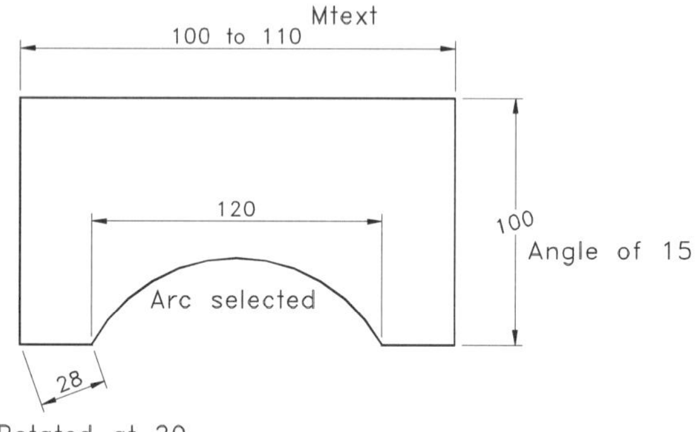

Fig. 10.11 Example 1

Fig. 10.12 The **Multiline Text Editor**

The **Multiline Text Editor** appears (Fig. 10.12). *Enter* in the text editor the required dimension and *left-click* on the **OK** button.
Dimension line location (Mtext/Text/Angle/Horizontal/Vertical/ Rotated): *pick* the required position
Command: *right-click*
Command: _dimlinear
First extension line origin or press ENTER to select: *right-click*
Select object to dimension: *pick* the right-hand line (Fig. 10.11)
Dimension line location (Mtext/Text/Angle/Horizontal/Vertical/ Rotated): *enter* a (Angle) *right-click*
Enter text angle: *enter* 15 *right-click*
Dimension line location (Mtext/Text/Angle/Horizontal/Vertical/ Rotated): *pick* the bottom left line (Fig. 10.11)
Dimension text <100>: *right-click*
Command: *right-click*
First extension line origin or press ENTER to select: *right-click*
Select object to dimension: *pick* the right-hand line (Fig. 10.11)
Dimension line location (Mtext/Text/Angle/Horizontal/Vertical/ Rotated): *enter* r *right-click*
Dimension line angle <0>: *enter* 20 *right-click*
Dimension line location (Mtext/Text/Angle/Horizontal/Vertical/ Rotated): *right-click*
Dimension text <28>: *right-click* (to accept 28)
Command:

Example 2 (Fig. 10.13)

This example shows the use of several of the tools from the **Dimension** toolbar. The following tool sequences describe the addition of dimensions to the outline of Fig. 10.13.

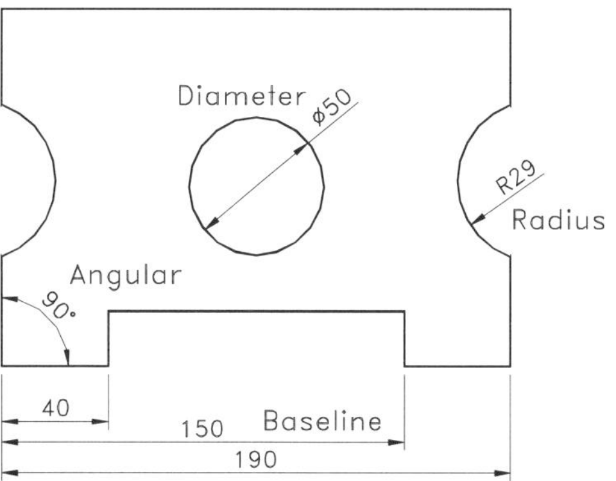

Fig. 10.13 Example 2

Fig. 10.14 Calling **Diameter Dimension**

Left-click on **Diameter Dimension** (Fig. 10.14). The Command line shows:

Command:_dimdiameter
Select arc or circle: *pick* central circle (Fig. 10.13)
Dimension text = 50
Dimension line location (Mtext/Text/Angle): *pick*
Command:

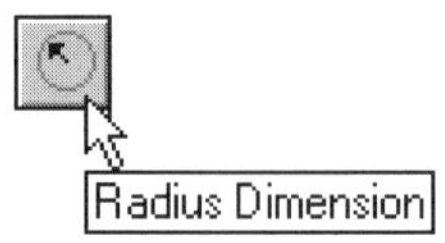

Fig. 10.15 Calling **Radius Dimension**

Left-click on **Radius Dimension** (Fig. 10.14). The Command line shows:

Command:_dimradius
Select arc or circle: *pick* right-hand arc (Fig. 10.13)
Dimension text = 29
Dimension line location (Mtext/Text/Angle): *pick*
Command:

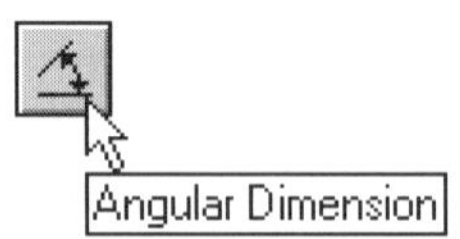

Fig. 10.16 Calling **Angular Dimension**

Left-click on **Angular Dimension** (Fig. 10.16). The Command line shows:

Command:_dimangular
Pick arc, circle, line or press ENTER: *pick* left horizontal bottom line (Fig. 10.13)
Second line: *pick* bottom left-hand upright line (Fig. 10.13)
Dimension arc line location (Mtext/Text/Angle): *pick*
Dimension text = 90
Command:

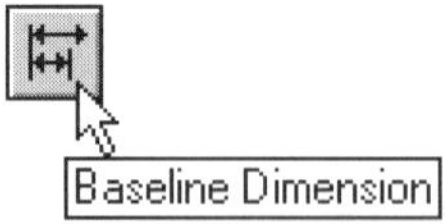

Fig. 10.17 Calling **Baseline Dimension**

For the next part of this example, first use **Linear Dimension** to place the 40 dimension (bottom right of Fig. 10.13).

Left-click on **Baseline Dimension** (Fig. 10.17). The Command line shows:

Command:_dimbaseline
Select base dimension: *pick* the 40 dimension
Select a second dimension line origin or (Undo/Select): *pick* the point on the outline ending the 150 dimension. The dimension automatically appears
Select a second dimension line origin or (Undo/Select): *pick* the point on the outline ending the 190 dimension. The dimension automatically appears
Select a second dimension line origin or (Undo/Select): *right-click*
Select base dimension: *right-click*
Command:

Example 3 (Fig. 10.18)

This example shows the uses of the text and dimension editing tools from the **Dimension** toolbar.

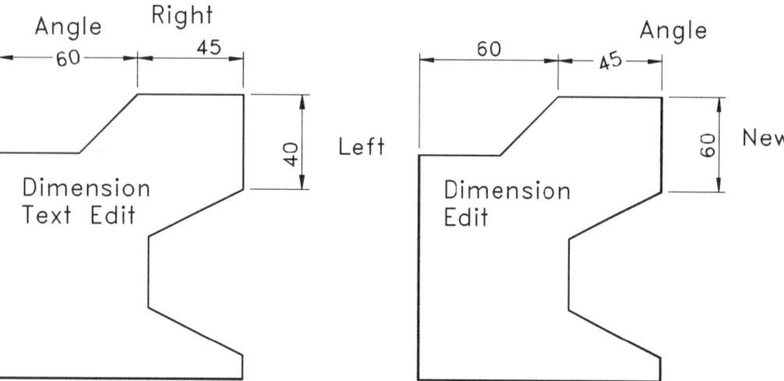

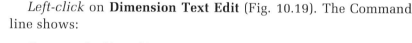

Fig. 10.18 Example 3

Left-click on **Dimension Text Edit** (Fig. 10.19). The Command line shows:

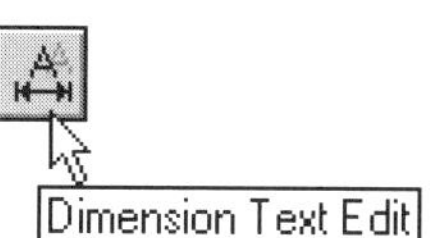

Fig. 10.19 Calling **Dimension Text Edit**

Command:_dimtedit
Select dimension: *pick* the 60 dimension
Enter text location (Left/Right/Home/Angle): *enter* a (Angle) *right-click*
Enter text angle: *enter* 30 *right-click*
Command: *right-click*
DIMTEDIT
Select dimension: *pick* the 45 dimension
Enter text location (Left/Right/Home/Angle): *enter* r (Right) *right-click*
Command: *right-click*
DIMTEDIT
Select dimension: *pick* the 40 dimension
Enter text location (Left/Right/Home/Angle): *enter* l (Left) *right-click*
Command: *right-click*

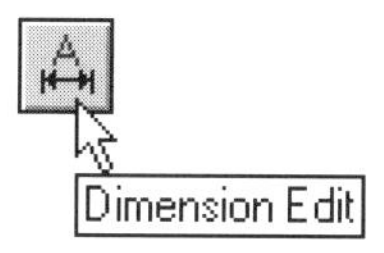

Fig. 10.20 Calling **Dimension Edit**

In a similar manner dimensions can be edited with the aid of the **Dimension Edit** tool from the **Dimension** toolbar (Fig. 10.20).

Associative dimensions

Dimensions are associated with the object to which the dimension is being added. If the object is changed, then any added dimensions change with the object. Examples of using **STRETCH** and **SCALE** on a dimensioned outline are shown in Fig. 10.21.

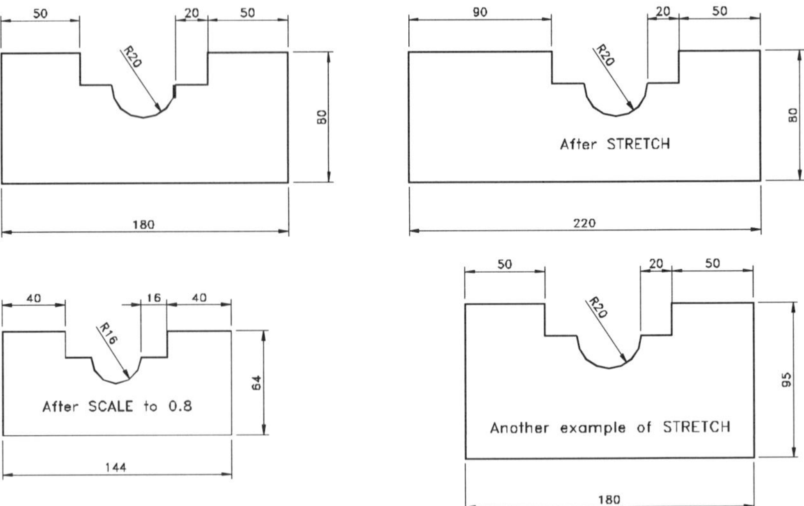

Fig. 10.21 Dimensions are associative

Tolerances

Arithmetic tolerances

Call the **Dimension Style** dialogue box (with ddim). *Left-click* on the **Annotation...** button and in the **Annotation** box, set **Primary Units** to **Precision** of **0.00** (Fig. 10, 22). Then, *left-click* on the arrow to the side of the **Method:** box to bring the popup list showing (Fig. 10.23).

Figure 10.24 shows some examples of tolerances applied to dimensions with the various methods selected in the **Tolerances** area of the **Annotation** box of **Dimension Style**.

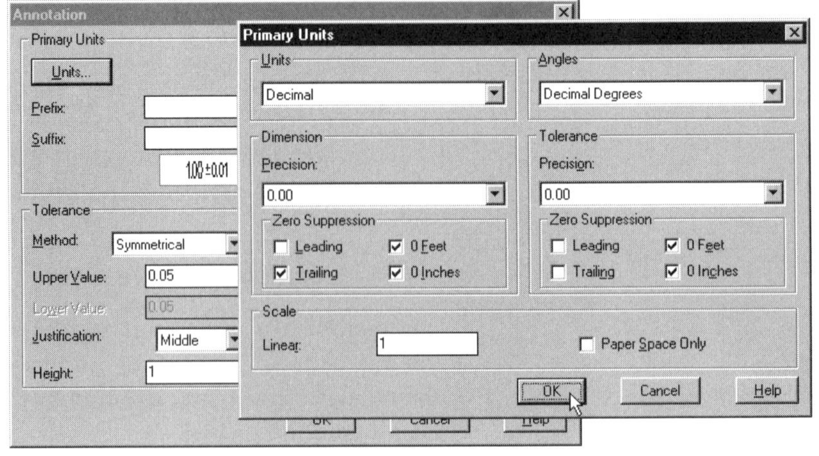

Fig. 10.22 Setting tolerances in the **Dimension Style** dialogue boxes

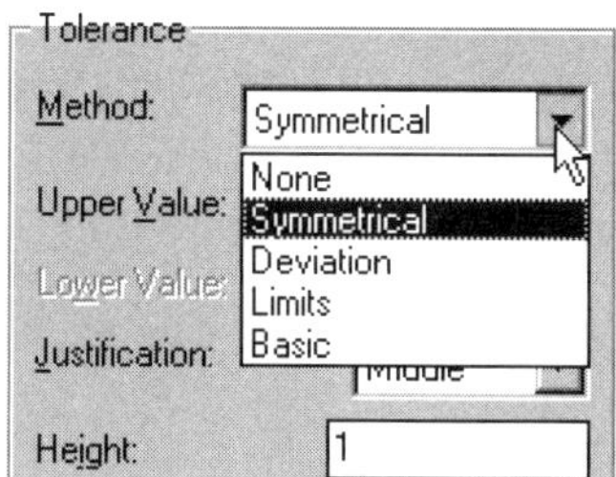

Fig.10.23 The popup list from the **Tolerance Methods** area of **Dimension Style**

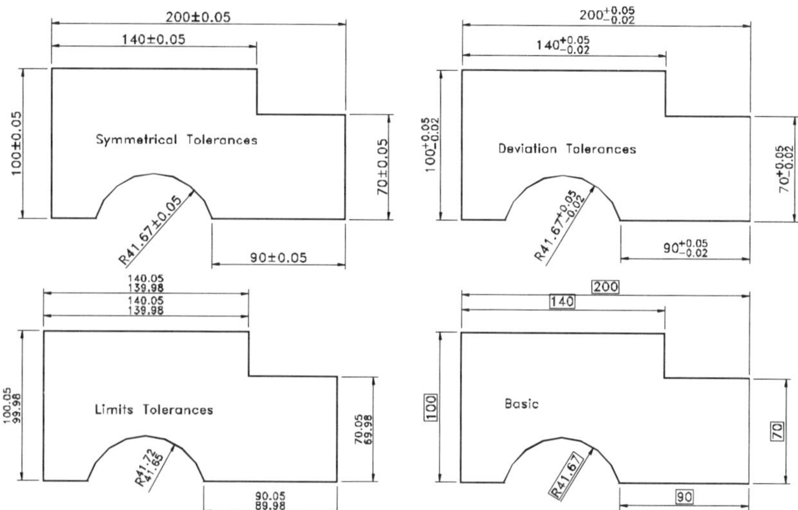

Fig. 10.24 Examples of dimensions with tolerances

Geometric Tolerances

Left-click on the tool icon **Tolerance** from the **Dimension** toolbar (Fig. 10.25. The **Symbol** dialogue box appears (Fig. 10.26). *Left-click* on the position symbol as shown, followed by another on the **OK**

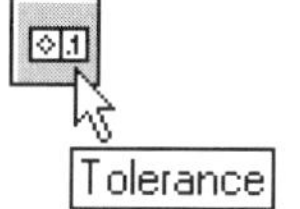

Fig. 10.25 Calling **Tolerance** from the **Dimension** toolbar

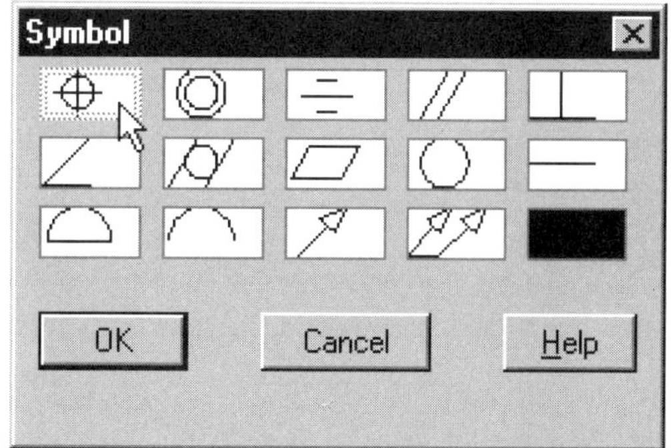

Fig. 10.26 The **Symbol** dialogue box

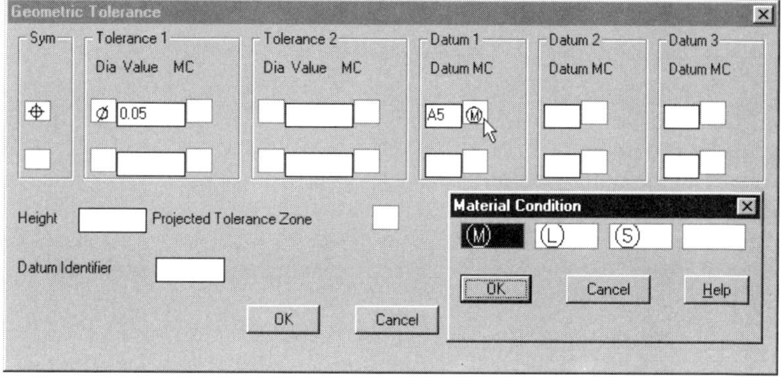

Fig. 10.27 The **Geometric Tolerance** dialogue box

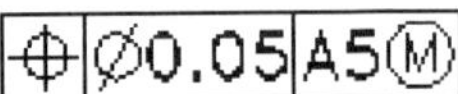

Fig. 10.28 The geometric tolerance from Fig. 10.27

button. The **Geometric Tolerance** dialogue box appears (Fig. 10.27). *Enter* letters and figures as shown in Fig. 10.27 and *left-click* on the **OK** button of the dialogue box. The geometric tolerance shown in Fig. 10.28 appears on screen. It can be *dragged* onto a dimension as required. Figure 10.29 shows some simple examples of geometric tolerances applied to dimensions.

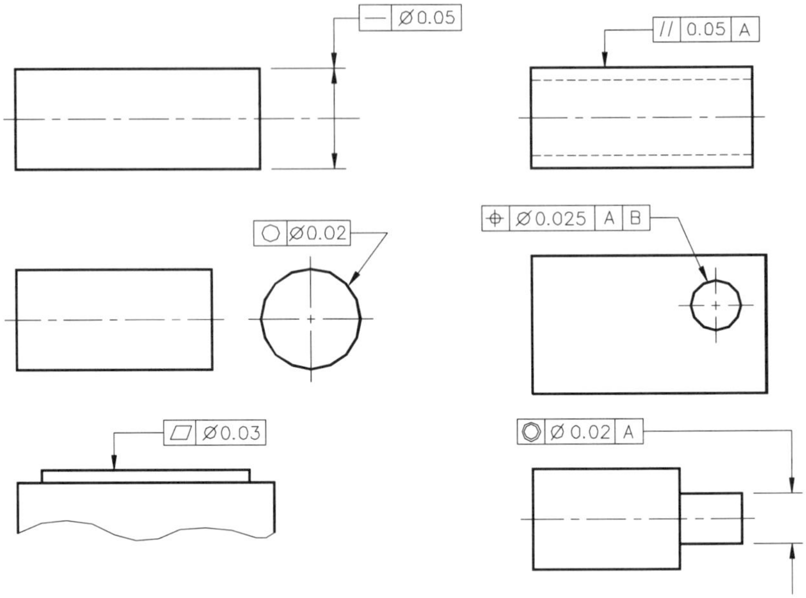

Fig. 10.29 Some examples of geometric tolerances applied to dimensions

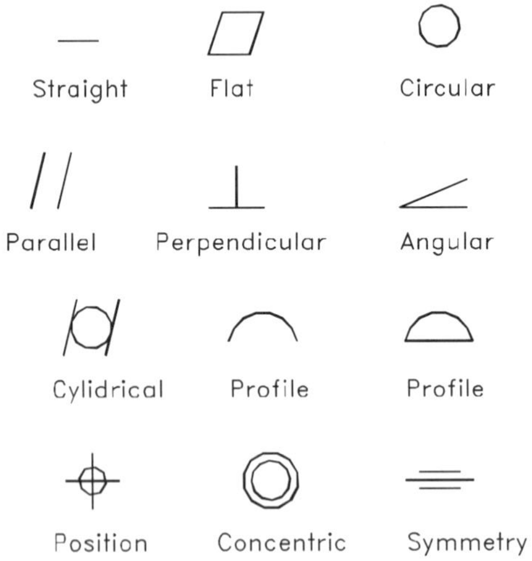

Fig. 10.30 The major geometrical tolerance symbols

Prefixes and suffixes

Prefixes and suffixes can be included with a drawing if thought necessary. Figure 10.31 shows the method of including these with

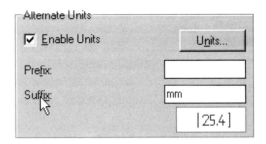

Fig. 10.31 setting a **Prefix** in the **Alternate Units** area

a dimension by ensuring the check box in the **Alternate Units** area of the **Annotation** box is set on (tick in box) and that the required prefix and/or suffix is *entered* in the appropriate boxes in the **Alternate Units** area. Some examples are given in Fig. 10.32.

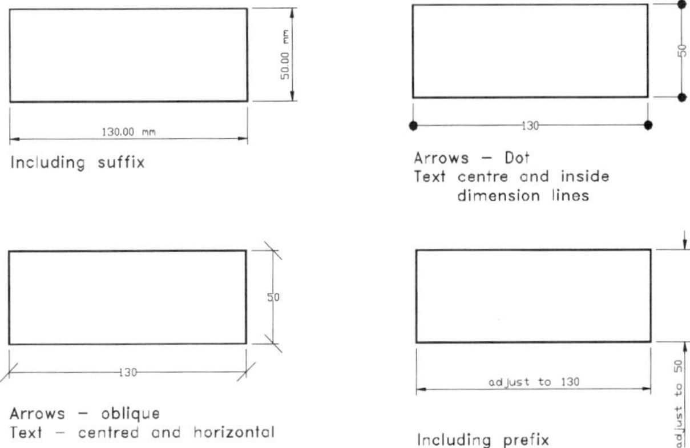

Fig. 10.32 Examples of different forms of dimensioning

Questions

1. What are the major differences between adding dimensions to a drawing by *entering* the command **dim** at the Command line and responding to prompts, compared with using the **Dimension** tools?
2. How is the **Dimension Style** dialogue box brought to screen?
3. There are three further dialogue boxes within the **Dimension Style** dialogue. Can you name them?
4. Can you describe the purpose of each of the three dialogue boxes associated with the **Dimension Style** dialogue box?
5. How are toleranced dimensions set up?
6. What are the differences between the several methods of including tolerances with dimensions in LT 97?
7. What is the difference between an arithmetic tolerance and a geometric tolerance?
8. What is meant by 'Associative dimensioning' in relation to LT 97?

9. If it is wished to add details of the dimensioning units to a dimension – e.g. mm or millimetres, ft or feet in or inches, how is this set up from the **Dimension Style** dialogue box?
10. If you wish to end dimension lines with ticks, instead of arrows, what action must be taken before the dimension is included with a drawing?

Exercises

Practise adding a variety of dimensions to any drawing using a variety of settings in the dialogue boxes associated with the **Dimension Style** dialogue box. Note the differences between each of the settings which have been made.

If drawings in answer to exercises from previous chapters have been saved to disk, now is the time to reload them and add dimensions. If the answers have not been so saved, go back through the previous chapters and construct drawings in answer to some of the exercises and this time include dimensions.

CHAPTER 11

Blocks and Inserting blocks

Blocks and the insertion of blocks

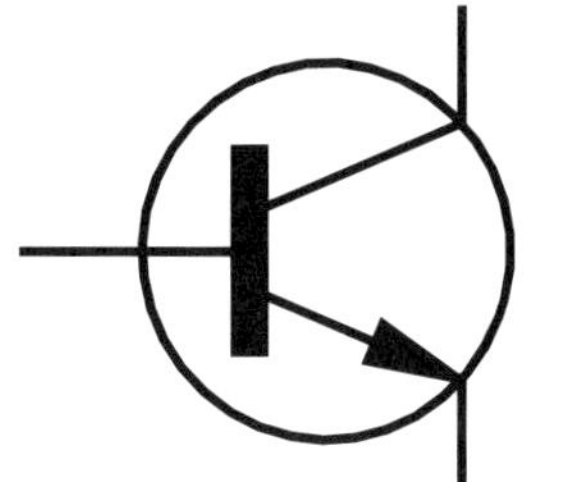

Fig. 11.1 Construct the symbol for an NPN transitor

Blocks are drawings which can be saved either within the data of the drawing in which they exist or as drawing files in their own right. Blocks which are part of the data of a drawing can only be recalled for insertion within the drawing of which they are part. Blocks saved as drawing files in their own right can be inserted as drawings within any other drawing or loaded as separate drawings. There are many uses for blocks. One particular use for blocks is in the construction of circuit drawings. To demonstrate how blocks can be constructed and inserted, examples from simple electronics or electrical circuits are given below.

Example 1

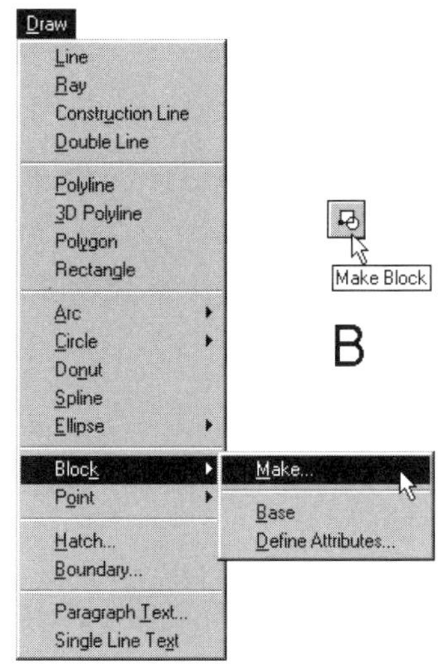

Fig. 11.2 Call the **Make Block** tool

1. Construct the symbol for the electronics symbol for an NPN transistor (Fig. 11.1).
2. Call the **Make Block** tool (Fig. 11.2). No matter which method is used – selection from the Insert pull-down menu, selecting the tool icon or *entering* b at the Command line, the **Create Block** dialogue box appears (Fig. 11.3).
3. In the dialogue box, make sure the **Internal block** check circle is on (dot in circle) and *enter* a name for the block to be created – in this example **NPN** in the **Name:** box of the dialogue box.
4. *Left-click* on the **Specify<** button. The dialogue box disappears. *Left-click* on a suitable point on the drawing.
5. The dialogue box reappears. *Left-click* on the **Select objects<** button. The dialogue disappears again.
6. Window the symbol and *right-click*. The dialogue box reappears with the symbol showing in a preview box to the right of the **Select objects<** button (as shown in Fig. 11.3).

Notes

1. If the block is to be saved as a separate drawing in its own right, the **DWG file** check circle should be set on (dot in the circle).

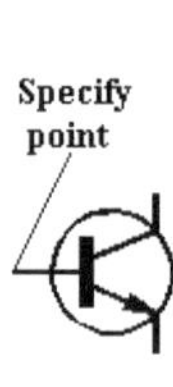

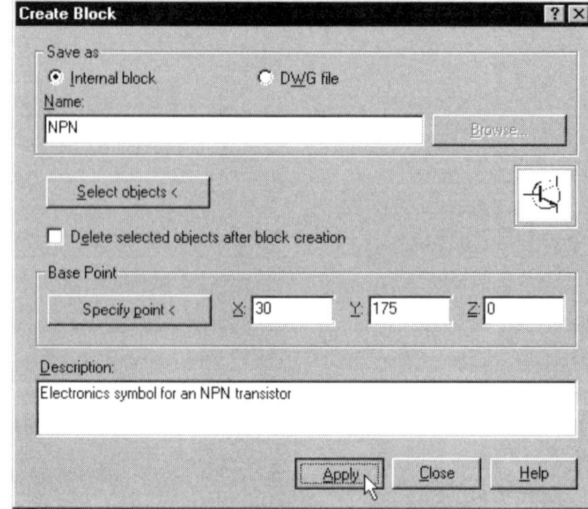

Fig. 11.3 Example 1. The **Create Block** dialogue box

2. When specifying a point (the insertion point of the block), take care to select a suitable point. In the case of symbols such as that for the NPN transistor, it is best to ensure **Snap** is on and select a point on the symbol drawing which would allow easy joining to other symbols in an electronics circuit.

Example 2

Figure 11.5 shows a small 'library' of electronic/electrical circuit symbols constructed in a single drawing and then each symbol made as a block within the drawing data. To demonstrate that the blocks have been made:

1. Call the **Insert Block** tool (Fig. 11.4). The **Insert Block** dialogue box appears (Fig. 11.6).

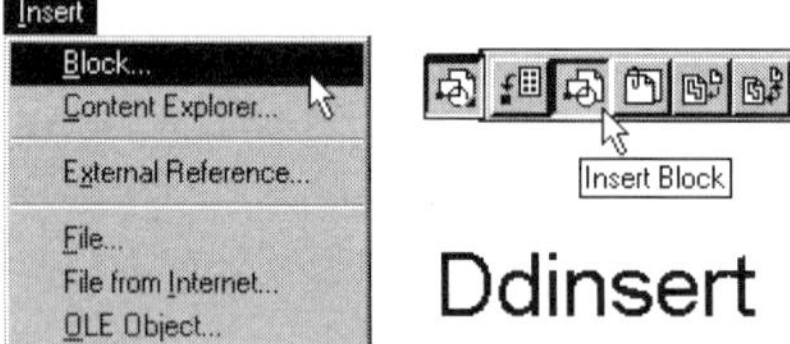

Fig. 11.4 Calling the **Insert Block** tool

2. *Left-click* on the **Block...** button of the dialogue box and the **Defined Blocks** dialogue appears as shown in Fig. 11.6.
3. In the dialogue box, select **NPN** and *left-click* on the **OK** button of the dialogue box. The **Defined Blocks** dialogue disappears and the block name appears in the **Block** window of the **Insert** dialogue box. *Left-click* on the dialogue box **OK** button.

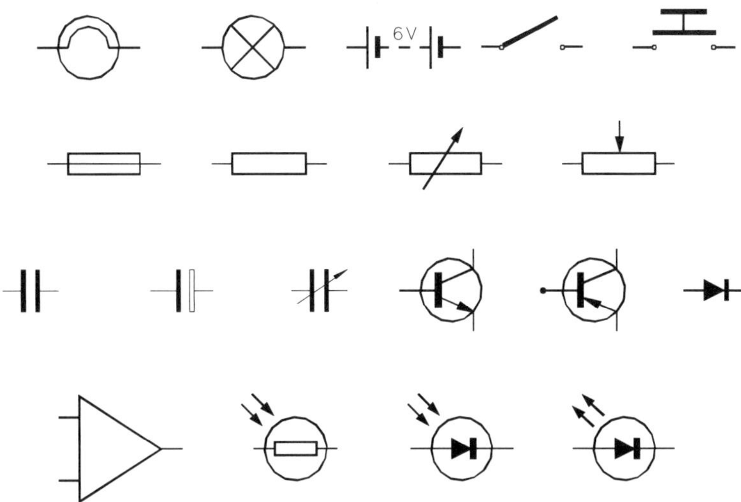

Fig. 11.5 Example 2

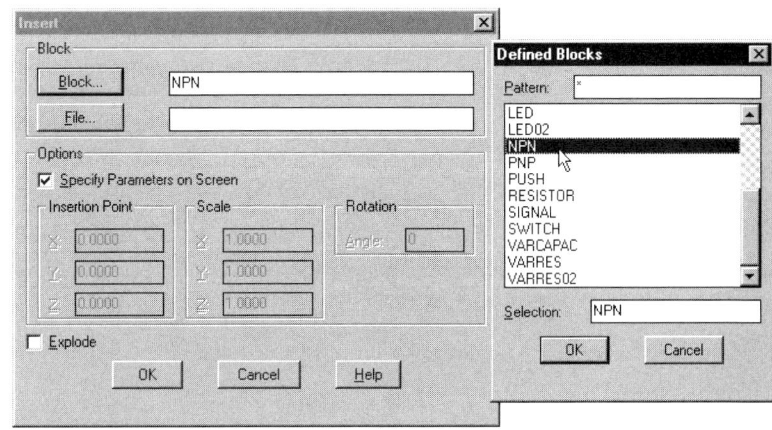

Fig. 11.6 The **Insert** dialogue box with **Defined Blocks** dialogue showing

4. The symbol appears on screen in a ghosted form with the cursor hair lines attached at the **Select point** of the symbol (Fig. 11.7) The symbol can be *dragged* to any position on screen. The Command line shows:

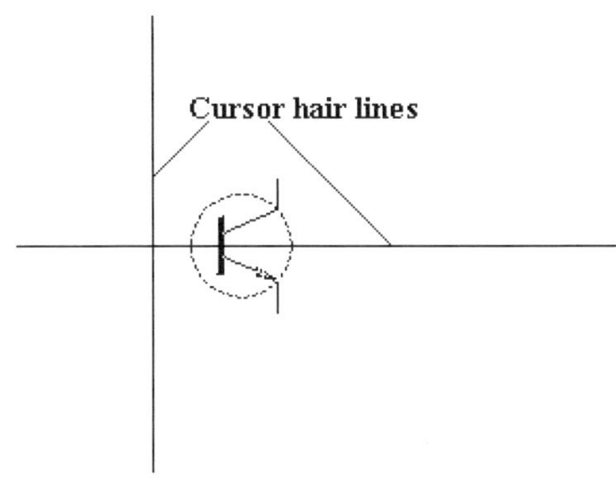

Fig. 11.7 The symbol appears in a ghosted form to be *dragged* into position

Command:_ddinsert
Insertion point: *pick* or *enter* coordinates and *right-click*
X scale factor <1>: *right-click* or *enter* a scale figure
Y scale factor (default = X): *right-click* or *enter* a scale figure
Rotation angle <0>: *right-click* or *enter* a rotation angle figure
Command:

Saving blocks to drawing files

If drawings, such as circuit diagram symbols, are to be saved as drawing files ensure that the **DWG file** check circle in the **Create Block** dialogue box is checked (dot in the circle). Then separate drawing files (extension ***.dwg**) are saved in the AutoCAD LT main directory with the names *entered* in the **Name:** box of the dialogue box. Remember the files are automatically saved to the AutoCAD LT 97 directory. If they are to be saved to another directory the full name of that directory must be *entered* with the **Name**. In the case of the symbol block files shown in Fig. 11.8, the full name would include **C:\Lt_97\Chap11\symbols**.

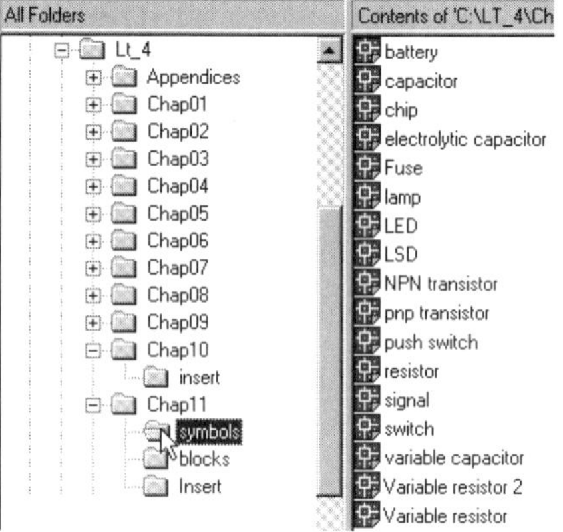

Fig. 11.8 The directory list from **Windows/Explorer** showing the symbol drawings in the symbols directory

When symbols are saved in this manner – as separate drawings in their own right – they can be used quickly to build up circuit drawings.

An example of drawing a circuit diagram

1. Call the **Insert** dialogue box to screen (Fig. 11.4). In the dialogue box, *left-click* on the **File...** button (Fig. 11.9). This brings up the **Select Drawing File** dialogue box as shown in Fig. 11.9.
2. Select the required directory – in this case **C:\Lt_4\Chap11\symbols** and from the file list which then appears select the name of the required symbol drawing – in this example **NPN_transistor**. *Left-*

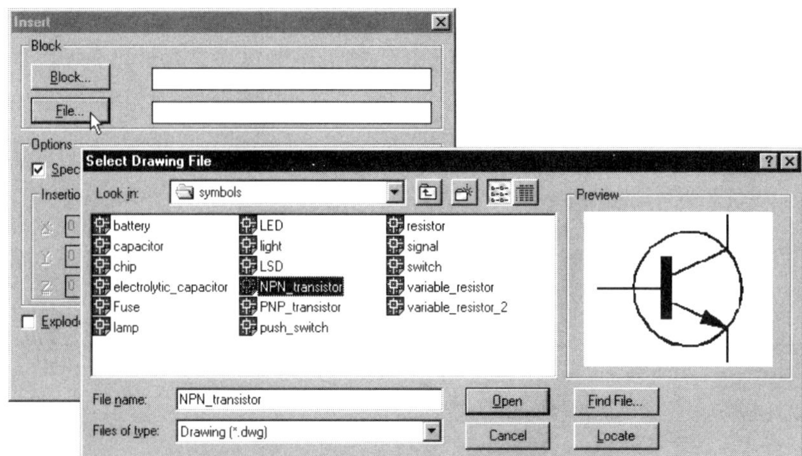

Fig. 11.9 *Left-click* on the **File...** button of the **Insert** dialogue box

click on the **OK** button and the name of the file appears in the **File...** box of the **Insert** dialogue box (Fig. 11.10).

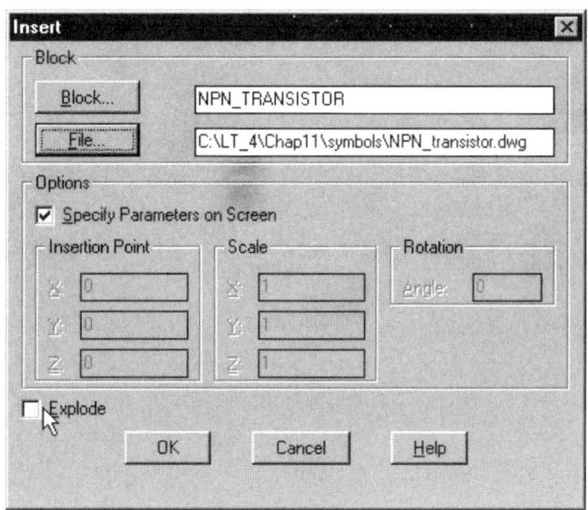

Fig. 11.10 The file name appears in the **File...** window of the **Insert** dialogue box

3. *Left-click* on the **OK** button of the dialogue box and the selected drawing appears attached to the intersection of the hair line cursors at the **select point** (insertion point) of the block.
4. *Drag* the symbol to its required position within the diagram, *left-click*, followed either by *right-clicks* or the *entering* of scale, rotation etc.
5. In this manner insert each symbol into the diagram in an approximate position (Drawing 1 of Fig. 11.11).
6. **Move** and/or **Rotate** symbols as necessary until they are in their required positions in relationship to each other in the diagram. See Drawing 2 of Fig. 11.11.

7. Join the symbols with lines. Any slight changes in position can be carried out with **Move** using **Osnaps** to achieve accuracy. See Drawing 3 of Fig. 11.11.
8. Complete the diagram by adding symbols not already saved as drawings – in this example the loudspeaker has had to be constructed

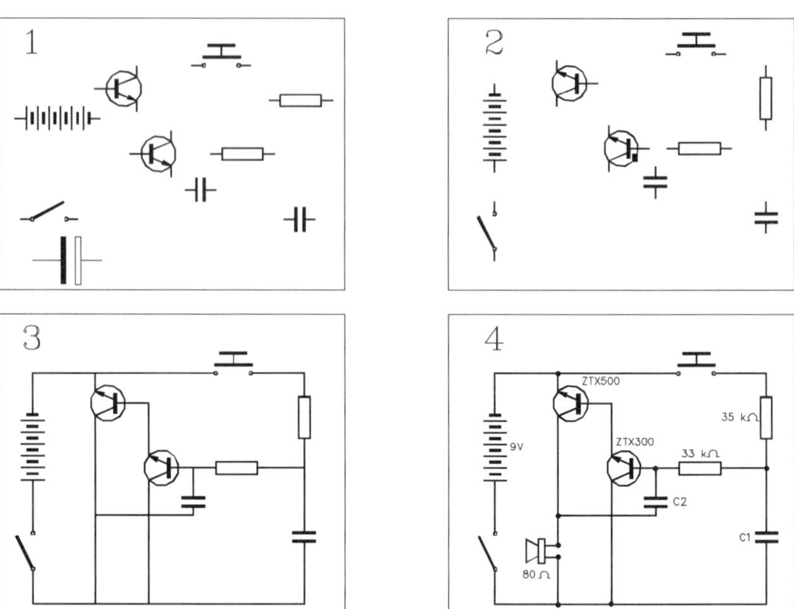

Fig. 11.11 An example of constructing an electronic circuit diagram from blocks

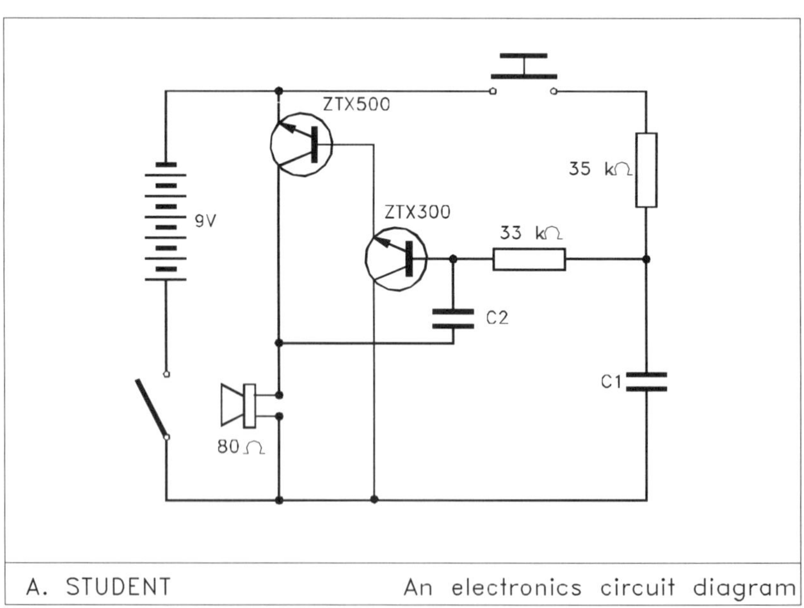

Fig. 11.12 The completed example including a title block and margins

separately to the other symbols. Add donuts at each point of intersection in the lines of the diagram. See Drawing 4 of Fig. 11.11.

9. Add the names of the symbols and include a title block with details and margins if thought necessary (Fig. 11.12).

Notes

1. Drawings for insertion are normal AutoCAD files with the file extension ***.dwg**.
2. A drawing to be inserted as a block must be named without breaks appearing in the name. **NPN transistor** is wrong, but **NPN_transistor** is correct. Failure to observe this rule will result in a warning appearing in the **Insert** dialogue box.
3. Blocks usually come onto screen as entities (objects) in their own right, so they can be moved, scaled, rotated etc. as with any other object. They can however be exploded into their constituent objects if the **Explode** check box of the **Insert** dialogue box is set on (tick in check box).
4. If a number of blocks have been saved within a drawing, their names can be seen by *entering* block, as follows:

Command: *enter* block *right-click*
Block(s) to list <*>: *right-click*

And an **AutoCAD LT Text Window** appears carrying the names of all blocks within the drawing. An example is given in Fig. 11.13.

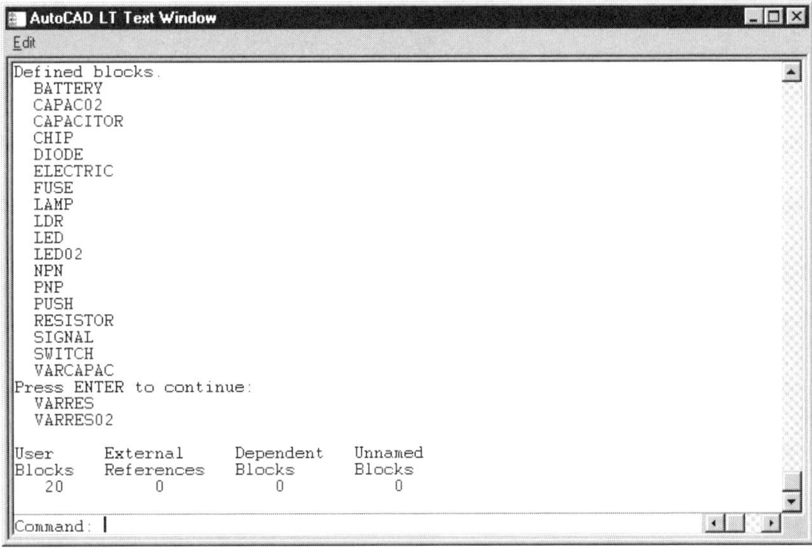

Fig. 11.13 The **AutoCAD LT Text Window** showing blocks held in the drawing Fig. 11.5

The Content Explorer

The **Content Explorer** is an LT 97 window from which blocks, drawings or Xrefs can be transferred quickly and easily into the drawing area of LT 97. More about Xrefs later. **Content Explorer** is a full Windows 95 window which, when in use, can be superimposed on top of the LT 97 window.

To call the **Content Explorer** to screen, either *left-click* on **Content Explorer...** in the **Insert** pull-down menu, *left-click* on the **Content Explorer** tool icon in the **Draw** toolbar, or *enter* content at the Command line. See Fig. 11.14. No matter which method is adopted, the **Content Explorer** window appears, an example of which is shown in Fig. 11.15. This is an example showing blocks of electronics symbols from a single LT 97 drawing file in a **Tree View**.

Fig. 11.14 Calling **Content Explorer**

Another example is given in Fig. 11.16. In this example, the **Tree View** is of the separate drawing in the **symbols** directory which contains separate drawing files, one for each symbol. It is this type

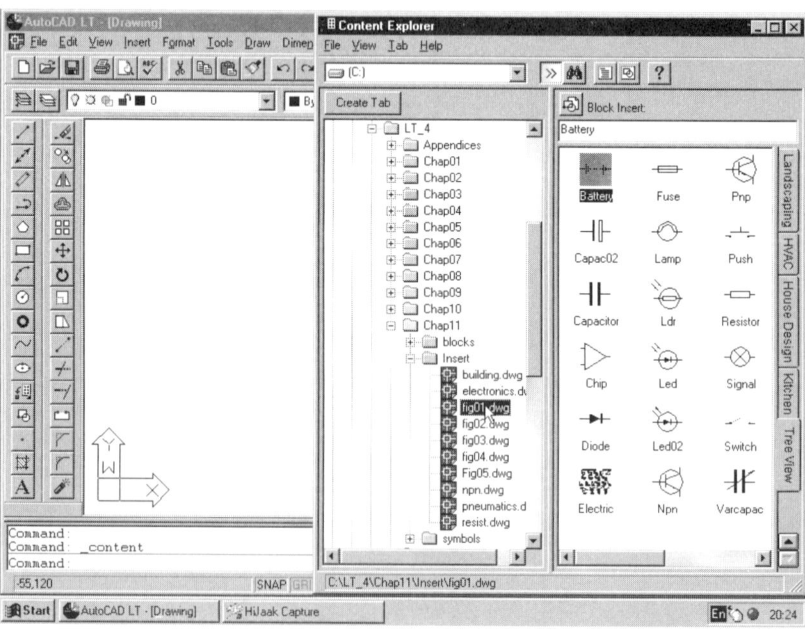

Fig. 11.15 The **Content Explorer** showing blocks in a drawing in a **Tree View**

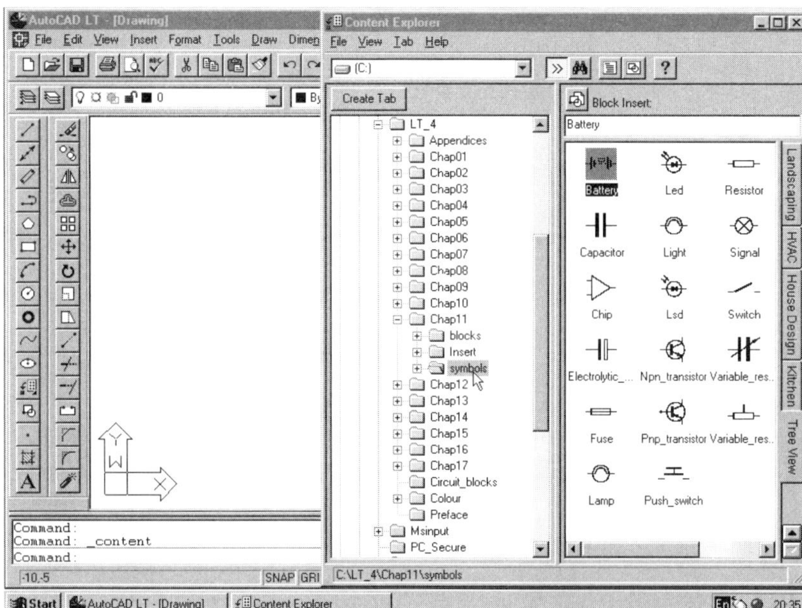

Fig. 11.16 The **Content Explorer** showing drawings from a directory in a **Tree View**

of directory from which drawings will be inserted into a current drawing.

Calling blocks or drawings from the Content Explorer

The left-hand part of the explorer is similar to the Windows 95 **Windows Explorer** in that directories from any disk in a computer can be shown and its files listed. When a file is selected, if it contains blocks, the blocks are shown in the right-hand half of the explorer as separate icons, with the names of the blocks, together with a single item showing the whole drawing. If a directory containing LT 97 drawing files is selected, the drawings in the directory are shown as icons, with the file names of the drawings.

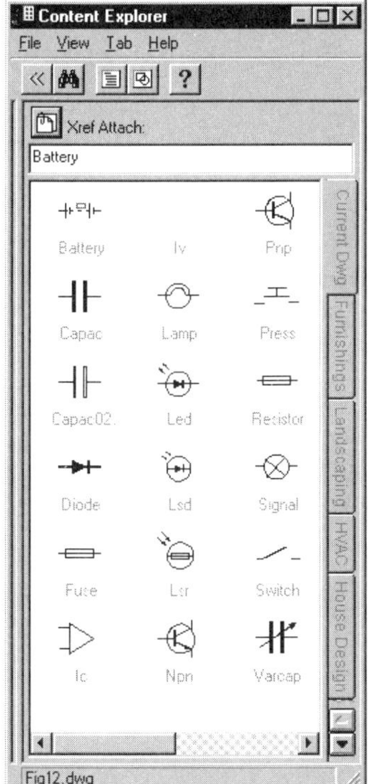

Fig. 11.17 The **Tree View** button

The tool icons in the Content Explorer

At the top right of the explorer window are five tool icons which are used as buttons to obtain the following effects:

Tree View: *Left-click* on the **Tree View** button. The icon changes to point to the right and the left-hand part of the explorer disappears and the icons representing the blocks which have been inserted in the current drawing are displayed (Fig. 11.17). *Left-click* on the button again and the icon points to the left and the right-hand part of the explorer reappears.

Find: *Left-click* on the **Find** button and the **AutoCAD LT Find** dialogue box appears in which a block or a drawing file can be found (Fig. 11.18).

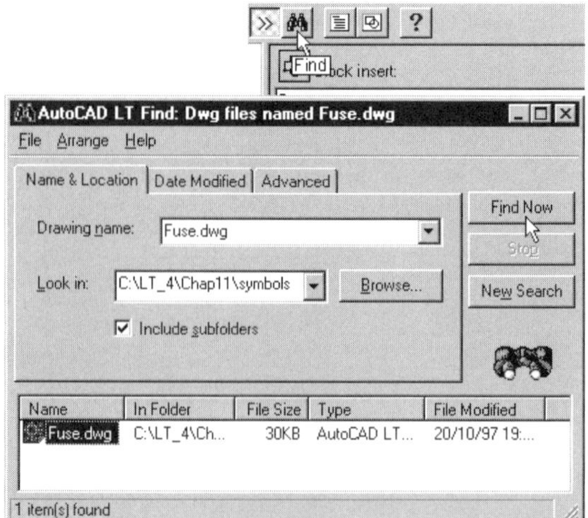

Fig. 11.18 *Left-click* on the **Find** button and the **AutoCAD LT Find** dialogue box appears

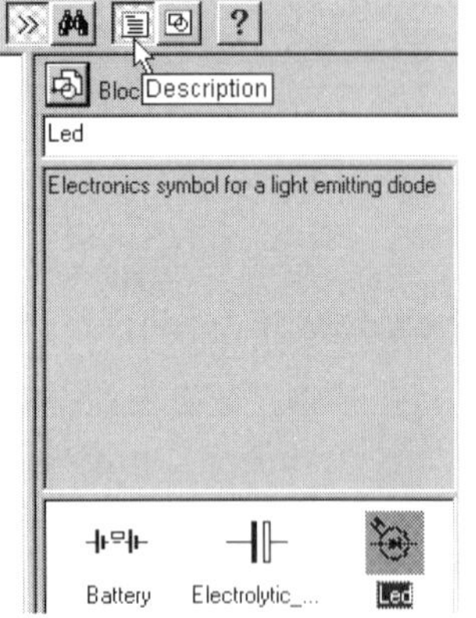

Fig. 11.19 The result of a *left-click* on the **Description** button

Description: *Left-click* on the **Description** button and the description of the selected block as *entered* in the **Description** box of the **Create Block** dialogue box when the block was created appears in a box just below the line of buttons (Fig. 11.19).

Preview: *Left-click* on the **Preview** button and a preview box opens showing an enlarged view of the block icon selected from those showing in the explorer (Fig. 11.20).

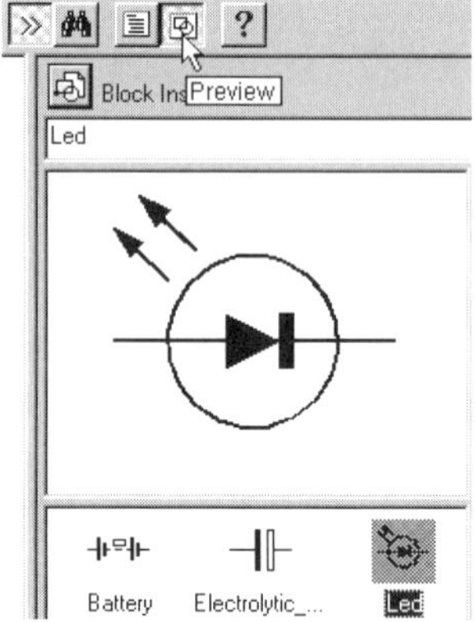

Fig. 11.20 The result of a *left-click* on the **Preview** button

?: A *left-click* on the **?** button and the **AutoCAD LT 97 Help System** window appears (Fig. 11.21).

Inserting blocks from the Content Explorer

To insert a drawing from the explorer:

1. Make sure the **Block Insert** icon is showing (Fig. 11.22). A *left-click* on this icon and it changes to **Xref Attach**.

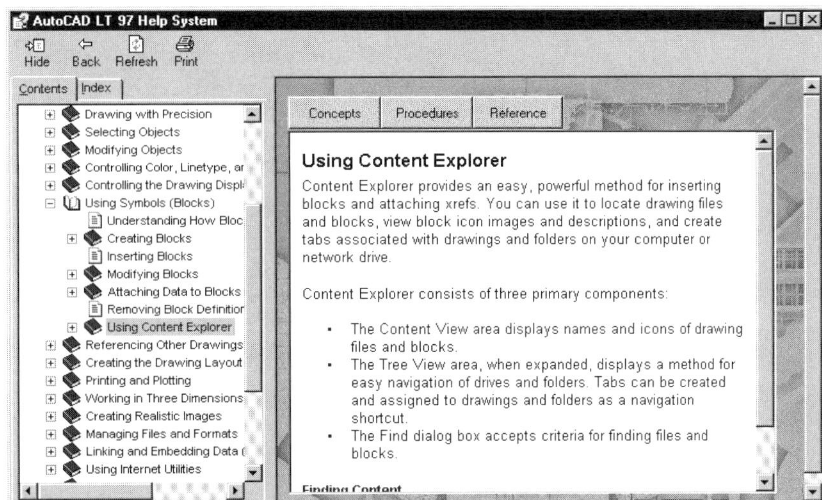

Fig. 11.21 The result of a *left-click* on the **?** button

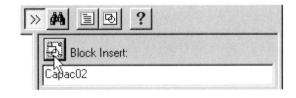

Fig. 11.22 Make sure the **Block Insert** icon is showing

Fig. 11.23 The icon for *dragging* a block into the current drawing

2. *Left-click* on the icon in the explorer which represents the block to be inserted. The LT 97 cursor changes to a circle with a bar icon Fig. 11.23).
3. *Drag* the icon into the drawing area. The explorer disappears. A ghosted version of the drawing appears in the LT drawing area and the Command line shows:

   Command:_xdrginsert
   Attach Xref CHIP: C:\LT_4\Chap11\symbols\Chip.dwg
   CHIP loaded
   Insertion point: *pick* or *enter* coordinates and *right-click*
   Command:

4. **OR:** *double-click* on the icon representing the drawing in the explorer. The explorer disappears and the drawing appears in the drawing area *dragged* at the cursor cross-hairs intersection. The Command line shows:

   Command:_xdrginsert
   Attach Xref CHIP: C:\LT_4\Chap11\symbols\Chip.dwg
   CHIP loaded
   Insertion point: *pick* or *enter* coordinates and *right-click*
   X scale factor <1>/Corner/XYZ: *right-click* or *enter* scale factor

Y scale factor (default = X): *right-click*
Rotation angle <0>: *right-click*
Command: *right-click*

And the explorer reappears.

Notes

There are several methods by which a block can be inserted into the current drawing:

1. From the **Content Explorer**.
2. By calling **ddinsert**.
3. By using the **Insert** tool.

The Content Explorer tabs

A number of tabs will be seen on the right-hand side of the explorer. The number of tabs depends upon how many types of symbols are available. When AutoCAD LT 97 is first loaded into a computer a large number of symbol drawings are loaded with the operational software. Symbols for Architectural, Furnishing, Landscaping, HVAC, House design and Kitchen design are included with the LT 97 software. To bring any of these groups of symbol drawings into the

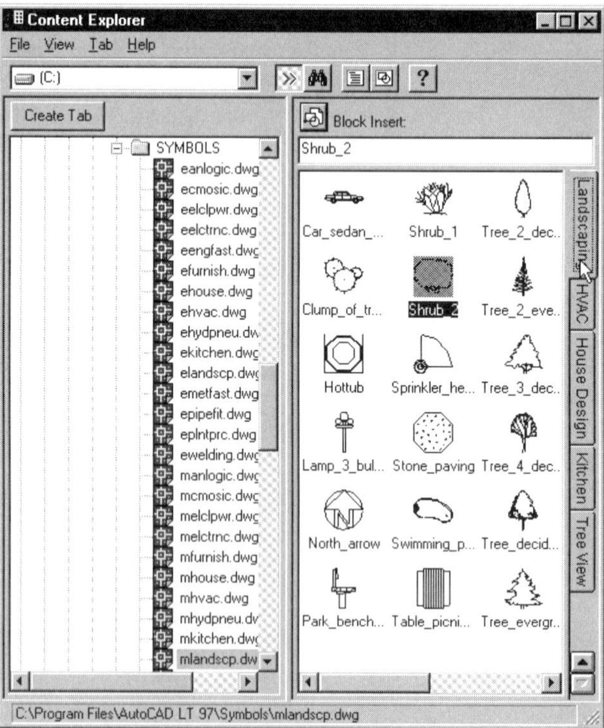

Fig. 11.24 Selecting the **Landscaping** tab

explorer, *left-click* on the tab carrying the name of the type of symbol required. The symbols automatically load into the explorer. Figure 11.24 shows some of the **Landscaping** symbols after a *left-click* on the appropriate tab.

Note that, at the same time, the directory carrying the names of the symbol drawings is automatically loaded into the left-hand part of the explorer window.

The pull-down menus

The explorer contains three pull-down menus, apart from a **Help** pull-down menu. The three pull-downs are shown in Fig. 11.25.

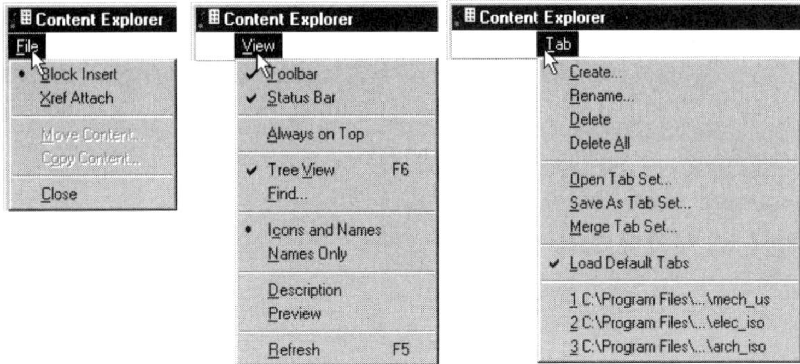

Fig. 11.25 The three pull-down menus of the explorer

External references

Drawings can be inserted into other drawings, or drawings can be opened as external references or **xrefs**. When xrefs are used, any changes in the original drawing are reflected in the drawing inserted or loaded as an xref. Xref is called either with a *left-click* on the **External Reference** tool icon in a flyout from the **Draw** toolbar, by a *left-click* on **External Reference...** from the **Insert** pull-down menu or by *entering* xref at the Command line (Fig. 11.26). No matter which method is used the **External Reference** dialogue box appears (Fig. 11.27).

Fig. 11.26 Calling **xref**

A *left-click* on the **Attach** button of the dialogue box brings the **Select file to attach** dialogue box on screen (Fig. 11.28).

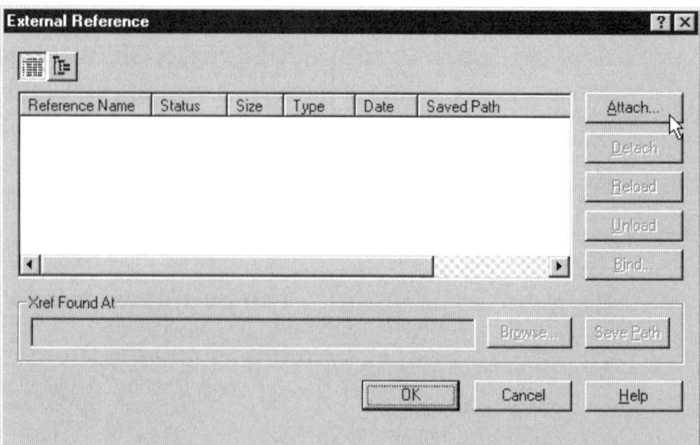

Fig. 11.27 The **External Reference** dialogue box

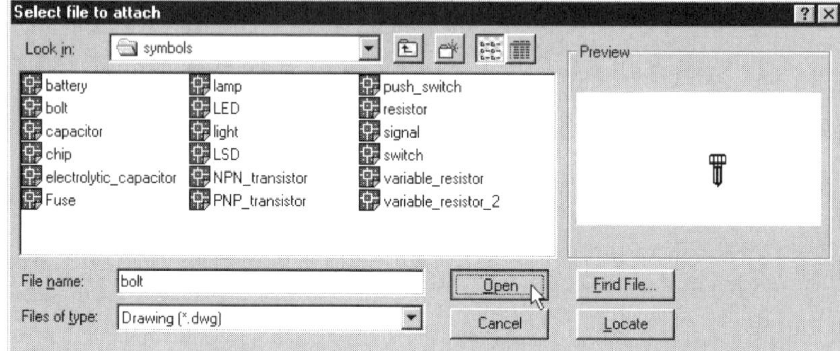

Fig. 11.28 The **Select file to attach** dialogue box

In the dialogue box, select the drawing **bolt** from the file list. *Left-click* on the **Open** button and the **Attach Xref** dialogue box comes on screen (Fig. 11.29) with the chosen drawing file's name in the **Xref Name** box.

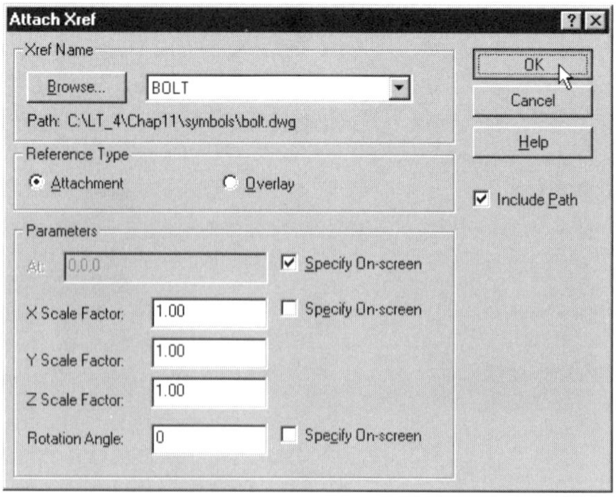

Fig. 11.29 The **Attach Xref** dialogue box

In this dialogue box, **X** and **Y** scale factors and rotation can be amended as when the **Insert** tool is used. *Left-click* on the **OK** button and the selected drawing appears on screen to be inserted into position within the current drawing as an **xref** (Fig. 11.30).

Figure 11.30 shows a sectional view through a component in which the bolts have been attached as **xrefs**.

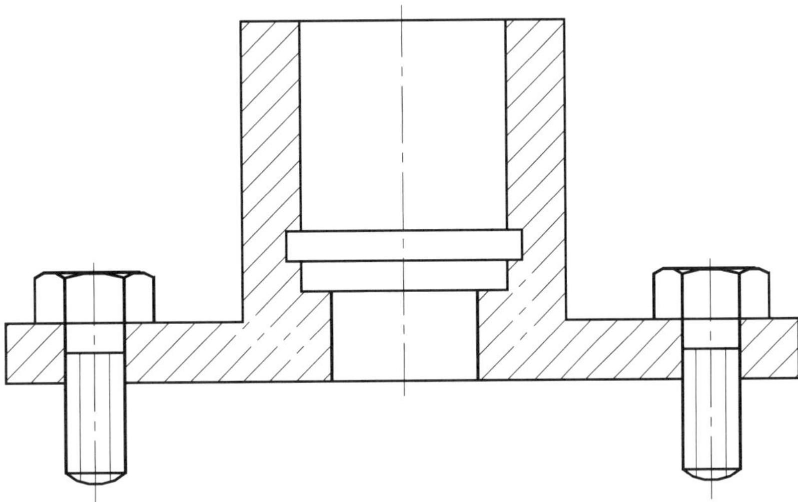

Fig. 11.30 A sectional view with bolts attached as **xrefs**

Figure 11.31 shows the same drawing after changes have been made to the drawing of the bolts which have been attached as **xrefs**. The changes in the bolt drawing are automatically changed in the original drawing in which the **xrefs** have been attached.

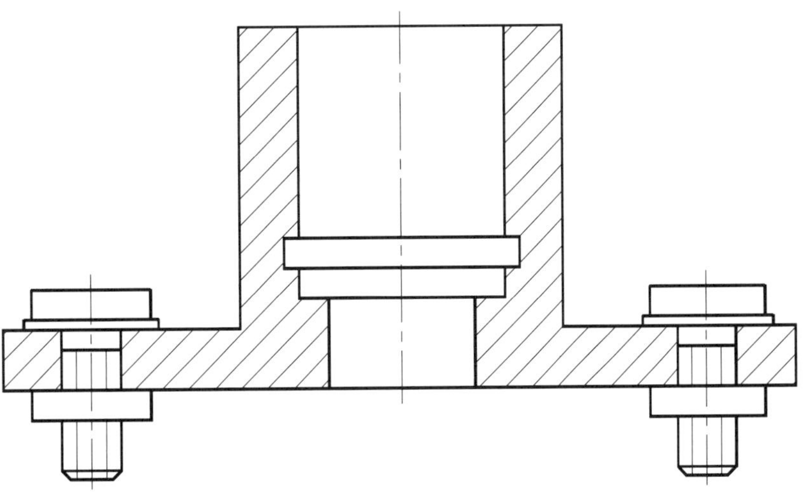

Fig. 11.31 Make changes in the bolts and the drawing changes

Notes

1. **Xrefs** cannot be exploded.
2. **Xrefs** can be removed from a drawing with a *left-click* on the **Detach** button appearing when an **xref** is selected from the **External Reference** dialogue box.
3. **Xrefs** are important in keeping design changes to a drawing up to date.
4. If the file name of a drawing being inserted as an **xref** is more than 8 characters in length, its name is automatically changed to a substitute name such as **XREF1**, **XREF2** etc. as indicated in Fig. 11.32.

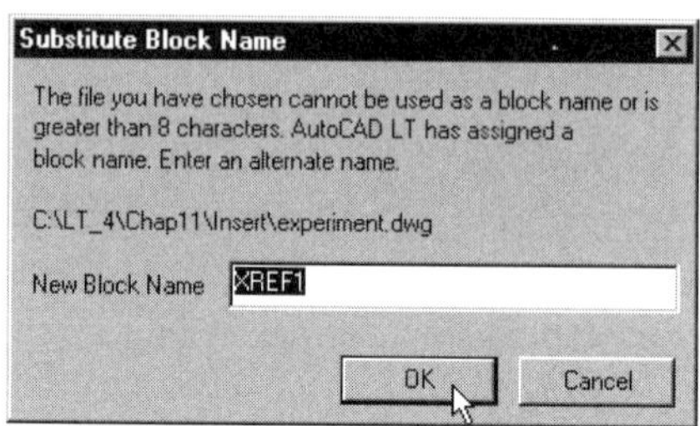

Fig. 11.32 The **Substitute Block Name** dialogue box

Questions

1. There are basically two types of blocks. Can you describe them and the differences between them?
2. What is meant by a library of symbols when using CAD software?
3. What is the difference between inserting a block and attaching an external reference to a drawing?
4. The Content Explorer can be used to insert blocks or to attach **xrefs**. When using the Content Explorer, what action must be taken to ensure that a drawing is inserted as a block or attached as an external reference?
5. Blocks can be exploded. Can **xrefs** be exploded?
6. What is meant by a **Tab** in connection with the Content Explorer?
7. What is the **Tree View** in the Content Explorer?
8. What are the differences between inserting a block and attaching an **xref**?
9. What happens if an LT 97 file with a name 15 characters long is attached as an **xref** to another drawing?
10. If an **xref** has been attached to a drawing by mistake, how can it be deleted from the drawing?

Exercises

1. Construct symbols from those given in Fig. 11.5 (page 173) and by insertion of the symbols you have constructed as blocks construct the circuit diagram represented by Fig. 11.33.

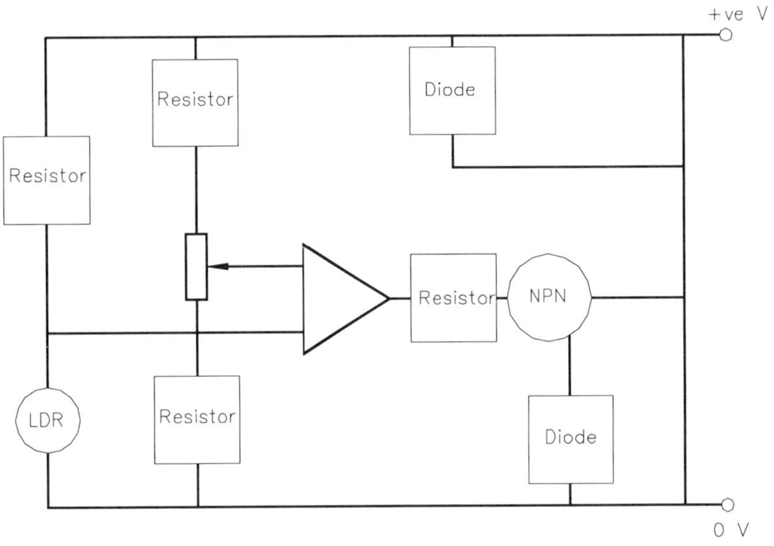

Fig. 11.33 Exercise 1

2. Figure 11.34 is a representative diagram for an electronics siren circuit. Using the symbol drawings constructed for Exercise 1, replace the numbered parts of Fig. 11.34 by the correct symbols in order to produce the correct circuit diagram.

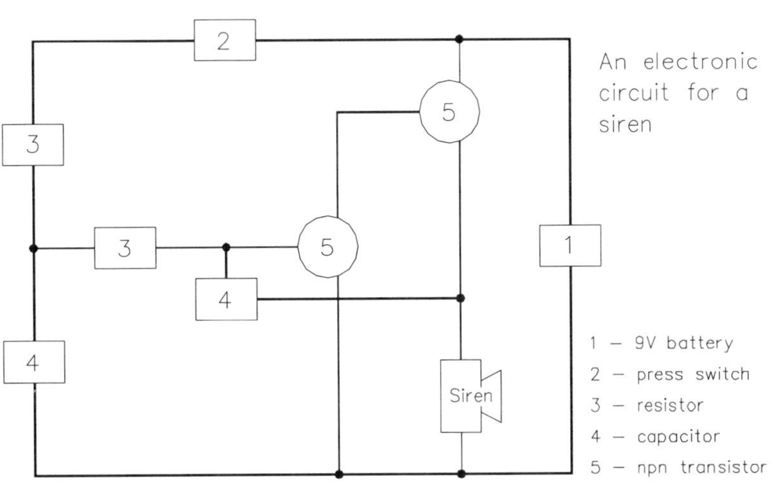

Fig. 11.34 Exercise 2

3. Figure 11.35 shows a two-view orthographic projection in third angle which includes two **xrefs** – the plugs in the holes around the flange and the spindle running centrally through the flange.

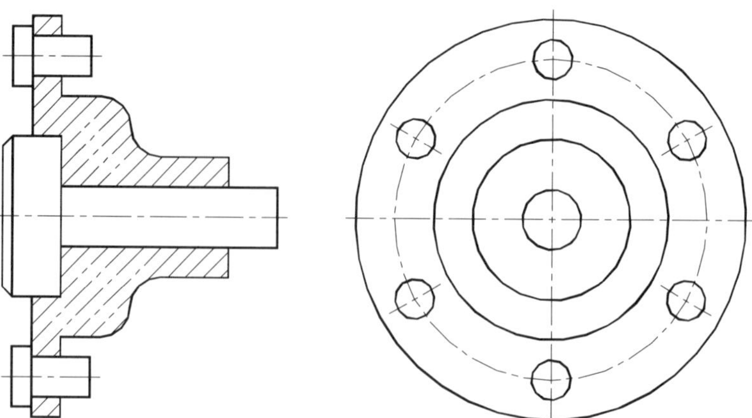

Fig. 11.35 The original drawing for Exercise 3

Figure 11.36 shows the same orthographic projection after changes have been made to the two **xrefs**.

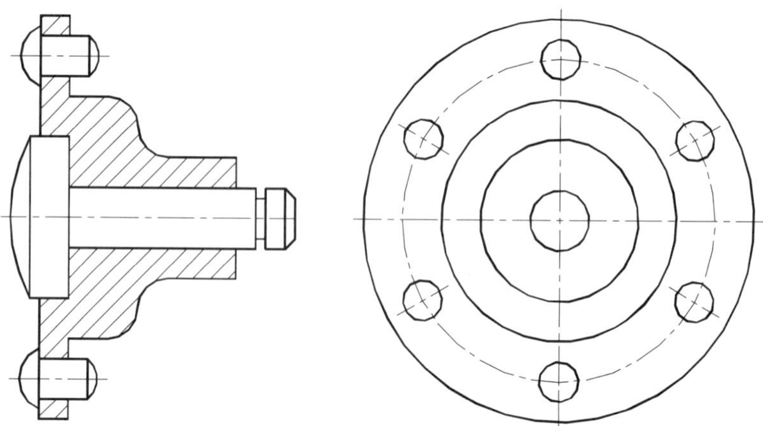

Fig. 11.36 Exercise 3

(a) Working to any suitable sizes of your own choice, construct the sectional view of Fig. 11.35 and then save your drawing. Construct two further drawings, one of the bolt, the second of the spindle. Then attach them in position into the main drawing as **xrefs**.
(b) Go back to the drawings of the bolt and of the spindle and amend their outlines to correspond to that shown in Fig. 11.36.
(c) Now reload the original drawing and note that the bolts and the spindle have automatically changed to the amended outlines.

4. Construct the drawing Fig. 11.37 in two parts.
   (a) First construct the two views of the clamp.
   (b) Save the drawing.
   (c) Construct a separate drawing of the bolt.
   (d) Save the bolt drawing.
   (e) Reload the two-view drawing of the clamp and attach the bolt drawing in position as an **xref**.
   (f) Save the new drawing.
   (g) Reload the bolt drawing and amend it as shown in Fig. 11.38. Then save the amended drawing to the same file name.
   (h) Reload the drawing which includes the **xref**. It should show the changes made to the drawing of the bolt (Fig. 11.38).

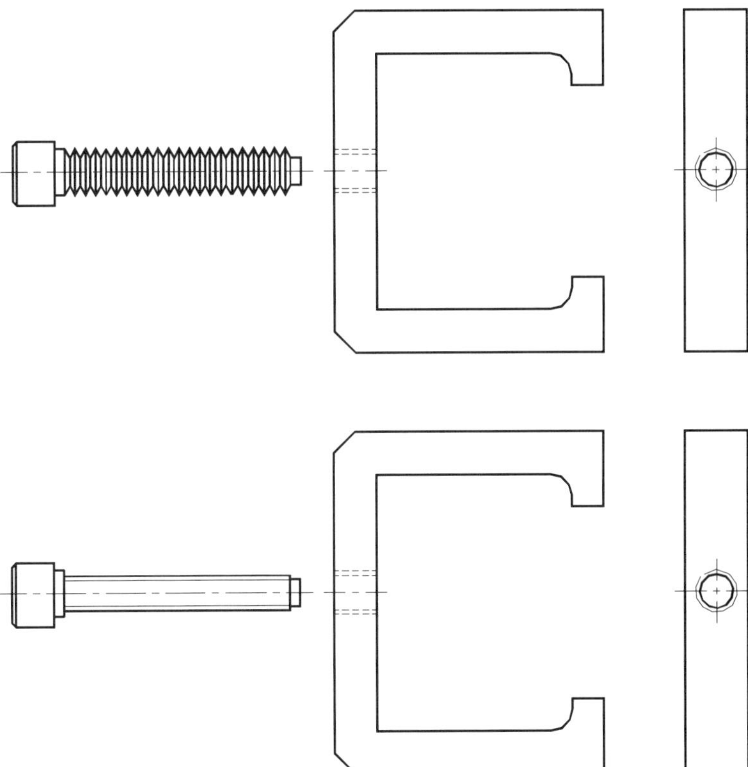

Fig. 11.37 The original drawing for Exercise 4

Fig. 11.38 Exercise 4

5. Figure 11.38 shows four separate drawings, each saved to a separate distinct file name.
   (a) Construct a drawing similar to the top left drawing of Fig. 11.39. Use any suitable text and any suitable border.
   (b) Save the drawing.

(c) Load a new template drawing and attach the text in its outline as an **xref**. Save this new drawing to another file name distinct from that used for the **xref**.

(d) Reload the original drawing and make changes to its text or/ and its outline frame.

(e) Reload the drawing containing the **xref** and note that it has changed.

(f) Repeat by changing the **xref** drawing and noting the changes in the drawing containing the **xref**.

Figure 11.39 shows the results in its four drawings of several changes to the **xref** drawing file.

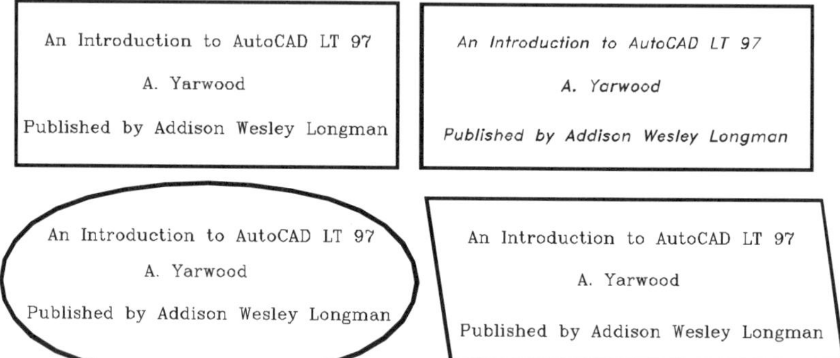

Fig. 11.39 Exercise 5

CHAPTER 12

Other modifying tools

The command Purge

Blocks within drawings inevitably take up some disk space. The space they occupy in a drawing can be deleted with the aid of the command **Purge**. Taking as an example the electronics circuit diagram Fig. 11.12 (page 176):

Command: *enter* purge *right-click*
Purge unused Blocks/Dimstyles/LAyers/LTypes/STyles/All: *enter* a (for All) *right-click*
Purge block DIODE <N>: *enter* y (for Yes) *right-click*
Purge block FUSE <N>: *enter* y (for Yes) *right-click*
Purge block CHIP<N>: *enter* y (for Yes) *right-click*
Purge block LAMP<N>: *enter* y (for Yes) *right-click*

and so on until all unwanted parts are purged. Then:

No unreferenced text styles found
No unreferenced shape file found
No unreferenced dimensions styles found
Command:

In the example given (Fig. 11.12) nearly 3 kilobytes of disk space was saved by purging all the blocks. Other features could have also been purged if thought necessary.

Purge can be used at any time during a drawing session. A second and even a third purging may be needed before all unwanted parts of a drawing file data have been completely purged.

Attributes

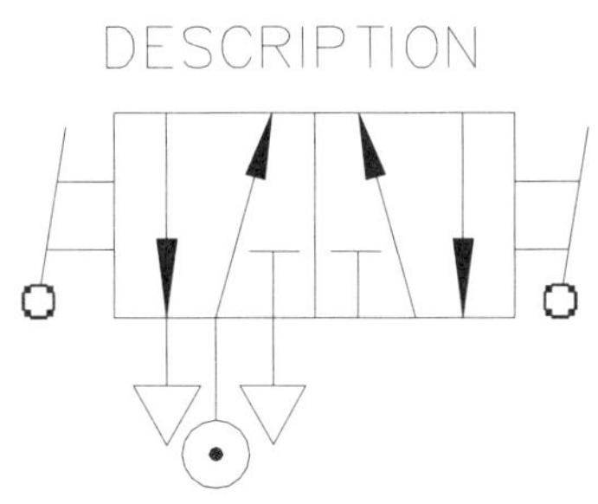

Fig. 12.1 A pneumatics symbol drawing with an **Attribute** tag

Construct the pneumatics symbol drawing Fig. 12.1. Then *enter* ddattdef at the Command line. The **Attribute Definition** dialogue box appears (Fig. 12.2). In the **Attribute Tag** box *enter* description and in the **Attribute Prompt** box *enter* describe. *Left-click* on the **Pick Point<** button, followed by the *picking* of a point just above the

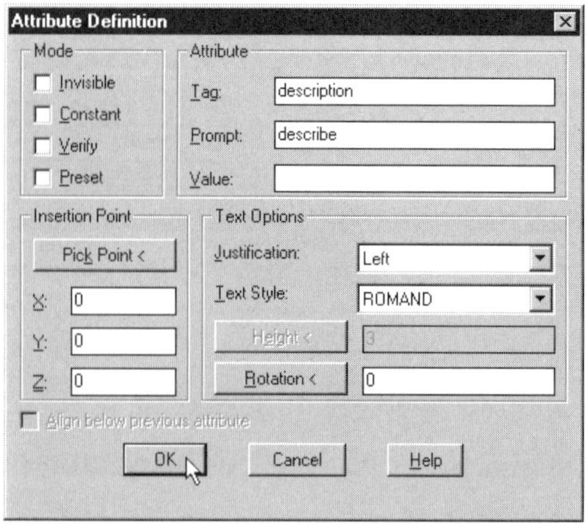

Fig. 12.2 The **Attribute Definition** dialogue box

pneumatics symbol drawing. The **Attributes Definition** box reappears. *Left-click* on the **OK** button. The word DESCRIPTION (in capital letters) appears above the symbol. Save the symbol and its attribute (DESCRIPTION) as a drawing file. Then when the symbol is required in another drawing as a block:

Command: *enter* i (Insert) *right-click*
In the **Insert** dialogue box select the symbol file (with its attribute)
Insertion point: *pick* **X scale factor <1>:** *right-click*
Y scale factor (default=X): *right-click*
Rotation angle <0>: *right-click*
Enter attribute values
describe: *enter* 5_port02 *right-click*
Command:

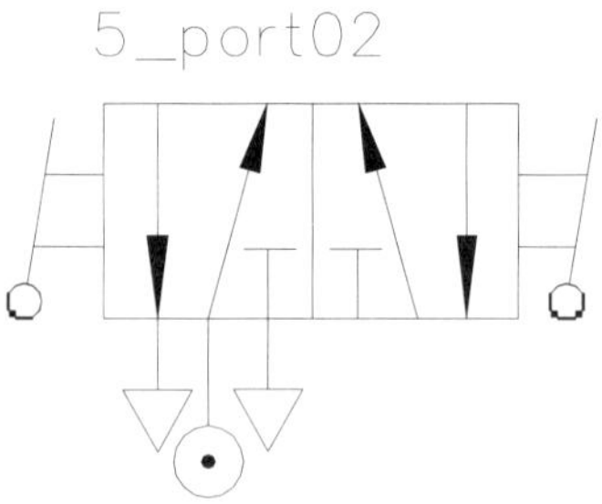

Fig. 12.3 The symbol inserted into a drawing with its description included as an attribute

Note that the prompt **describe:** is that which was entered in the **Attribute Prompt** box of the **Attribute Definition** dialogue box. The resulting attribute 5_port02 appears in its correct position – Fig. 12.3.

Another example of attributes

Figure 12.4 shows another example of the addition of attributes to a block inserted several times into a drawing. In this example two tags and prompts – **Student's name** and **Student's group number** – were included with the block of the rectangle of the desk positions of the students.

Other attributes could have been included in this example such as the student's address, home telephone number, college tutor etc. Each attribute will need to be entered in separate **Attribute Definition** dialogue boxes and, if the **Align below previous attribute** box is checked, the attributes will line up one below the other. Each attribute will have its own prompt appearing in turn one after the other in the command prompt sequence at the command line.

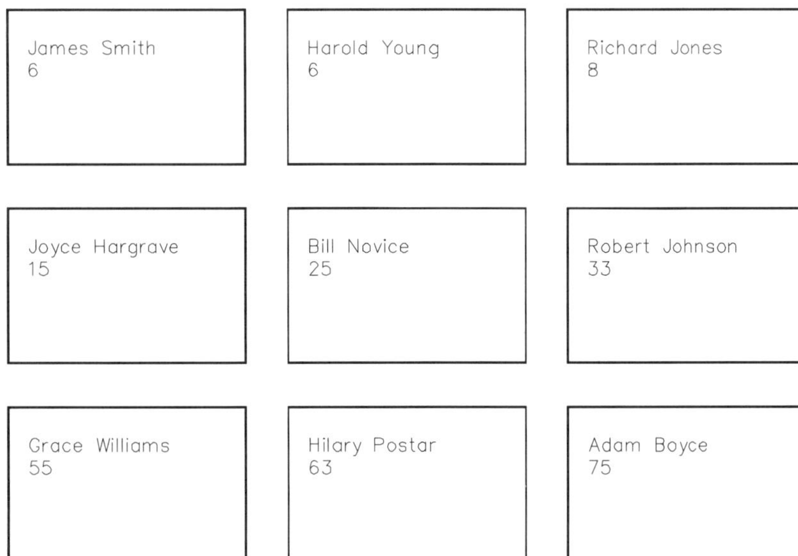

Fig. 12.4 An example of repeated insertion of attributes

The Modify II toolbar

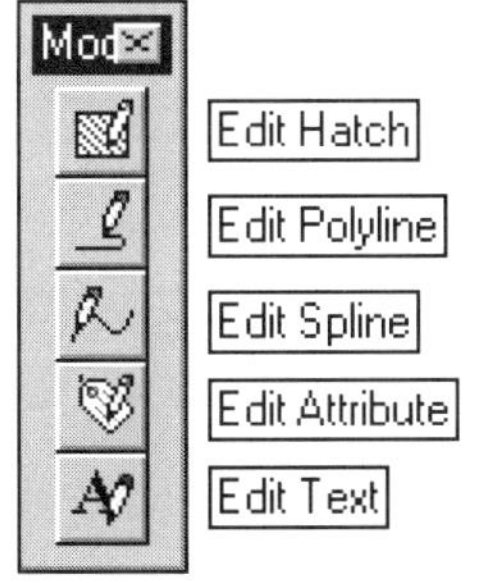

Fig. 12.5 The **Modify II** toolbar

Right-click in a part of any toolbar on screen and from the **Toolbars** dialogue box which then appears, select the **Modify II** toolbar. Figure 12.5 shows not only the toolbar as it appears on screen, but also the names of the tools in the toolbar.

The Edit Attribute tool

Taking the **Edit Attribute** tool first because attributes have been briefly described above, either *left-click* on the tool icon, or at the Command line:

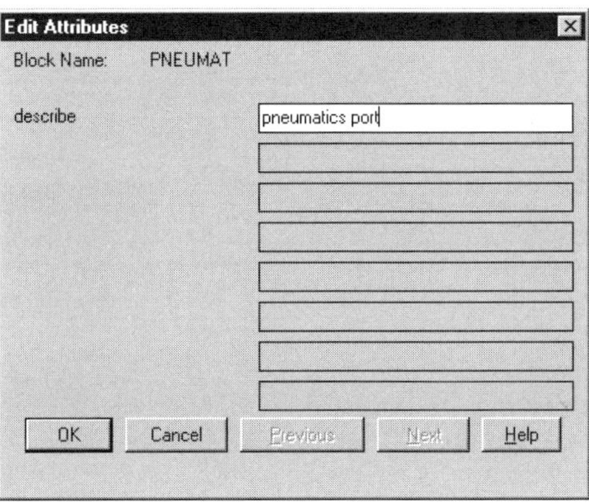

Fig. 12.6 The **Edit Attribute** dialogue box with a new name *entered* in the **describe** box

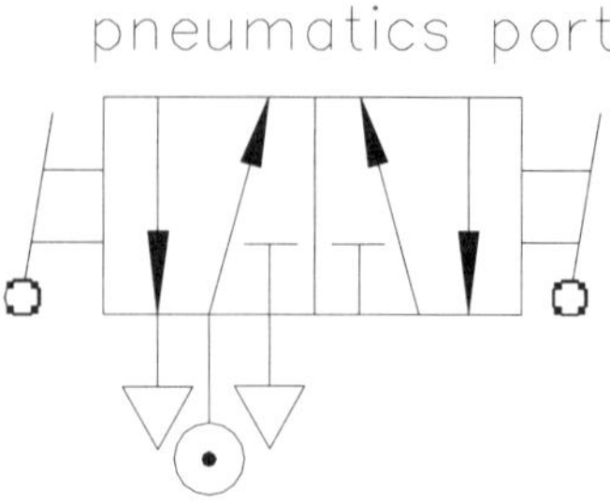

Fig. 12.7 The edited attribute as it appears on the drawing

Command: *enter* ddatte *right-click*

Select block: *pick* the drawing of the symbol with the attribute **5_port02** (Fig. 12.3). The **Edit Attribute** dialogue box appears (Fig. 12.6). In the **describe** box of the dialogue box, the attribute **5_port02** will be seen. Change this to say **pneumatic port** and *left-click* on the **OK** button. The attribute on the drawing changes to what has been *entered* in the **describe** box (Fig. 12.7).

Command:

Note Attributes connected with a block within a drawing cannot be edited unless they have been exploded into their constituent parts, either by using the **Explode** tool, either from the **Modify** toolbar (Fig. 12.8), or by *entering* x at the Command line and then *picking* the unexploded block.

Fig. 12.8 The **Explode** tool from the **Modify** toolbar

The Edit Hatch tool

With drawing Fig. 11.35 on screen, *left-click* on the **Edit Hatch** tool or *enter* hatchedit at the Command line. The Command window shows:

Command: _hatchedit

Select hatch object: *pick* the hatched area of the sectional view which has been hatched with the **ANSI31** pattern. The **Hatch Edit** dialogue box appears on screen. In the **Hatch Edit** dialogue box, *left-click* on the **Pattern...** button and from the resulting **Hatch pattern** dialogue box, select the **ANSI32** pattern. Then

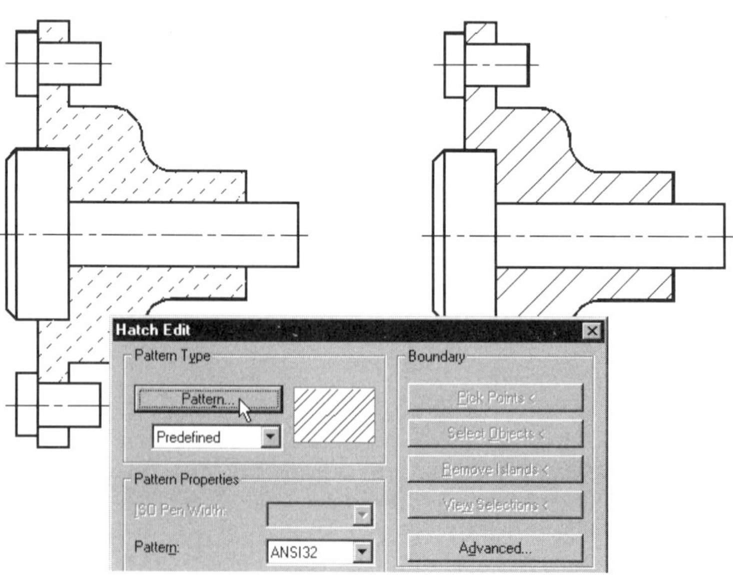

Fig. 12.9 An example of the use of the **Edit Hatch** tool

Left-click on the **Preview** button to check that the hatching has been edited as required and if satisfied, *left-click* on the **Apply** button.

Command:

Figure 12.9 shows the original sectional view and the resulting hatch editing.

The Edit Polyline tool

Either select the **Edit Polyline** tool from the **Modify** toolbar, or *enter* pe at the Command line. The Command window then shows:

Command:_pedit Select polyline: *pick* the polyline to be edited
Open/Join/Width/Edit vertex/Fit/Spline/Decurve/Ltype gen/Undo/eXit <X>: *enter* the initial letter of one of the editing prompts and respond to the further prompts as they appear

Figure 12.10 shows examples of the results of editing in response to some of the prompts from the **Edit Polyline** sequence.

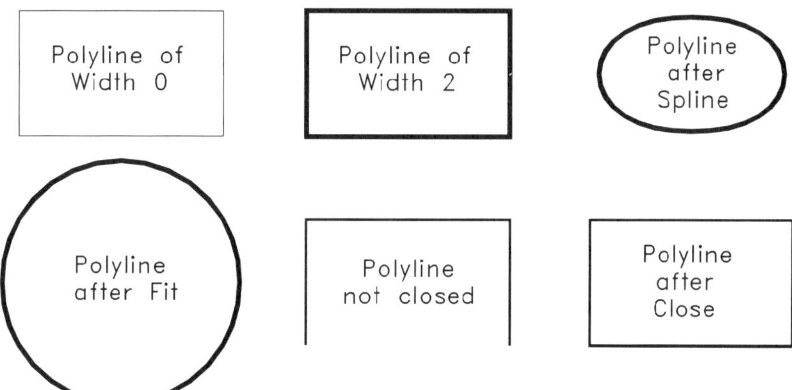

Fig. 12.10 Examples of the use of **Edit Polyline**

The Edit Spline tool

Select the **Edit Spline** tool or *enter* splinedit at the Command Line. The Command window then shows:

Command:_splinedit
Select spline: *pick* the spline to be edited
Fit/Data/Close/Move Vertex/Refine/rEverse/Undo/eXit <X>:

enter the initial letter of the required prompt and then respond to the prompts which follow.

Figure 12.11 shows two of the results of responding to the prompts of the **Edit Spline** prompts sequence.

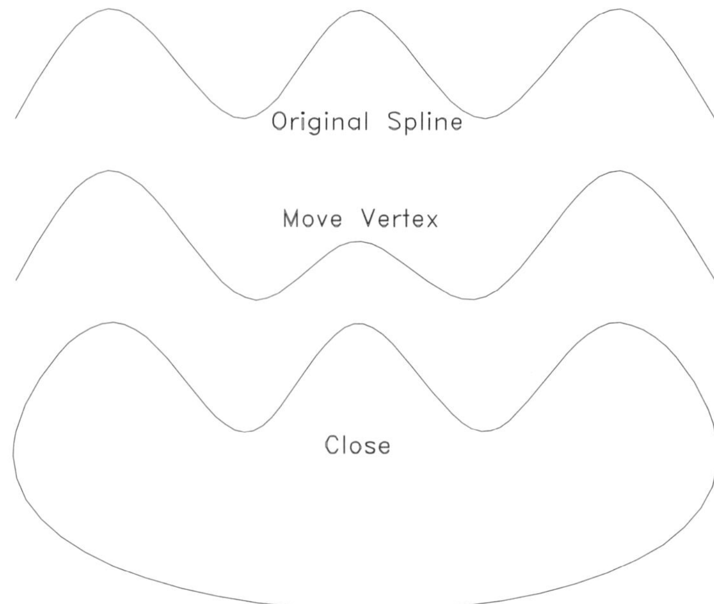

Fig. 12.11 Some examples of the use of **Edit Spline**

The Edit Text tool

Either select the **Edit Text** tool from the **Modify II** toolbar, or *enter* ddedit at the Command line. The Command window then shows:

Command:_ddedit
<Select an annotation object>/Undo: *pick* the text to be edited. The **Edit Text** dialogue box appears with the line of selected text showing in its **Text:** box. Change any letters that need changing and *left-click* on the **OK** button of the dialogue box. The edited text appears in place of the original text (Fig. 12.12).

This is texst to be edited

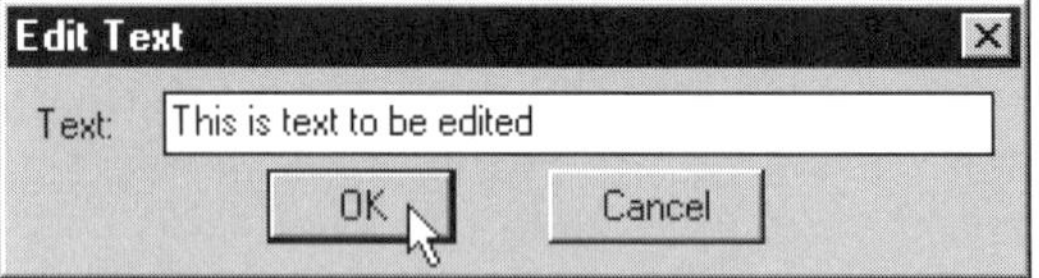

This is text to be edited

Fig. 12.12 The **Edit Text** dialogue box

Grips

Select **Grips...** from the **Tools** pull-down menu (Fig. 12.13). If the **Enable Grips** check box is set in the **Grips** dialogue box (Fig. 12.14),

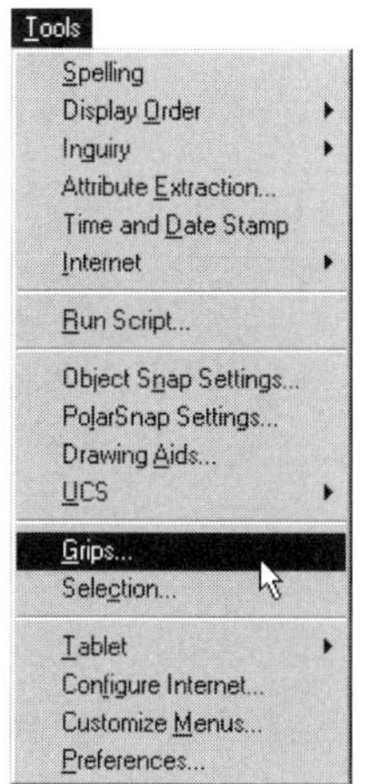

Fig. 12.13 Select **Grips...** from the **Tools** pull-down menu

grip boxes appear whenever an entity is selected without a command being in action. **Grips** allow the use of the tools **STRETCH**, **MOVE**, **ROTATE**, **SCALE** and **MIRROR** without having to call them in any way.

There are two types of **Grip** boxes – **Unselected**, which usually appears in a blue colour, and **Selected**, which usually appears in red. To use **Grips**, first make sure the **Enable Grips** check box is checked, then *left-click* on the entity to be modified. Blue grip boxes appear around the entity, which also highlights (Fig. 12.15). *Left-click* on the grip box to be used as a base point. It becomes a **Selected** box and turns red. The command line changes to:

****STRETCH****

with a corresponding series of stretch prompts. A *right-click* and the command line changes to:

****MOVE****

with another series of move prompts. *Right-click* again.

****ROTATE****

appears with its set of prompts. This continues with ****SCALE**** and ****MIRROR****. The operator decides which of these modify tools he/she wishes to use. The results of some of these **Grips** modifications are shown in Fig. 12.16.

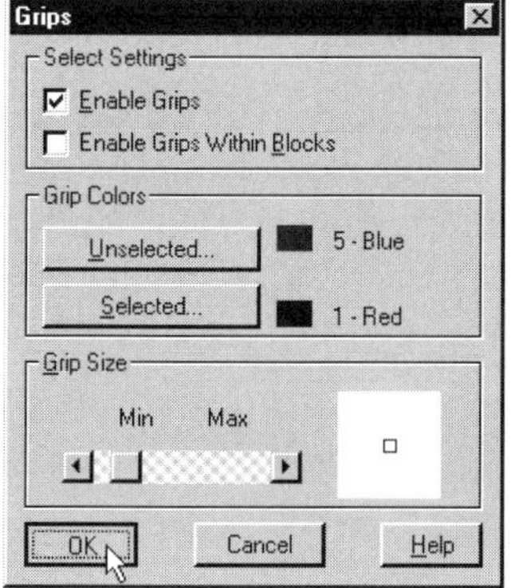

Fig. 12.14 The **Grips** dialogue box with **Enable Grips** set on

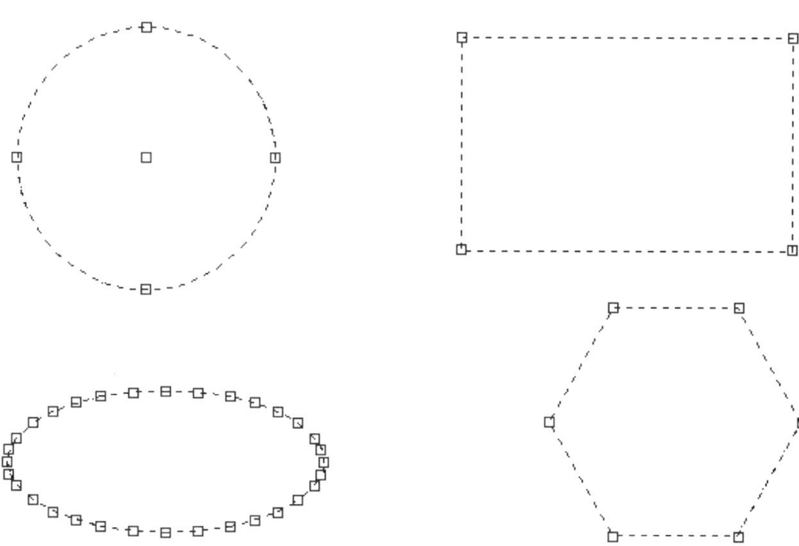

Fig. 12.15 Grips appears whenever an object is selected without a tool being called

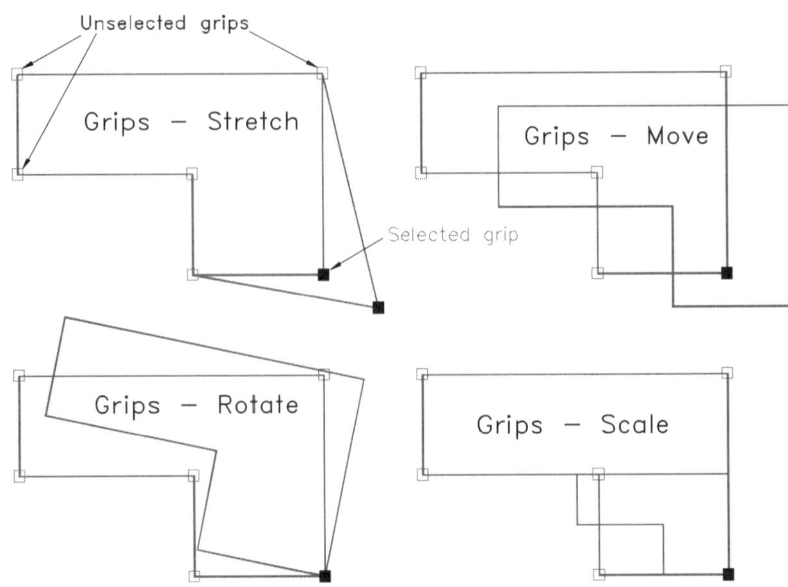

Fig. 12.16 The effects of using **Grips**

Undo, Redo, Redraw and Regen tools

These four tools are in fairly constant use when constructing drawings in LT 97. The four tools are called either by selection from the **Edit** or **View** pull-down menus (Fig. 12.17), or by *entering* u (for **Undo**),

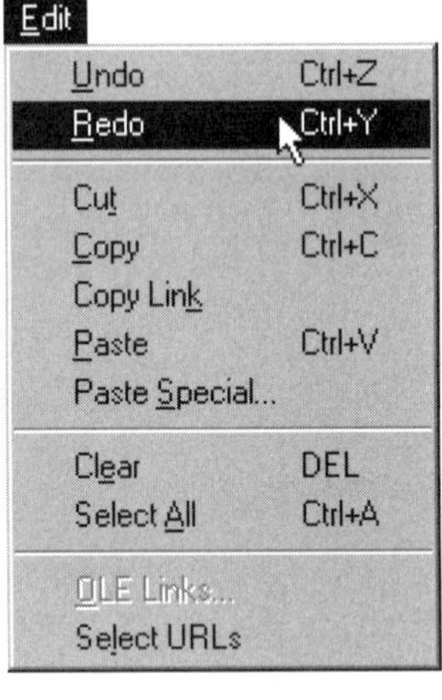

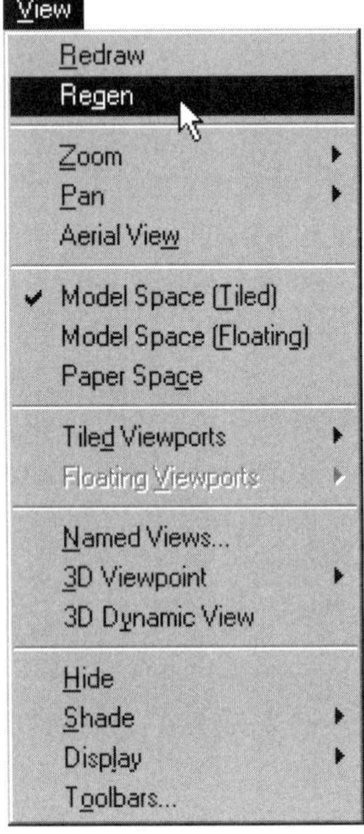

Fig. 12.17 The **Edit** and **View** pull-down menus

redo, r (for **Redraw**) or re (for **Regen**). The four tools have the following action:

Undo: Undoes the last tool action. Repeated use of u (for Undo) will eventually undo everything in a drawing which has been added during the current drawing session.
Redo: Undoes the action of **Undo**, but only the one last undo. Redo cannot be used repeatedly as can Undo.
Redraw: Redraws the screen in its entirety.
Regen: Regenerates the viewport currently in use. See Chapter 14 for details of viewports.

Questions

1. What is the purpose of the **Purge** tool?
2. How can the wording of an attribute be changed?
3. If a wrong hatch pattern has been selected when applying hatching to a drawing, how can the mistake be remedied?
4. When using **Grips** how many commands can be used before quitting from the command sequence?
5. What are the Command line abbreviations for Undo, Redo, Regen and Redraw?

Exercises

1. (a) Working to any convenient dimensions construct the outline of the rivet shown in the top left-hand drawing of Fig. 12.18.

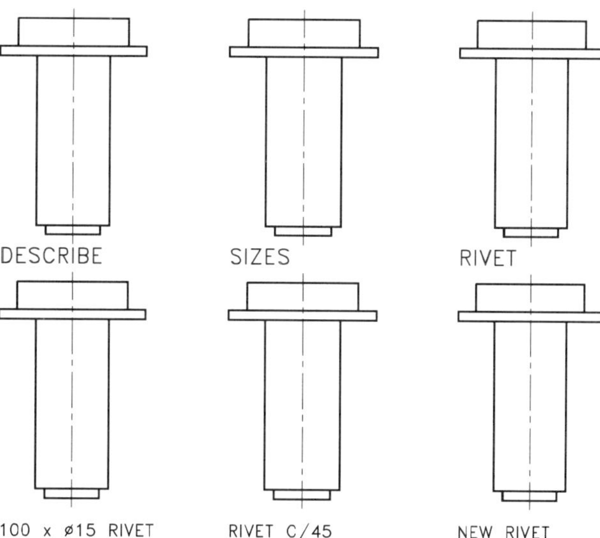

Fig. 12.18 Exercise 1

(b) Save your drawing and **Insert** it into a new drawing.
(c) Using the **ddattdef** command add the attribute **DESCRIBE**.
(d) Using the **Edit Attribute** tool edit the attribute as shown in the drawing below that with the attribute **DESCRIBE**.
(e) Repeat the exercise using the centre to right top drawings, editing the attributes to those shown in the bottom line of drawings.

2. Figure 12.19.
(a) Draw pline **1** of Width **0**. Using **Edit Polyline** edit its Width to **4**.
(b) Draw pline **2** of Width **0**. Edit the polyline to Width **2**.
(c) Draw the circle **3** using a pline of Width **1**. Use the **Arc** prompt of the **Polyline** tool, following the hints given with Drawing **3** of Fig. 12.19.
(d) Draw pline **4**. Edit the pline to a **Spline**.
(e) Draw pline **5**. With **Edit Polyline** and using the **Close** prompt, close the rectangle.
(f) Draw the pline **6**.

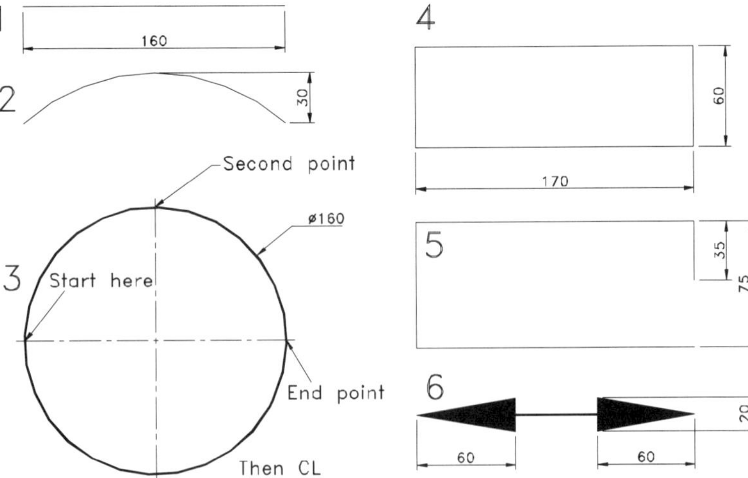

Fig. 12.19 Exercise 2

3. Construct nine rectangles of any convenient dimensions as shown in Fig. 12.20, using suitable scales for the patterns. Hatch each rectangle with the patterns named within the rectangles.
Using the **Edit Hatch** tool, edit each of the hatch patterns as follows, taking care that suitable scales for each pattern are *entered* in the **Boundary Hatch** dialogue box:

ANGLE to **ANSI37**.
ANSI31 to **AR-B816**.

AR-PARQ1 to **AR-BRELM**.
AR-SHAKE to **AR-BRSTD**.
AR-SAND to **EARTH**.
HONEY to **GRATE**.
HEX to **INSUL**.
NET to **NET3**.
STARS to **TRIANG**.

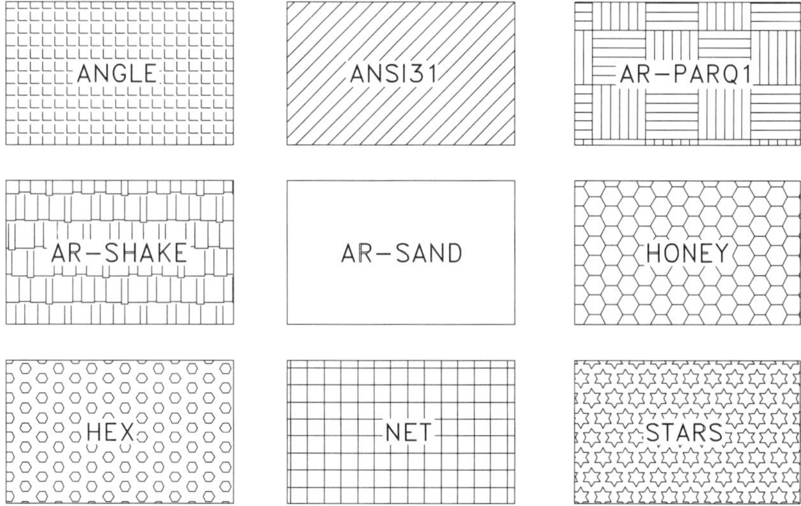

Fig. 12.20 Exercise 3

4. Construct two splines as shown in Fig. 12.21. Then using the **Edit Spline** tool practise using the various prompts in the **Edit Spline** sequence to edit the splines.

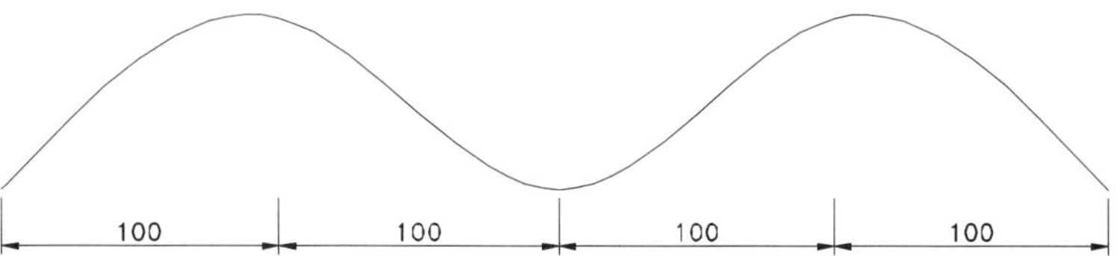

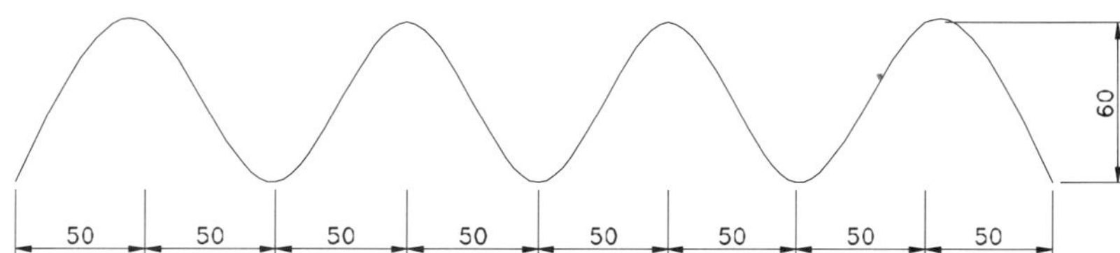

Fig. 12.21 Exercise 4

CHAPTER 13

Importing and exporting files

Types of files

AutoCAD LT 97 can make use of a number of different types of file formats. Those most likely to be used are:

The AutoCAD drawing file: This has the extension ***.dwg**. LT 97 can save AutoCAD drawing files in AutoCAD R14, R13 or R12 formats, or in LT R2 or LT R3 formats.

The AutoCAD LT template file: This has the extension ***.dwt**. LT 97 can save template files in either LT 97 or in LT R3 formats.

Windows Metafiles: These have the extension ***.wmf**. These are a mix of raster type and vector type data. Raster type data includes the data of pixels showing in a graphic image. Vector type data includes the geometrical data of features such as lines. Thus a ***.wmf** file will produce a graphic image of an AutoCAD LT drawing which is a true representation of objects such as lines, arcs, plines, circles, etc.

Bitmap files: These have the extension ***.bmp**. Bitmap files contain only raster type data and the graphic images from ***.bmp** files do not truly represent AutoCAD drawings.

Data eXchange Files: These have the extension ***.dxf**. These files allow the saving of drawing files from most CAD software systems to be loaded into most other CAD systems. This format was originated by Autodesk, but has been universally accepted as the standard for the exchange of drawing files between CAD systems. LT 97 can save **DXF** files in either AutoCAD R14, R13 or R12 formats as well as in LT R2 or LT R3 formats.

Encapsulated Postscript files: These have the extension ***.eps**. These files can be saved in AutoCAD LT 97 and loaded into documents produced by other applications. They will, however, only print to Postscript type printers.

Drawing Web Format files: These have the extension ***.dwf**. These files are for publishing or downloading drawings from the Internet using a Web Browser. They have the advantage that they do not require LT 97 to be running for the DWT drawings to be downloaded.

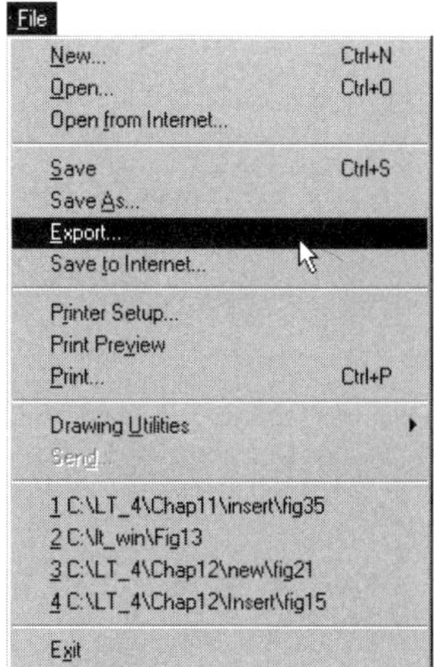

Fig. 13.1 The **File** pull-down menu

Saving, Exporting and Importing files

Saving files

Left-click on **Save As...** from the **File** pull-down menu (Fig. 13.1). The **Save Drawing As** dialogue box appears (Fig. 13.2). *Left-click* in the **Save as type:** box and the popup menu which then appears shows the type of files to which the current drawing on screen can be saved.

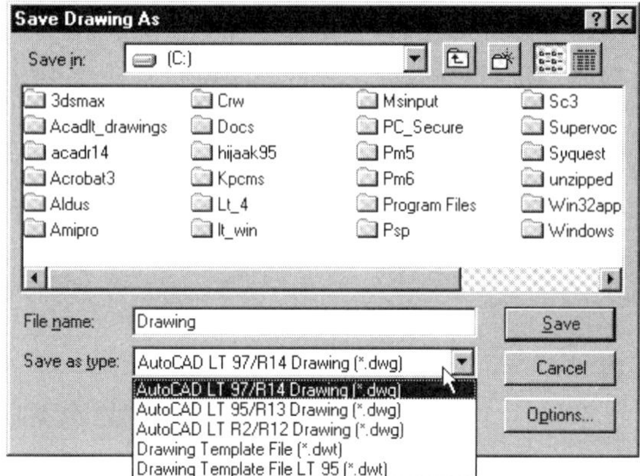

Fig. 13.2 The **Save Drawing As** dialogue box

Exporting files

Left-click on **Export...** in the **File** pull-down menu and the **Export Data** dialogue box appears. A *left-click* in its **Save as type:** box brings up a popup list showing the types of file which can be exported.

To import a DXF file use *enter* dxfin at the Command line.

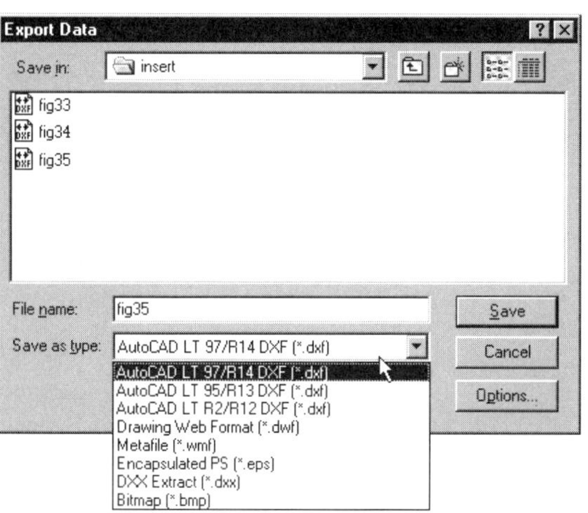

Fig. 13.3 The **Export Data** dialogue box

Importing files

Either *left-click* on **Open File...** from the **File** pull-down menu, which brings the **Select File** dialogue box on screen (Fig. 13.4) or *enter* import at the Command line, which brings the **Import File** dialogue box on screen. It can be seen from the popup menus associated with these two dialogue boxes the types of files which can be imported into LT 97.

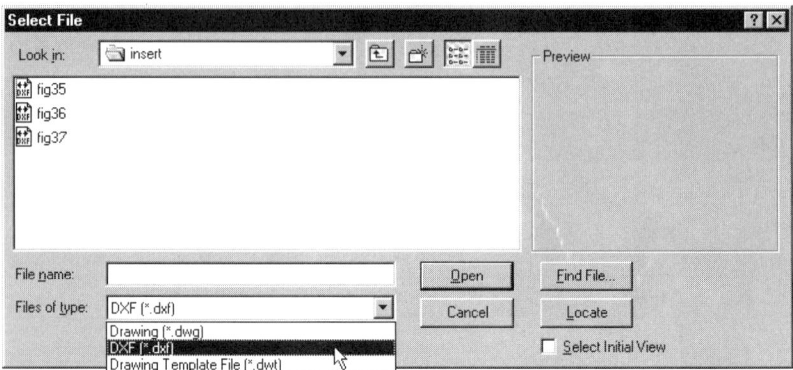

Fig. 13.4 The **Select File** dialogue box

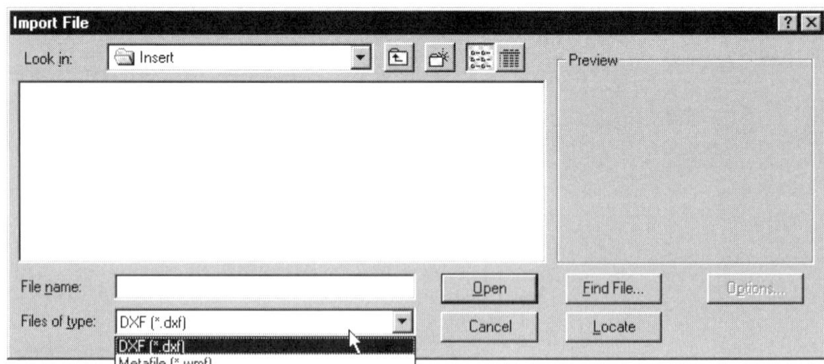

Fig. 13.5 The **Import File** dialogue box

Pasting

Bitmaps such as those from graphics files with the extensions ***.bmp** or ***.pcx** can be pasted into LT 97 drawings and printed with the drawing. An example is given in the three illustrations Figures 13.6 to 13.8.

Figure 13.6: A 3D model of a part from a machine is rendered with a material assigned to the model in AutoCAD Release 14. With the aid of a screen dump software programme such as **Hijaak 95**, the 3D rendered model is saved as a bitmap file (extension ***.bmp**).

Figure 13.7: The bitmap is opened in the Windows 95 programme **Paint**. While in the **Paint** programme, **Select All** is selected from the **Edit** pull-down menu, followed by **Copy** from the same menu.

Figure 13.8: The copied bitmap is pasted into a drawing in LT 97. To paste a bitmap in this fashion, select **Paste** from the LT 97 **Edit** pull-down menu.

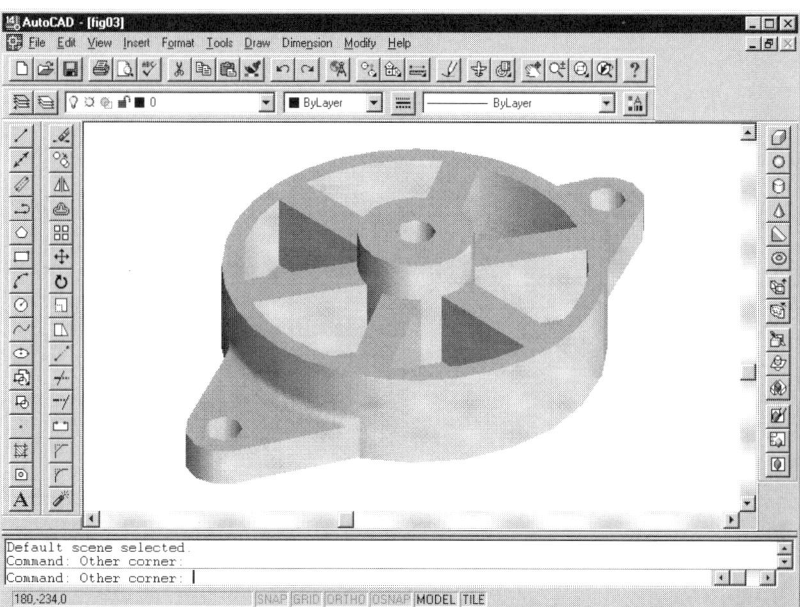

Fig. 13.6 The 3D model constructed and rendered in AutoCAD Release 14

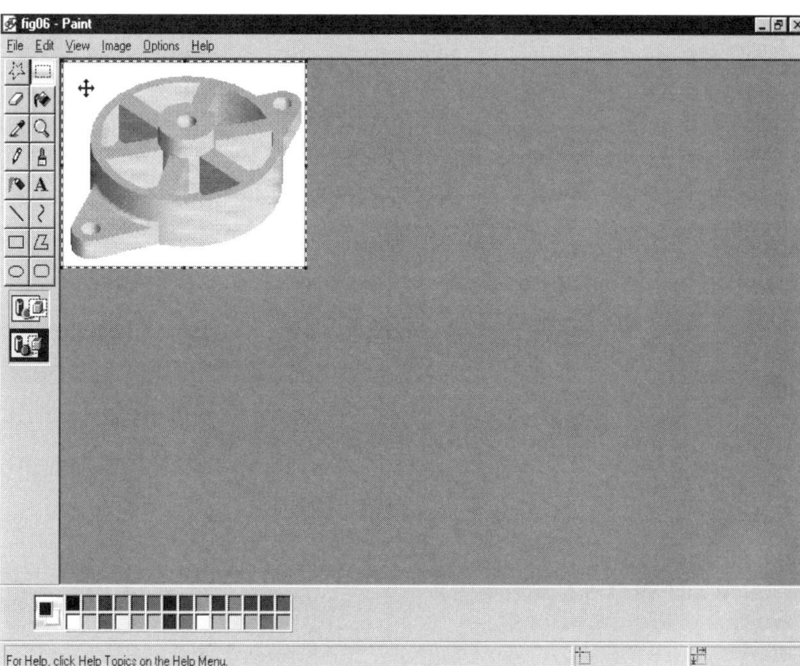

Fig. 13.7 The bitmap opened in **Paint**, and copied

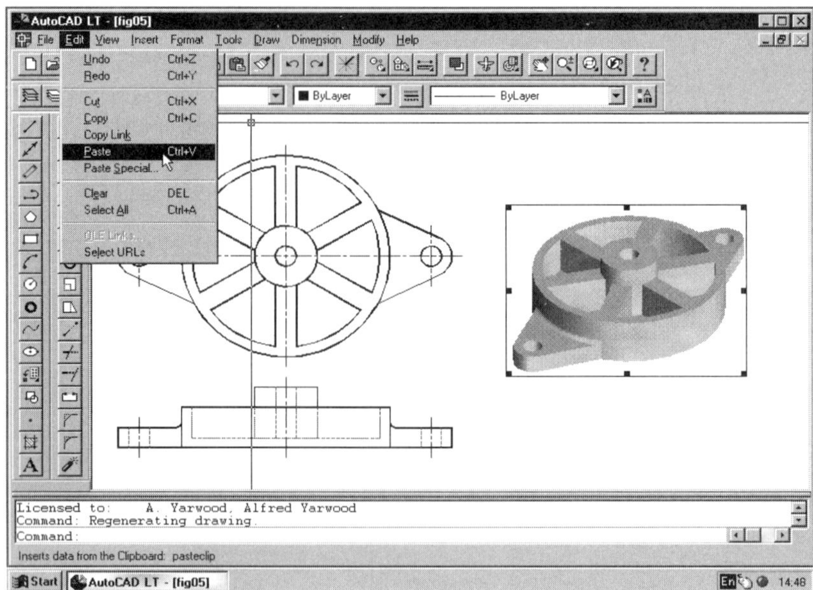

Fig. 13.8 The bitmap **Pasted** into an LT 97 drawing

The Date and Time Stamp tool

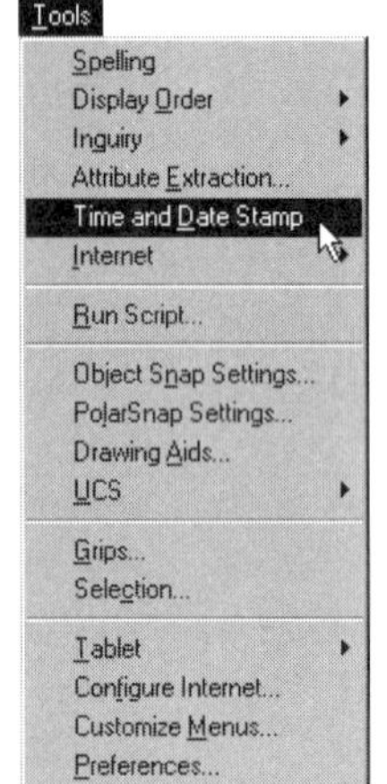

Fig. 13.9 Select **Time and Date Stamp** from the **Tools** pull-down menu

Either select **Date and Time Stamp** from the **Tools** pull-down menu (Fig. 13.9), or *enter* revdate at the Command line.

Command:_revdate
REVDATE block insertion point<0,0>:

appears at the Command line. *Pick* a suitable point on screen and details of the operator, the current date, the current time and the file name of the drawing appear at the *picked* point as shown in the lower part of Fig. 13.10.

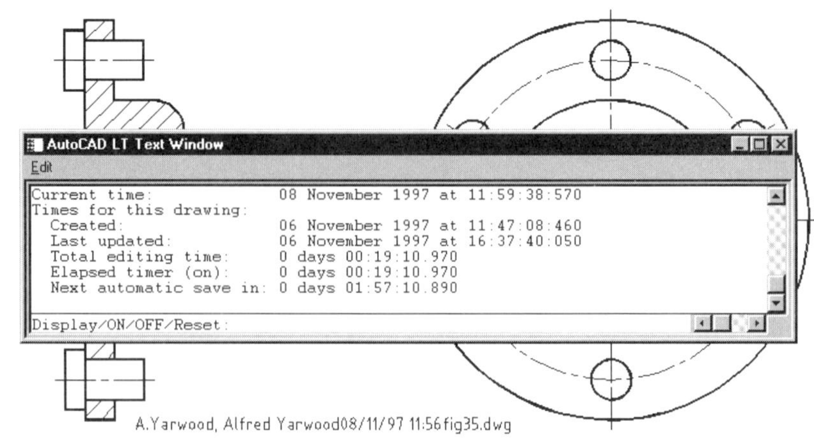

Fig. 13.10 The **LT 97 Text Window** and the **Time and Date Stamp** showing with a drawing in LT 97

The Time tool

Enter time at the Command line. An **AutoCAD LT Text Window** appears showing details of the times when the drawing was updated and edited. Figure 13.10 shows the window when **Time** was called with a drawing in the LT 97 window.

The Inquiry toolbar

Fig. 13.11 The **Inquiry** toolbar

From the **Toolbars** dialogue box, select **Inquiry**. The **Inquiry** toolbar appears (Fig. 13.11). The tools from the **Inquiry** toolbar can also be selected from the flyout which appears when a *left-click* is held on the **Distance** tool icon in the **Standard** toolbar (*docked* at top of the LT 97 window). Figure 13.12 shows the names of the tools from this flyout.

The Distance tool

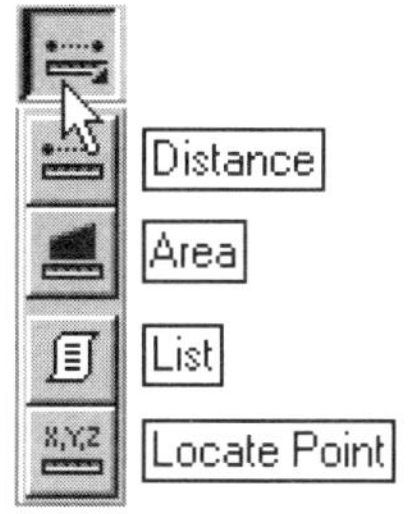

Fig. 13.12 The tools in the **Distance** flyout

For finding the distance between any two selected points in the LT 97 graphics window, either *left-click* on the tool icon, or *enter* di at the Command line (Fig. 13.13). The Command line then shows:

Command: *enter* di *right-click*
DIST First point: *pick* **Second point:** *pick*
Distance = 259, Angle in XY Plane = 326, Angle from XY plane = 0
Delta X = 215, Delta Y = -145, Delta Z = 0
Command:

showing information about the distance, angles in and from the plane of the graphics window and the X and Y distances between the two points.

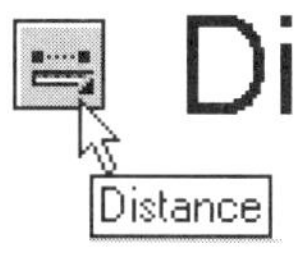

Fig. 13.13 Calling the **Distance** tool

The Area tool

This tool allows the operator to find the area enclosed within selected points on the screen. To call the tool, either *left-click* on the tool's icon or *enter* aa at the Command line (Fig. 13.14). The Command line then shows:

Command: *enter* aa *right-click*
<First point>/Entity/Add/Subtract: *pick*
Next point: *pick*
Next point: *pick*
Next point: *pick*, followed by a *right-click* after selecting as many points as there are at the vertices of the boundary within the area being found.

Fig. 13.14 Calling the **Area** tool

Area = 100000 Perimeter = 400
Command:

The above shows the area enclosed in a square of 100 units side length. The area is in units², the length of the perimeter is in units.

If the area of an **Entity** such as a circle, ellipse or closed polyline is required, use the **e** response. If areas are to be added or subtracted use the **a** or the **s** response.

The List tool

Fig. 13.15 Calling the **List** tool

If **List** is called (Fig. 13.15), an AutoCAD LT R3 text window appears listing all the details about the entities within the current drawing in the graphics window (Fig. 13.16).

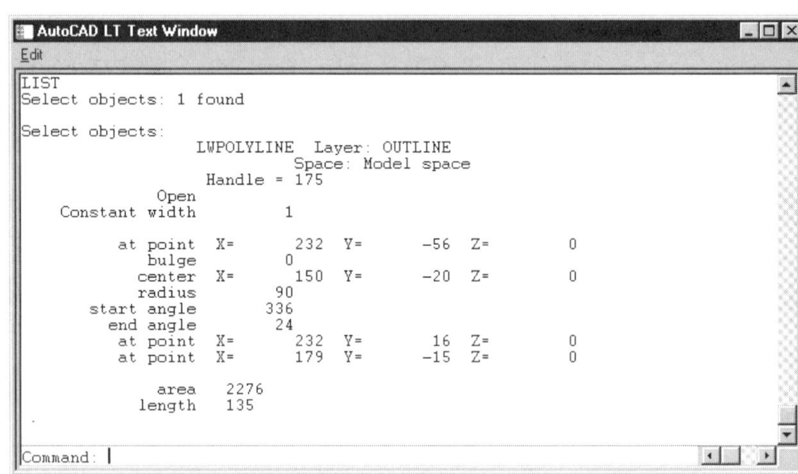


```
LIST
Select objects: 1 found

Select objects:
                  LWPOLYLINE  Layer: OUTLINE
                            Space: Model space
                   Handle = 175
              Open
    Constant width         1

          at point  X=      232  Y=      -56  Z=        0
             bulge         0
            center  X=      150  Y=      -20  Z=        0
            radius        90
       start angle       336
         end angle        24
          at point  X=      232  Y=       16  Z=        0
          at point  X=      179  Y=      -15  Z=        0

              area   2276
            length   135

Command:
```

Fig. 13.16 The **AutoCAD LT Text Window** appearing when **List** is called

The Locate point tool

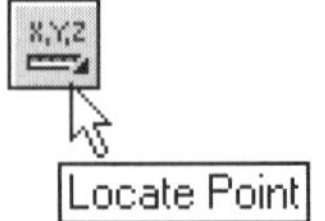

Fig. 13.17 Calling the **Locate Point** tool

Select the **Locate Point** tool (Fig. 13.17), followed by *picking* a point (say 110,90) on screen and the Command line shows:

Command:_id Point: X=110 Y=90 X=0
Command:

Questions

1. What are the file-name extensions for the following types of files:

   AutoCAD drawing; Template file: Bitmap file: Data Exchange file: Encapsulated Postscript file?

2. What is the purpose of the Data Exchange file format?

3. In how many AutoCAD Release formats can LT 97 drawings be saved?
4. How is a graphics file such as a bitmap file loaded into an LT 97 drawing?
5. What is the difference between using the **Time** tool and the using **Date and Time Stamp** tool?

Exercises

1. Practise using the four tools from the **Inquiry** toolbar.
2. Load any LT 97 drawing you have constructed, save in to a DXF format and reload it in DXF format.
3. Place a **Time and Date Stamp** on any drawings you have saved.
4. Use the **Time** tool to check when a drawing you have constructed was started, ended and the time taken to construct.

CHAPTER 14

3D Facilities in LT 97

Introduction

AutoCAD LT 97 includes limited 3D facilities, which allow the loading of 3D solid model drawings created in AutoCAD, together with limited editing of the loaded 3D models. In order to facilitate the loading and part editing of 3D models, the coordinate system of AutoCAD LT 97 includes a third axis – the Z axis – with an imaginary direction positively outwards perpendicularly from the graphics window. Figure 14.1 illustrates the positive and negative directions of the three coordinate axes.

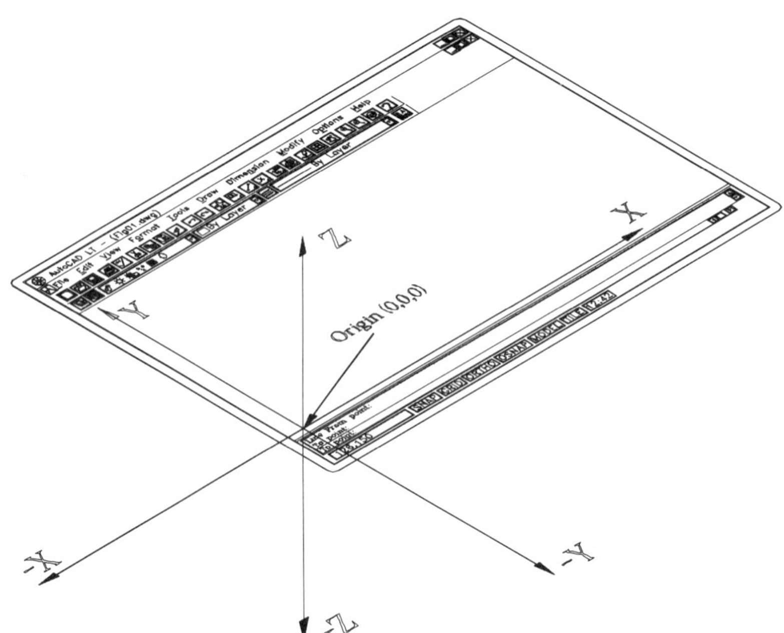

Fig. 14.1 The X,Y,Z coordinate axes of LT 97

An example of a solid model drawing

Figure 14.2 is an AutoCAD Release 14 rendering of the 3D solid model drawing shown in Fig. 14.3. This simple solid model will be

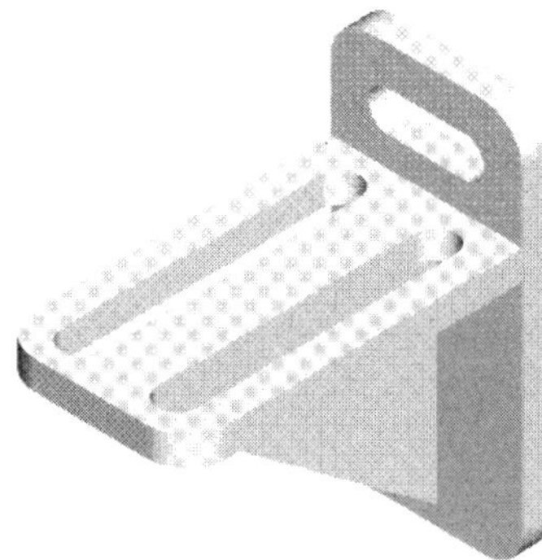

Fig. 14.2 An AutoCAD Release 14 rendering of a simple solid model to be loaded into LT 97

used to show some of the 3D capabilities of LT 97. To start with it can be loaded as a drawing into AutoCAD LT 97. It can then be acted upon by the following tools.

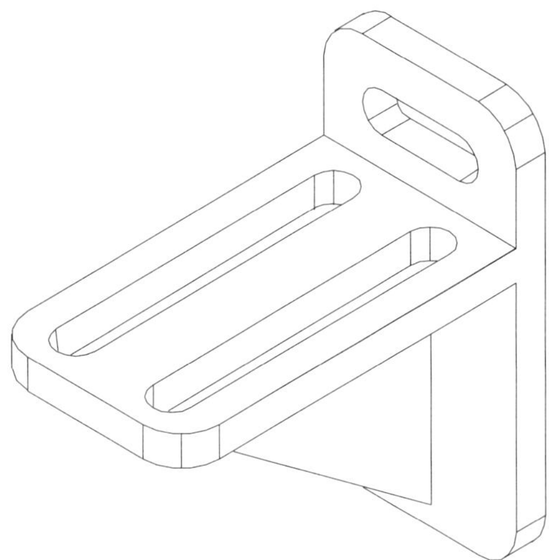

Fig. 14.3 A simple 3D solid model constructed in AutoCAD Release 14 and loaded into LT 97

The Hide tool

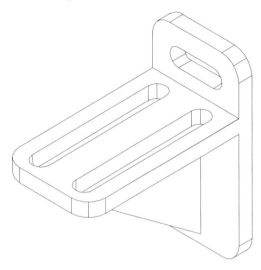

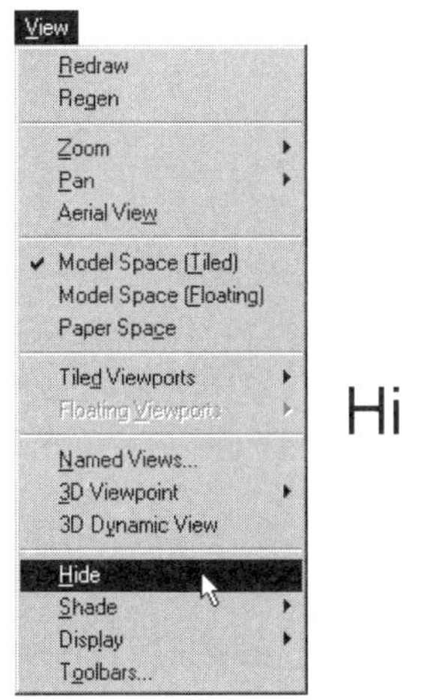

Hi

Fig. 14.4 Calling the **Hide** tool

The solid shown in Fig. 14.3 has already been acted upon by the tool **Hide**. When the tool is called, hidden lines will automatically be hidden behind the surfaces showing to the front. To call **Hide**, either select the tool name from the **View** pull-down menu (Fig. 14.4), or *enter* hi at the Command line:

Command: *enter* hi *right-click*
HIDE Regenerating drawing
Command:

If the drawing is complex, the removal of hidden lines from the graphics window will take some time. To bring back the hidden lines:

Command: *enter* re (for Regen) *right-click*

The Shade tool

A very limited form of rendering is available in LT 97 with the aid of the **Shade** tool. Call the tool from the **View** pull-down menu (Fig. 14.5). The shaded solid model Fig. 14.6 was the result of using the **16 Color Filled** option from the **Shade** sub-menu. The Command line shows:

Command: _shade Regenerating drawing
Shading complete
Command:

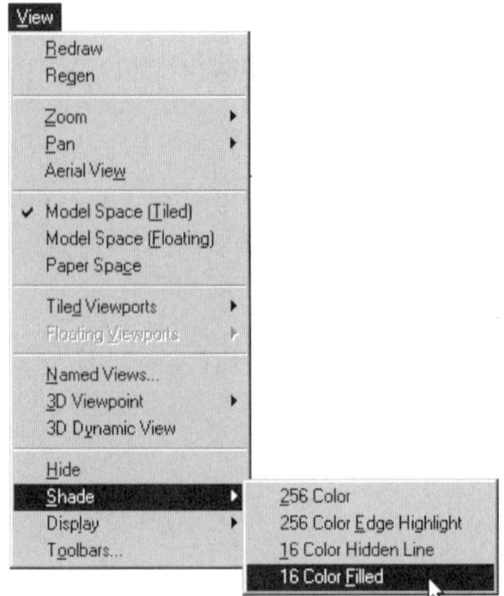

Fig. 14.5 Calling **Shade**

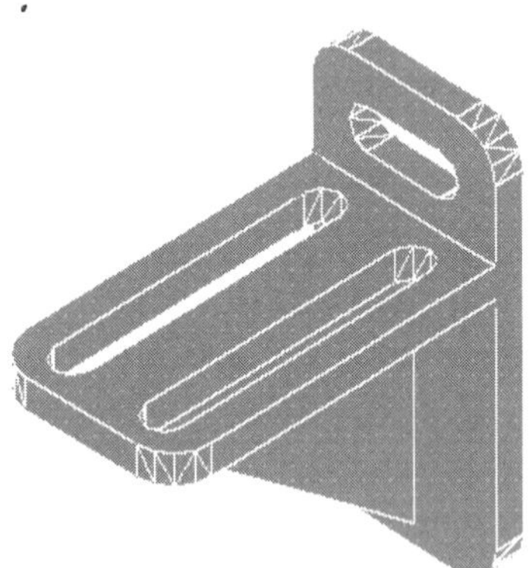

Fig. 14.6 The results of using **Shade** with the **16 Color Filled** option

The reader is advised to attempt using the tool applying the other options in the **Shade** sub-menu from the **View** pull-down menu.

The Vpoint tool

Vpoint allows a 3D drawing to be viewed from any direction in the *X,Y,Z* coordinate area. To call the tool:

Command: *enter* vp *right-click*
VPOINT Rotate/<Viewpoint>:<0,0,1>:

The figures **<0,0,1>** indicate the position from which the 3D drawing is currently viewed. The coordinate figures represent only the angle of the direction from a viewing point, not the distance of the viewing point from the 3D model. Thus the **<0,0,1>** indicates that the viewing point is +Z from the model, i.e. from above. In other words the view as seen is a plan view.

Some examples of other viewing points would be:

–1,–1,1 From the left (–X), from the front (–Y) and above (+Z);

1,1,1 From the right (+X), from behind (+Y) and above (+Z);

–1,–1,–1 From the left (–X), from the front (–Y) and below (–Z)

If either **Tripod** is selected from the **3D Viewpoint** sub-menu (Fig. 14.7), or if the prompt **Rotate/<Viewpoint>:** is answered with a *right-click*, the graphics window changes and a tripod marked with X, Y and Z together with a double circle with a small cross within its outline (the World icon) appear – Fig. 14.8. As the mouse is moved, so the axes of the tripod change and the cross within the World icon moves. The three axes represent the directions of the axes of the 3D model which reappears with a *right-click* in the window once the axes have been determined under mouse control. The model position is now seen to be based upon the directions of the three axes. The World icon represents a view of the world from above with the smaller circle representing the equator. The tiny cross represents the position of the viewing point in relation to the world plan. Move the cross and the tripod axes respond.

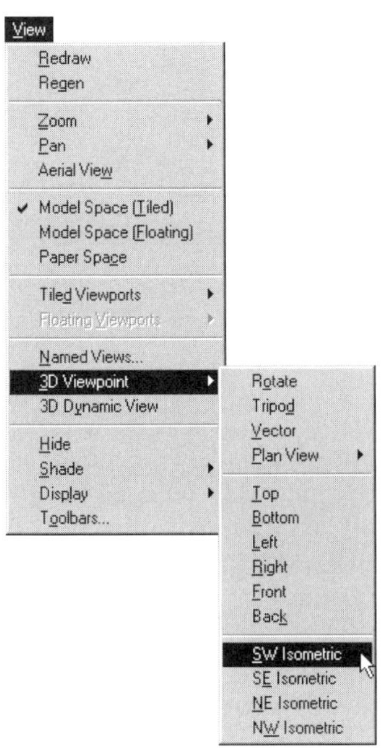

Fig. 14.7 Calling **3D Viewpoint** from the **View** pull-down menu

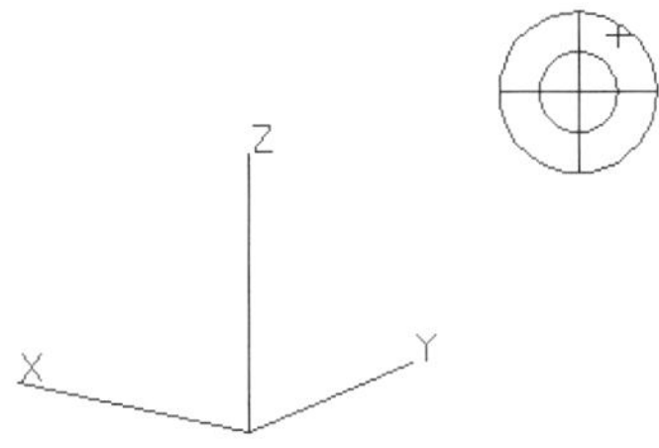

Fig. 14.8 The **Vpoint** tripod

The Rotate prompt of Vpoint

Another way of setting the axes is to answer the **Vpoint** prompts by *entering* an r (for Rotate), followed by setting angles for the rotation of the 3D model in both the XY plane itself and the angle from the XY plane. The command line changes to:

Enter angle in XY plane: *enter* 30 (say) *right-click*
Enter angle from XY plane: *enter* 30 (say) *right-click*
Command:

The 3D model then assumes a position which is 30° in the XY plane and 30° from the XY plane.

3D Viewpoint

Yet another way of setting viewing points is to *left-click* on one of the items in the **3D Viewpoint** sub-menu of the **View** pull-down menu as shown in Fig. 14.7. Figure 14.9 shows a 3D model in each of the four 3D **Isometric** positions. These are equivalent to the following Rotation angles in the XY plane and to the XY plane:

Viewpoint Iso SW:	or	**angle in XY plane:** 225
		angle to XY plane: 35
Viewpoint Iso SE:	or	**angle in XY plane:** 315
		angle to XY plane: 35
Viewpoint Iso NE:	or	**angle in XY plane:** 45
		angle to XY plane: 35
Viewpoint Iso NW:	or	**angle in XY plane:** 135
		angle to XY plane: 35

Each of the views in Fig. 14.9 have been acted upon by **Hide**.

In addition, the viewpoints can be set to show a 3D model from the **Top**, **Front**, **Bottom**, **Left**, **Right**, **Front** or **Back** by selection from the **3D Viewpoint** sub-menu of the **View** pull-down menu. Figure 14.10 illustrates these views.

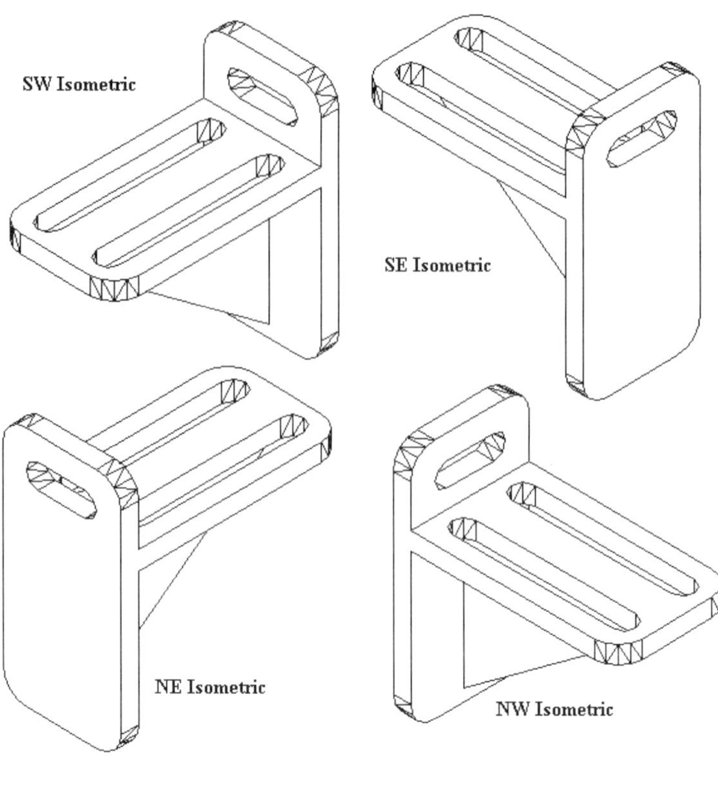

Fig. 14.9 The four **Isometric** views as selected from the **3D Viewpoint** tools

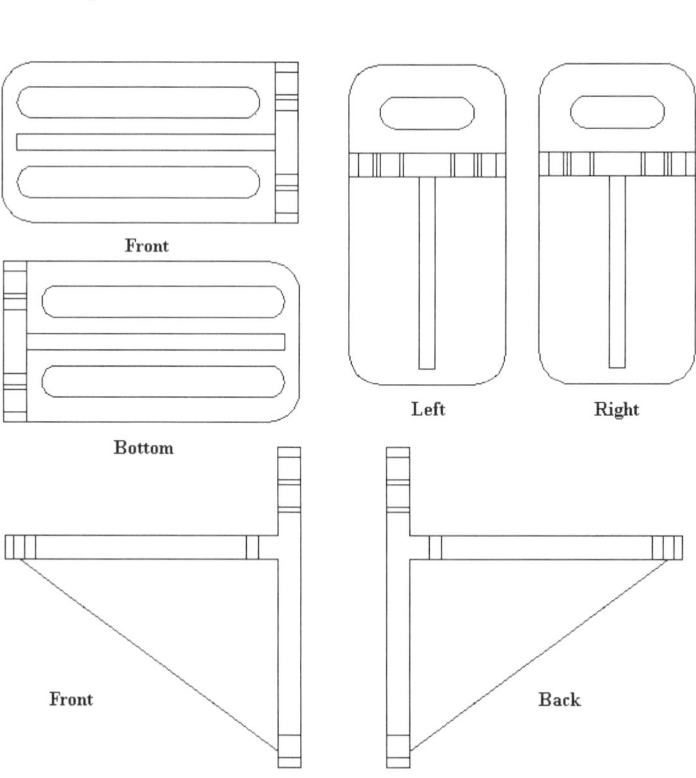

Fig. 14.10 More **3D Viewpoint** views

The User Coordinate System (UCS)

When setting the viewing position for viewing a 3D model with **Vpoint**, the 3D model with the XY plane is moved. When viewing a 3D model in the **User Coordinate System (UCS)** the XY plane moves with the model. The UCS allows the operator to place the XY plane at any angle or slope.

The set variable Ucsfollow

Before the XY plane can be changed with the aid of the UCS, the variable **Ucsfollow** must first be set on (to 1), as follows:

Command: *enter* ucsfollow *right-click*
New value for UCSFOLLOW<0>: *enter* 1 *right-click*
Command:

The UCS icon

It is also advisable to have the UCS icon showing at the bottom right-hand corner of the AutoCAD LT graphics area. If the UCS icon is not already showing then:

Command: *enter* ucsicon *right-click*
ON/OFF/All/Noorigin/ORigin <OFF>: *enter* on *right-click*
Command:

The icon can take a variety of forms as illustrated in Fig. 14.11.

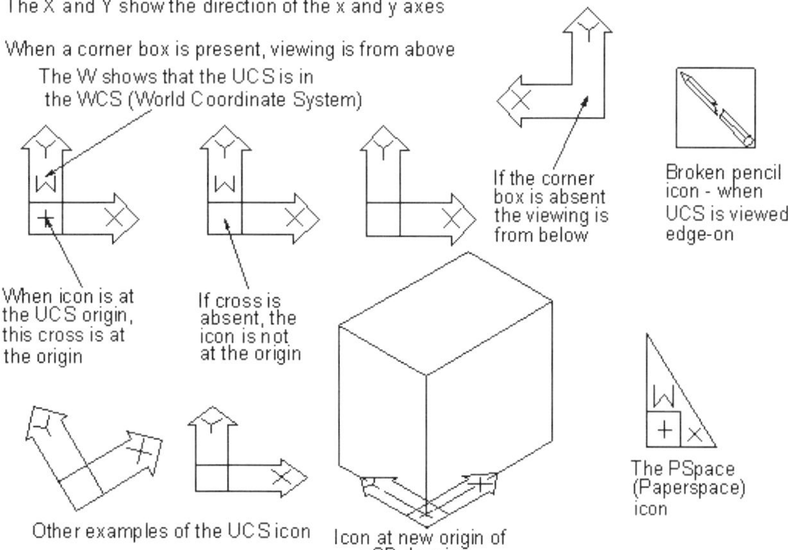

Fig. 14.11 The variety of shapes of the UCS icon

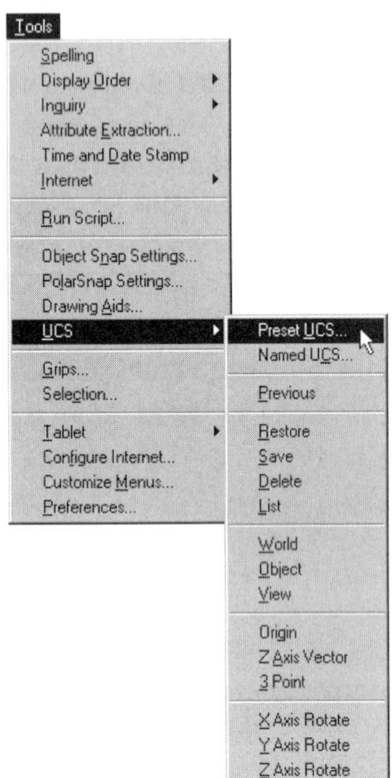

Fig. 14.12 Select **UCS Presets...** from the **Tools** pull-down menu

Setting the UCS

The UCS can be set using a number of methods. For setting the UCS at orthogonal angles – at right angles to each other, *left-click* on **Set UCS...** in the **Tools** pull-down menu (Fig. 14.12), followed by a *left-click* on **UCS Presets...** in the sub-menu which appears. The **UCS Orientation** dialogue box comes on screen – Fig. 14.13.

Fig. 14.14 shows a rendering of a 3D solid model from AutoCAD Release 14. Figure 14.15 shows the model before rendering as it would appear in several of the **UCS** orientations from the dialogue box – **Top**, **Bottom**, **Left** and **Right**. A *left-click* in the relevant box of the dialogue box, followed by another *left-click on* the **OK** button and the model changes to its new UCS orientation. Make sure the **Absolute to WCS** (World Coordinate System) is checked. The **WCS** is the original XY plane as it appears when AutoCAD LT is first opened.

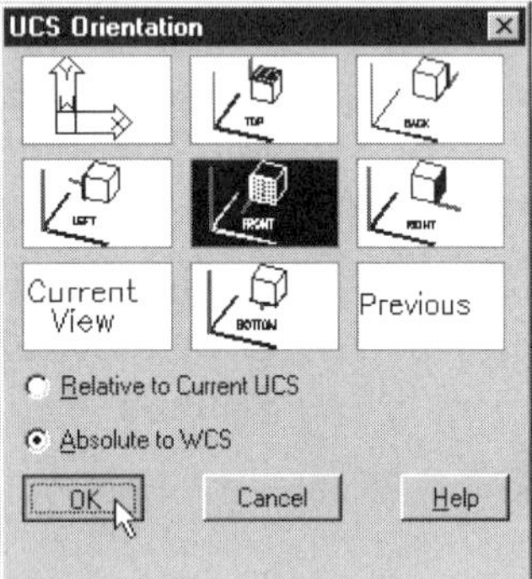

Fig. 14.13 The **UCS Orientation** dialogue box

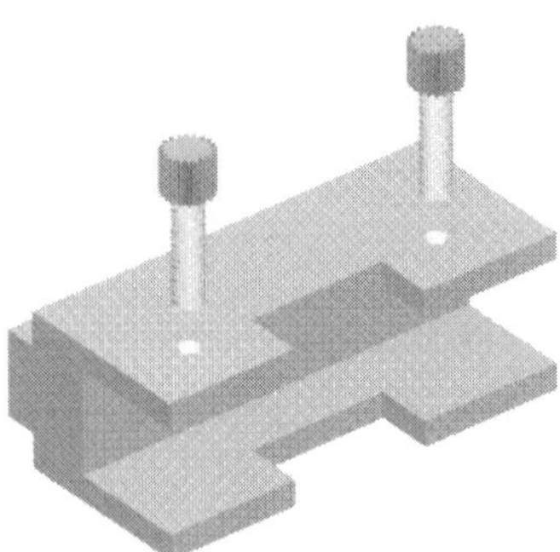

Fig. 14.14 An AutoCAD Release 14 rendering of a 3D solid model

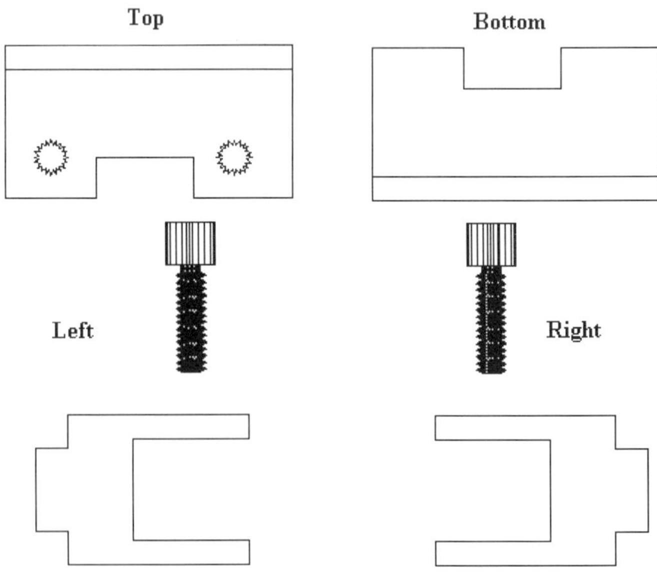

Fig. 14.15 Four settings from **Preset UCS**

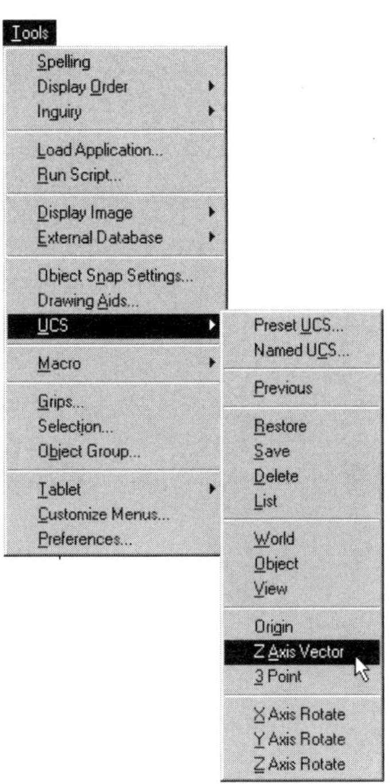

Fig. 14.16 The **UCS** sub-menu from the **Tools** pull-down menu

Other settings of the UCS

Left-click on **UCS...** in the **Tools** pull-down menu (Fig. 14.16). Figure 14.17 shows the results of working to some of the options within this sub-menu. The actions of the various options are:

World: No matter in which UCS the model is placed, it reverts to the **WCS** – the original LT 97 XY plane (Fig. 14.17).

Origin: Providing the **UCSICON** setting is for **OR** (Origin), a new origin can be picked on a 3D model (Fig. 14.17).

3 Point: Follow the prompts which appear at the command line when this selection is made. The **3 Point** view shown in Fig. 14.17 has resulted in a front view of the model.

View: Places the hair line cursors so that the X hair line is horizontal and the Y line vertical, no matter what the viewing position of the model.

X, **Y** and **Z Rotates:** Follow the prompts at the command line which request a rotation angle. These three prompts can be used one after the other to obtain a view as seen when the UCS is rotated around one, two or all three coordinate axes.

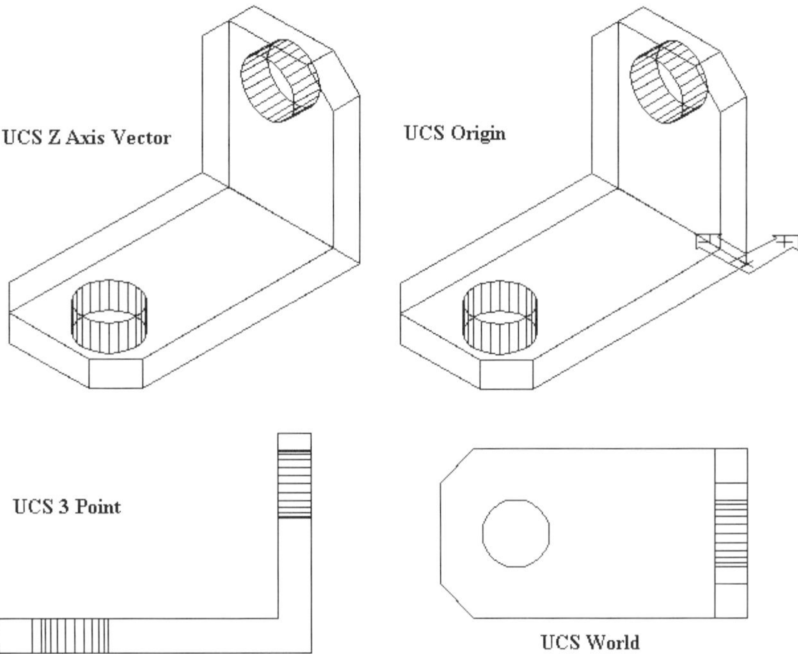

Fig. 14.17 Some **UCS** views

Notes

1. After using any of the **UCS** tools it may be necessary to **Zoom** back to 1 (scale at which the drawing was constructed). This is because

after using any of these tools, the screen reverts to a **Zoom Extents** situation, which may not be convenient for the operator to continue working with the model.

2. It will be found that the **.XY** filter may be required when setting a **3 Point** setting. As an example when **3 Point** is called, the command line shows:

   Command: UCS
   Origin/ZAxis/3point/OBject/View/X/Y/Z/Prev/Restore/Save/Del/ ?/<World>: _3point
   Origin point<0,0,0>: *pick*
   Positive point of X-axis: *pick*
   Point on positive-Y portion of the UCS XY plane: *enter* .xy **.XY of** *pick* **(need Z):** *enter* 1 *right-click*
   Command:

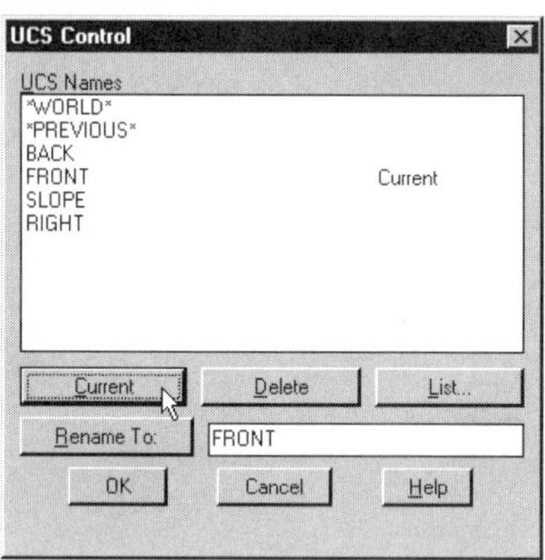

Fig. 14.18 The **UCS Control** dialogue box

3. Note the **(need Z)** response is 1 (could be –1). This is because this Z coordinate figure only gives the direction along the Z axis and not the distance;
4. When a UCS is saved, it should be given a name. A named view which has been saved can be recalled by a *left-click* on **Named UCS...** in the **UCS...** sub-menu of the **Tools** pull-down menu (Fig. 14.12 page 216). This brings up the **UCS Control** dialogue box (Fig. 14.18) from which a saved UCS can be recalled.

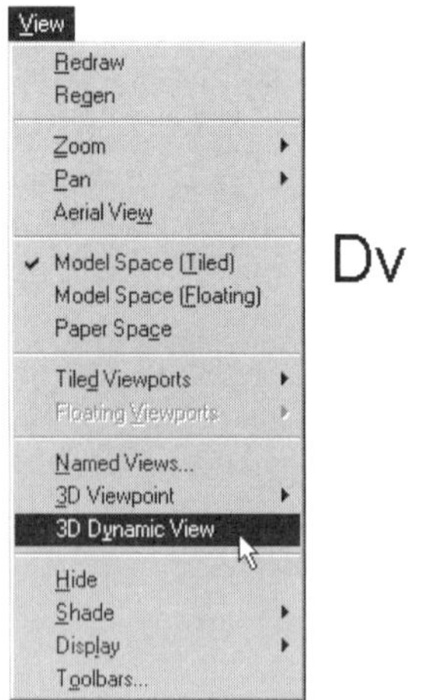

Fig. 14.19 Calling **Dynamic View**

3D Dynamic View

When **3D Dynamic view** is selected from the **View** pull-down menu (Fig. 14.19), the Command line shows the following:

Command: _dview
Select objects: *pick* usually by windowing

CAmera/TArget/Distance/POints/PAn/Zoom/TWist/CLip/Hide/Off/ Undo/<eXit>:

When the response is either **CAmera**, **TArget** or **TWist**, a rubber band line becomes attached to the 3D model and as the mouse is moved a ghosted model replaces the 3D model and moves under mouse control giving the operator an indication of the outcome of the view. In other words, the model is responding dynamically to mouse movement.

Figure 14.20 shows some of the results of adopting the various responses. In each of the given examples, **Hide** has been called to hide all hidden lines. Note the perspective icon in the **Distance** view.

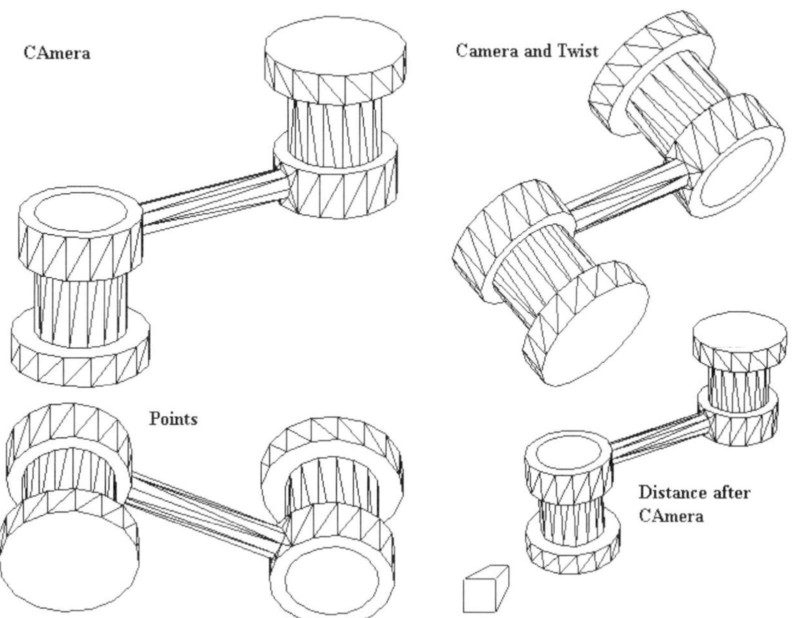

Fig. 14.20 Some Dynamic views

The Elevation tool

The settings for Elevation and Thickness are set from the Command line by *entering* elev (for elevation) at the command line:

Command: *enter* elev *right-click*
ELEV New current elevation<0>: *right-click* (accepts the 0)
New current thickness<0>: *enter* 50 *right-click*

With the aid of these settings simple 3D models can be built up from entities drawn with the aid of the **Draw** tools. Examples are given in Fig. 14.21. An example of a simple block constructed on differing

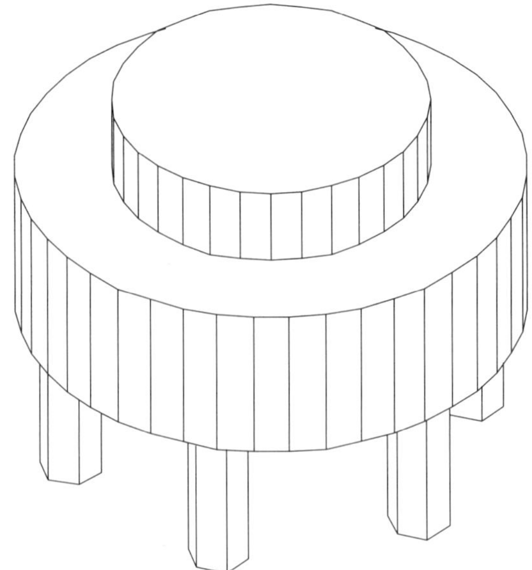

Fig. 14.21 A simple 3D solid model built up with the use of **Elevation**

elevations is given in Fig. 14.22. The given examples have all been acted upon by **Hide**. Note that the circle and the plines have tops behind which lines are hidden, whereas the other examples are open at their upper faces. Note also that the plines, which in plan view would be solid filled lines, are no longer solid filled when in an elevation situation.

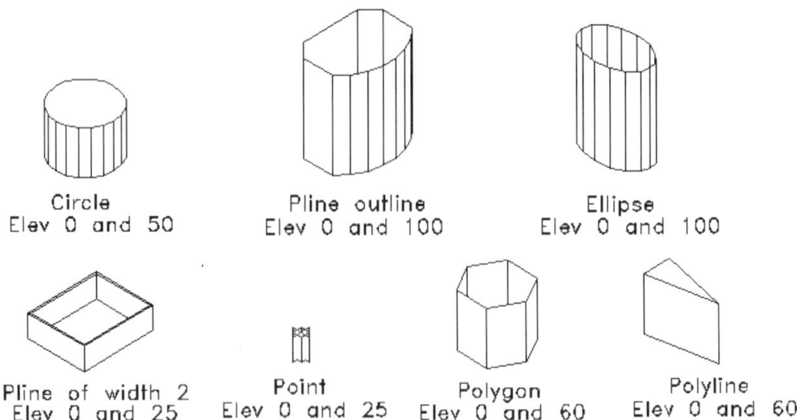

Fig. 14.22 Some examples of the use of **Elevation**

Viewports

Model Space and Paper Space

Figure 14.11 on page 215 shows the variety of possible shapes of the UCS icon when it is set on. The majority of the UCS icons shown in that illustration are for MSpace (Model Space). One of the icons in that illustration is the PSpace or Paper Space icon. So far throughout this book, all working has been carried out in MSpace. To change from MSpace to PSpace, select **Paper Space** from the **View** pull-down menu (Fig. 14.23).

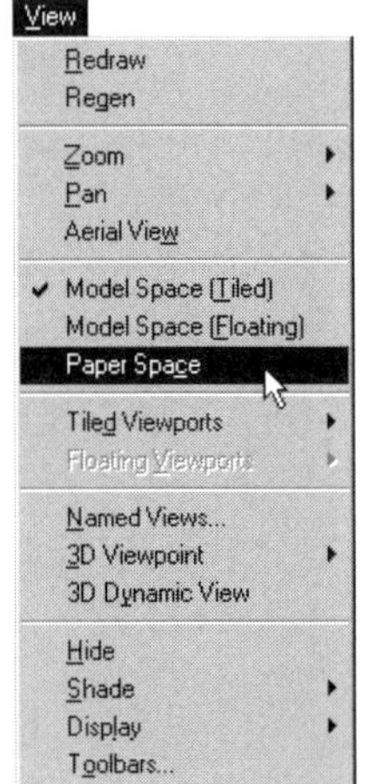

Fig. 14.23 Select **Tiled Viewports...** from the **View** pull-down menu

If in MSpace a *left-click* on **Tiled Viewports** in the **View** pull-down menu brings up the **Tiled Viewports** sub-menu (Fig. 14.24). Select **Layout...** from the sub-menu and the **Tiled Viewport Layout** dialogue box appears (Fig. 14.24). A variety of different viewport layouts is available from the dialogue box from which a selection may be had. In the example given in Fig. 14.25 the LT 97 window becomes divided into four viewports spaced as shown in Fig. 14.26. The current viewport in which construction could proceed is outlined in a thick line. The current viewport can be changed by moving the cursor under mouse control into the required viewport, followed by a *left-click*. The selected viewport then becomes the current viewport. Before using viewports it is necessary to understand Model Space and Paper Space. The following seven examples of using viewports in both PSpace and MSpace should clarify their uses.

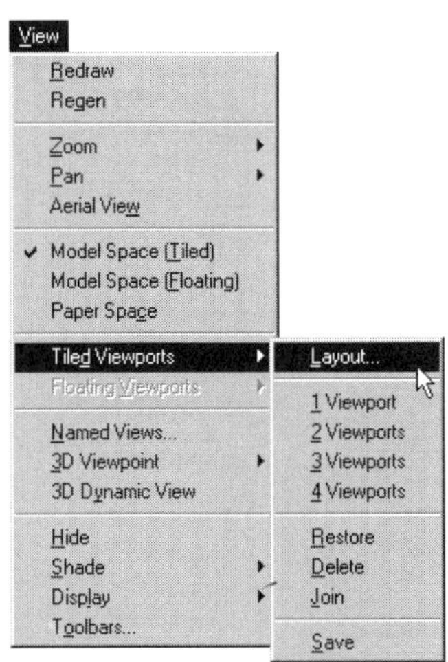

Fig. 14.24 Select **Layout...** from the **Tiled Viewports** sub-menu of the **View** pull-down menu

Examples of the use of viewports

Throughout this book, the LT 97 window in which 2D drawings are shown are in Model Space (MSpace). Some operators may prefer working 2D drawings in Paper Space (PSpace). When editing 3D models in LT 97, a suggested method of working is:

1. Open the drawing file containing the 3D model data. This will load into MSpace if the drawing was constructed in MSpace.

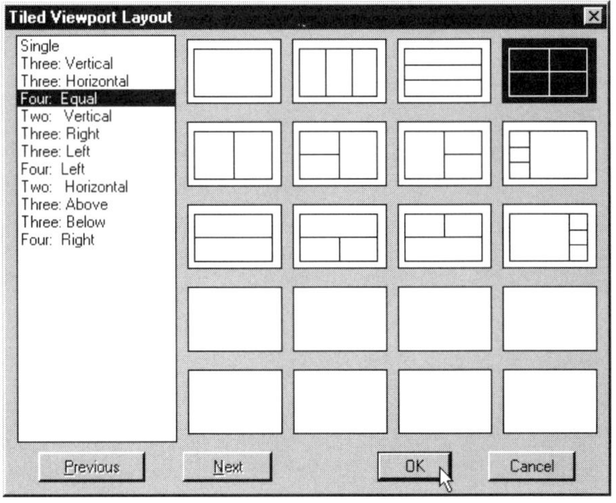

Fig. 14.25 The **Tiled Viewport Layout** dialogue box

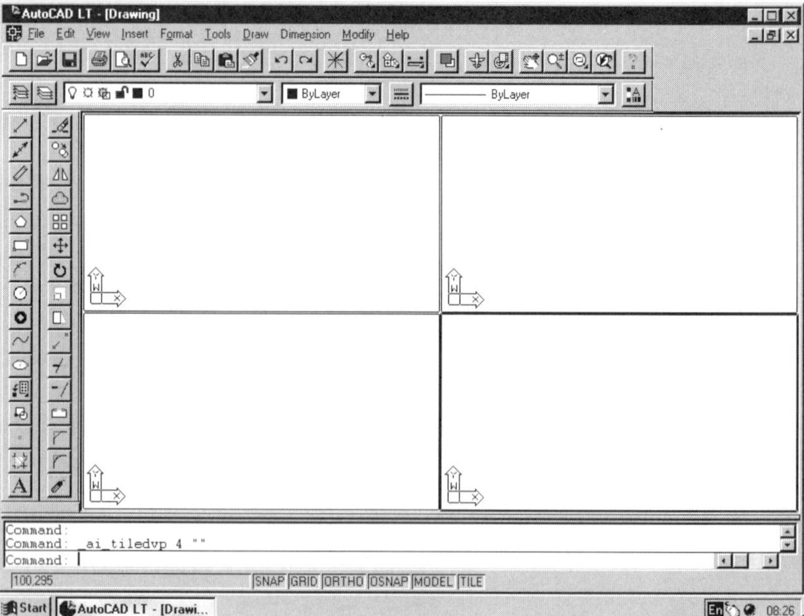

Fig. 14.26 The LT 97 window with a four-viewport layout

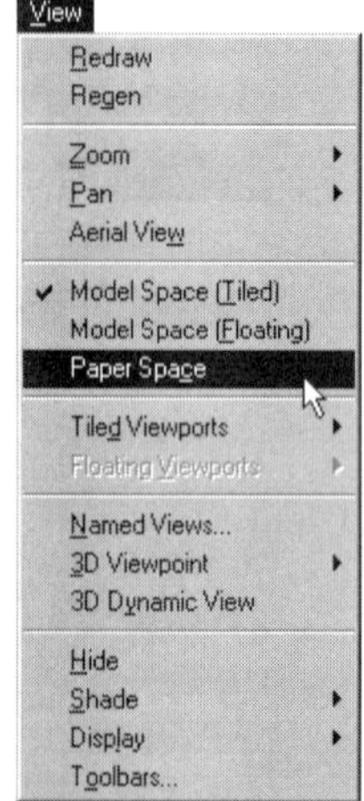

Fig. 14.27 Select **Paper Space** from the **View** pull-down menu

2. *Left-click* on **Paper Space** in the **View** pull-down menu (Fig. 14.27). The 3D model in MSpace disappears from the window, which becomes blank, with a prompt at the command line:

   Command:
   Regenerating paperspace.
   Command:

   or:

   Command: *enter* tm (for Tilemode) *right-click*
   New value for TILEMODE<1>: *enter* 0 *right-click*
   Regenerating paperspace.
   Command:

3. Call **MVIEW** as follows:

   Command: *enter* mv (for Mview) *right-click*
   ON/OFF/Hideplot/Fit/2/3/4/<First point>: *enter* four *right-click*
   Fit/<First point>: *enter* f (Fit) *right-click*
   Command:

   Figure 14.28 shows the results of entering MVIEW in four viewports.

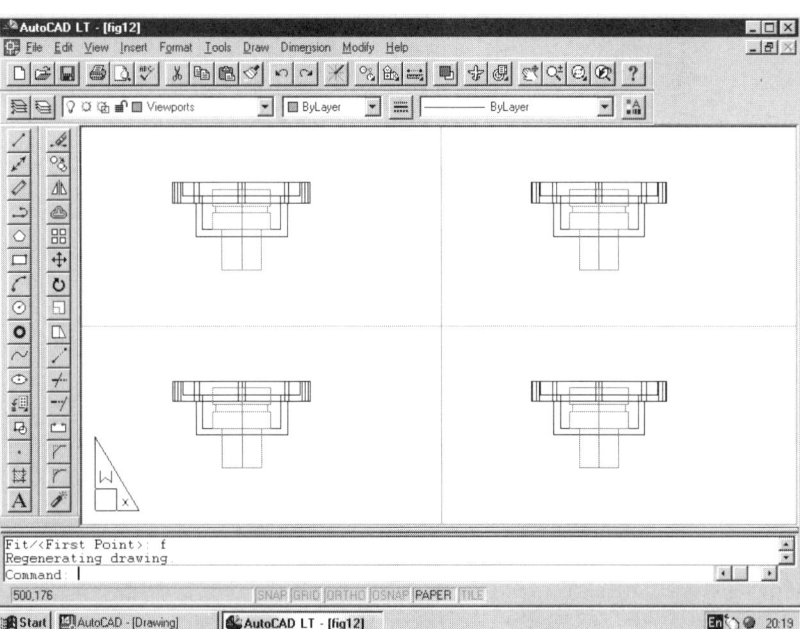

Fig. 14.28 Entering **MVIEW** with four viewports

4. Go back to MSpace (Model Space):

   Command: *enter* ms (MSpace) *right-click*
   MSPACE
   Command:

5. In the viewports, from **3D Viewport** sub-menu in the **View** pull-down menu:

   Top right – **NE Isometric**
   Bottom left – **Back**
   Bottom right – **Right**
   In all viewports **Zoom** to 1.

   The results are shown in Fig. 14.29.
6. Now go back to **PSpace** by:

   Command: *enter* ps *right-click*

   The result is shown in Fig. 14.30.

While in **PSpace** the viewports containing the different views of the 3D model can be copied, moved, mirrored, stretched or scaled. It is the viewport on which the action of these tools takes place, the 3D model in the viewport being unchanged. To move a viewport, *left-click* on one of its edges and, holding the left button down, *drag* the viewport to its new position under mouse control. Figure 14.31 shows the result.

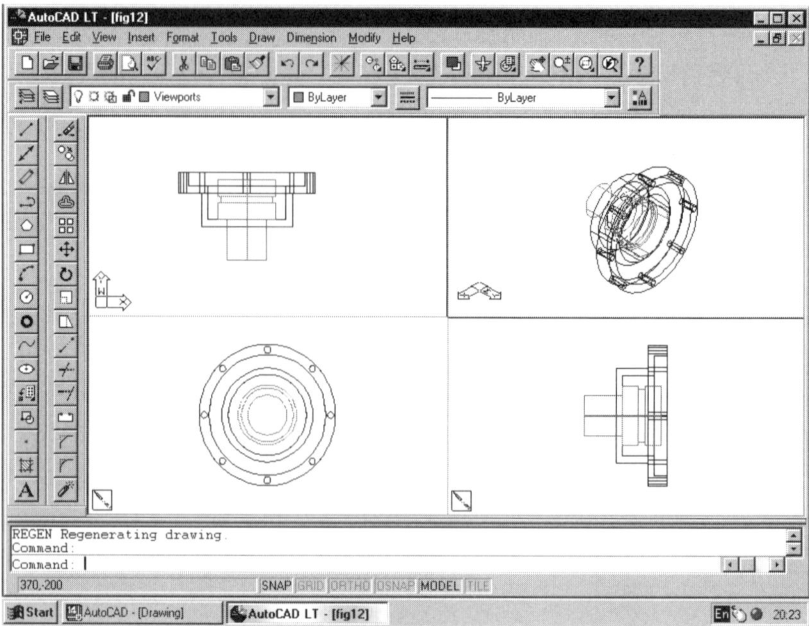

Fig. 14.29 The 3D model in a four viewport setting in MSpace

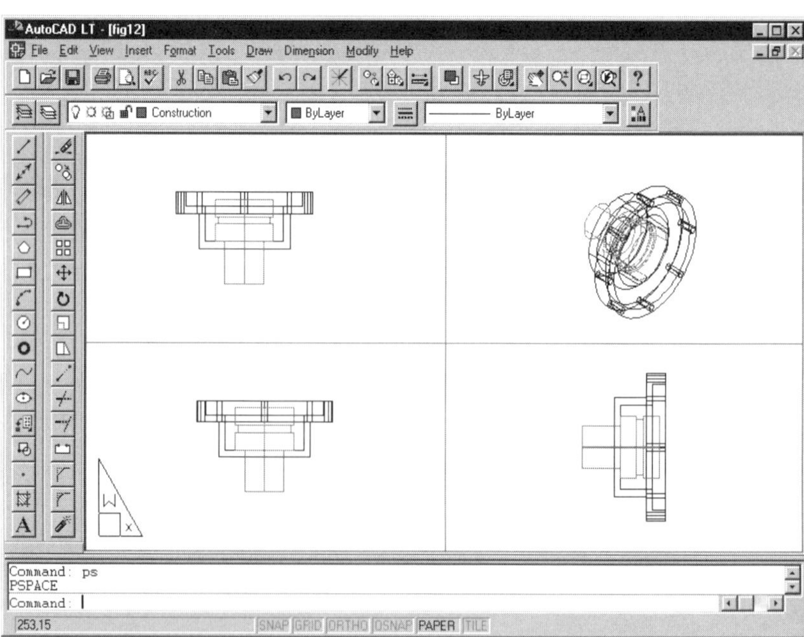

Fig. 14.30 Back into **PSpace**

Hiding viewport edges

The edges of the viewports can be hidden by:

1. When in **PSpace** before calling **Mview** to determine the number of viewports, make a new layer named **Viewports** preferably of a

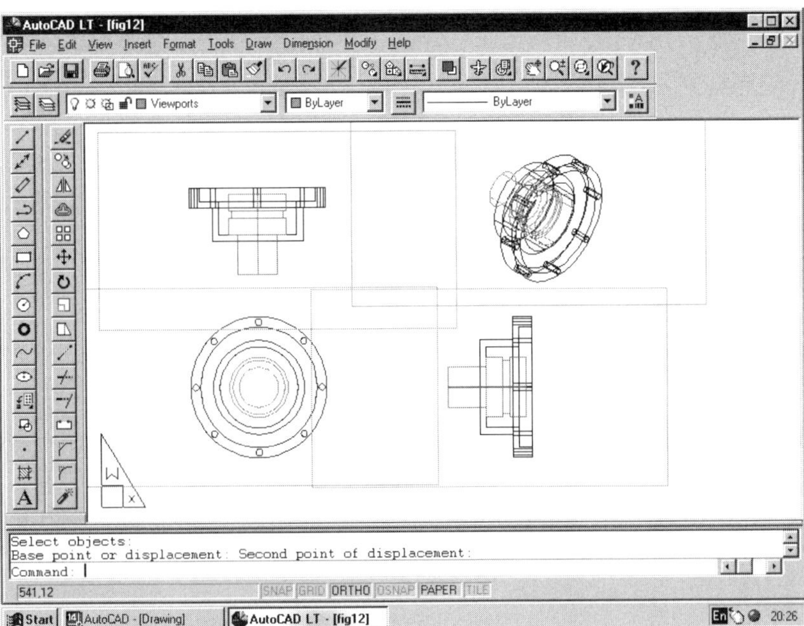

Fig. 14.31 In **PSpace** after moving the viewports

different colour to the entities making up the 3D model. Make the layer **Viewports** current.

2. Call **Mview** and set the number of viewports. The 3D model appears in **PSpace**.
3. Turn layer **Viewports** off. The edges of the viewports disappear from the graphics window, but the 3D model still shows in the spaces where the viewports were.

Figure 14.32 is an example of the 3D model in 4 viewports **PSpace** after moving the viewports and then turning the layer **Viewports** off.

The value of these operations between **MSpace** and **PSpace** allows the operator to set up a 3D model ready to be printed/plotted as an orthographic projection.

Hideplot

If a plot or print is required with the hidden lines of a 3D model removed, use the **Hideplot** prompt of the **MVIEW** command sequence. If with **Hideplot** in operation any edge of a viewport is picked while in **PSpace** the view in that viewport is printed or plotted with hidden lines removed. An example of a plot from a 3D model in which the viewport edges have been hidden and **Hideplot** put into action is given in Fig. 14.33.

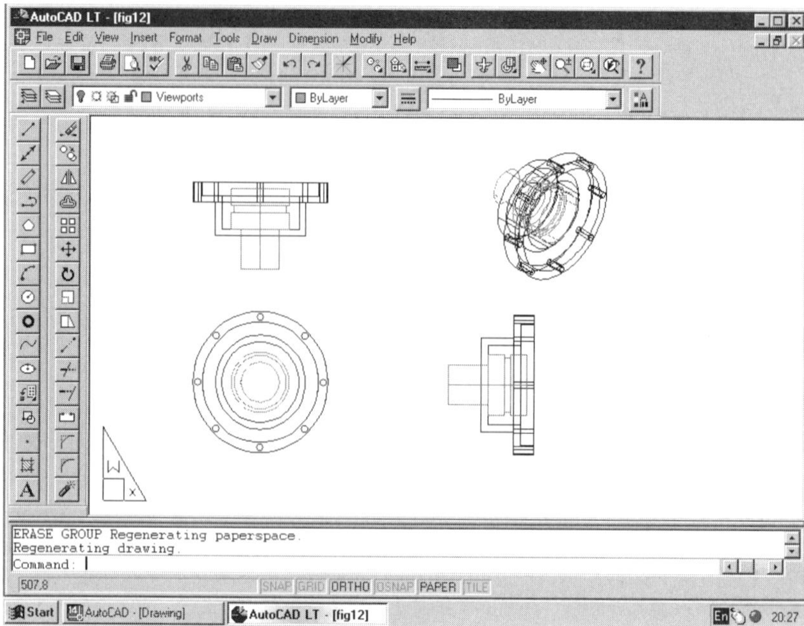

Fig. 14.32 A 3D model in **PSpace** with the viewport edges turned off

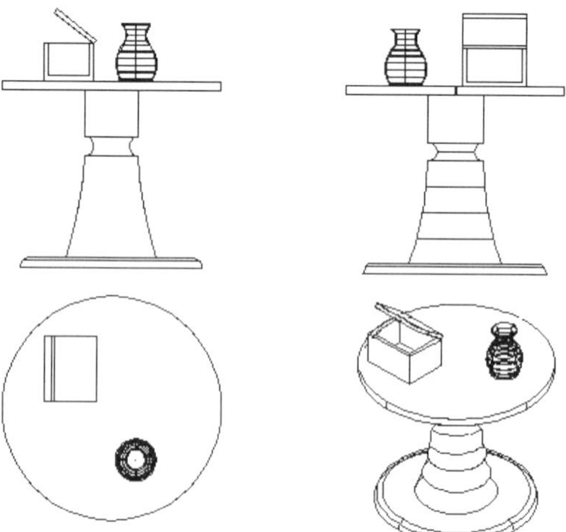

Fig. 14.33 A plot in which viewport edges have been hidden and **Hideplot** put into action

Bitmap files inserted into viewport areas

In **PSpace**, viewports can be erased by calling the **Erase** tool and *picking* an edge of the viewport to be erased. Once the viewport is erased, a bitmap can be pasted in its place if desired. Figure 14.34 shows an example of a bitmap from a rendering of the model in AutoCAD Release 14. See page 204 about the pasting of bitmaps.

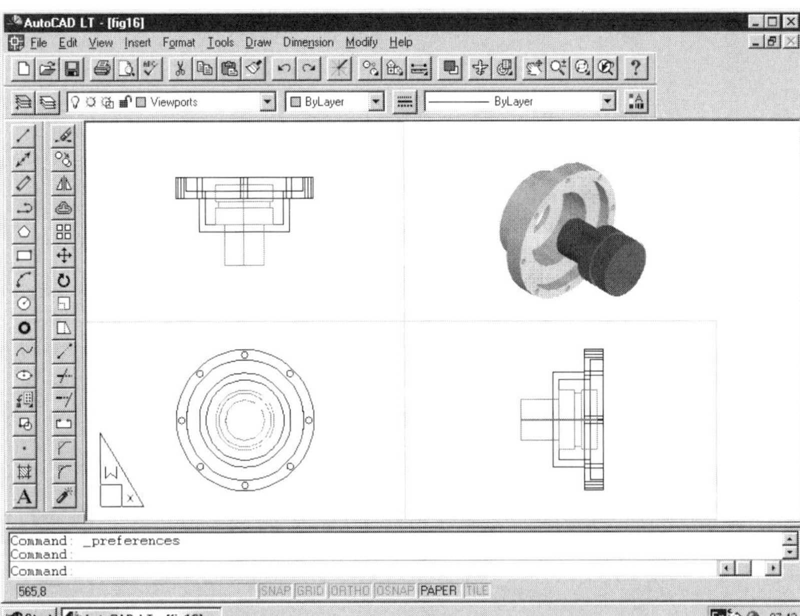

Fig. 14.34 A bitmap inserted into a viewport area

Questions

1. In which direction is the +ve Z axis in relation to the AutoCAD LT graphics window?
2. LT 97 is a 2D CAD software package. Yet this chapter has dealt with 3D. Why is that?
3. What is the purpose of the tool **Hide**?
4. What is the purpose of the tool **Shade**?
5. If the response to **Vpoint** is –1,–1,1, from which directions would you expect a 3D model to be viewed?
6. A limited type of 3D model drawing can be constructed in AutoCAD LT 97. With which tools can such models be constructed?
7. What is the purpose of the **3D Viewpoint** tools from the **View** pull-down menu?
8. What is the difference between viewing a model using the **Vpoint** tool and viewing it with the aid of a **UCS Preset**?
9. What is meant by **Paper Space**? What are the differences between **Paper Space** and **Model Space**?
10. How can a drawing in PSpace in a number of viewports be plotted without the edges of the viewports showing?

Exercises

Because AutoCAD LT 97 is not equipped to construct full 3D models, no exercises will be set for this chapter. The reader is, however, advised to load any 3D models he/she may have constructed in AutoCAD and practise using the variety of 3D tools and commands in AutoCAD LT 97.

CHAPTER 15

Object linking and embedding (OLE)

Introduction

Several applications can be loaded in Windows 95 to run concurrently. For example, one could have AutoCAD LT 97, Adobe PageMaker 6.0, Windows 95 Paint and Windows 95 Write all loaded, ready for use. Loaded applications show in the **Task Bar** at the bottom of the window of any loaded application as indicated in Fig. 15.1. A *left-click* on any of the names of the loaded applications showing in the Task Bar brings the selected application on screen ready for use. If all the loaded applications are brought onto the screen and the windows holding them are made small enough several can be seen on the screen at the same time, as shown in Fig. 15.2.

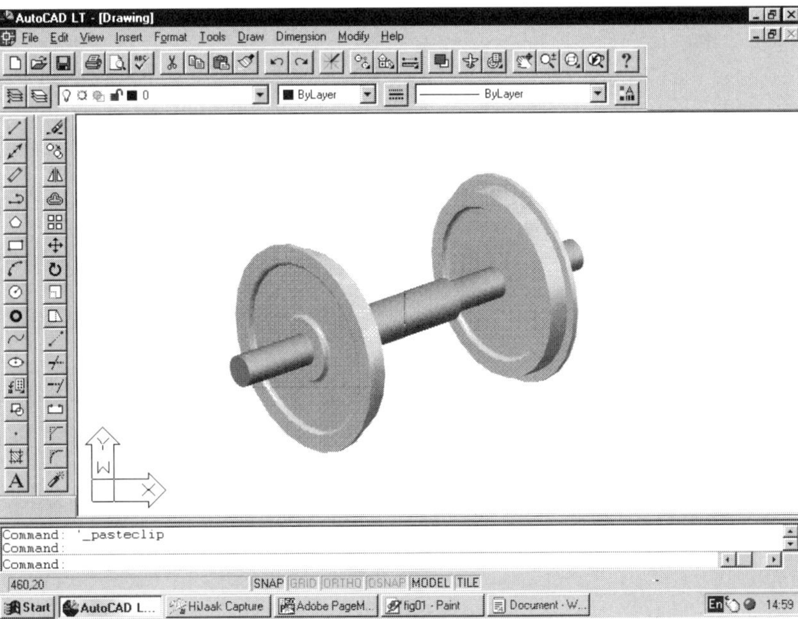

Fig. 15.1 The **Task bar** at the bottom of Windows 95 showing loaded applications

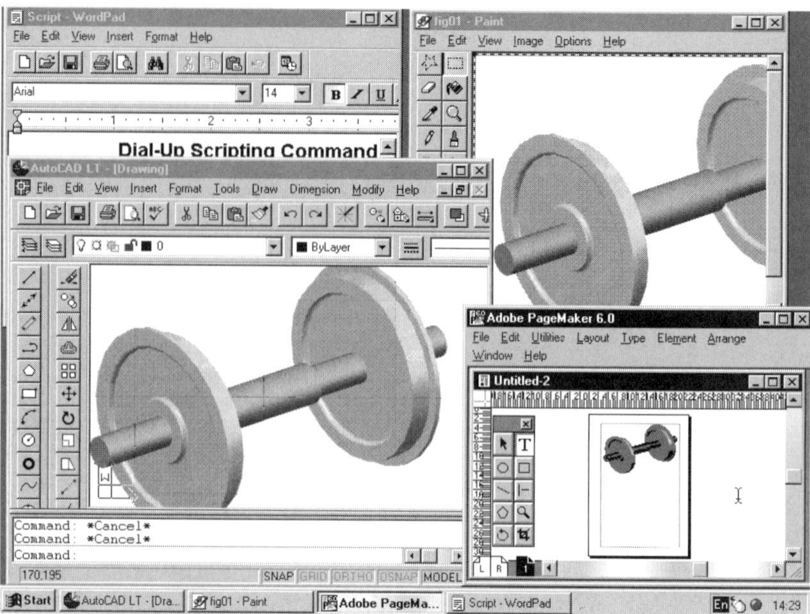

Fig. 15.2 If all application windows are made small enough they will all be seen

Thus Windows 95 allows easy switching between any applications which have been loaded. Switching between loaded applications can be carried out in one of two ways:

1. *Left-click* on any one of the application names in the **Task Bar**. The application window comes on screen.
2. Press the key marked **Alt**, together with the **Tab** key (two arrows). One of the application names in the Task bar highlighted as **Alt+Tab** is repeatedly pressed. At the same time a box appears in the window with the names of the applications appearing one after the other as **Alt+Tab** keys are pressed. Stop pressing the keys when the name of the required application name is highlighted and its window comes up on screen.

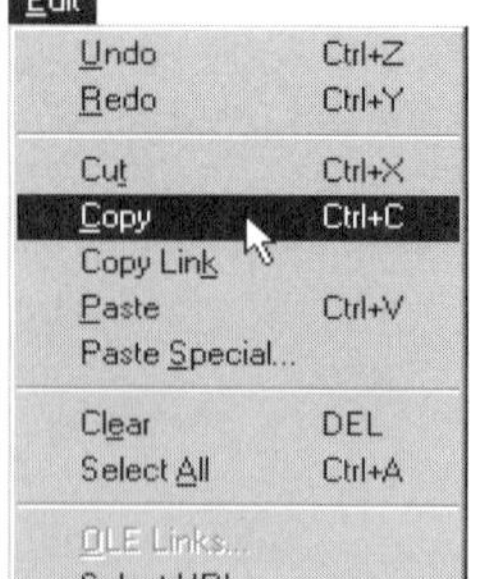

Fig. 15.3 The tools in the **Edit** pull-down menu

Object Linking and Embedding

Some tools from the Edit pull-down menu

The three tools **Cut**, **Copy** and **Copy Link** from the **Edit** pull-down menu can be used for copying or linking drawings from LT 97 into other applications. These three tools are common to all true Windows 95 applications. The use of these three tools allows text and graphics from one application to be loaded into another application. There is a distinct difference between text or graphics embedded in another application compared with text or graphics linked from one application into another:

Embedding: When text or graphics is embedded from one application into another, the embedded text or graphics becomes part of the data of the application file into which the embedding takes place. If the text or graphics are amended in the original application, it will make no difference to the text or graphics in the application into which it is embedded.

Linking: When text or graphics are linked from one application into another, any change in the original will automatically take place in the application into which the text or graphics are linked.

To embed an LT 97 drawing into another application, use the **Copy** tool. To link an LT 97 drawing with another application use the **Copy Link** tool.

To embed part of a drawing from LT 97 into another application use the **Cut** tool.

The Cut tool

When the tool is selected, the Command line shows:

Command: _cutclip
Select objects: *enter* c (crossing) *right-click*
First corner: *pick* **Other corner:** *pick* **2 found:**
Command: and the objects within the crossing window disappear from screen. *Entering* oops brings them back.

The cut parts can now be pasted into another application.

The Copy tool

When the tool is selected, the Command line shows:

Command: _copyclip
Select objects: *enter* w (window) *right-click*
First corner: *pick* **Other corner:** *pick* **3 found**
Select objects: *right-click*
Command:

The selected objects can now be pasted into another application.

The Copy Link tool

Copy Link works in a different manner. All the **Copy** tools are part of the **Object Linking and Embedding** (OLE) facility of Windows 95. Whereas the first two mentioned (**Cut** and **Copy**) can be used to embed a copy of a drawing by **Pasting** in an application, **Copy Link** links an LT 97 drawing to the copy in the application document as well as pasting it into the document. When **Copy Link** is selected from the **Edit** menu (see Fig. 15.3 on page 230), the Command line shows:

Command: _copylink
Command:

And the whole of the LT 97 drawing is copied.

The real difference between **Copy Link** and the other two copy tools is that if the copy is then pasted into a document in an application the drawing is then linked between LT 97 and the application document. Figure 15.5 is an example of the front view of a house shown in the LT 97 drawing (Fig. 15.4) pasted into a document in the desktop programme PageMaker 6.0.

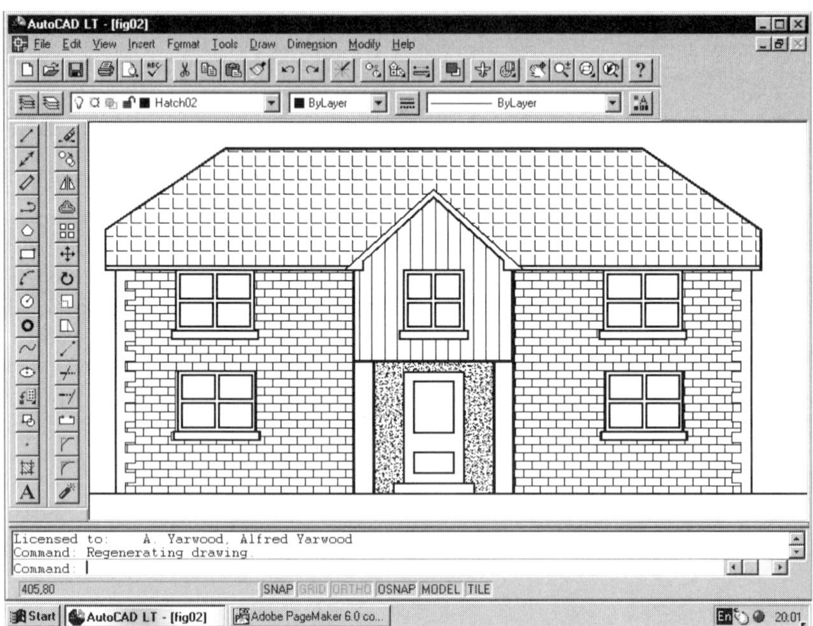

Fig. 15.4 A 2D drawing of a house loaded into LT 97

In the PageMaker 6.0 window a *double-left-click* within the drawing brings back the AutoCAD LT window with its drawing. If the LT 97 programme is not currently loaded it will automatically be loaded with the drawing linked to PageMaker 6.0. The two drawings are linked together – the LT 97 drawing is linked in the PageMaker document. Changes made to the drawing in LT 97 will appear in the PageMaker 6.0 document using the **Links...** facility of PageMaker, providing the LT 97 drawing with any amendments has first been saved. This form of linking does not occur with the other two copy tools, although they can be used to copy drawings or parts of drawings from AutoCAD LT into other applications. The drawings will not, however, be linked.

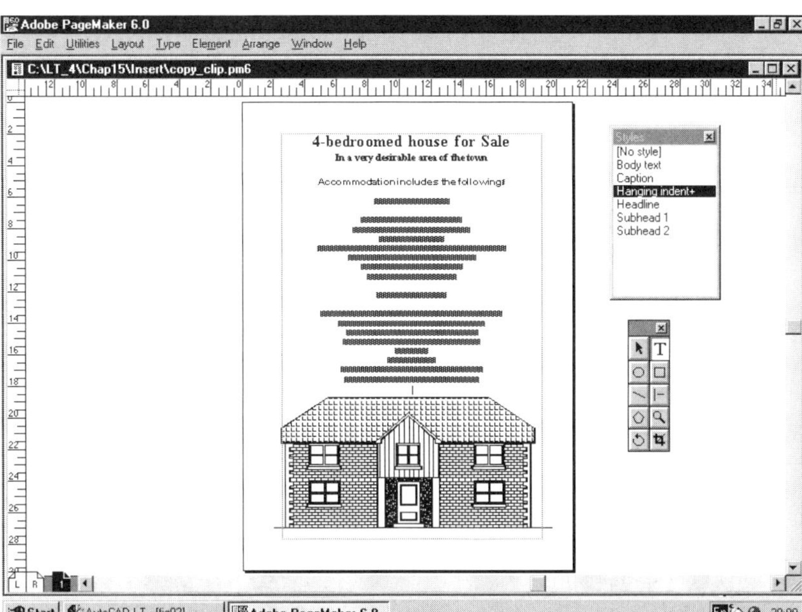

Fig. 15.5 The LT 97 drawing pasted into a PageMaker 6.0 document with the aid of the **Copy Link** tool (LT 97) and **Paste** (PageMaker)

Any of the **Copy** tools can be used to paste AutoCAD drawings in other Windows 95 applications as necessary. They can also be used to **Paste** (**Edit** menu) an LT 97 drawing into another AutoCAD drawing. A drawing pasted into another, using a Copy tool, will be in the form of a block, which will need to be exploded if individual parts of the pasted drawing are to be modified.

Several LT 97 windows can be loaded concurrently

Figure 15.6 shows that a number of LT 97 windows can be loaded concurrently. In Fig. 15.6 the Task bar shows six LT 97 drawings have been loaded.

Questions

1. What are the two methods of switching between applications in Windows 95?
2. What are the differences between **Copy Link** and the **Cut** or **Copy** tools?
3. How many copies of LT 97 can be running at the same time?
4. If an LT 97 drawing is linked in an application document, how can amendments in the drawing be included in the application document?
5. Can 3D drawing models loaded into LT 97 be copied to another application?

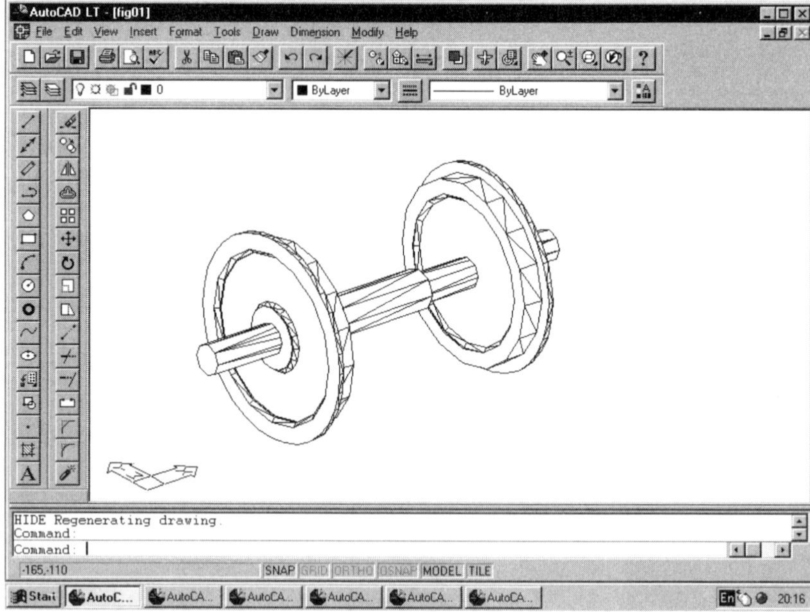

Fig. 15.6 A number of LT 97 windows can be loaded concurrently

Exercises

These exercises are included here as revision exercises, but the reader is advised to use the **Copy** tools to copy and/or link the drawing obtained as answers to any Windows 95 application which is on the hard disk of the computer in use. The following could be attempted:

(a) Copying the drawings to another drawing opened in LT 97.
(b) Linking the answers to another application and updating links through the Object Linking feature of Windows 95 and LT 97.

1. Figure 15.7 is a two-view first angle projection of part of a pipe bending machine. Construct the two views, but working in third angle projection.
2. Figure 15.8 is a two-view first angle projection of a clamping device. Construct the two-view drawing in third angle projection with the holding screws half way into their respective positions.
3. Figure 15.9 is a two-view first angle projection of a coupling. Working in third angle projection construct the two views.
4. Figure 15.10 is a front view of part of a holding device. Construct the view to the given dimensions.

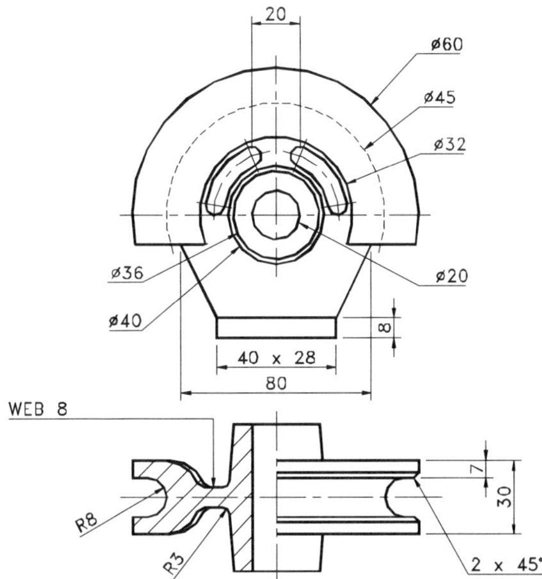

Fig. 15.7 Exercise 1

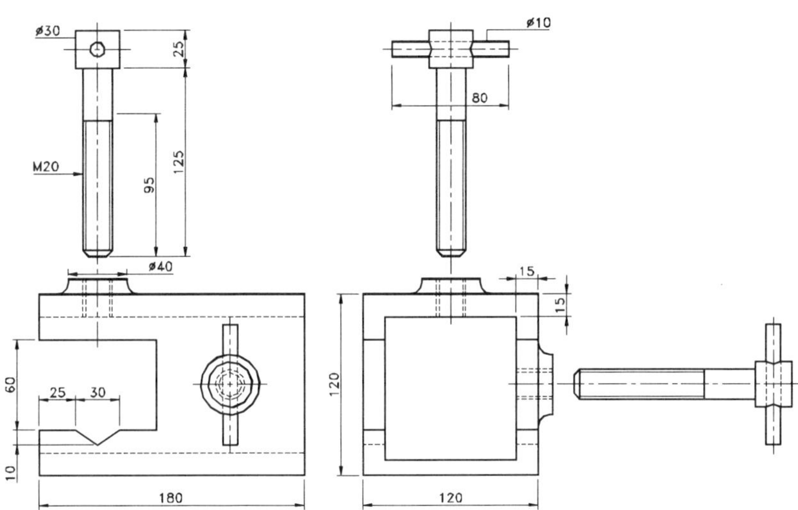

Fig. 15.8 Exercise 2

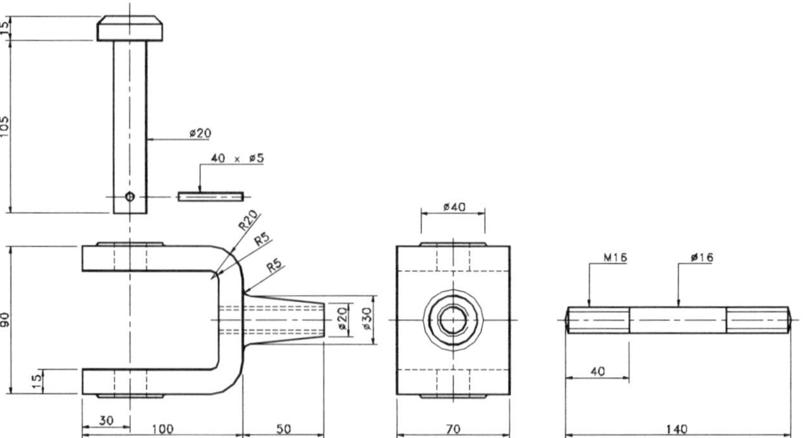

Fig. 15.9 Exercise 3

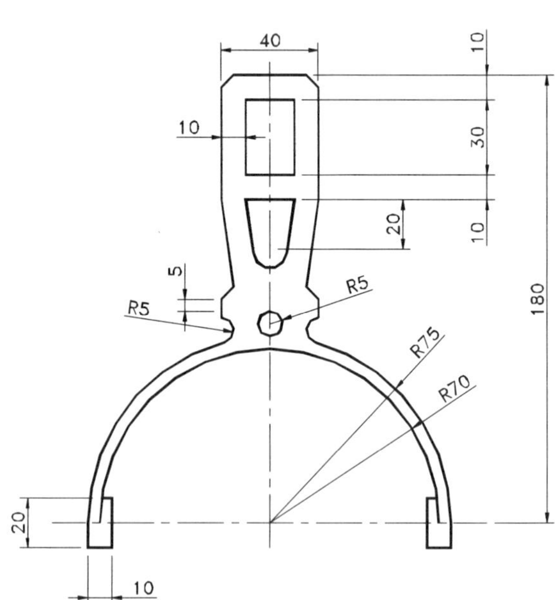

Fig. 15.10 Exercise 4

CHAPTER 16

The LT 97 Internet tools

The Internet

LT 97 includes tools for accessing the Internet to obtain up-to-date information for **Help** and for the sending and receiving of drawings through URLs (User Resource Locators). The **Help** information available for LT 97 comes via the URL site

http://www.autodesk.com/acltuser

or via

http://www.autodesk.com/autocadlt

Drawings in ***.dwf** format can be sent or received over the Internet via URLs.

The HTML language

HTML (Hyper Text Markup Language) is a reasonably simple computer language designed for the setting up of pages which can be sent or received via the **www** (World Wide Web) system on the Internet. Pages made up using HTML must be sent via a Web server on an URL. In general, to set up a server is too expensive for the single user of LT 97. Space can, however, usually be rented or hired if necessary from some firms who have Web servers.

Although the HTML language is an easily learned and easy to use computer language, it is beyond the scope of this book to describe the language and how pages can be set up in HTML for sending and receiving information via the Internet.

URLs

A URL (Uniform Resource Locator) is an address on a server to which and from which LT 97 drawings can be sent or received in ***.dwf** format. In order to be able to send or receive to or from a URL, it is necessary for the computer in use to be on line to the Internet via software such as is provided by Compuserve, AOL, British Telecom,

Microsoft, or a similar company. The company providing the on line service will make a monthly charge for the use of the servers providing the facility. The computer being used must also be equipped with a modem to a telephone line through which pages on the Internet can be sent or received.

Web Browser

A Web Browser such as Microsoft Internet Explorer or Netscale Navigator must also be loaded on the computer. Because the Internet is being constantly updated, it is advisable to have the latest available version of the net browser being used.

URL addresses

A URL address consists of three parts. Taking as an example that given above **http://www.autodesk.com/acltuser**:

http:// – is the service descriptor.
www.autodesk.com/ – is the Internet address at which the required resource is to be found.
acltuser – location at the Internet address where the resource can be found.

Another common service descriptor is **ftp:** There are others.

Passwords

In order to ensure privacy it is necessary to use passwords to protect what is sent or received by the World Wide Web. The request for *entering* a password will frequently be seen when using URLs. When typing in a password, the letters or numbers being *entered* will show in password boxes as asterisks, further guarding against anybody learning the password being *entered*.

Note Addresses and passwords are usually case sensitive.

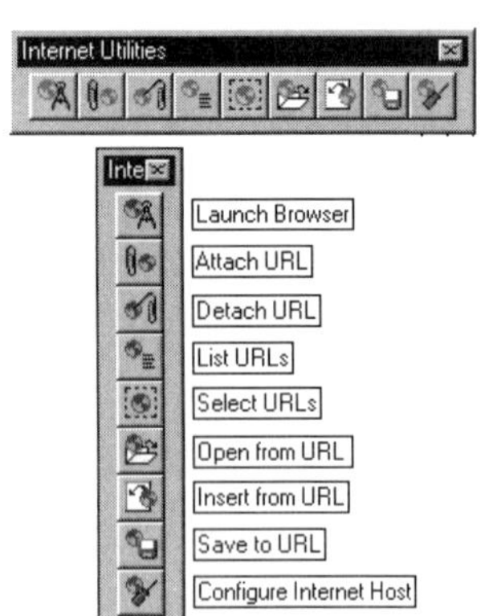

Fig. 16.1 The **Internet Utilities** toolbar with the names of its tools

The LT 97 Internet tools

Right-click anywhere in a toolbar on screen, except in a tool icon and from the **Toolbars** dialogue box, *left-click* in the check box against **Internet Utilities**. The toolbar appears on screen (Fig. 16.1). Figure 16.1 also includes the names of the tools.

In the toolbar *left-click* on the **Configure Internet Host** tool icon. The **Internet Configuration** dialogue box appears. In the **Name:** and **Password:** boxes *enter* the name by which you are known to your server company and the password by which you are recognised by that company (Fig. 16.2). *Left-click* on the **OK** button of the dialogue box.

Then, from the **Help** pull-down menu, *left-click* on **Connect to Internet** (Fig. 16.3). The **Connect To** dialogue box appears, followed by the required web page appearing in a **Microsoft Internet Explorer** window (Fig. 16.5). Selection of the required information can be made from this page.

A similar result can be obtained with a *left-click* on the **Launch Browser** tool icon in the **Internet Utilities** toolbar (Fig. 16.1).

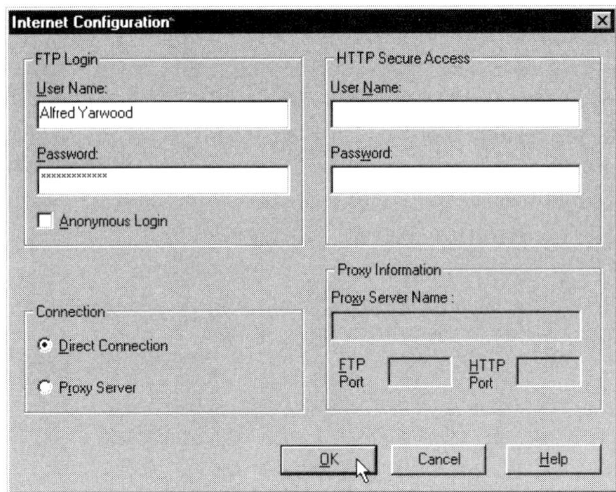

Fig. 16.2 The **Internet Configuration** dialogue box

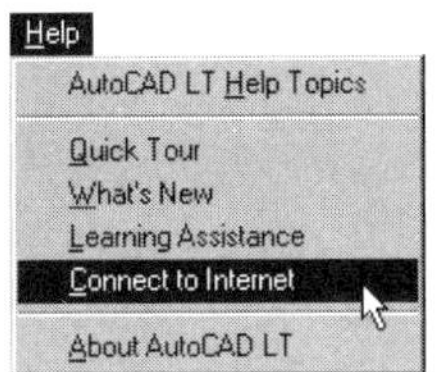

Fig. 16.3 Select **Connect to Internet**

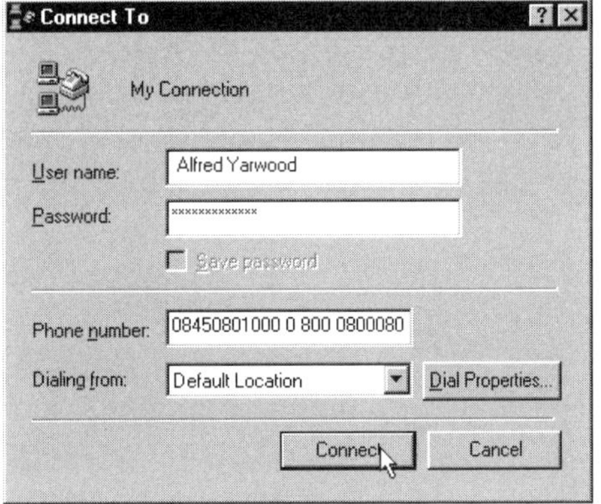

Fig. 16.4 The **Connect To** dialogue box

Other Internet Utilities tools

The other tools in the toolbar are associated with URLs. As an example, *left-click* on the **Insert from URL** icon and the dialogue box **Insert DWG from URL** appears (Fig. 16.6) into which the address of the URL server can be *entered*, together with the required location

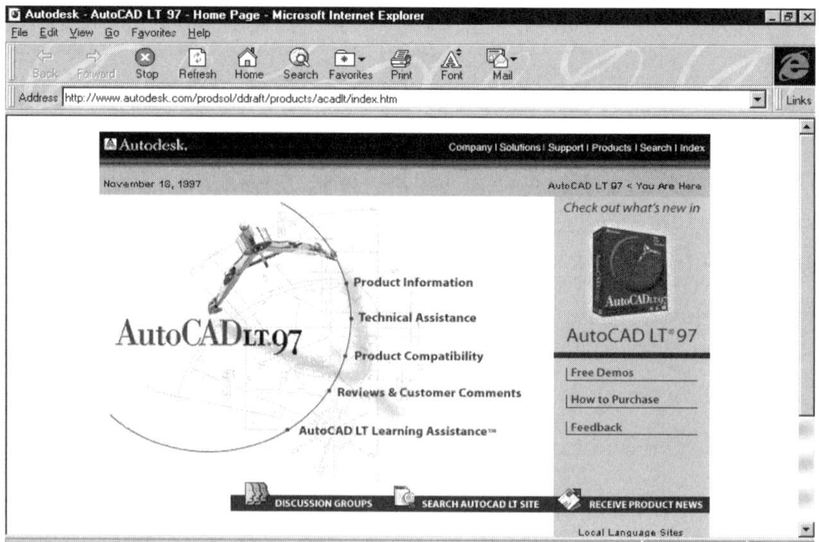

Fig. 16.5 The **Microsoft Internet Explorer** window carrying LT 97 information

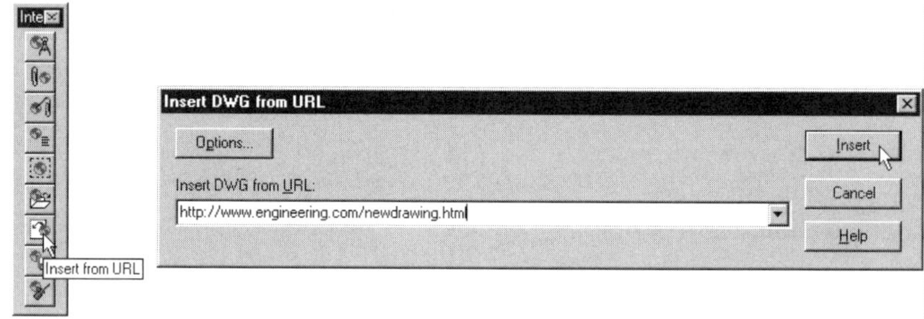

Fig. 16.6 The **Insert DWG from URL** dialogue box

of the text or drawing required from the server the address of which has been *entered*. A *left-click* on the **Insert** button and the required text or drawing appears on screen from the Internet.

LT Help

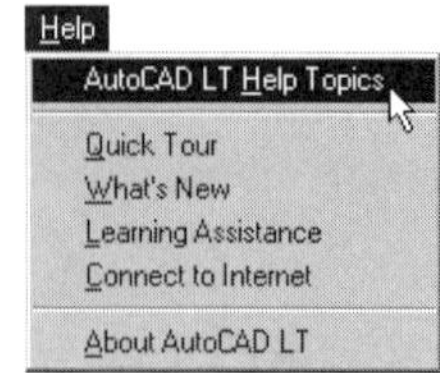

Fig. 16.7 Select **AutoCAD LT Help Topics** from the **Help** pull-down menu

Either select **AutoCAD LT Help Topics** from the **Help** pull-down menu (Fig. 16.7), or *enter* help or a **?** at the Command line. The **AutoCAD LT 97 Help System** window appears (Fig. 16.8).

Left-click on the **Index** tag and *enter* html in the **Index** box. The window changes as shown in Fig. 16.8.

The set variable INETLOCATION

Enter inetlocation at the Command line and the name of the Web page showing information connected with LT 97 shows. Another

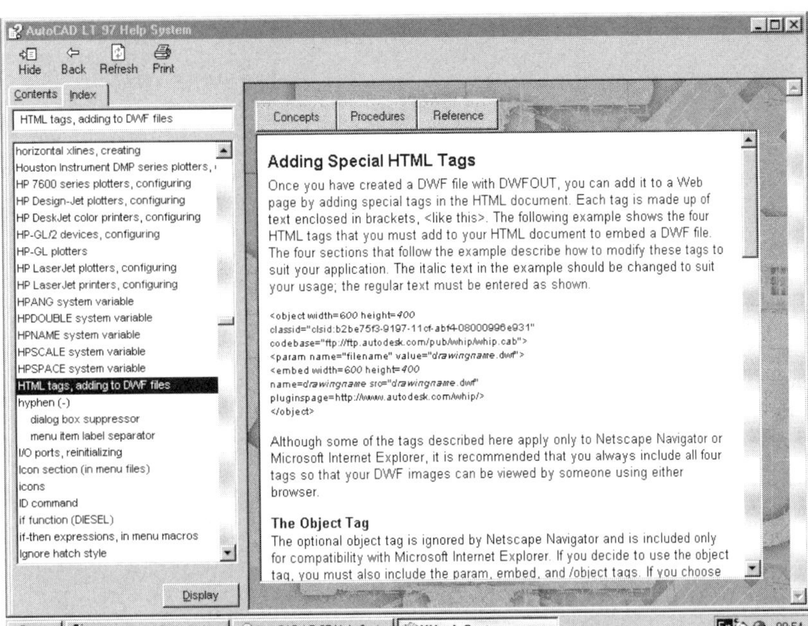

Fig. 16.8 The **AutoCAD LT Help System** window with help for **HTML tags** selected

URL can be *entered* if thought necessary in place of the one which appears at the Command line. As an example:

Command: *enter* inetlocation
New value for INETLOCATION <http://www.autodesk.com/acltuser>: *enter* http://www.autodesk.com/autocadlt *right-click*
Command:

And the next time a connection is made through LT 97 it will use that address.

Questions

1. What is the name of the language for setting up pages to be sent over the Internet?
2. What does the abbreviation **www** stand for?
3. What do the initials URL stand for?
4. What is meant by an URL?
5. Can you name two URL service descriptors?
6. Why is it necessary to have to use passwords when sending drawings to another computer via the Internet?

CHAPTER 17

Printing and plotting

Introduction

Drawings constructed in LT 97 can be printed or plotted to a large range of different types of printers or plotters, such as pen plotters, laser printers, inkjet plotters or printers or electrostatic plotters. Before you can print or plot your drawing the printer or plotter must be correctly connected, switched on and loaded with the required paper, plastic sheet or other type of material on which your drawing is to be printed. In this book, however, we will only be concerned with printing with the default Windows 95 printer, already connected to the computer in use. Methods of printing or plotting are similar even if you are not using the default printer.

The Windows 95 Printers

The printer or plotters set up with Windows 95 can be seen and added to in the following manner:

1. *Left-click* on the **Start** button in the Windows 95 start-up window.
2. *Left-click* on the **Settings** icon in the list which appears.
3. *Left-click* on **Printers** (Fig. 17.1) and the **Printers** window appears (Fig. 17.2). The printers and plotters already set up in Windows 95 are shown in the **Printers** window by named icons. To add further printers or plotters:
4. *Double-click* on the **Add Printers** icon in the window. The **Add Printers Wizard** dialogue box appears (Fig. 17.2). A *left-click* on the **Next** button and a list of printers or plotters appears from which choices can be made for adding printers or plotters either from the manufacturer's disk or from those currently available in Windows 95 (Fig. 17.2).

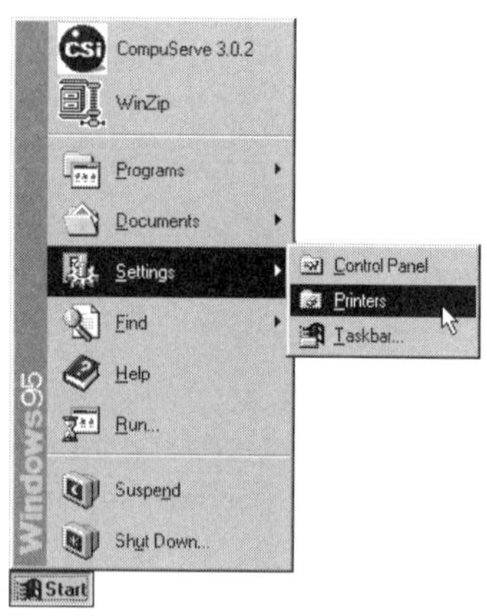

Fig. 17.1 Calling **Printers** from the **Settings** menu

Note As shown in Fig. 17.2 the default current printer in use with the computer being employed for this book is an HP Laser Jet IIIP. This is the printer we will use in illustrations in this chapter.

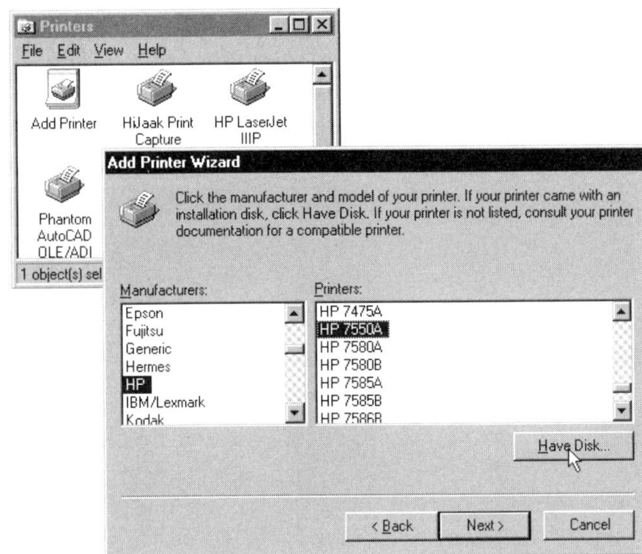

Fig. 17.2 The **Add Printers Wizard**

Printing a drawing

To print (or plot) a drawing:

1. Either *left-click* on **Print...** in the **File** pull-down menu, or *left-click* on the **Print** tool icon in the **Standard** toolbar, or *enter* pp at the Command line (Fig. 17.3).
2. The **Print/Plot Configuration** dialogue box then appears (Fig. 17.4). It will be seen that a number of parameters can be set for printing or plotting a drawing in the **Additional Parameters** area of the dialogue box. Note in particular the **Hide Lines** and **Plot to File** check boxes. We will be printing a windowed part of our drawing.

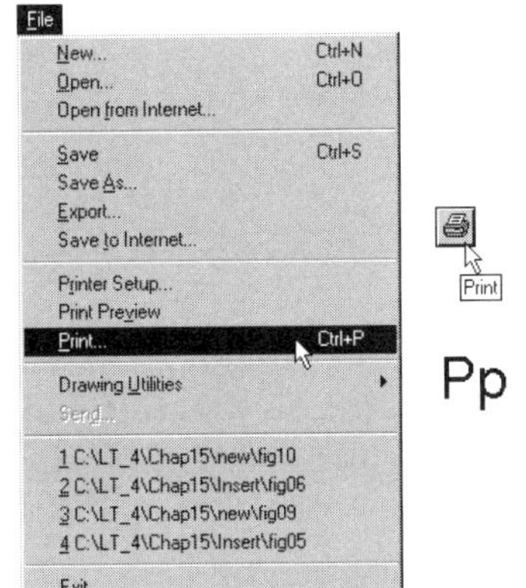

Fig. 17.3 Calling the **Print** tool

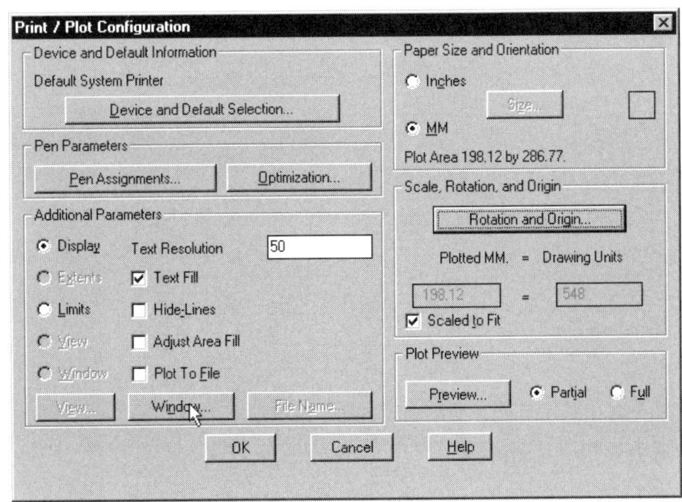

Fig. 17.4 The **Print/Plot Configuration** dialogue box

A *left-click* on the **Window...** button brings up the **Window Selection** dialogue box (Fig. 17.5). *Left-click* on the **Pick** button and window the part of the drawing to be printed. *Left-click* on the **OK** button and the **Plot Configuration** dialogue reappears.

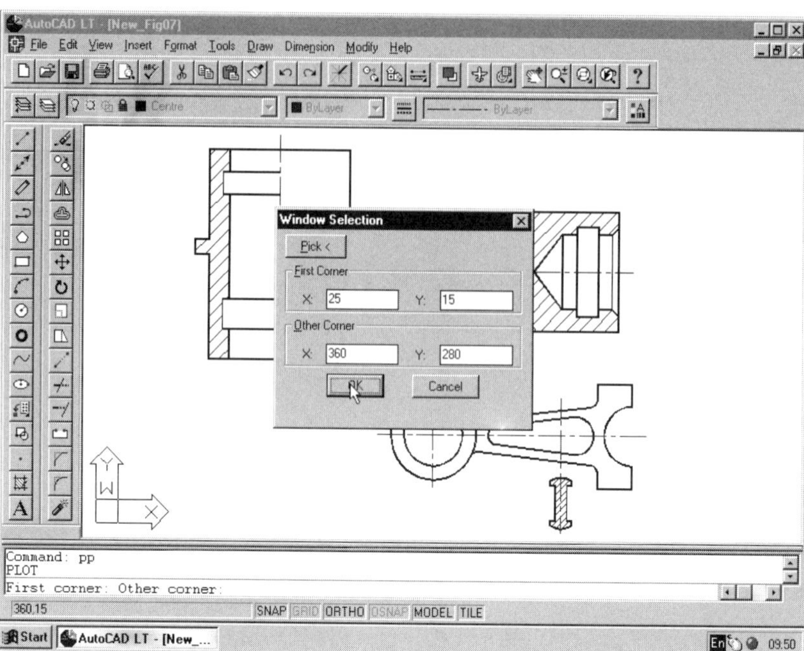

Fig. 17.5 The **Window Selection** dialogue box

3. In the dialogue box, set **MM** on (dot in its check circle).
4. In this example, set rotation to 90 by first selecting the **Rotation and Origin...** button of the dialogue box, followed by setting the check

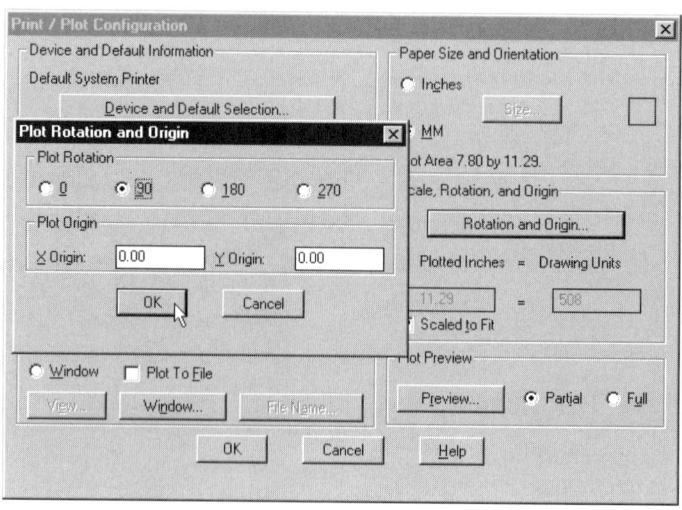

Fig. 17.6 The **Plot Rotation and Origin** dialogue box

box against **90** on in the dialogue box which appears. *Left-click* on the **OK** button of the **Plot Rotation and Origin** box (Fig. 17.6).

5. The **Plot Configuration** dialogue box reappears. Set the check circle on against **Full** in the **Plot Preview** area of the dialogue box, followed by a *left-click* on the **Preview...** button. A preview of the plot appears (Fig. 17.7). If satisfied *right-click* followed by a *left-click* on the name **Exit** in the small menu which appears, as shown in Fig. 17.7.

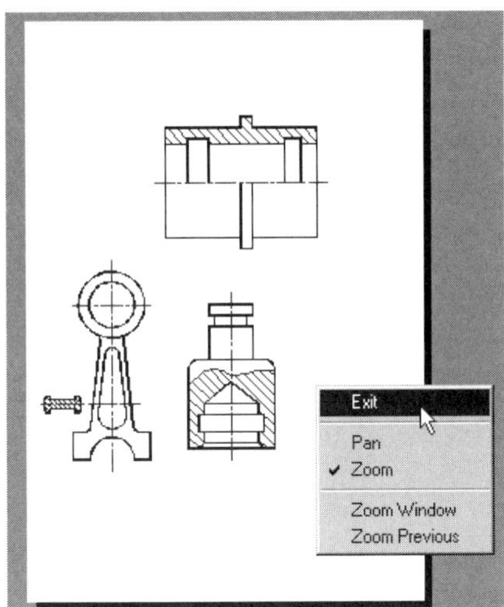

Fig. 17.7 The **Full Preview** of the drawing to be printed

6. Now *left-click* on the **OK** button of the **Print/Plot Configuration** dialogue box. A message box appears showing the percentage of data being sent to the printer (Fig. 17.8). When **%age** reaches **100**, the message box disappears from screen and the printing commences.

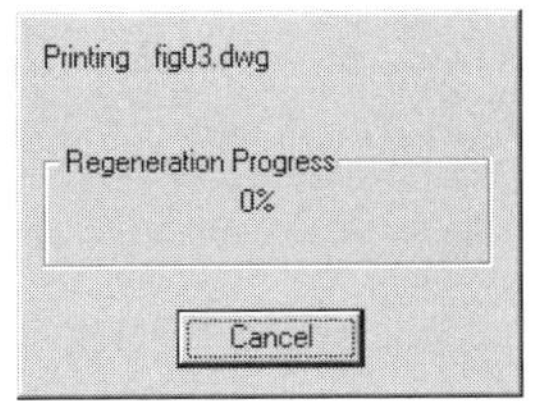

Fig. 17.8 The message box informing the operator of the **%age** of print/plot completed

Changing the printer or plotter

If desired, the printer or plotter in use can be changed while still in LT 97. Bring the **Preferences** dialogue box on screen (*right-click* within the Command window) and in the dialogue box, *left-click* on the **Printer** tag at the top of the dialogue box and the **Reconfigure a Printer** dialogue box appears (Fig. 17.9). To reconfigure the printer or plotter *left-click* on the **Reconfigure...** button and proceed from there in an **AutoCAD LT Text** window which appears.

Or, if a different printer or plotter is required, *left-click* on the **New...** button in the **Printer** dialogue from **Preferences** and select a new printer or plotter from the **Add a Printer** dialogue box which then appears (Fig. 17.10).

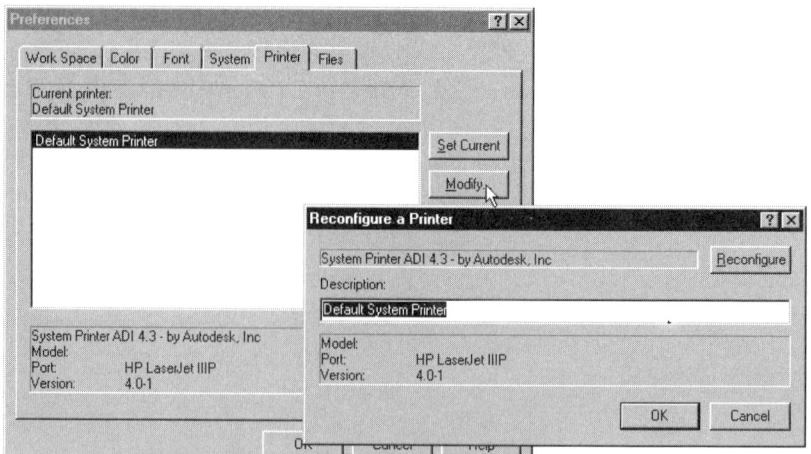

Fig. 17.9 The **Reconfigure a Printer** dialogue box from **Preferences**

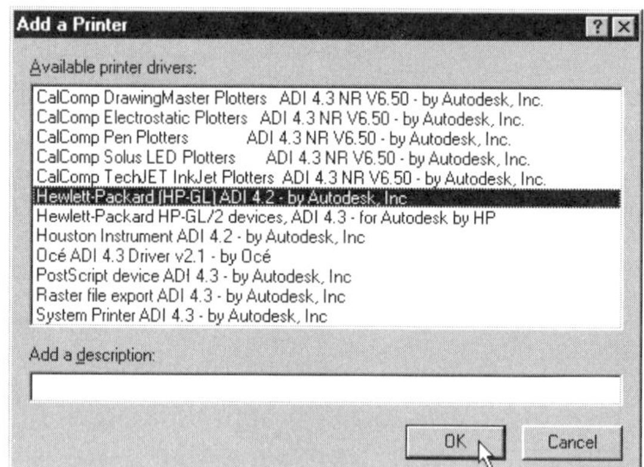

Fig. 17.10 The **Add a Printer** dialogue box

APPENDIX A

Command abbreviations

Introduction

The following tool abbreviations can be used in place of selecting a tool icon from a toolbar or a tool name for a pull-down menu:

A	**Arc**	**EL**	**Ellipse**	**PS**	**Pspace**
AA	**Area**	**EX**	**Extend**	**PU**	**Purge**
AR	**Array**	**F**	**Fillet**	**PT**	**Point**
B	**Make Block**	**G**	**Grid**	**QT**	**Qtext**
BA	**Base**	**HI**	**Hide**	**R**	**Redraw**
BM	**Blipmode**	**IN**	**Insert**	**RC**	**Rectang**
BR	**Break**	**IS**	**Isoplane**	**RE**	**Regen**
C	**Circle**	**L**	**Line**	**RO**	**Rotate**
CH	**Change**	**LA**	**Layer**	**S**	**Stretch**
CHA	**Chamfer**	**LM**	**Limits**	**SC**	**Scale**
CL	**Copylink**	**LS**	**List**	**SD**	**Shadedge**
CO	**Color**	**M**	**Move**	**SH**	**Shade**
CP	**Copy**	**MI**	**Mirror**	**SN**	**Snap**
D	**Dim**	**MS**	**Mspace**	**SO**	**Solid**
D1	**Dim1**	**MV**	**Mview**	**T**	**Dtext**
DI	**Distance**	**OO**	**Oops**	**TI**	**Time**
DIB	**Divide**	**OF**	**Offset**	**TR**	**Trim**
DL	**Dline**	**OR**	**Ortho**	**U**	**Undo**
DO	**Donut**	**P**	**Pan**	**VP**	**Vpoint**
DR	**Draworder**	**PE**	**Pedit**	**VL**	**Vplayer**
DT	**DTEXT**	**PG**	**Polygon**	**X**	**Explode**
DV	**Dview**	**PL**	**Pline**		
E	**Erase**	**PP**	**Plot**		

Dialogue box abbreviations

When some of the abbreviations are entered at the command line a dialogue box appears in the AutoCAD LT graphics window. These are listed below.

AT	**Attribute Definition**
DAD	**Attribute Definition**
DC	**Change Properties**
DM	**Dimension Styles**
DX	**Create DXF File**
ED	**Edit Attribute Definition**
GR	**Grips**
H	**Boundary Hatch**
I	**Insert**
LT	**Layer and Linetype Properties**
O	**Osnap Settings**
OP	**Select File**
OS	**Running Object Snap**
PR	**Preferences**
SA	**Save Drawing As**
SE	**Object Selection Settings**
ST	**Text Style**
UC	**UCS Control**
V	**View Control**
VS	**Select Slide File**
W	**Create Drawing File**
WI	**Import WMF**
WO	**Export WMF**
XB	**Xbind**
XR	**External Reference**

Function key calls

Pressing the function keys give the following results:

F1 Brings up a **Help** window with help for current command.
F2 Toggles between LT 97 drawing area and LT 97 Text window.
F3 Brings up the **Osnap Settings** dialogue box.
F5 Toggles Isoplane between **Top/Right/Left** in that order.
F6 Toggles **Coords** on/off.
F7 Toggles **Grid** on/off.
F8 Toggles **Ortho** on/off.
F9 Toggles **Snap** on/off.
F10 Followed by *Return* Brings down the **File** pull-down menu.

Key calls

The following key combinations result in:

Esc Cancels last command.
Ctrl/C Copyclip.
Ctr/E Toggles Isoplane **Top/Right/Left** in that order.
Ctr/D Toggles **Coords** between **on/absolute/relative**.
Ctr/G Toggles **Grid** on/off.
Ctrl/B Toggles **Snap** on/off.

APPENDIX B

Glossary of tools

Introduction

Many of the tools shown in this glossary have not been described in the pages of this book. This book is intended for those learning how to use LT 97. In order to keep the book to a reasonable size on the grounds of cost to the reader, it has been necessary to restrict description of tool usage to those considered to be essential to the beginner. It is hoped this glossary will encourage readers to experiment with those tools not described earlier:

ARC – Creates an arc.
AREA – States in square units of the area selected from a number of points.
ARRAY – Creates **Perpendicular** or **Polar** arrays in 2D.
ATTDEF – Allows editing of attributes from the Command line.
ATTEDIT – Allows editing of attributes from the Command line.
AUDIT – Checks and fixes any errors in a drawing.

BLIPMODE – Sets blips on or off (1 or 0).
BLOCK – Saves a drawing to a block within the drawing in which it was saved.
BMAKE – Brings the **Create Block** dialogue box on screen.
BMPOUT – Brings the **Create BMP File** dialogue box.
BOUNDARY (BO) – Brings the **Boundary Creation** dialogue box on screen.
BREAK – Breaks an object into parts.

CHAMFER – Creates a chamfer between two entities.
CHPROP – Change properties of an entity through the **Change Properties** dialogue box.
CIRCLE – Creates a circle.
COPY – Creates a single or multiple copies of selected entities.
COPYCLIP – Copies part of a drawing to other Windows 95 applications.

COPYLINK – Forms a link between an LT 97 drawing and its appearance in another application such as a word processing package.

DDATTDEF – Brings the **Attribute Definition** dialogue box to screen.
DDATTE – Edits individual attribute values.
DDATTEXT – Brings the **Attribute Extraction** dialogue box on screen.
DDCOLOR – Brings the **Select Color** dialogue box on screen.
DDEDIT – Select text and the **Edit Text** dialogue box appears.
DDGRIPS – Brings the **Grips** dialogue box on screen.
DDIM – Brings the **Dimensions Styles** dialogue box on screen.
DDINSERT- Brings the **Insert** dialogue box on screen.
DDOSNAP – Brings the **Osnap Settings** dialogue box on screen.
DDPTYPE – Brings the **Point Style** dialogue box on screen.
DDRENAME – Brings the **Rename** dialogue box on screen.
DDRMODES – Brings the **Drawing Aids** dialogue box on screen.
DDSELECT – Brings the **Object Selection Settings** dialogue box on screen.
DDUCS – Brings the **UCS Control** dialogue box on screen.
DDUCSP – Brings the **UCS Orientation** dialogue box on screen.
DDUNITS – Brings the **Units Control** dialogue box on screen.
DDVIEW – Brings the **View Control** dialogue box on screen.
DDVPOINT – Brings the **Viewpoint Presets** dialogue box on screen.
DIM – Starts a session of dimensioning.
DIM1 – Allows the addition of a single addition of a dimension to a drawing.

Note: There are a large number of set variables controlling methods of dimensioning. These are not included here.

DIST – Measures the distance between two points in coordinate units.
DIVIDE – Divides an entity into equal parts.
DONUT – Creates a donut.
DTEXT – Creates dynamic text. Text appears in drawing area as it is entered.
DVIEW – Instigates the dynamic view prompts sequence.
DXBIN – Brings the **Select DXF File** dialogue box on screen.
DXFOUT – Brings the **Create DXF File** dialogue box on screen.
DXFIN – Brings the Select DXF File dialogue box on screen.

ELLIPSE – Creates an ellipse.
ERASE – Erases selected entities from a drawing.
EXIT - Ends a drawing session and closes AutoCAD down.
EXPLODE – Explodes a block or group into its various entities.
EXPORT – Brings the **Export Data** dialogue box on screen.
EXTEND – To extend an entity to another.
EXTRUDE – Extrudes a closed polyline.

FILLET – Creates a fillet between two entities.

HATCH – Allows hatching by the *entry* responses to prompts.
HELP – Brings the **Help Topics** dialogue box on screen.
HIDE – To hide hidden lines in 3D models.

ID – Identifies a point on screen in coordinate units.
IMPORT – Brings the **Import File** dialogue box on screen.
INSERT – Allows the insertion of a block by response to prompts at the Command line.
ISOPLANE – Sets the isoplane when constructing an isometric drawing.

LAYER – Brings the **Layer and Linetype** dialogue box on screen.
LENGTHEN – Lengthen an entity on screen.
LIMITS – Sets the drawing limits in coordinate units.
LINE – Creates a line.
LINETYPE - Brings the **Layer and Linetype** dialogue box on screen.
LIST – Lists in a text window, details of any entity or group of entities selected.
LTSCALE – Allows the linetype scale to be adjusted.

MEASURE – Allows measured intervals to be placed along entities.
MIRROR – Creates an identical mirror image to selected entities.
MOVE – Allows selected entities to be moved.
MSLIDE – Brings the **Create Slide File** dialogue box on screen.
MSPACE – Changes from Paperspace to Modelspace.
MTEXT – Brings the **Multiline Text Editor** on screen.
MVIEW – When in PSpace brings in MSpace objects.

NEW – Brings the **Create New Drawing** dialogue box on screen.

OFFSET – Offsets selected entity by a stated distance.
OOPS – Cancels the effect of using **Erase** and brings back a drawing after **WBlock**.
OPEN – Brings the **Select File** dialogue box on screen.
ORTHO – Allows ortho to be set ON/OFF.

PAN – Pans the LT 97 drawing editor in any direction.
PEDIT – Allows editing of polylines.
PLAN – Allows a drawing in 3D space to be seen in plan (UCS World).
PLINE – Creates a polyline.
PLOT – Brings the **Plot/Print Configuration** dialogue box to screen.
POINT – Allows a point to be placed on screen.
POLYGON – Creates a polygon.
POLYLINE – Creates a polyline.
PREFERENCES – Brings the **Preferences** dialogue box on screen.
PREVIEW – Brings the print/plot preview box on screen.

PSPACE – Changes Modelspace to Paperspace.
PURGE – Purges unwanted data from a drawing before saving to file.

QSAVE – Quicksave. Saves the drawing file to its current name.
QUIT – Ends a drawing session and closes down AutoCAD.

RAY – A construction line from a point and (usually) at an angle.
RECOVER – Brings the **Select File** dialogue box on screen to allow recovery of selected drawings as necessary.
RECTANG – Creates a pline rectangle.
REDEFINE – If an AutoCAD Command name has been turned off by **Undefine** turns the command name back on.
REDO – Cancels the last **Undo**.
REDRAW – Redraws the contents of the R14 drawing area.
REGEN – Regenerates the contents of the R14 drawing area.
ROTATE – Rotates selected entities around a selected point.

SAVE – Brings the **Save Drawing As** dialogue box on screen.
SAVEAS – Brings the **Save Drawing As** dialogue box on screen.
SCALE – Allows selected entities to be scaled in size – smaller or larger.
SCRIPT – Brings the **Select Script File** dialogue box on screen.
SETVAR – Can be used to bring a list of the settings of set variables into an LT 97 Text window.
SHADE- Shades a selected 3D model.
SOLID – Creates a filled outline in triangular parts.
SPLINE – Creates a spline curve through selected points.
SPLINEDIT – Allows the editing of a spline curve.
STRETCH – Allows selected entities to be stretched.
STYLE – Brings the **Text Styles** dialogue box on screen.

TEXT – Allows text from the Command line to be entered into a drawing.
THICKNESS – Sets the thickness for the Elevation command.
TOLERANCE – Brings the **Symbol** dialogue box on screen from which geometric tolerance symbols can be selected.
TOOLBAR – Brings the **Toolbars** dialogue box on screen.
TRIM – Allows entities to be trimmed up to other entities.

UNDO – Undoes the last action of a tool.

VIEW – Allows a view to be controlled – deleted, restored or saved.
VPLAYER – Controls the visibility of layers in paperspace.
VPOINT – Allows viewing positions to be set by x,y,z entries.
VPORTS – Allows viewport settings to be made.
VSLIDE – Brings the **Select Slide File** dialogue box on screen.

WBLOCK – Brings the **Create Drawing File** dialogue box on screen.
WMFIN – Brings the **Import WMF File** dialogue box on screen.
WMFOPTS – Brings the **Import Options** dialogue box on screen.
WMFOUT – Brings the **Create WMF** dialogue box on screen.

XATTACH – Brings the **Select file to attach** dialogue box on screen.
XLINE – Creates a construction line.
XREF – Brings the **External Reference** dialogue box on screen.

ZOOM – Brings the zoom tool into action.

APPENDIX C

Set Variables

Introduction

LT 97 is controlled by a number set variables, many of which are automatically set when making entries in dialogue boxes. Many are also automatically set or read only variables depending upon the configuration of LT 97 .

Below is a list of those set variables which are of interest in that they often require to be set by *entering* figures or letters at the Command line. To set a variable, enter its name at the Command line and respond to the prompts which are seen.

To see all the set variables, *enter* set (or setvar) at the Command line:

Command: *enter* set *right-click*
SETVAR Variable name or ?: *enter* ? *right-click*
Variable(s) to list <*>: *right-click*

A Text window opens showing a list of the first of the variables. To follow on the list press the **Return** key when prompted.

ANGDIR – Sets angle direction. **0** counter clockwise; **1** clockwise.
APERTURE – Sets size of pick box in pixels.
ATTDIA – Set to **1** INSERT uses a dialogue box; set to **0** no dialogue box for INSERT.
BLIPMODE – Set to **1** marker blips show; set to **0** no blips.

Note: DIM variables – There are between 50 and 60 variables for setting dimensioning, but most are in any case set in the **Dimension Styles** dialogue box or as dimensioning proceeds. However, one series of the **Dim** variables may be of interest:

DIMBLK – Sets a name for the block drawn for an operator's own arrowheads. These are drawn in unit sizes and saved as required.
DIMBLK1 – Operator's arrowhead for first end of line.
DIMBLK2 – Operator's arrowhead for other end of line.

EDGEMODE – Controls the use of **Trim** and **Extend**. Set to **0** does not use extension mode; set to **1** uses extension mode.

FILEDIA – Set to **0** disables dialogue boxes; set to **1** enables dialogue boxes.

FILLMODE – Set to **0** entities created with **Solid** are not filled; set to **1** they are filled.

MIRRTEXT – Set to **0** text direction is retained; set to **1** text is mirrored.

PELLIPSE – Set to **0** creates true ellipses; set to **1** polyline ellipses.

PICKBOX – Sets selection pick box height in pixels.

PICKDRAG – Set to **0** selection windows picked by two corners; set to **1** selection windows are dragged from corner to corner.

QTEXTMODE – Set to **0** turns off Quick Text; set to **1** enables Quick Text.

SAVETIME – Sets Automatic Save time. Initially 120. Set to **0** disables Automatic Save time.

SHADEDGE – Set to **0** faces are shaded, edges are not highlighted; set to **1** faces are shaded, edges in colour of entity; set to **2** faces are not shaded, edges in entity colour; set to **3** faces in entity colour, edges in background colour.

TEXTFILL – Set to **0** True Type text shows as outlines only; set to **1** True Type text is filled.

TILEMODE – Set to **0** Paperspace enabled; set to **1** tiled viewports in Modelspace.

TOOLTIPS – Set to **0** no tool tips; set to **1** tool tips enabled.

TRIMMODE – Set to **0** edges not trimmed when **Chamfer** and **Fillet** are used; set to **1** edges are trimmed.

UCSFOLLOW – Set to **0** new UCS settings do not take effect; set to **1** UCS settings follow requested settings.

UCSICON – Set **0FF** and the UCS icon does not show; set to **ON** and it shows.

Index